LEARNING FROM THE GLOBAL FINANCIAL CRISIS

HIGH RELIABILITY AND CRISIS MANAGEMENT
Series Editors: Karlene H. Roberts and Ian I. Mitroff

LEARNING FROM THE GLOBAL FINANCIAL CRISIS

Creatively, Reliably, and Sustainably

Edited by
Paul Shrivastava
and Matt Statler

STANFORD BUSINESS BOOKS
An Imprint of Stanford University Press
Stanford, California

Stanford University Press
Stanford, California

Special discounts for bulk quantities of Stanford Business Books are available to corporations, professional associations, and other organizations. For details and discount information, contact the special sales department of Stanford University Press. Tel: (650) 736-1782, Fax: (650) 736-1784

Printed in the United States of America on acid-free, archival-quality paper

Library of Congress Cataloging-in-Publication Data

Learning from the global financial crisis : creatively, reliably, and sustainably / edited by Paul Shrivastava and Matt Statler.
    pages cm
  Includes bibliographical references and index.
  ISBN 978-0-8047-7009-5 (alk. paper)
    1. Global Financial Crisis, 2008–2009.   2. Crisis management.   3. Sustainable development.   4. Economic policy.   I. Shrivastava, Paul, editor of compilation. II. Statler, Matthew, editor of compilation.
  HB37172008 .L43 2012
  330.9′0511—dc23

2011030083

Typeset by Newgen in 10/14 Minion

To the well-being of future generations

Contents

Acknowledgments

A book such as this is not possible without the support and help of many people and organizations. We thank all the participating authors and commentators for their hard work, their patience, and their thoughtful writing. They did all the extra editing work we asked for with diligence and good spirits.

We acknowledge the support of several institutions and individuals. We thank the students and faculty at Bucknell University, Concordia University, and New York University, the institutions where this project lived for nearly two years. Andrew Ross of the David O'Brien Centre for Sustainable Enterprise at Concordia University did a wonderful job of coordinating authors and compiling the final manuscript.

We thank Karlene Roberts and Ian Mitroff as the editors of the Stanford University Press series High Reliability Organizations and Crisis Management. Margo Beth Crouppen and her able team including Jessica Walsh provided tremendous support and encouragement throughout the process.

Finally, a big thank-you to our spouses, Michelle Cooper and Roxanna Sooudi, for helping us sustain a healthy balance of work and life.

Paul Shrivastava
Montreal

Matt Statler
New York

Introduction

Paul Shrivastava and Matt Statler

This book is motivated by the simple hope that the cloud of the global financial crisis may yet have a silver lining. In short, we hope that political leaders as well as economists and management scholars might seize the opportunity to reflect critically on the assumptions, practices, and infrastructures that have precipitated the crisis, and thereby to imagine and enact new conceptual models as well as new forms of organization that sustainably enhance the well-being of all global stakeholders.

We must admit, however, that this hope has been dampened somewhat by the reactions of world economic political leaders and the economics community since the crisis began several years ago. Leading economists—including Alan Greenspan, and the British Economics Association, in response to the queen—have acknowledged that they did not anticipate the crisis or understand exactly how and why it could have happened. One after another, sovereign leaders as well as industry titans have sought to restore their national economies and marketplaces to some semblance of their precrisis conditions by relying on political and economic strategies that are grounded in that same blind spot. These strategies, and the arguments through which they are advanced in public discourse and policy, rest on a set of basic assumptions that must be subjected to critical scrutiny, lest the seeds of the next crisis be sown precisely in the market stabilization policies themselves.

Raising Basic Questions

According to the prevailing narrative, the global financial crisis originated in the U.S. real estate and financial sectors in the first few years of the twenty-first century. The failures of the financial icons Lehman Brothers and Merrill Lynch in September 2008 were the highest-profile manifestations of crisis onset. Within two months, more than an estimated $10 trillion, fully 40 percent of the wealth in the global financial markets, had been lost. The U.S. economy went into a deep recession and pulled other interdependent economies with it. Over the past two years, desperate attempts have been made to revive economies, stabilize markets, bolster financial regulations, and shore up near-bankrupt banks and financial companies. Despite huge infusions of cash by governments, the economies of many nation-states continue to face tremendous pressures. Iceland declared bankruptcy in 2009; Greece was bailed out by Germany in 2010; and as we write, Spain, Portugal, Ireland, Italy, and Hungary all find themselves in dire economic straits. The current financial crisis is clearly not over yet, and there are compelling reasons to believe that it may intensify and spread to other regional economies and industry sectors in the coming years.

In this light, a series of very basic questions remain unanswered. What exactly was the process through which the crisis emerged? What were its causes? What are its consequences? Could it have been avoided? How can it be managed? What can companies and governments do about it? What kinds of organizations and economies do we need to create to resolve the crisis and avoid similar crises in the future? What kind of leadership do we need to raise and collectively address these difficult questions?

As noted above, these questions are commonly answered by economists and financial experts in ways that do not involve or require any critical reflection on underlying ontological, epistemological, and ethical assumptions. For example, "market stabilization" and "containment" solutions have proliferated around the world over the past two years. In the United States alone, the range of proposed solutions included the bailout of banks (valued at $900 billion), an increase of the money supply ($1 trillion), government purchase of short-term commercial paper ($700 billion), and short-term loans by the Federal Reserve Bank to money-market mutual funds ($500 billion), totaling about $3 trillion by the end of 2008. Similarly dramatic measures have been taken by government-run central banks around the world, including in the United Kingdom, China, European Union, and the United Arab Emirates.

For example, in October 2008, the EU "directive on credit guarantees" was modified to safeguard all deposits. Dozens of European and U.S. financial companies have been bailed out with government funds (e.g., BNP Paribas, Northrock, AIG, Goldman Sachs). Hungary, Latvia, and Romania have received loans totaling €25.5 billion, €7.5 billion, and €20 billion, respectively, from the International Monetary Fund, the World Bank, and the European Union. Finally, all major economies, including the United States and the European Union, have issued new regulations on transparency and risk management in the financial services industry. It is only the most superficial irony that such measures have under other circumstances been derided as socialist or communist, as pertaining more appropriately to planned economies than to liberalized market economies.

As economists and finance experts struggle to put the Humpty Dumpty of the global financial system back together, we suggest humbly that the sources of knowledge that guided the design and operation of those same markets may be insufficient to the task. Indeed, the open question—currently being debated as we write—concerning the potential value of regulatory oversight in the derivatives markets seems relatively simple to resolve compared to the deeper questions concerning the systemic risk involved with a globalized financial system. Not only does the neoliberal Washington consensus on the merits of privatization and deregulation seem suddenly inadequate, but commonly accepted assumptions concerning the scope and exercise of national sovereignty, the balance of public and private interests, and the capacity of economic actors to act rationally on the basis of available information must be critically reevaluated in light of the current crisis.

Moreover, the challenges confronting the evolution of the global political economy go beyond the concepts and methods associated with the academic discipline of economics. The economy of the future will increasingly have to be designed to contend with limitations and constraints associated with the physical situation of the earth. Physical and biological ecosystems that provide the basis for all economic value creation are already under severe pressure, disruption, and outright extinction. These phenomena include depleting oil reserves, overharvesting of forests and fisheries, loss of agricultural land, loss of biodiversity, and polluting emissions at the root of global climate change (Worldwatch Institute 2007; Brown 2006; Brown and Carver 2009). And beyond ecological constraints, the future global economy will also need to contend with the rampant poverty and social inequity that threaten political stability (Thorbecke and Charumilind 2002). The current situation in which nearly 4 billion people live on less than $10 per day, and nearly 1 billion live on less than $1 per day, is simply untenable. What will happen to these economic systems, and to the ideologies that frame our management of these systems, if current demographic forecasts come true and 9 billion people live on the earth within the next thirty years? Today already, even the core supporters of the past economy, the 40 percent in the so-called middle classes, are stagnating at 1970-level living standards (Baker 2007). Indeed, as income disparities widen in the United States, how much longer will government and business leaders be able to muster the political will to support business as usual on Wall Street?

More broadly, should we struggle to re-create an economy with easy credit, high debt, and leverage? Should we re-create an economy where the ecological footprint is wildly unsustainable? Should we continue in the ideology of untrammeled "growth" without concern for the optimal size of the economy and the equitable distribution of wealth?

Articulating New Responses

This volume originated not in a coherent, theoretically grounded response to these basic questions but in a conviction that there must be other sources of knowledge from which to draw. Provocatively put, political questions about the global economy are too dangerous to be left exclusively to either economists or politicians. Our attempt to mitigate this risk by integrating other voices into the dialogue about the principles that will guide the design of the future economy rests on three basic premises.

The first premise is that the global financial crisis shows the limits of very specific and very pervasive metaphysical and epistemological assumptions that reduce the complexity of organizational (and economic) life, zero out the richness of lived experience in production function equations, and ultimately engender more quantity rather than better quality. These assumptions function at an individual and intersubjective level as constraints on the possibilities for thought and action. They beg for philosophical and aesthetic critique and for a renewed understanding of economies and organizations that includes emotional and somatic dimensions of human experience.

The second premise is that at the heart of the financial crisis is the issue of failures caused by lack of organizational and institutional resilience and reliability. In more than twenty years of research on high-reliability systems and crisis management, organizational scholars have accumulated a large amount of knowledge about regulation, surveillance, preparedness, risk management, safety in depth, rescue and emergency response, crisis communication, and conflict resolution. These principles, systems, and structures give shape and meaning to group-, firm-, and industry-level organizational phenomena, and they are relevant to the global financial crisis.

The third premise is that past levels of excessive credit and leverage, overconsumption by a few, and unfettered economic growth are not physically viable nor morally justifiable. There is growing research on the global ecological situation and the need for sustainability at the enterprise level and the economywide level. We need to build toward sustainable and equitable development appropriate for the world's 6.7 billion people.

Working from these basic premises, we seek to develop responses to the crisis that are creative, reliable, and sustainable. Rather than drawing on traditional source theories from economics, finance, organizational theory, and political science, this volume draws on arts and aesthetics, crisis management, and sustainability studies. Again, we do not intend to present this grouping of alternative approaches as a fully integrated set of theoretical propositions. Instead, we present the volume as a provocation to engage in inter- and multi-disciplinary dialogue.

There is a huge reservoir of human creativity in the arts and aesthetics, but this source has remained almost entirely untapped by politicians, economists, and business leaders because of metaphysical and epistemological assumptions about how knowledge is and should be developed. Similarly, as the complexity of organizational life has intensified in recent years, so, too, has the potential for multiple types of failures, including human errors, misjudgments, equipment and materials failures, policy and regulatory failures, infrastructure failures, and so on. An interest in practical wisdom (Statler and Roos 2006) has developed among practitioners as well as academic researchers around these problems, but the lessons that have been learned have not yet been integrated into the overall considerations about how to design and manage economies. Finally, a diverse community of scholars and innovative practitioners have long recognized that the design of economic systems is not just about managing financial outcomes but about managing equitable financial and economic evolution under conditions of extreme ecosystem stress, using human creativity and organizational resilience. And yet the challenge of sustainable development has only begun to be addressed seriously by mainstream political economists, and the potential of human creativity to build new fulfilling relationships with nature (Brown and Carver 2009) remains untapped.

By seeking insights from these three disciplines, we hope to foster a dialogue among economics and finance experts about alternative solutions to the global crisis. This attempt is hardly as radical as it may seem—indeed, the economy is anchored in natural ecosystems and inextricably linked to them. From a design perspective, the purpose of any economy is to fulfill human needs within the constraints of natural ecology. In this light, the appropriate size of the global economy has to be pegged to the earth's capacity to sustainably produce and reproduce goods and services. To be truly sustainable, the value generated by the exchange of those goods and services must be distributed equitably among stakeholders, including present and future generations, as well as the millions of other species that inhabit the earth.

In this light, the practices associated with art and aesthetics, crisis management, and sustainability may provide intellectual as well as emotional resources that support the design and management of future economies and organizations.

Structure of the Book

The subtitle of this volume—"Creatively, Reliably, and Sustainably"—serves as an organizing structure for the various contributions. The basic logic behind this structure is a progression of scale from the microlevel issues that pertain to individuals and teams who act creatively to the mesolevel issues that pertain to the structures, practices, and processes associated with reliable organizations, and to the macrolevel issues that pertain to the interdependent ecological systems that are sustainable in various contexts and over time.

We recognize that these distinctions exist to facilitate the analysis of phenomena that, in practice, remain difficult, if not impossible, to separate. And yet we believe that together they emphasize the importance of developing holistic responses to the financial crisis that do not attempt to solve a relatively local problem while ignoring other problems that may exist in other localities or at the level of the entire global system.

The three sections each contain full-length chapters exploring key issues in depth as well as shorter commentaries that focus on more practical issues. This structure serves to create a textured discourse, and it also offers a reality check on the chapters and extends the appeal of the book to practitioners.

Creatively

In "Truth, Beauty, and the Financial Crisis: Evaluating What Works," Robert Richardson and Matt Statler take as a point of departure the claim made by the Nobel laureate Paul Krugman (2009) that the global financial crisis resulted from a confusion among economists who have allowed their own appreciation of the beauty of theoretical models to cloud their judgment about the truth of those models. Although organizational theorists have considered the relationship between truth and beauty periodically over the years, few attempts have yet been made to take stock of and integrate the debates among contemporary philosophers about the distinction between facts and values (see Putnam 2002). In this chapter, Richardson and Statler trace out the history of these philosophical debates, seeking to develop a pragmatic theory of meaning that has general implications for organizational theory and specific implications in view of the ongoing financial crisis.

In "Aesthetic Leadership: Walking Toward Economic Recovery," Ralph Bathurst and Margot Edwards explore the idea of communitarian artistic co-creativity and partnership as a means of addressing the global financial crisis. Beginning with the notion that an excessive emphasis on instrumental rationality and economic growth has resulted in an unsustainable contemporary situation, they explore the potential for leadership practice that is demonstrated by aesthetic engagement between "self" and "other." Specifically, they focus on the aesthetic practices demonstrated by the Maori artist Peter Robinson and the Detroit-based artist Tyree Guyton, who engage in dialogic art that helps create community by provoking critical reflection. They close by inquiring into how this dialogical notion of leadership might be applied to the situation currently faced by U.S. President Barack Obama and the chair of the U.S. Federal Reserve Bank, Ben Bernanke.

In "Smashing Moneytheist Mirrors: How Artists Help Us Live with Financial Schizophrenia," Pierre Guillet de Monthoux reflects critically on what he refers to as moneytheism, an ideology that represents the world in exclusively financial terms and reduces the value of human life to matters that can be measured in terms of money. He explores art and aesthetics as an alternative approach to value, focusing on insider artists who work within organizational and economic systems and seek using gestures and provocations to open up new public spaces for dialogue and experience. The chapter closes with an illustration by artist Michelangelo Pistoletto, who staged a performance at the

2009 Venice Biennale in which he used a sledgehammer to smash a number of huge mirrors hung in gilded frames.

In the provocatively titled "Hence God Exists," Skip McGoun offers a historically anchored and trenchant critique of the mathematization of finance and its disastrous consequences. He suggests that beginning in the first quarter of the twentieth century and continuing to date, mathematics has moved from being a tool of analysis to being an end in itself. Finance research and practice uncritically use mathematical models to ineffectively represent reality, which leads to false and ideologically biased conclusions. He argues that mathematical equations are not axiomatic laws but rather interpretive metaphors. They are not the truth, although they may express useful ideas. The finance profession needs to recognize the limits of mathematics and the metaphors that have been used to implement mathematics in the management of financial systems.

In "The Art of Finance," Steven S. Taylor picks up this thread and introduces a distinction between art and craft to reflect on the practices associated with accounting and finance. Where craft involves the use of skills in an established process to produce a desired result, art involves engaging the senses as well as the imagination to depart in a new direction. Viewed in this sense, the creation of financial derivatives appears as a form of art, albeit one that has become unmoored from its material and ethical ground to an extent that it has invited both academic critique and moral condemnation. Taylor argues that unless finance can embrace its own roots as a craft that produces sustainable growth for societal stakeholders, we have learned nothing from the crisis.

In "The Play Ethic and the Financial Crisis," Pat Kane considers how bankers and traders have placed the infinite game of creative innovation in the service of the finite game of winner-take-all shareholder capitalism and points out that the increased importance of regulators and arbiters in sports as well as finance is driven by a similar tendency to innovate beyond the application of existing rules. Whereas free-market advocates have tended to rely on game theory and complex adaptive systems theory to justify the evolutionary creation and destruction of specific organizational and institutional forms, Kane raises a series of questions about the ground of play in embodied, materially potentiating human beings. Indeed, what is the healthiest arrangement between the free play of financial speculation and the rule-based structure of financial regulation for human life? In response to this question, Kane frames stakeholder capitalism in terms of the Danish phrase *leg godt* (good play), which he interprets as "sharing nicely."

In "Cassim's Law," the Berlin-based artist and management scholar Henrik Schrat presents an account of what he calls Cassim's law, referring to Ali Baba's brother in the classic fable, who greedily escalates a situation until it extends beyond his own understanding and ends up chopped into pieces by thieves. On Schrat's reading of the crisis, it is not sufficient to cast the bankers as thieves; instead, we must reflect on greed as such, on consumerism, and on the counting imperative that drives us all to want more and more over time. Schrat recalls the notion articulated by the Austrian economist Wilhelm Ropke that moral reserves must be built up in areas such as the environment and the family to counterbalance the rapacious tendencies that market systems tend to unleash. But ultimately, Schrat argues, following Georges Bataille, that the crisis exemplifies a kind of potlatch in which cosmic energy is expended catastrophically, and the captains of the financial industry as well as the small-time investors and market participants literally expend themselves in tragedy.

Reliably

In "Managing the Global Financial Crisis: Lessons from Technological Crisis Management," Paul Shrivastava, Bill Gruver, and Matt Statler take lessons from the past thirty years of research on technological crisis management and apply it to the current global financial crisis. They illustrate parallels and similarities in technological and financial crisis antecedent conditions, crisis causes, and prevention and management strategies. They suggest policies for mitigating the impacts of financial crisis, including long-term planning for managing the crisis process, regulating risk and leverage, building surveillance systems, improving global communications, and redesigning a new sustainable global economic order.

Nathaniel I. Bush, Peter F. Martelli, and Karlene H. Roberts, in their chapter "Failures of High Reliability in Finance," examine the deep organizational problems in the culture and tools of high finance that limit reliable performance only within a very narrow set of system conditions. They suggest that overspecialization, control and conformity, insensitivity to unknown risks, and lack of flexibility in response contribute to systemic failures in the financial services industry. To prevent future systemic breakdowns, they recommend process auditing, long-term-oriented reward systems, monitoring of quality, multiple (and even conflicting) perspectives on risk assessment and mitigation, redundancy in auditing systems, and training on high-reliability issues.

Ian I. Mitroff and Can M. Alpaslan, in "Wrong Assumptions and Risk Cultures: Deeper Causes of the Global Financial Crisis," examine the incorrect assumptions and risk cultures that are the deep and hidden root causes of the financial crisis. They argue that the crisis was caused not simply by technical economic and regulatory failures but rather by the unconscious psychological assumptions and cultural assumptions prevalent in financial companies and financial markets. These assumptions are reductionist and incomplete in portraying human motivation reduced to self-interest, complex human emotions reduced to fear and greed, all available information about asset values reduced to market prices, and all information about the riskiness of assets reduced to asset price volatility. Such obsessive reductionism created a fatally flawed approach to defining and measuring risk, and eventually led to the failure of risk management. As a solution, they propose moving financial companies from a culture of risk, selfishness, and narcissism to a culture of trust.

Michael Berkowitz, in "A Busy Decade: Lessons Learned from Crisis Planning and Response from 1999 to 2009," presents an account of the lessons that have been learned from the past decade of practice in the field of crisis management. This discipline, which in organizational contexts often focuses on operational risks, has undergone a series of significant transformations in response to the rise of global terrorism as well as the myriad threats associated with flu pandemics and climate change. Berkowitz was working for the New York City Office of Emergency Management on September 11, 2001, and he subsequently transitioned into the private sector, where he currently serves as the director of business continuity and crisis management for Deutsche Bank in Asia. He focuses his chapter on the tension between all-hazards and hazard-specific protocols, on the relevance of testing the crisis management system on low-grade incidents, and on the importance of communications. These lessons appear generically applicable to the ongoing management of the global financial crisis, although it remains to be seen whether functional crisis management systems can be built across institutional and national boundaries within the financial markets, much less in other markets.

Brett Messing, in "A Critique of Managing the Global Financial Crisis: Lessons from Technological Crisis Management," provides an insightful critique of the comparison of financial and technological crises. He goes further into exploring the ultracomplexity of some trading businesses, such as debt securitization and derivatives. These, he explains, have evolved in complexity beyond the understanding of risk managers and bank chief executive officers. He suggests that transparency into the balance sheets of investment banks can lead to a more optimal capital structure that is better equipped to handle financial market meltdowns.

Sustainably

Perry Sadorsky's chapter, "Green Financing After the Global Financial Crisis," focuses on the critical topic of green financing. This type of financing (often part of the stimulus spending) is increasingly necessary for the world economy to move toward sustainability. He examines four economic recovery scenarios (U-shaped recovery, V-shaped recovery, stagflation, and deflation) and the impacts that each of these scenarios will have on the future of green financing. Some countries are seeing stimulus investing as an opportunity to morph into sustainable economies. South Korea, for example, has devoted 20 percent of its stimulus spending to environmental measures and thus has the greenest fiscal stimulus package.

Aida Sy and Tony Tinker, in "Leveraging Ourselves out of Crisis—Again!" frame the ongoing crisis as only the most recent instantiation of a recurrent phenomenon, a flaw that is intrinsic to capitalist economies that encourage leveraged speculation. They identify three contradictions that consistently jeopardize the process of growth through which capital is accumulated: the falling rate of profit, the need to dispose of overproduction, and the concentration and centralization of capital. Most poignant, they argue that the stabilization strategies that have been employed to mitigate the current crisis have not only deferred the impacts but also have increased the potential for systemic risk and thus increased the likelihood that other "time bombs" will soon implode, especially in nations such as Switzerland, where bank leverage vastly exceeds the gross domestic product.

Andreas Georg Scherer and Emilio Marti, in their chapter "The Normative Foundation of Finance: How Misunderstanding the Role of Financial Theories Distorts the Way We Think About the Responsibility of Financial Economists," provide a trenchant critique of how financial economists have misunderstood the role of financial models and abdicated their intellectual responsibilities. They draw on the philosophy of science to clarify these responsibilities to include critical reflections on the problems of practice and closely tie theories to practical problems. In pursuing the widely adopted, largely abstract efficient market hypothesis, based on unrealistic assumptions, financial economists have largely neglected this responsibility.

Mark Starik, in his chapter "A Multilevel, Multisystems Strategic Approach to a Sustainable Economy," analyzes the recent global financial crisis at these levels, focusing on natural environment-related inputs, processes, and outputs. He also explicates other systems-oriented phenomena at each level to provide a holistic systems framework for understanding the financial crisis and its connections to sustainability. This permits a more comprehensive analysis of crisis causes and necessity of multifocal solutions that include residential, commercial, industrial, and institutional investments in improving the quality of air, water, land, and other natural resources. He argues for greater emphasis on eating lower on the food chain, for both human and natural environmental health benefits, both of which may have long-lasting financial effects.

In "The Global Financial Crisis: A Perspective from India," Murali Murti and N. V. Krishna focus their analysis on resilience to the global financial crisis based on experiences of the Indian economy. Through assessment of commonly used measures such as gross domestic product growth rate; unemployment rate; fall in property values; value destruction of financial assets; current account deficits; and the failure of institutions, corporations, banks, and so on, they consider the relatively high resilience of the Indian economy (as compared to that of the United States and Europe). In this resilience lie some lessons. They include high savings rate and lower credit exposure, a strong regulatory framework and an effective central bank responsible for monetary policy, policy emphasis on stability rather than growth, and lowering of economic dependence on exports. Although these lessons may not be applicable universally, they contain kernels of wisdom that many developing countries can implement in building economic resilience.

Opening a New Conversation

The Chinese symbol for crisis has two characters that signify both danger and opportunity. Hard as it might be to imagine at this time, the ongoing global financial crisis is also an opportunity to conceptualize and reach global consensus around the principles that can guide the design and operation of financial systems that can truly contribute to the well-being of all participants in the global economy.

The book raises some fundamental questions about how to reconstruct the global economy from multiple disciplinary perspectives. We don't have any clear and definite solutions. Our goal is to gather and present these perspectives in the hopes of provoking a conversation in response to vital questions about how to re-create the global economy. It is this conversation—engaging managers, employees, customers, and the public at large—that can develop local solutions to global challenges. We hope these chapters will open up a vibrant and much needed dialogue that breaks down the conventional disciplinary silos and bridges the academic–practitioner divide.

Pragmatically, the book includes lessons for managers working in a broad range of industries affected by the global financial crisis, including financial services, insurance, real estate, infrastructure, economic development, and so on. The book also contains ideas for shaping economic and financial policies and regulations that can be used by policy makers, including members of executive and legislative branches of local, regional, and national governments, as well as national and international regulatory agencies. The book also contains a set of provisional strategies that managers and affiliates of third-sector organizations, including nonprofits, activism groups, and associations can use to address the impacts of the global financial crisis through direct service and/or advocacy. Finally, the book provides managers of organizations already engaged in practices associated with the three source disciplines (i.e., arts and aesthetics, sustainability, and high reliability and crisis management) with new responses to the basic questions that arise in view of the future of the global economy.

The global financial crisis is also a global financial opportunity. But the opportunity is not for some countries to rush back to the growth economics of the past. It is not in uncritically building resource- and energy-intensive, wasteful consumer societies. The opportunity is to rethink creatively the parameters of a globally sustainable economy. Such an economy will limit the size and scale of its eco-footprint. It will provide work opportunities that effectively use the creative potential of human resources. It will have organizational and social systems that offer high reliability and deep resilience. The chapters in this book open up a new series of possibilities to develop that future economy, and we hope that they move readers to experiment and transform their own lives and organizations in ways that are creative, reliable, and sustainable.

References

Baker, Dean. 2007. *The United States since 1980.* Cambridge: Cambridge University Press.

Brown, L. 2006. *Plan B 2.0: Rescuing a planet under stress and a civilization in trouble.* Washington, D.C.: Earth Policy Institute.

Brown, Peter G., and G. Carver. 2009. *Right relationship: Building the whole earth economy.* San Francisco: Berrett-Koehler Publishers.

Intergovernmental Panel on Climate Change. 2007. *Fourth synthesis report.* Geneva: IPCC.

Statler, M., and J. Roos. 2006. Re-framing strategic preparedness: An essay on practical wisdom. *International Journal of Management Concepts and Philosophy* 2 (2): 99–117.

Stern, N. 2006. *The Stern review on the economics of climate change.* London: HM Treasury. http://www.hm-treasury.gov.uk/sternreview_index.htm.

Thorbecke, Erik, and Chutatong Charumilind. 2002. Economic inequality and its socioeconomic impact. *World Development* 30 (9): 1477–95.

Worldwatch Institute. 2007. *State of the Earth report.* Washington, D.C.: Worldwatch Institute.

CREATIVELY

1 Truth, Beauty, and the Financial Crisis

Evaluating What Works

Robert Richardson and Matt Statler

Paul Krugman (2009) recently attributed the ongoing global financial crisis to a confusion among economists who have, he alleged, allowed an appreciation of the beauty of certain theoretical models to cloud judgment about their truth. Although organizational theorists have considered the relationship between truth and beauty periodically over the years (e.g., Astley 1985; Weick 1989; Nonaka 1993), no attempts have yet been made to consider the debates among contemporary philosophers about the distinction between facts and values (Putnam 2002). In this chapter, we trace out the history of these philosophical debates, seeking to develop a pragmatic theory of meaning that has general implications for organizational theory and specific implications in view of the ongoing financial crisis.

Framing the Problem: The Financial Crisis as a Confusion of Beauty and Truth

In a *New York Times* column titled "How Did Economists Get It So Wrong?" the Nobel laureate Paul Krugman (2009) alleges that economists have, first and foremost, mistaken beauty for truth. Falling under the woozy sway of predictive power, they have mistaken their models for the real world. As a matter both of disposition and practice, they have gathered data from the world that confirm the veracity of these models, and they have discounted data that do not support them. These mistakes, Krugman claims, set up the global markets for a crisis, and so long as we do not critically examine and learn from those mistakes, we will continue to perpetuate the situation in which we find ourselves: choked with debt as a nation, interrogating financial executives in congressional hearings, but still trying to generate models that predict a free collective of self-interested market participants growing in perpetual balance with the resources available in the natural world. Such claims merit more careful examination.

The notion of mistaking beauty for truth calls forth a particular tangle of metaphysical, epistemological, and ethical problems. At a glance, it may signal a faulty metaphysics in which the model is mistaken for the world. It may employ a faulty epistemology in which a distinction between facts and values is blurred. It may be driven by a hubristic ethos in which economists and management scholars seek a theory of everything to describe and predict all action in the human social world. Such hubris may legitimize an equally flawed practice of management and governance, in which the will to profit is asserted as a natural law. Then on top of it all, the straws that break the camel's back appear to be the emergence of derivatives markets, the corollary postulate that all risk can be effectively hedged, and an unexpected free-fall collapse of trust across global markets as well as across Wall Street in lower Manhattan.

The problem Krugman points to is thus illustrated by, but not limited in scope to, the current global financial crisis. It has at least also to do with the foundations of capital, with the emergence of new technologies, with the exercise of power through organizational and institutional systems, and with the sustainability of human activities within the natural environment. Responding to the current crisis, we have an interest in creating and developing more reliable and sustainable systems of organization and governance. How, then, to address the confusion between beauty and truth that has allegedly given rise to this crisis?

. . .

The topic of the problems that follow from confusing beauty and truth has surfaced periodically over the years among organizational theorists. It has been argued that the entire discipline of administrative science consists not of objective truth but of socially constructed artifacts of language that acquire an institutional stamp of legitimacy (Astley 1985). It has similarly been argued that organization studies rests on foundations both within the sciences and within the humanities (Zald 1993). Others have claimed that the process of constructing organizational theories involves imagination, and that rather than validation, the interests of researchers provide the standard for truth (Weick 1989). Management studies, like other social sciences, has been viewed through a postmodern lens as consisting less of facts than of a series of reflexive fictions (Berg 1989; Chia 1996). More specifically, knowledge management researchers have noted how qualitative judgments (e.g., of beauty, of goodness) can be as important as quantitative judgments (e.g., of return on investment, of efficiency) in the creation of organizational knowledge (Nonaka 1993). A stream of research has recently emerged that approaches organizations primarily as an aesthetic phenomenon (see Brady 1986; Strati 1992 1996, 1999; Gagliardi 1996; Taylor and Hansen 2005; Guillet de Monthoux and Statler 2008). Management storytelling has, for example, been analyzed in aesthetic terms (Taylor et al. 2002), as has leadership (Ladkin and Taylor 2010). Finally, we cannot ignore the contributions of behavioral economics (Kahneman and Tversky 1979), which proceeds from a cognitive psychological perspective and explores the ways in which perfect rationality is bounded (Simon 1982) by irrational desires and other factors, thus suggesting that individual decisions about utility maximization are always shaped by perceptions of beauty, fit, appropriateness, and so on.

Reflecting on these various attempts to differentiate beauty from truth, some appear to invert the logical priority of the terms, privileging beauty over truth as a criterion of value within the discipline of management, whereas others appear to assert the simultaneous relevance of beauty and truth, with one term functioning as a kind of limit, frame, or boundary for the other. None of these attempts, however, has traced out the history of the distinction within the discipline of philosophy, where the concepts of truth and beauty have been subjected to rigorous critique and where debates about the fact–value dichotomy (Putnam 2002) have in recent years yielded some advances that are relevant to organizational theory. Similarly, there has yet been no attempt (to our knowledge) to bring this critical tradition to bear on the circumstances surrounding the global financial crisis that has played out over the past few years.

In this chapter, we articulate the difference between truth and beauty in terms of a distinction drawn by contemporary philosophers between description (i.e., assertions about facts) and evaluation (i.e., judgments of value, including beauty and goodness). We focus on the critique of certain metaphysical assumptions about referentiality and the correspondence between language and the world. But instead of framing the end of metaphysics as a collapse of the possibility of truth, we unfold a pragmatic theory of meaning and introduce "workingness" as a criterion by which both beauty and truth can be objectively judged. In closing, we consider the implications of this pragmatic theory for organizational theory, as well as for the development of more creative, reliable, and sustainable approaches to managing the financial crisis.

To whom are we writing? In deference to the scope and scale of the ongoing financial crisis, we write to the people who we assume read Krugman's *New York Times* column—that is, to fund managers, institutional investors, macroeconomists, policy makers and strategists, decision makers in large financial and other business organizations—and to the economists and organizational theorists who both offer expert guidance to these practitioners and reflect on the conceptual foundations of management practice. In particular, we contribute these reflections to the stream of organizational research concerned with the ways in rational decisions are framed by fundamental assumptions (see Tversky and Kahneman 1986). Scholars have described these assumptions variously in terms of frames of reference (Shrivastava and Schneider 1984), interpretative frames (Bartunek and Moch 1987), mental models (Argyris and Schon 1978), scripts (Gioia 1986), paradigms (Kuhn 1970), and so on. Although the philosophical language that we employ may seem esoteric to scholars familiar with this literature, it is required to identify and reflect on the specific metaphysical, epistemological, and normative assumptions that sustain the fact–value distinction within the domain of organizational theory.

But rest assured, by attempting to deconstruct the fact–value dichotomy, we need not collapse all knowledge into social constructionism or into another, more normative form of idealism. Although we concede to Krugman that many things people have taken to be factual may be shot through with value, we maintain that many things people have taken to be merely expressions of value offer a different snapshot of the truth. In this sense, the environment of the current crisis affords us an occasion to explore how our true representations of the facts include modes of evaluation about what is best, while our evaluations about what is best can also be true.

Truth, Beauty, and the End of Metaphysics

Friedrich Nietzsche (1990, 46) famously traced out a genealogy of metaphysics stretching from the pre-Socratics to German idealism, calling it the "history of an error." The "death of God" became perhaps the most notorious phrase associated with Nietzsche's philosophical project, but his primary objective was to critique a basic assumption about the existence of something (e.g., God, Being) eternal and unchanging that provides an ultimate grounding for statements of fact that are free from corruption by values, preferences, or beliefs. Although the broad implications of this critique continue to be worked out by philosophers and social theorists, we here focus on the rise and eventual collapse of logical positivism as the basis for the empirical social sciences, especially including the project of scientific management.

The Origins of Truth

To uncover the theory of truth shared by traditional economic modelers, the risk managers who follow their lead, and Krugman himself, we need to first understand the role truth plays within the traditional theory of linguistic meaning.

One of the most enduring traditional theories of meaning is referentialism, sometimes called the Augustinian view of language (Wittgenstein 1968). Referentialism is built from several intuitions we have about the nature of language acquisition. In reflecting on our own language learning or in observing the same in children, it often appears to us that language is founded on individual words used as the names of, or as labels for, objects. Anyone who has spent a significant amount of time with a two-year-old will be especially given to this impression. The full theory of meaning, then, is merely an extrapolation from the case of names to more complex forms of linguistic expression: just as names refer to objects, so do phrases refer to states of affairs, and so do sentences refer to facts (Russell 1973). It is important to note, however, that this extrapolation is fed by another very basic assumption: that the meaning of a sentence is a function of the meaning of the simpler elements of which it is composed (i.e., phrases and words). The basic idea is that if words mean by referring to objects, and if words are the compositional elements of sentences, and if sentences are functions of their compositional elements, then sentences also mean by referring (Frege 1980b). But if appealing to reference is going to be truly explanatory of meaning, we ought to be able to give some more fundamental account of the phenomenon of reference, even if it is merely descriptive rather than itself further explanatory.

The attempt to give a further account of this phenomenon has led philosophers in many different directions, but the best elucidations have pursued the idea that reference is a matter of representing and/or picturing. The feature that all pictures and representations share in common is that they are "about" something. That is, they "point to" some object, state of affairs, or fact beyond themselves or other than themselves. To understand this last point, we need only observe that no picture can picture itself (Wittgenstein 1961). Thus, if meaning is a matter of reference, and reference a matter of picturing, and picturing a matter of "being about," then meaning is a matter of "being about."

That said, there are yet further aspects of linguistic meaning, further aspects of "being about" that we need to add to our analysis for it to be fully explained and elucidated. More specifically, when we compare pictures with sentences, it becomes clear that we require an account of truth to fill out the traditional theory of meaning. We first have to begin by laying out the terms in which pictures and sentences can be compared. Pictures vary, from those that represent with a high degree of accuracy to those that represent in only the vaguest way. Think, for example, of the difference between a photograph and an abstract painting. Both can be regarded as pictures, of course. In fact, it's not uncommon for us understand pictures of each sort as being about one and the same event. In such a case, if we ask which is the "true" representation of the event—the photo or the abstract painting—we may end up with as many opinions as there are parties to the debate.

What conclusion are we to draw from this fact? The simple way to put it is that "being about" is not really a function of accuracy; it's almost entirely, if not entirely, a function of our having understood the picture as a picture in the first place. To put it even more bluntly, something's being a picture is entirely subjective (Wittgenstein 1961). In fact, with enough time and imagination, we can take just about any state of affairs as the representation of another. What does this tell us? In short, no one is in a position to say to another that what he or she has understood as a picture is no picture at all by appeal to some greater or lesser degree of accuracy, or to some similar criterion. So if it turns out that someone is, in fact, committed to the "truth" of a particular picture as opposed to any alternative, what they are really committed to is some property or properties possessed by the picture that they believe pictures must have in order to be of the best sort (Collingwood 1958). Art history is filled with these debates, but these are not debates about truth. They are debates about subjective preferences and how they are satisfied, to a greater and lesser extent, by objects understood as pictures—which requires that some objects will never be understood by certain people as pictures at all for having failed to satisfy their preferences to even the most minimal degree. But is all of this also the case for sentences?

Let us take for granted that sentences are also pictures, in that they are objects understood as "being about" some state of affairs different from themselves. Like all pictures, then, this implies that a sentence can fail to be a sentence for having failed to be understood as one. Unlike pictures, however, there is the possibility that we might take some object to be a sentence that is not one. How are we to account for the difference between the case of pictures and that of sentences? Simply put, the very possibility of mistaking certain objects for sentences means that not only is there a subjective condition of sentencehood, there is also an objective condition. This is not so with pictures generally. So what is the objective condition?

We need only examine cases of things that look like sentences but fail to be so to discover this objective condition. Some objects fail to be sentences by failing to be logically well formed, despite being grammatically well ordered. They fail to be logically well formed because they fail to follow the standard rules for logically well-formed formulations of a given language (Wittgenstein 1961; Russell 1996). To put it in terms of meaning per se, such objects appear to mean something, but they fail to mean for failing to be sentences; and they fail to be sentences for failing to be logically well formed, that is, for failing to follow the rules. In contrast, the principal indication that an object has satisfied the objective condition of sentencehood in being logically well formed is that the sentence has a property that the mere picture does not in only having to satisfy a subjective condition for its picturehood. The property in question is truth evaluability, sometimes called "truth aptness." More simply, it is the property of being either true or false, which is an absolute distinction and does not admit of degrees. It is one or the other. This is not the case with pictures generally.

The traditional theory of truth, called the correspondence theory, takes together these two features of the special pictures that we call sentences: their "being about"–ness and their truth evaluability. Briefly, the correspondence theory of truth says that truth consists in a relation of correspondence to reality or that truth is a relational property holding between propositions and facts that they picture (Russell 1971). We might also say that truth is a relation such that propositions are truth bearers and the facts that they picture are their truth makers (Moore 1953).

Let's take a simple example to illustrate this point: "The Dow Jones index lost two hundred points today." This proposition is true if and only if it is a fact that the Dow Jones index lost two hundred points today. The example makes the correspondence theory appear intuitively clear, because the fact that serves as the proposition's truth maker is of a fairly simple nature that can be verified by empirical observation. The fact for which we are looking is limited in temporal scope, that is, limited to one day, and can be verified with just one confirming instance by checking the ticker that aggregates the market's results.

Things become more difficult when we consider a proposition that asserts a fact of a more complicated nature. For instance, "Theoretical models can help generate predictive knowledge about the probability of future events." The truth-making fact for which the proposition asks us to look, while still empirically verifiable in principle, would require observation over time and generalization from many confirming instances. The latter example begins to trouble the intuitive clarity of the correspondence theory. That said, the basic underlying structure—an assumption about the nature of the truth relation—remains fundamentally the same in both of the previous cases, even if determining the truth of a given proposition turns out to be very difficult.

It is worth providing a few more details about the correspondence theory. It says that in being logically well formed, the sentence does two things at once: (1) it shows that it is possible for there to be a fact composed of nonlinguistic elements exhibiting the same structure as the linguistic elements of the sentence; and (2) it asserts that such a fact actually exists (Wittgenstein 1961). It is this last point about asserting that such a fact exists that makes for the truth evaluability of the sentence, because in making that assertion, the sentence forces us to consider whether or not the truth-making fact exists. If there is an existing fact with a structure that is mirrored by the structure of the sentence, then the sentence is true. If there is no such fact, then the sentence is false. What is interesting to notice about this, though, is how great a number of unquestioned (metaphysical) assumptions have to be held in place if this theory of meaning and truth is going to hold. To understand the point from the opposite direction, we need only observe that if an object fails the objective condition for sentencehood, it will be nonsense, that is, without any truth evaluability, because there is no possible fact with the structure asserted by a sentence that is not well formulated. It is this last point that forms the foundation of the logical positivists' transformation of the traditional theory of meaning and truth into a critical tool for what, in their opinion, was the total elimination of metaphysics.

The preceding examples can be used to illuminate what is for us the key point about the nature of metaphysics. We assumed earlier that our first example was metaphysically uncomplicated, as do positivists when giving their favored examples. But we can see that when considered metaphysically, things are not quite so simple. When we say, "The Dow Jones index lost two hundred points today," we have implicitly proposed the existence of all kinds of things that would have to play a role in composing the fact that confirms the proposition—the point being that these are not things we will necessarily be able to observe "right now" or "easily." As a result, there must be a whole raft of tacit assumptions at work to support our isolation of a given proposition for consideration as to its meaning, that is, as to its truth. In turn, these tacit assumptions are undergirded by a raft of tacit agreements between individuals about what can and what cannot be asked, lest the entire collective edifice of inquiry collapse. That said, there is still variability about just which of these background assumptions and agreements is necessary to make the inquiry about the truth of a given proposition at all possible. Because not all the things proposed by a sentence are currently observable, not every interpretation or reading of the full meaning of that proposition will agree about what must exist for the sentence to be true.

In the Dow Jones case, it seems clear that stretches of time must exist, measurable into units; so, too, the Dow Jones index must exist; and there must be a relation called "loss" to which the Dow Jones index is subject relative to some other property it possesses, such that it can be measurably diminished. Thus far, we are at the very bare minimum of what is required. As to *what* the Dow Jones index is, however, we might well disagree about which interpretation of it is sufficient. We could disagree, for instance, about whether the best interpretation is realist, such that the numbers refer to yet further facts in the world having to do with the organization of economic activity, or about whether the best interpretation is nominalist, such that the number itself is the only relevant fact from which to conclude about proper action. In fact, the market practitioner's theory-in-use is frequently nominalist, but, as Hardy said of most mathematicians, they are realists at night when their heads hit the pillow (Hardy 1992)—especially when it comes to the predictive power of their investment portfolio models.

In the following section, we consider the faith in that principle by which such a truth could be verified.

Positivism, Verification, and Nonsense

The logical positivists were first and foremost empiricists of a healthy variety, assuming in a reasonably modern way that all existence is circumscribed by the causal closure principle (James 1950), which holds that in order to explain the as-yet-unexplained phenomenon, it will be explained only insofar as we can appeal to the physical causes that brought it about. To appeal to causes other than physical causes will be to appeal to a second order of causation, which ultimately would be to scuttle all explanation in terms of causes. The faith in this principle is not irrational for the very reason that appeal to physical causes has been the hallmark of scientific progress, which is measured by our ability to predict future events along a causal chain. Appeals to causes of another order, say, God's will, in no way increase our ability to predict and thereby control outcomes for the human well-being and flourishing. We can see here the perfectly admirable foundation of modern scientific management. In all this, though, we need to know what counts as a cause, which is to say, what counts as existing. The short answer is anything observable by means of perception, maybe including introspection of our own mental states—but this last point was and is hotly contested among scientific empiricists specifically and philosophical naturalists generally. To exist, then, is to be perceivable. It does not take very much reflection to understand that this is a very strict criterion for existence.

When we combine this robust commitment to empiricism with the referential theory of meaning and the correspondence theory of truth, we arrive at the positivists' principle of verification (Ayer 1952; Carnap 2003), which is essentially an ingenious way of telling whether a sentence is truth evaluable and possibly meaningful. In very rough outline, the principle says that a sentence is meaningful only insofar as we can say what steps would need to be taken to verify either its truth or its falsity, where what counts as verification is the evidence of the senses. If we can neither say nor imagine what we would *do* to verify the sentence's truth value, the sentence is meaningless, despite appearances to the contrary, despite its having fulfilled the subjective condition of being understood as a picture about a possible way the world might be. In essence, the positivists claim that the way such a sentence fails is that it expresses an arrangement of elements that is not logically possible; hence, there could be no such fact to which it corresponds, because no fact can violate the order of logical possibility (Wittgenstein 1961). The positivists then draw some general conclusions from the application of the principle of verification, conclusions that ultimately constitute what goes by the name "elimination of metaphysics."

To illustrate, let's begin with a sentence that would likely be validated by the positivists as meaningful: "The volume of trading is down at the New York Stock Exchange." When we survey observable facts to verify the truth value of an empirical assertion, we do so by verifying that there exists an observable marketplace that possesses the observable property of having a lower trading volume. We might also imagine that it has the properties of being located in lower Manhattan, regulated by the Securities and Exchange Commission, and so on. All of these properties we discover by means our various senses. At the same time, when we undertake this verification or imagine undertaking it, we also discover that there is a set of procedures that we can outline that would, if carried out by any possible observer, allow them to conclude definitively whether the assertion under consideration is true.

In a sentence where the predicate expresses a value, however, say "good" or "beautiful," we are faced with two difficulties. Let's take a basic aesthetic claim like "The economic algorithm is beautiful," which has all the features of a traditional empirical assertion, principally a subject–predicate structure. First, in attempting to verify that to which the value term refers, we cannot simply appeal to the use of our senses; whereas my vision allows me access to the market's location in Manhattan and, thus, gives me the sense of its being among or "alongside" the marketplace's other properties, the same will not be true of my evaluation of the algorithm's beauty: I am not able to identify the perceptual channel through which beauty is perceived, and furthermore, I do not have the sense that beauty exists alongside the algorithm's other proper-ties, like being composed of logical operators, being used by risk managers, and so on. There are many questions to be asked about this, but the positiv-ists move quickly to the second difficulty to help elucidate and explain the initial difficulty. Second, we simply are unable to imagine and articulate a set of procedures that any possible observer could undertake that would lead him or her to conclude definitively whether the sentence is true (Schlick 1985; Ayer 1952).

On these grounds, positivists draw very particular conclusions about the nature of moral and aesthetic discourse, that is, evaluative discourse. To put it simply, they conclude that such discourse is only apparently meaningful, but actually *nonsense*. We may take sentences of the evaluative variety to repre-sent some facts in the world, but they do not represent (or picture, or refer) to reality. (As we will see here, there is also the option that moral and aesthetic discourse is reducible to statements that are about value-neutral, empirically observable facts.) Given our account to this point, we can see that there are weaker and stronger claims mixed together here. There is either a (weaker) semantic claim being drawn, or there is a (stronger) ontological claim being drawn.

On the one hand, the merely semantic conclusion is that an evaluative claim is not truth apt for the reason that we cannot provide a set of procedures through which any observer might go and arrive at a definitive conclusion about the claim's truth. However, this leaves open whether there might exist a realm of moral and aesthetic facts to which we simply do not have access. In other words, the conclusion is epistemologically stringent but metaphysically permissive. It is the philosophical equivalent of either mysticism or agnosticism, depending on one's temperament (Wittgenstein 1961).

On the other hand, the robust ontological conclusion is that an evaluative claim's being meaningless gives us every reason to abandon any supposition that there exist moral or aesthetic facts that could make our evaluative claims true. This is because the range of our epistemic capacities is generally thought to be specially suited to gaining access to what can genuinely be said to exist. Thus, the rational person will conclude that there are no facts that have moral and aesthetic properties. This is the philosophical equivalent of atheism (Carnap 2003).

Whatever else may be the case, however, the two positivist positions share some important features in common: both regard evaluative discourse as non–truth apt, and thus both regard evaluative discourse as doing something semantically different than referring; likewise, both regard evaluative discourse not as referring to the world but as expressing either one's emotions with regard to certain aspects of the world or one's attitudes of approval or disapproval of those aspects (Ayer 1952; Stevenson 1944).

In turn, both varieties of positivism present a challenge to anyone who remains committed to the meaningfulness of moral and aesthetic discourse: to provide a position that is epistemologically and metaphysically simpler than positivism for explaining the nature of evaluative discourse. To be metaphysically simple, a theory needs to refer to only one kind of thing—in the positivist's case, concrete things, that is, objects existing at a location in space and time and observable by the senses. To be epistemologically simple, a theory needs to refer to only those perceptual modalities used for accessing concrete things. As it stands, though, it would appear that to account for the meaningfulness of moral and aesthetic discourse, we would need to posit both a realm of facts that is abstract (rather than concrete) and a mode of access to those facts that involves something like moral or aesthetic intuition (rather than perception). This is neither metaphysically nor epistemologically simple. Is there any way out of this bind?

. . .

Consider the following assertion: "The current financial crisis is bad." As against a claim like Krugman's—which identifies as crippling an aestheticization of financial judgment that eschews any reference whatsoever to grounding facts—one might well want to reestablish the soundness of financial judgment on the basis of some guarantee that our assertions about what's best are grounded in observable facts. Of course, this is a perfectly admirable desire, except insofar as it partakes in the positivism that we mean to question here—that is, insofar as it proposes that the realm of facts is value neutral. The problem with proposing a value-neutral realm of facts to which our assertions correspond for their meaning is that an assertion so clearly true as "the current financial crisis is bad" must, by the positivist account, go without any verification. That is, such claims turn out to be neither true nor false; they turn out to be meaningless, such that the imperative, in fact, is to contest them as somehow empty or unhelpful, as we see them contested in all manner of popular and scientific discourse.

To correct this problem, "badness" and "the financial crisis" would have to be rendered meaningful by way of correlating them with observable facts that we must explicitly agree constitute the empirical ground of the otherwise purely evaluative and abstract terms at play. And yet, inevitably, there will be wide disagreement about what observable facts, if any, constitute the empirical ground of evaluative discourse and/or discourse referring to facts so large as to be unavailable to any observation except as an induction from instances occurring between arbitrarily chosen points in time. The arbitrariness of such a choice asks for a further making explicit of the grounds of our assertions—for instance, the assertion "the start of the financial crisis occurred in 2007." To gather evidence for such a claim, we would need to leave unquestioned yet some more fundamental assumption, lest we risk a regress that would scuttle all meaning and truth.

The best way to avoid the regress is to never take the first step, whereby some manner of evaluative discourse is reduced to a set of observation statements. Instead, we must take for granted and as fundamental what is already intuitively clear: that the assertion "the current financial crisis is bad" is true, simpliciter. (In fact, almost no one will disagree with this.) It is interesting to note that the intuition about its truth, especially these days, is never very far from people's minds. Even when engaged in a semantic reduction in positivist terms, we suspect that the truth of this assertion is more than merely a function of the truth of the empirical observations to which it might be reduced—assuming, of course, that we could even agree as to how such a reduction would happen.

But if we reject as empty the reduction of evaluative discourse to empirical discourse, are we then allowed to suppose that evaluative discourse appeals to nonobservable facts in order to be true, which, in turn, would require some extraperceptual intuition by which we would have access to these facts? The answer would seem to be very clearly no; on this point, the positivists are correct. We cannot appeal to anything quite so metaphysically and epistemically challenging as moral facts and moral intuition. We must show that "the current financial crisis is bad" is true without appeal to the phenomenon of correspondence and, at the same time, without positing anything more metaphysically and epistemologically complicated than concrete facts and simple perception. And, again, we must do all this without reducing this clearly true claim to what would have to be agreed is a more fundamental level of empirical discourse. The positivists do give us another choice.

Is the only path left open to us, then, to assume that evaluative discourse is the expression of mere attitudes of pleasure and displeasure toward situations with which we are presented in thought or perception? Are we to understand such an expression as "the current financial crisis is bad," especially out the of mouths of a nonexperts, as nothing more than the extreme displeasure of finding oneself behind the eight ball?

The answer here too seems clearly to be no, because in positing as much, we would lose the normative power of our evaluative judgments, the genuine power of such judgments to require our action to change the world. On both counts, we are faced with a multifaceted challenge: (1) to reject any reduction of evaluative discourse to more fundamental empirical discourse, but (2) at the same time, to provide a theory of meaning and truth that does not suppose either the existence of moral facts and intuitions or that moral discourse is simply the expression of merely subjective attitudes of pleasure and displeasure.

This challenge has been faced in many different ways, but we need only recall what the purpose of our account here is: to provide a genealogy that gives some perspective on how scientific management came to trade on the absolute distinction between factual and evaluative discourse. It turns out that most of the discourse built up around the recent crisis retains a generally positivist set of assumptions about the relationship between propositional knowledge and empirical reality. The problem, as we will continue to show in the following section, is that positivism is a radically weak position, subject to criticisms from many directions and generally untenable.

Moving Beyond the Fact-Value Dichotomy

We turn now to a review of the criticisms that strike at the heart of the positivist project and thereby undermine the theory of truth to which both

Krugman and his opponents tacitly appeal as the correction to the econo-mists' addiction to the beauty of their models.

The simplest way to present all the criticisms at once is to point out how the position outlined here leads us to what many regard as the horns of a di-lemma, that is, a situation in which you're damned if you do and damned if you don't. Simply put, positivism requires either that you attain to metaphysi-cal and/or epistemological complexity in explaining the meaning of evalu-ative discourse or that you conclude that evaluative discourse is "merely" expressive of private attitudes. (Notice that this is what Krugman is accus-ing his opponents of.) In the eyes of most, this is simply unacceptable. Philo-sophically speaking, ending on the horns of a dilemma is to fail to offer a proper explanation and requires that we review the health of the assumptions on which the conclusions are drawn. In the positivist case, the assumptions are myriad: the referentiality of meaning, the correspondence of truth, the verification principle, and so on. We could go back to review all the assump-tions we've named already, but the list here is sufficient for us to arrive at a damning conclusion.

We first reflect critically on the verification principle. The easiest objection to it—and in some sense the cheapest, but also the most important—is that when we use the principle as a criterion of meaning and apply it to the very statements that articulate and elucidate the principle itself, it turns out that the principle is meaningless on its own terms. We can make the same point by asking a simple rhetorical question or two: What observation procedures might one engage in—either in fact or in principle—to confirm the truth or falsity of the verification principle itself? Where might I go in this world or any possible world to observe the facts that I would use to confirm that the verification principle is true? The answer to both questions is clear. There are no observation procedures by which I could verify or falsify the verification principle, which says that an assertion is meaningful only to the extent that it is verifiable or falsifiable. In this sense, the verification principle is itself meaningless. If this is true, however, the principle is inconsistent maybe to the point of self-contradiction and cannot be used as a criterion for meaning.

The harder objection, the one that brings us closer to the heart of what we want to illuminate here, is that the brand of empiricism from which the veri-fication principle springs rests on a questionable distinction between analytic and synthetic statements (Popper 1977; Quine 1980). A mathematical example will illuminate this point and help us further establish a strategy for facing the positivist challenge for evaluative discourse.

If a statement is well formed according to the rules of the formal language that constitutes mathematics, then that statement must be either true or false. The problem is that on the theory of meaning and truth held by the positivists, although such statements have the property of being truth evaluable, there is no set of procedures that will, if carried out by any possible observer, lead them to a definitive conclusion as to the statement's truth. For a true mathematical statement, one might very well go through a set of procedures constructed by a knowledgeable practitioner to reveal the statement's truth, and yet not arrive at that conclusion for simply failing to understand. In this case, the positivists have two choices: (1) they can conclude that all mathematical discourse is like evaluative discourse, that is, meaningless and actually expressive of attitudes about states of the world; or (2) they can conclude that true mathematical discourse is actually a disguised variety of analytic statement making—that is, statements true by definition and, therefore, necessarily true. (Synthetic statements, by contrast, are made true by the facts of the world and are therefore only contingently true.) Again, we are faced with an untenable dichotomy. The positivists themselves more or less rejected the first option out of hand because mathematics is so clearly truth evaluable, and not only apparently so (Ayer 1952).

At the same time, pursuing of the second option puts positivists on rocky terrain for two reasons. First, mathematical assertions are very frequently ampliative or informative; that is, they are clearly more than merely conceptual analyses wherein the predicates are shown to be contained in the subject by definition (Moore 1953); so that, second, if mathematical discourse is going to be understood as a variety of analytic statement making, we first need to show how it can be reduced to some other discourse that is clearly and completely analytic—in this case, logic. The problem is that logicism, the project of reduction, stalled out on several fronts (Russell 1996; Gödel 1992).

The logical reduction basis on which mathematics is supposed to rest must itself be true by definition, but this is an ambiguous requirement. Either it means that logical discourse is true by means of conventional agreement (Hilbert 1996)—in which case, it loses any claim to having a priori status, that is, any claim to necessary truth, which does seem very clearly to be a hallmark of logic (Quine 1980). Or it means that we retain logic's a priori status and, instead, work out an explanation such that logical assertions actually express the universal and immemorial structures that the (immaterial) human mind brings to the organization of experience (Kant 1965; Brouwer 1981), or an explanation such that logical assertions mean by reference to facts that are themselves comprehensible, although not observable (Bernays 1983). Neither of the latter options is available to the positivists, because it would require foregoing either metaphysical or epistemological simplicity, or both. However, the former option begs us to ask: If logic is true by convention and not necessarily true, then if we reduce mathematics to it, won't we also forgo the necessary truth of mathematics that we wanted to preserve? The answer is clearly yes. So where does this leave positivism?

It leaves positivists, as we have claimed above, in the position of having to make an unenviable decision. First, do we throw off our concern with maintaining metaphysical and epistemological simplicity to secure mathematical truth? If we do, then we have to forgo the only brand of empiricism that validates our holding apart evaluative from factual discourse, because there is no nonarbitrary reason we couldn't then consider that there are a set of nonnatural facts that make moral and aesthetic statements true. Alternatively, second, do we throw off the concern with explaining mathematical truth, thereby capitulating tacitly to the idea that mathematical discourse is not truth apt, like the evaluative forms of discourse? In addition to being patently absurd—throwing off mathematical truth as a way to maintain a theory in the face of criticism is an incredibly high price to pay for consistency—there is the further disadvantage that we then lose the ability to explain a further aspect of mathematical discourse: its clear applicability for the solution to empirical problems. That phenomenon would, under the condition of taking this second path, become completely inexplicable. For the record, this phenomenon would also be inexplicable by following the initial path: there is simply no way to explain how mathematics is applicable to empirical problems if what such discourse is really about is a realm of existence populated not by concrete particulars but by abstract universals (Maddy 1992, 2000).

Wittgenstein's solution was to create a special category into which mathematical assertions fit, called the "senseless." "Nonsense" included any genuinely meaningless assertions, whereas assertions with "sense" could be empirically verified. "Senseless" assertions could not be verified, but they were nonetheless true or false—and necessarily so. For him, every necessarily true mathematical assertion had an underlying logical form akin to "a = a," despite any appearances to the contrary. Although elegant, his solution for mathematical assertions depends on a fundamentally faulty assumption: no mathematical assertion is genuinely informative. But Wittgenstein's solution per se is not the interesting fact; instead, it's the way his solution speaks to several of the issues that we have in mind regarding evaluative discourse: (1) he rejects any kind of reduction to more fundamental empirical discourse; (2) he finds a solution that does not require the supposition of metaphysical or epistemological complexity, by simply denying that mathematical assertions refer at all to their truth; and (3) he rejects the reduction to merely subjective states, thereby giving their objectivity its proper due. The parallel to evaluative discourse is clear, so we simply need to see how the advantages of Wittgenstein's approach can be maintained without also having to assume the fundamentally noninformative character of mathematical assertions.

What we want is a theory of meaning and truth that allows mathematical discourse (and, by implication, all evaluative discourse) its truth evaluability and applicability without any further reference to specious metaphysical entities or unfamiliar forms of epistemic access to reality. At the same time, we clearly need a theory of meaning and truth not born of the brand of empiricism that has now been shown to be untenable for requiring that we abandon certain discourse as meaningless or requiring that in saving it we abandon certain of its defining features. To put it bluntly, the strategy is a simple one: if referentiality is ultimately what backs us into this corner, then we need to question whether meaning is a function of referentiality at all. The less radical strategy in the same direction would be not to question referentiality but to rethink that to which such sentences actually refer, thus opening up the possibility that they refer to facts of the social world rather than facts of the natural world, where social facts are nonetheless observable.

We will pursue the more radical alternative below, but first, the less radical approach is worth some further consideration. Let's take our example again: "The current financial crisis is bad." Rather than referring to a fact composed of a globally large, abstract object ("financial crisis") and an evaluative property ("bad")—a fact that garden-variety empiricism implicitly asks us to understand as similar to more prosaic facts, for instance, a local and concrete object ("chair") possessing a physical property ("three legged")—the idea here is that such assertions actually refer to dynamic facts, social facts rather than objectlike static facts. This has the advantage of not forcing us into the positivist's trap of having to suppose a strange variety of static facts to which such evaluative assertions correspond; it instead gets us looking for the appropriate corresponding facts from among those composed of the local and concrete actions of agents in particular and qualitatively specifiable circumstances.

For instance, we can imagine much more easily being able to render explicit our agreements about what observable actions constitute the meaning of statements like "the current financial crisis is bad." We can illustrate this simply by pointing to the actions that we understand as counting against the observable well-being of those whose lives are directly affected by such actions, that is, the stakeholders. For instance, to say that the crisis is bad is to mean in part that "selling mortgages to subprime borrowers in 2007 led to a measurable decrease in homeowners' well-being." It also means in part that "selling mortgages to subprime borrowers in 2007 made hedging risk measurably more difficult." And it might well mean a whole raft of other action-based, social facts bearing on the well-being of stakeholders, even to the point that the decrease in well-being is so large—as in this case—as to draw new and originally unaffected individuals into the stakeholder's position (i.e., "the American taxpayer"). The problem remains, of course, that this procedure will nonetheless require explicit agreement about the equivalency of terms and might involve so large a set of facts that we run the risk of never being able to finally specify the total number of facts to which any given evaluative assertion refers. But we can nonetheless see how the progress toward that agreement is more easily begun because we are focused on finding referents from among social facts.

If we had more space, we would review all these possibilities in turn, but we will instead simply follow the line of argument that considers the nature of truth. With regard to truth, we have a similar option as we did with meaning: if meaning is not referential, then truth simply cannot be a matter of correspondence but rather a function of some other kind of relationship, identity, or process; but if we maintain some variety of referentiality, then truth can remain correspondence to reality, but now understood as correspondence to a set of social facts, which, unlike natural facts, have a nonfoundationalist structure of coherence (Davidson 2001). Again, we will be pursuing the first path for reasons of economy. What, then, does such a theory of meaning and truth look like?

What Works? Toward a Pragmatic Theory of Meaning and Truth

We first need to review quickly the reasons we should abandon referentiality, because in doing so, we also show reasons for abandoning correspondence as the criterion of truth. The earliest forms of the referentiality thesis ultimately required that we understand all complex sentences as functions operating over constituent elements—that is, names—but this leads to serious problems. To put it more simply, sentences were regarded as the functional total of the referential power of their constituent parts to name objects. This would require, however, that any list of names is meaningful, but we can easily imagine a list that is not meaningful. The revision of the referentiality thesis required that there must be truth-preserving contexts into which names were put to attain to their full meanings (Frege 1980a), such that not just any list of names will be meaningful (Wittgenstein 1961). This revision has its advantages, but it loses the ability to say how some lists of names are actually meaningful—that is, any list of names without the supporting logical mechanism of subject–predicate structure—or it could maintain that capacity but require that the meaning of the constituent terms is a function of reference to specious metaphysical entities.

To use a famous example (Wittgenstein 1968), "five red apples" would require for its meaningfulness that, in addition to the concrete apples, we posit the abstract objects of redness and fiveness to which the respective words refer and thus mean. But this runs afoul of our commitment to metaphysical and epistemological simplicity. We could also just conclude that such lists of names are not meaningful at all, under any circumstances. But this is patently false. Under the pressure exerted by our commitment to metaphysical simplicity, then, we have to think seriously about dropping reference as belonging to the analysis of meaning at all. Why?

The reason it is suspect that reference belongs to the proper analysis of meaning is because appealing to it happens only on the basis of an unquestioned assumption about what type of linguistic expression is paradigmatically meaningful: assertions, which are defined by predicating a subject. On this account, then, a whole range of linguistic expressions is left out as meaningless, unless they can be shown to be disguised assertions: imperatives, interrogatives, exclamations, and so on. What is curious, however, is that with regard to use, assertions make up relatively little of our daily discourse by comparison to the emphasis placed on them within the theory of meaning considered here. In using language, we are as frequently, if not more frequently, imperative, interrogative, ironic, and expletive. The pragmatic approach to meaning and truth, then, begins by looking at how we use language in practice, looking at our utterances and inscriptions in context rather than considering assertions as objects outside any use-context whatsoever (Austin 1962; Searle 1969).

The appeal of this new strategy is augmented by the observation that there are also assertions that are explicable only by appealing to the context of their use, for instance, "That is a nice red one" (and other uses of demonstratives and indexicals). And it is augmented yet again by appealing to the imperative quality both of evaluative discourse and of mathematical discourse. In the case of evaluative discourse, although it is difficult to understand how the positivist's reduction of it to the expression of subjective attitudes could possibly maintain the normative force that we believe such discourse to have, it is much easier to see that moral and aesthetic statements are disguised imperatives directing another's actions under given conditions. Likewise, although it preserves the quality of its being necessarily true, it is difficult to understand that mathematical discourse is just a disguised version of analytic statement making; it seems so clearly applicable to the real world, seems so much about it, that it would make more sense to understand the appeal to its necessary truth as again a variety of imperative for what someone ought to do under certain circumstances.

Thus, what we see when we really begin to look at meaning from the perspective of our ordinary use of language is that, for the most part, it is not at all referential and truth is not a matter of correspondence. Imperatives are not about anything, nor are questions, nor are outbursts, nor is fiction, nor are jokes—certainly not in the sense implied by referentialism. Yet all these uses of discourse clearly mean something, as long as they are expressions used in a way that follows the rules of the language game in which they are played as moves (Wittgenstein 1968). With no initial appeal to reference, we thus also lose the capacity to appeal to representation or picturing as a concept by which to illuminate meaning. And, in turn, we lose the motivation to describe truth as a correspondence between the structure of the proposition's constituents and those of the fact.

And yet, the problem is even more radical than that. It is not simply that we lose the motivation, but that we additionally lose the ground for doing so. If we take as paradigmatically meaningful those expressions that are nonreferential or nonrepresentational, then we have lost the ability to distinguish between the representation and the represented—that is, nonidentical entities that can serve as the arguments that satisfy the variables that define the two-place relation called truth. In a far less rigorous mood, some worry that we then have to do without these vital concepts, meaning and truth, such that we end in nihilistic relativism. It is no surprise that this is the accusation often made against Nietzsche. All we are really faced with, though, is the problem of offering workable theories of each—theories that respect the fact that meaning and truth are very real properties of our expressions and experiences. So what are we to say of meaning and truth now?

We will get at the new account of truth only by way of a new account of meaning that rejects the compositionality thesis that frames an expression's meaning as a function of the meaning of its constituent parts. This traditional perspective on language understands assertions as static objects that can be analyzed into constituent parts, much like physical atomism. In fact, science is the model for the analytic paradigm in the early twentieth-century theorizing about language. At any rate, the parts of which assertions are composed are, straightforwardly enough, phrases and individual words. We recognize, of course, that these smaller constituents of assertions are meaningful in some incomplete way, for instance, "the current financial crisis" understood outside of its use in an assertive context, likewise for "crisis." At the same time, there must be some smallest meaningful part, because we equally well recognize that c has no meaning whatsoever. (Many linguistics think that minimal part is the phoneme, an expression made of more than one letter sound but technically less than a full word—although they frequently regard this as belonging, strictly speaking, to spoken language.) As such, the meaning of an assertion is a function of the meaning of its constituent parts; so, too, for any complex construction whereby assertions are combined by means of logical connectors. The compositionality thesis requires, then, every assertion with the same logico-grammatical form has the same meaning, insofar as it is meaningful. But this flies in the face of what is observably the case.

From the newer perspective that we are encouraging here, where meaning is partially or wholly a function of its use within a context (Wittgenstein 1968), we introduce the theoretical possibility—which reflects actual linguistic practice—that two different instances of an expression with identical syntactical structures could have contradictory meanings. Likewise, it is possible that expressions with two different syntactical structures could mean the same thing in a single context. Technically speaking, this possibility is left open to the referentialist as well, who will simply say that in both cases—of synonymous and ambiguous expressions—we resolve these defects by ignoring certain misleading features of the surface grammar and attending to the underlying logical formation of the expression. But for the theorist attending to meaning from the perspective of use, there is a further possibility for which the referentialist is unable to account: that expressions can be synonymous and ambiguous even if these are perfectly simply expressions, that is, single words, parts of words, or vocal gestures.

In this case, although the expressions are meaningful, referentialism fails because it cannot avail itself of the analysis of the expression into its parts to resolve the seeming conundrum presented by the surface grammar about an expression's literal and univocal meaning (Searle 1979). They have no analyzable composition. It remains the case, however, that the instance of a given expression—that is, on a single occasion of its use—has to mean one thing rather than another. It might be ambiguous or synonymous across uses, but in the moment, it must mean only one thing to be genuinely meaningful. If we now must go without an appeal to analysis as a way to resolve an expression's literal meaning, what, then, is the criterion that decides an expression's meaning? That an expression has a univocal meaning still requires in principle that it is decidable to which side of an absolute divide the expression falls, a divide that mirrors the normative distinction between truth and falsity for assertions: correctness or incorrectness (Wittgenstein 1968). This commitment, taken as key to constructing a theory of meaning and truth, however, must be fulfilled with an eye to metaphysical and epistemological simplicity, such that the result appeals to neither specious entities or capacities. What, then, is the theory of truth revealed from within this insight?

Truth as Evaluation: What Can We Really Afford?

Let us begin by recalling that we are now on a terrain that asks us to consider all meaningful expressions, including evaluative expressions—as well as questions, interrogations, imperatives, and the like—as actions of utterance or inscription in given contexts. Moreover, we have recognized that such expressions have the meanings that they do for being correct uses in that context. We have to ask, then, what is the criterion of correctness, say, for evaluative language? Notice already how it is automatically a reasonable working assumption of the theoretical endeavor undertaken here that there are correct or incorrect uses of evaluative language (Blackburn 1984; Gibbard 1992). Moreover, we will find that claims of truth per se involve an epistemic value—an achievement of sorts, if you will.

So, then, what happens if we approach meaning from the perspective of evaluation rather than assertion? Every evaluative judgment implies, in its expression, that others ought to believe in the same way and come to the same conclusion (see Kant 1986)—and, just as important, that so believing will stand both as a reason for acting in a particular way and a motivation to so act. In offering our evaluations, however, we do not take ourselves to be expressing merely subjective desires and opinions. We take ourselves to be offering a belief that has the advantage of being objectively true or objectively correct.

What, then, makes such an evaluation true? To put it simply, any such evaluation is true when it expresses a belief that would be formed by an observer at the conclusion of an inquiry under ideal conditions (Peirce 1992).

For this theory to be able to take account of assertions, which it must if it is not going to suffer from the same defects as the theories rejected above, we have to see that assertions also share the feature we've outlined here: when we assert a fact, we are essentially asking another to come to same belief—which will, in some admittedly attenuated way, be a reason to act in a particular way and serve as the motivation to so act. This sounds odd, of course, but if we combine it with the idea that the meaning of such a statement is objectively determined by its being the belief to which a capable person will come under ideal conditions, then we can see that what is recommended is that under conditions of disagreement—which is often the setting in which genuine assertions with any import are made—someone ought to act so as to bring themselves closer to the (ideal) position in forming their beliefs. Of course, the question that is often asked of this view is what constitutes the ideal conditions (Evans 1982; Merleau-Ponty 2002)?

Traditional theorists of behavior and game theory will say, "Thanks, but we already have a notion of what constitutes an ideal position: fully informed and fully rational." This ideal position is understood in the absolute sense, such that it is ideal as well in the sense of being unachievable in practice. We have to be satisfied, then, with policies that encourage second-best approximations of an ideal that is not measured in genuinely human terms. Pragmatists would, in view of the ongoing financial crisis, respectfully dispute this traditional notion of economic rationality. Instead, the pragmatic ideality to which we are appealing has to do with what is expedient (James 1997) for the achievement of observable advances in well-being within given contexts.

In other words, inquiring toward truth involves raising questions about the adaptation of our capacities to what the environment affords (Gibson 1979). It is to understand that the primary sense of truth is not being "consistent with a fact" but instead "conforming with a rule," where the rules are developed over time within shared forms of life (or spheres of activity) and directed toward the maintenance of the values and understandings that help keep the organization of collective activity aimed at the achievement of the very goals that define the sphere of activity—and all these goals, no matter the form of life, are geared toward the achievement of human well-being (Wittgenstein 1968).

. . .

To see what this might look like in practice, let us examine the activity of an expert within his environmental context. In Wittgenstein's (1966)

"Lectures on Aesthetics," he regards aesthetics broadly as a domain that includes all manner of evaluation. The domain is so broad, in fact, that evaluation is taken to include the noncognitive attitudes and practices of the expert craftsman. For our purposes—and taking much of our analysis to this point into account—we can understand "noncognitive attitude" to be a subjective mental state of the expert's that does not have the character of (an explicit) belief, such that the attitude does not represent the world as being one way rather than another. Likewise, a "noncognitive practice" is an active or behavioral expression of such an attitude. More radically, we might claim that the line between attitude and practice is amorphous or nonexistent. In the first case, there would be no priority given to attitudes of which practices are expressions; we could as much say that attitudes are—as they often are—the expression of our practices. In the second case, where the line between attitudes and practices is, from the theoretical perspective, eliminated, it would be because there is no discernable line at work in our experience. Think about how often we reflexively find our way through a whole series of practices or behaviors that simply *are*, in the metaphysical sense, our attitudes of pleasure and displeasure toward an object or situation; for instance, walking to the refrigerator during the commercial break. Where is the line between the desire and the action? It is in exactly this respect that Wittgenstein's several examples help illuminate his point that such practices are not merely reliant on evaluations but, in themselves, constitute a mode of truth-apt evaluations.

Before turning to his examples, it is worth emphasizing again that as a mode of evaluation, the practices of the expert craftsman are normative—such that their manipulation of an object in their environment with which they are concerned is guided by the noncognitive judgment they "ought" to be "like this" rather than "like that." The reason we need to reemphasize this point is because it helps us distinguish our position from one that we considered earlier. A traditionalist would simply take our position as a brand of expressivism, which is one of the horns of the dilemma supposedly forced on us by the positivists. Remember that they require that their position means either that we propose the existence of normative facts and the capacities for discerning them or that our evaluations are simply expressive of non-truth-evaluable attitudes, like subjective pleasure and displeasure. We have just now implicitly proposed that (linguistically formulated) evaluations would be the expression of noncognitive attitudes, which are themselves neither true nor false. But that is exactly what is in question here. We propose—with the pragmatists and Wittgenstein—that there is an important class of evaluative attitudes and/or practices—which "exhibit" or "show" that one option is better than another or that we ought to do this rather than that—which are themselves truth evaluable. In fact, they are at the foundation of what is truth evaluable exactly because the attitudes and/or practices engaged by the rule-following expert practicing his or her craft within the context of an environment shared with others—defined by rules that each holds as a set of background assumptions about useful behavior—are the original for which there is a criterion of correctness.

In this respect, combining Wittgenstein's elaboration with that of the pragmatists shows that what we ought to have in mind here as truth is not only the beliefs of the ideal observer at the conclusion of inquiry but also, and primarily, the practices (and only secondarily the beliefs and assertions, understood as derivative, linguistic practices) of the rule-following expert operating within the context of his mastery.

So, if we want to know what how to avoid a financial crisis, one simple answer is not merely to do what the algorithm dictates but to watch what the expert decides for himself or herself as against the algorithm. It is the true measure of which actions are required to meet the goals that already define the sphere of activity in which the expert operates, the only one that provides any standard of correctness. And again, all goals genuinely shared by humans are aimed at the achievement of well-being, even if the explicit ideas of such differ from one form of life to another. This is largely an Aristotelian point about eudaimonia borrowed by Wittgenstein. At any rate, Wittgenstein's further examples are instructive as to how we might make sense of certain actions or practices being noncognitive, that is, affective and genuinely truth-apt evaluations. In fact, they help us identify exactly which actions are pertinent for consideration in managing risk in the financial sector, for instance.

The first example is of an architect who corrects the design of a door. Wittgenstein claims that such correction is a matter of "instinct." From the context in which the example is given, it is reasonable for us to conclude that the use of "instinct" here is meant to be understood as over and against the interpretation of skillful behavior in question as dependent on a mode of "intuition," a manner of inarticulate knowing-that. In his estimation, appealing to intuition is a mystification of a process that is in many ways perfectly concrete and, to some degree, discernable. As such, the appeal to instinct names a certain bodily knowing-how. So the architect's correction of the door's design is an instinctive reaction to objects in his environment—but because the features of the environment to which he is reacting are observable, as are his reactions themselves, the entire evaluation can both be taught and learned. It is not a mysterious and natural capacity somehow interior to the craftsman.

How, then, are we to approach an analysis of the phenomenon in question? Simply put, we need merely to observe and describe what we see when an expert craftsman offers a correction. We can identify five distinct features of this embodied practice. The architect (or tailor, another of Wittgenstein's favorite examples) is first and foremost absorbed in his environment and, by all reports, no cognitive distance from the objects with which he is concerned. Other philosophers have referred to this absorption or engagement as nondeliberative or nonpropositional (see Merleau-Ponty 2002). As such, a second feature is that the expert's appreciation appears publicly in the very practice of reacting, not as a private state available only to the craftsman's reflection. In fact, it is important that the craftsman himself will often report an inability to find such states among his cognitive store when made to reflect on it. It only appears in practice. Taken all together, these other features suggest a third feature, which is that deliberation is itself a mark of the failure of the expert's appreciation, a moment to be overcome by delving again into a working engagement with the materials at hand.

The example of the architect reveals a fourth feature, though, that is particularly interesting. Insofar as the architect's appreciation is directed on making a correction, it requires that the architect appreciate the relation of the object to its environment, not simply the object per se. This door corrected in thus and such a way will not be an appropriate correction for that door over there. The fifth feature, then, is that we will never be able to articulate fully or entirely the features of that appreciation, because what constitutes an immediate environment, the variety of features in an environment, and the variety of environments per se are all too complex to be generalized. What we see here is that, although there are rules that cover what to do generally under certain circumstances—rules that the expert has fully internalized in order to be an expert—the expert himself is an important source of normativity, in the sense that what is correct is whatever satisfies the expert in a situation defined by the complexities that are the hallmark of daily life.

So what do we see when looking at the expert per se working in his environment, if we look to him as the source of normativity? Again, the behaviors are important. We do not typically see the expert give a linguistic report of his appreciation of an object within its environment; instead, we see what Wittgenstein (1966, 13) calls "aesthetic reactions" of "discontent, disgust, discomfort." The way we see these reactions is in the expert's bodily postures, gestures, and expressions. In this way, we can observe easily what matters to the expert within his environment. We literally have to see what the expert is doing.

Moreover, Wittgenstein points out that these aesthetic reactions are "directed" at an object. In philosophical terms, this means that the relation between the expert's reaction and the object is intentional and, therefore, internal, rather than external, as would be the case if the relation were merely causal. Causal relations are merely accidental, in that things could easily have been otherwise, whereas internal relations are such that the items so related are intrinsically so. The relation is necessary and, in that respect, normative. So, then, what might we conclude about the global financial crisis in view of these reflections?

In Conclusion: Evaluating What Works as Truth

Both Wittgenstein's notion of aesthetics and the pragmatic theory of truth that we have identified and articulated suggest a series of conclusions that might be used as a set of criteria or standards for formulating an appropriately qualitative way to think about how to manage a financial institution or, for that matter, how to design the principles for a sustainable, reliable global economy.

The first conclusion is that anything that can be regarded as possibly true or correct necessarily involves the exercise of evaluative judgment. Contrary to Krugman's suggestion, we will not move beyond the crisis simply by ridding ourselves of aesthetic judgment and reverting to a notion of objective truth. At the same time, no individual judgments or decision procedures aimed merely at the maintenance of consistency and/or coherence—two of the features associated with beautiful models—can be regarded as appropriately contributing to the possibility of truth. Why so? Because these judgments or decisions are exercised entirely outside of the human context by being divorced from the practice, by being disembodied representations that have lost the link to human action or never had it. In such cases, we lose any connection to the context that provides a criterion of correctness, and everything expressed thereafter is literally meaningless. Only those evaluations enacted by rule-following experts mutely engaged with their environments bear any direct relation to what deserves the name "truth." We can make this same point by saying that no decision can be true unless it is one exercised by a human within a context defined by rules directed on the achievement of shared goals, because it lacks the necessary evaluative component of truth.

Again, this requires that we turn our attention from the conclusions produced by algorithmic decision procedures to the decisions of the inventors of the algorithms, especially when they are faced with quandaries in the building of their models that need solutions. That which can be generalized on the basis of the judgment exercised under those conditions would, we propose, maintain the link to the human context necessary in elaborating a model of right action. In an important sense, we need to watch and learn from the dissatisfied modeler—which assumes, of course, that he needs to continue building models—to find just what he does to alleviate that dissatisfaction, not so that we can then take the model for reality but so that we can extrapolate on the basis of that decision to a qualitative model firmly established on the mute expertise of the rule-following practitioner giving expression to a shared commitment to our well-being.

· · ·

If anything possibly true or correct necessarily involves an evaluative judgment, then we can draw a second conclusion that the shared context in which the decision takes place must somehow be maintained—otherwise the judgment will not and cannot make sense to some of those affected by it and is, therefore, without any possible truth. We could just as well say that the practices we have in mind must be sustainable, but here *sustainable* actually has a concrete meaning. The idea is simply that embodied judgments exercised by experts in response to dissatisfaction produced by their engagement with their environment has to be tempered by observance of the rules that allow their actions to be interpreted as meaningful by those with whom they share the context. Put differently, the shared values and understandings that are necessary for the organization of collective behavior toward a shared goal have to be supported rather than corroded by those evaluative practices from which the qualitative action strategy is extrapolated. To wit: the architects of the political and economic system that has destroyed many trillions of dollars of wealth and (arguably) perpetuated or exacerbated the human impacts of resource-driven conflicts in many regions of the world may one day be called on to account for their decisions and actions.

This brings us to our third and final conclusion, which involves an extension of the implicit appeal to public comprehensibility to include an additional, explicit appeal to the public or observable nature of the well-being in question. According to the epistemological notions that we have articulated above, anything possibly true or correct necessarily involves an evaluative judgment that sustains the context from which the judgment arose and is about *observable* human well-being.

Of course, there are many "experts"—in the sense that they exhibit rule-following mastery for a given form of life or sphere of activity—whose practices have the effect of sustaining the context in which they take place but who are not circumscribed by an obvious commitment to observable human well-being. For instance, the pastor of a church might encourage his congregation to establish a relationship to an invisible entity who must be pleased to secure some advantage that is largely intangible. Of course, we could interpret this commitment in a materialist manner and focus on the material advantages won by organization into a closely bonded community, but these advantages are often difficult to observe. Likewise, we might identify experts whose rule-following practices are clearly directed toward observable well-being but whose judgments are suspect. Take, for instance, the economist who establishes a reasonable quantitative measure of the increase and decrease of human well-being in some regard but who, in adapting his model in light of counterevidence, chooses to pursue a correction on the basis of a satisfaction that follows from the establishment—from the macro perspective—of an advantage for the economy per se. This kind of correction would not be that one could possibly be true from the perspective that we are encouraging here and, therefore, could not be embraced as a basis for any reliable and sustainable organization. As such, for any expert decision that's exercised in such a way that the conclusions are not observable in terms of human well-being, these, too, are without the genuinely evaluative dimension that makes them possibly true or false.

In this sense, rather than tinkering with the model again to correct for an unexpected variation, the architects of the global financial system should begin talking much more expertly about the multiple facets of human well-being (Sen 2009).

Implications

In this chapter, we have presented a critique of the assumptions that undergird Paul Krugman's (2009) claim that the financial crisis has arisen because economists have mistaken beauty for truth. We have traced out a series of philosophical debates about the primacy of assertion in theories of meaning, the concept of referentiality in language analysis, and the correspondence theory of truth. In so doing, we have attempted to show how the positivism that continues to provide the basic epistemology for economics as well as mainstream management theory is inadequate to describe the financial crisis because it rests on a series of untenable metaphysical assumptions. As an initial step beyond these assumptions, we articulated an alternative, pragmatic theory of meaning that characterizes the truth of claims about facts as well as values in terms of their "workingness."

Working with the pragmatic account of the relationship between truth and value outlined above, we can acknowledge the extent to which judgments of value have shaped economic policy and will continually and unavoidably shape policy. Such judgments should be subjected to critical reflection as a provisional measure of caution in the face the possibility of future so-called crises of capitalism. By the same token, we can also acknowledge that specific notions of beauty in the domain of economics have, in view of the current crisis, ceased to work. Under certain conditions, there is a fittedness between the model and the world that gives the model's proponent the benefit of being able to say, "See, the model reflects the facts! This is truth, empirically demonstrated scientific truth!" But as soon as the conditions shift, and whenever reality is suboptimal (e.g., when executives are not able to buy enough public relations to prevent a run on the bank), then what you have is a sort of unmasking of what was always the reason that the model seemed to work (e.g., because it is beautiful when judged by the standard of people that operate with assumptions about the exponential increase in profit). In particular, it seems that while an aesthetic preference for "balance" has undergirded the putative objectivity of economic risk models, the crisis has called that preference into question by showing the extent to which it has ceased to fulfill the truth criterion of "workingness."

Krugman suggests that beauty cannot provide the basis for rational economic policy. He seems to presuppose an ontological difference between truth and beauty—namely, that truth is fact and beauty a sentiment that can bias our approach to the facts. In view of the philosophical arguments outlined above, we suggest that Krugman's critique can only go so far, and that if he continues to affirm truth as opposed to beauty, he will eventually arrive back at the same set of problems having to do with the breakdown of economic models of the world. In this light, addressing the root causes of the crisis is not as simple as following Krugman's suggestion that beauty should not be mistaken for truth. The challenge for economists, investors, and organizational theorists is more complex than rooting out a bias for beauty that colors descriptive assertions about facts. Instead, it is a matter of sorting through the various ways in which descriptive claims about fact are inevitably riven with preferences and determining the extent to which those preferences can be considered correct in terms of how they may manifestly be afforded by the social and material world around us.

The potential implications of this pragmatic theory of meaning for economics and management research are broad and far reaching. In this sense, our attempt to respond creatively, reliably, and sustainably to the financial crisis involves a longer-term theoretical project. Regulators cannot simply pull a lever or two, nip an interest rate here, and incentivize a little consumer spending there. Investors cannot simply maintain a balanced portfolio of long and short positions on commodities here while leaning on emerging markets for supranormal returns there. So long as the metaphysical ideology enacted by Krugman (2009) continues to hold sway over theorists, policy makers, and organizational leaders, there will be more crises. In other words, we are dealing not only with the madness of crowds but also with the madness of metaphysical dualisms among the very scientists who study the behavior of market participants. As the sociologist Donald MacKenzie has argued (2008), the volatility of the markets may result directly from the models that are enacted by economists.

· · ·

The most important implication of this chapter is that economists and organizational theorists can no longer afford to sustain the metaphysical assumption of referentiality. As we have argued, the problem with economic models of the world lies not with economists' preferences for the aesthetics of balance, nor even with their preferences for pure, unbounded rationality as a basis for intentional human action. The problem is that the correspondence theory of truth, and the referential relationship between language and world that it is based on, engenders an illusion that knowledge about the world (including statements of fact as well as risk management algorithms) exists somewhere outside of or apart from the world to which it refers.

As noted above, the closest that economists and management theorists have come to calling the ontological difference between facts and values into question and affirming evaluative claims (whether about aesthetic "beauty" or the ethical "good") as relevant sources of knowledge is behavioral economics (Kahneman and Tversky 1979). As is well known, this stream of research approaches evaluative claims in terms of affective dynamics, framing them as decision biases (i.e., suboptimality) that must be accounted for by theory precisely because they cannot be fully eliminated from practice. But this simple opposition between rational-optimal and affective-suboptimal suggests that the Nietzsche's metaphysical "death of God" has not yet been felt in the disciplines of economics and management theory.

Indeed, although the concept of bounded rationality acknowledges the limitations of this fantastic, metaphysical realm of pure knowledge, behavioral economists continue to seek to develop models of human behavior that account for these limits in such a way as to arrive at predictions of future behavior. For example, experiments designed to determine the ways in which certain desires affect how people frame and perceive risk rest on the essentially positivist foundations of the tradition of scientific management, which legitimize the search for universal, context-free principles and laws that govern human social behavior in the same way that the laws of physics govern the natural world.

To date, critics of the positivist tradition in organizational theory have sought to deconstruct its presuppositions while advancing an alternative epistemology in which complex organizational systems are socially constructed by participating actors and, in turn, interpreted by organizational theorists (see Tsoukas and Hatch 2001). One influential variation on this theme suggests that organizations are enacted as collective capacities (Orlikowski 2002) in an environment through processes of interpretation and narrative sense-making (Daft and Weick 1984). This notion has been further elaborated with regard to the management of organizations in crisis situations and under conditions of uncertainty (Weick 1988). It has additionally been suggested that market crises are themselves enacted phenomena (Abolafia and Kilduff 1988). Stretching the horizon of the crisis situation somewhat, the discourse of sustainable development has been analyzed from a Foucauldian perspective to emphasize the importance of ethical choice for business (Fergus and Rowney 2005).

Such attempts to offer alternative explanations of organizational behavior, often drawing on the tradition of the *Geisteswissenschaften* within the human sciences, frustrate scholars who seek predictive knowledge through empirical scientific methods. And in effect, conversations at the Academy of Management Annual Meetings (as well as in the halls of elite business schools) tend to run in parallel on either side of this chasm of disagreement, with occasional potshots fired from one camp into the other to maintain hegemony. But for better or worse, as Karen Knorr-Cetina (2001) has argued, these debates "tend to assume science is a unitary enterprise to which epistemic labels can be applied across the board . . . [when in] fact it is not one enterprise but many, a whole landscape—or market—of independent epistemic monopolies producing vastly different products" (4).

What is therefore most interesting about the pragmatic theory of meaning that we have developed here is that it subjects both of these traditions—each rooted in metaphysical assumptions about the nature of facts and values—to the same criterion of truth. The notion of "workingness" serves notice to the most radical interpretativists and to the most hard-nosed empiricists, calling them both to reflect on how their respective claims about facts and values remain always provisional, subject to revision and critique in view of observable reality. Broadly speaking, behaviorist models of risk decision making should be reconsidered in light of the extent to which their existence as such depends on the affordances of the social and natural world. And by the same token, organizational theories about how to manage uncertainty through sensemaking should be reconsidered in light of the extent to which narratives appear as true or false based on the embodied, material dimensions of the enacted mind.

· · ·

With regard to the ongoing financial crisis, some readers may object that these humble corrections on relatively arcane bodies of organizational theory, articulated in reference to even more arcane philosophical debates, will have little or no effect on practice because, at root, they do not address greed and human fallibility. We respond to this objection by suggesting simply that theories, concepts, and mental models of markets and organizations do not exist metaphysically apart from the markets and organizations to which they putatively refer. Instead, they are enacted by managers and economists in the world and are thus afforded by the world, or not.

In this light, we close this chapter with a measure of hope that, over time, sustainability will increasingly come to be appreciated both as a qualitative imperative that integrates moral and aesthetic values and as a true description of how management can enact a balance with the social and natural world. To realize this hope, we must invest money, attention, and energy in the creation, acculturation, and development of individuals who are able to exercise aesthetic and ethical judgments. We need leaders who, faced with a crisis, do not simply run to an algorithm and on that basis decide against or independently of human well-being to pursue unsustainable strategies. Thus, programs that develop professional responsibility and leadership need not amount simply to an exercise in instilling prescribed values in people. Instead, they can be designed to train people how to appreciate the truth, namely, to make embodied judgments about the sustainable fit and appropriateness of a given representation, characterization, response, or strategy within a given context. At the globalized tail end of metaphysics, where truth emerges in practice, we must strive desperately to educate people who are not only sensitive to the contexts in which they act but also capable of creatively producing well-being within them.

References

Abolafia, M., and M. Kilduff. 1988. Enacting market crisis: The social construction of a speculative bubble. *Administrative Science Quarterly* 33 (2): 177–93.

Astley, W. G. 1985. Administrative science as socially constructed truth. *Administrative Science Quarterly* 30 (4): 497–513.

Austin, J. L. 1962. *How to do things with words*, edited by J. O. Urmson. Oxford: Clarendon Press.

Ayer, A. J. 1952. *Language, truth, logic*, 2nd ed. New York: Dover Publications.

Berg, P. O. 1989. Postmodern management? From facts to fiction in theory and practice. *Scandinavian Journal of Management* 5 (3): 201–17.

Bernays, P. 1983. On Platonism in mathematics. In *Philosophy of mathematics: Selected readings*, edited by P. Benacerraf, 258–71. Cambridge: Cambridge University Press.

Blackburn, S. 1984. *Spreading the word: Groundings in the philosophy.* Oxford: Oxford University Press.

Brady, F. N. 1986. Aesthetic components of management ethics. *Academy of Management Review* 11 (2): 337–44.

Brouwer, L. E. J. 1981. *Brouwer's Cambridge lectures on intuitionism*, edited by D. van Dalen. Cambridge: Cambridge University Press.

Carnap, R. 2003. *The logical structure of the world and pseudoproblems in philosophy*, translated by Rolf A. George. LaSalle, IL: Open Court Publishing.

Chia, R. 1996. The problem of reflexivity in organizational research: Towards a postmodern science of organization. *Organization* 3 (1): 31–59.

Collingwood, R. G. 1958. *The principles of art.* New York: Oxford University Press.

Daft, R., and K. Weick. 1984. Toward a model of organizations as interpretation systems. *Academy of Management Review* 9 (2): 284–95.

Davidson, D. 2001. A coherence theory of truth and knowledge. In *Subjective, intersubjective, objective*, 137–53. Oxford: Oxford University Press.

Dean, J. W., Jr., E. Ottensmeyer, and R. Ramirez. 1997. An aesthetic perspective on organizations. In *Creating tomorrow's organizations: A handbook for future research in organizational behavior*, edited by G. Austin, J. L. Cooper, and S. E. Jackson, 419–37. New York: John Wiley.

Evans, G. 1982. *The varieties of reference*, edited by John McDowell. Oxford: Clarendon Press.

Fergus, A., and J. Rowney. 2005. Sustainable development: Epistemological frameworks and an ethic of choice. *Journal of Business Ethics* 57 (2): 197–207.

Frege, G. 1980a. *The foundations of arithmetic*, translated by J. L. Austin. 2nd ed. Evanston, IL: Northwestern University Press.

———. 1980b. On sense and reference. In *Translations from the philosophical writings of Gottlob Frege*, edited and translated by P. Geach and M. Black. 3rd ed. Oxford: Blackwell.

Gagliardi, P. 1996. Exploring the aesthetic side of organizational life. In *Handbook of organization studies*, edited by S. R. Clegg, C. Hardy, and W. R. Nord, 565–80. London: Sage.

Gibbard, Allan. 1992. *Wise choices and apt feelings.* Cambridge, MA: Harvard University Press.

Gibson, J. J. 1979. *The ecological approach to visual perception.* Boston: Houghton Mifflin.

Gödel, K. 1992. *On formally undecidable propositions of* Principia Mathematica *and related systems*, translated by B. Meltzer. New York: Dover Publications.

Guillet de Monthoux, P. 2004. *The art firm: Aesthetic management and metaphysical marketing.* Stanford, CA: Stanford Business Books.

Guillet de Monthoux, P., and M. Statler. 2008. Aesthetic play as an organizing principle. In *The Sage handbook of new approaches in management and organization*, edited by D. Barry and H. Hanson, 423–435. London: Sage.

Hardy, G. H. 1992. *A mathematician's apology.* Cambridge: Cambridge University Press.

Hilbert, David. 1996. The logical foundations of mathematics. In *From Kant to Hilbert: A sourcebook in the foundations of mathematics*, 2 vols., edited by William B. Ewald, 1134–47. Oxford: Oxford University Press.

James, William. 1950. *The principles of psychology.* New York: Dover Publications.

James, William. 1997. *The meaning of truth.* New York: Prometheus Books.

Kahneman, D., and A. Tversky. 1979. Prospect theory: An analysis of decision under risk. *Econometrica* 47 (2): 263–91.

Kant, I. 1965. *Critique of pure reason*, translated by Norman Kemp Smith. New York: St. Martin's Press.

Knorr-Cetina, K. 2001. *Epistemic cultures: How the sciences make knowledge.* Cambridge, MA: Harvard University Press.

Krugman, P. 2009. How did economists get it so wrong? *New York Times*, September 2. http://www.nytimes.com/2009/09/06/magazine/06Economic-t.html.

Ladkin, D., and S. S. *Taylor.* 2010. Enacting the true self: Towards a theory of embodied authentic leadership, *Leadership Quarterly* 21 (1): 64–74.

MacKenzie, D. 2008. *An engine not a camera: How financial models shape markets.* Boston: Massachusetts Institute of Technology Press.

Maddy, Penelope. 1992. *Realism in mathematics.* Oxford: Oxford University Press.

Maddy, Penelope. 2000. *Naturalism in mathematics.* Oxford: Oxford University Press.

Merleau-Ponty, M. 2002. *Phenomenology of perception*, translated by Colin Smith. London: Routledge.

Moore, G. E. 1953. *Some main problems of philosophy.* London: George Allen and Unwin.

Nietzsche, F. 1990. *Twilight of the idols,* translated by R. J. Hollingdale. New York: Viking.

Nonaka, I. 1994. A dynamic theory of organizational knowledge creation. *Organization Science* 5 (1): 14–37.

Orlikowski, W. 2002. Knowing in practice: Enacting a collective capability in distributed organizing. *Organization Science* 13 (3): 249–73.

Ottensmeyer, E. J. 1996. Too strong to stop, too sweet to lose: Aesthetics as a way to know organizations. *Organization* 3 (2): 189–94.

Peirce, C. How to make our ideas clear. In *The essential Peirce: Volume 1. Selected philosophical writings, 1867–1893,* edited by Nathan Houser and Christian J. W. Kloesel, 124–41. Bloomington: Indiana University Press.

Popper, K. 1977. *The logic of scientific discovery.* 2nd ed. London: Routledge.

Putnam, H. 2002. *The collapse of the fact/value dichotomy and other essays.* Cambridge, MA: Harvard University Press.

Quine, W. V. O. 1980. Two dogmas of empiricism. In *From a logical point of view.* 2nd ed. Cambridge, MA: Harvard University Press.

Russell, B. 1971. *Problems of philosophy.* Oxford: Oxford University Press.

Russell, B. 1973. On denoting. In *Essays in analysis.* London: George Allen and Unwin.

Russell, B. 1996. *The principles of mathematics.* New York: W. W. Norton.

Schlick, M. 1985. *General theory of knowledge,* translated by Albert E. Blumberg. LaSalle, IL: Open Court Publishing.

Searle, J. 1969. *Speech acts: An essay in the philosophy of language.* Cambridge: Cambridge University Press.

Searle, J. 1979. *Expression and meaning: Studies in the theory of speech acts.* Cambridge: Cambridge University Press.

Sen, A. 2009. *The idea of justice.* Cambridge, MA: Harvard University Press.

Simon, H. 1982. *Models of bounded rationality,* Vol. 12. Boston: Massachusetts Institute of Technology Press

Stevenson, C. L. 1944. *Ethics and language.* New Haven, CT: Yale University Press.

Strati, A. 1992. Aesthetic understanding of organizational life. *Academy of Management Review* 17 (3): 568–81.

Strati, A. 1996. Organizations viewed through the lens of aesthetics. *Organization* 3 (2): 209–18.

Strati, A. 1999. *Organization and aesthetics.* London: Sage.

Taylor, S., D. Fisher, and R. Dufresne. 2002. The aesthetics of management storytelling: A key to organizational learning. *Management Learning* 33 (3): 313–30.

Taylor, S. S., and H. Hansen. 2005. Finding form: Looking at the field of organizational aesthetics. *Journal of Management Studies* 42 (6): 1211–32.

Taylor, S. S., and D. Ladkin. 2009. Understanding arts-based methods in managerial development. *Academy of Management Learning and Education* 8 (1): 55–69.

Tsoukas, H., and M. J. Hatch. 2001. Complex thinking, complex practice: The case for a narrative approach to organizational complexity. *Organization Studies* 54 (8): 979–1013.

Weick, K. 1988. Enacted sensemaking in crisis situations. *Journal of Management Studies* 25 (4): 305–17.

Weick, K. 1989. Theory construction as disciplined imagination. *Academy of Management Review* 14 (4): 516–31.

Wittgenstein, L. 1961. *Tractatus logico-philosophicus*, translated by D. F. Pears and B. F. McGuinness. New York: Humanities Press.

Wittgenstein, L. 1966. *Lectures and conversations on aesthetics, psychology and religious beliefs*, edited by Cyril Barrett. Oxford: Basil Blackwell.

Wittgenstein, L. 1968. *Philosophical investigations*, translated by G. E. M. Anscombe. Oxford: Basil Blackwell.

Zald, M. 1993. Organization studies as a scientific and humanistic enterprise: Toward a reconceptualization of the foundations of the field. *Organization Science* 4 (4): 513–28.

2 Aesthetic Leadership

Walking Toward Economic Recovery

Ralph Bathurst and Margot Edwards

In this chapter, we explore the idea of communitarian artistic cocreativity and partnership as a means of solving the current global economic crisis. In light of the challenges that face leaders who are working to solve problems as a result of the crisis, we present an aesthetic approach to leadership that values heightened sensation and provocative insight through the works of the installation artists Peter Robinson and Tyree Guyton. The works of these artists help surface experience of past, painful histories and help turn our focus from financial concerns to those of much deeper and much more important human interest. How, through the aesthetic engagement that dialogic art inspires, individuals move from self-absorption to develop humility and a focus on the Other and to build toward diverse communities are key issues that this chapter addresses.

Crisis and Transformation

The experience of overwhelming crisis often raises existential questions about the nature and meaning of life. Such questions lead us to reassessments of our current activities and to changes in our values and behaviors. Crisis comes in many different forms, including job loss, the betrayal of a friend, or the death of a loved one. The anthropologist Ronald Wright (2005) makes these links between loss and the quest for personal meaning in his provocative text based on the 2004 Massey Lectures. He opens with a discussion of

Thanks to Merle Turner for her generous help and advice in preparing this chapter.

Paul Gauguin's large mural painting *D'où venons nous? Que sommes nous? Où allons nous?* Wright cleverly juxtaposes Gauguin's despair at hearing of the death of his daughter with his own despair at the degradation of the earth's environment by successive generations of voracious human settlement. Hence, Gauguin's three questions of existential import (Where do we come from? What are we? and Where are we going?) become, for Wright, key points of inquiry into how to sustain human existence on planet Earth in the twenty-first century.

Now we as global citizens are asking similar questions. We have experienced such a dramatic collapse of the economic system that commentators talk in terms of meltdown. The losses of property, retirement savings, and employment by millions of citizens in Western countries have provoked in us the same questions on which Gauguin ruminated. We ask, "How have we got ourselves into this precarious position, and what can be done about it?"

It is significant that both Gauguin and Wright turned to art as a means of exploring and explaining questions of ultimate meaning and concern. For Gauguin, painting was a vehicle through which he could express his angst, yet for Wright, art seems secondary to his call for urgent action to turn back the tide of voracious human consumption. Art and the need for accurate scientific understandings necessary for achieving sustainable human existence seem at odds, with neither bearing any significance to the other.

So it is for us—we have separated engagement with art from the rest of our lives, allocating it to the museum, art gallery, or concert hall, thus making us less sensitized to the provocative and transformative nature of the aesthetic experience. How, then, might art speak to business leaders confronted with complex balance sheets, the uncertainties of economic forecasting, and the problems of maintaining an upward growth trajectory in the midst of a turbulent global economic system? To address this, we discuss that, despite the rigors of scientific methods adopted by experts in finance and economics, ultimately it is art that speaks most powerfully.

Broughton (2008) describes this eloquently in his ruminations as a student at Harvard Business School studying for his MBA. A journalist by profession, Broughton believed that learning the multitude of business skills that an MBA offers would equip him for a life outside of the declining newspaper industry. Six weeks into his course, Broughton describes encountering "finance" for the first time. His professor came to lectures replete with graphs and formulas, but he ultimately failed in his quest to make the subject an entirely rational pursuit. Broughton (2008, 101) writes: "There seemed to come a point in every class involving the use of numbers when the professor would say, 'This is an art not a science.' And there always seemed to be a note of regret in his voice. Valuing companies, for all the sweat and effort people put into it, always ran into immeasurable uncertainties."

The "note of regret" sounding from the professor is paradigmatic of our perceptions of the value of art: it is something done by people who are regrettably not able to communicate scientifically. Broughton goes on to claim that pure accounting principles are often not able to explain the nuances of a company's value, and yet implications gained by leaps of judgment may make sense. He likens this to "the difference between a formal studio photograph that failed to capture the sitter's character and a portrait in thick, crude oils that summed up a person in a few brushstrokes" (Broughton 2008, 105).

Here Broughton himself turns to art to describe a kind of knowing that is beyond statistical data. Such a turn has its precedents in Greek antiquity. For instance, Aristotle in his *Poetics* (sec. VI) writes of the tragic theater as a vehicle for the audience to experience a "catharsis" or purgation of emotions. This catharsis allowed for the audience members to gain insights into their own behavior and to return, purified, to normal life (Boal 1979, 37).

In like fashion, this chapter explores a similar aesthetic approach with the aim of offering a critique of unbridled consumption and hope for a sustainable future, beyond the tradition that privileges economic rationality over other measures of human advancement.

Although, as discussed above, Wright's agenda was to discuss the problem of environmental degradation, our concern is the problem of economics. In this chapter, we argue that art is more than illustrative in that it provides a springboard from which to explore the essence of what it means for humans to live sustainably in this age. Art invites an investigation of the past and, on that basis, suggests how we might live in the future, all the while offering tools for thoughtful critique of social practices.

In this way, artistry and leadership join together as complementary processes, for both rely on actions that recruit the goodwill and creative involvement of groups of people. Visual and performing artists rely on a community of actants who work together to bring projects to fruition. Similarly, leaders rely on group cooperation and involvement, a process that Kort (2008) calls plural action.

Hence, understanding how artists communicate among themselves to bring works into existence is an example to contemporary leaders of how to approach a crisis situation like the current financial situation. For in solving this crisis, leaders must act beyond self-interest and see the global community of nations as stakeholders in and beneficiaries of sustainable business practices.

What is required, then, is an aesthetic awareness that is alert to both inner sensate responses and an ability to decipher symbols. Aesthetics, which can be defined as "sense perception" (Williams 1988, 31), places the emphasis on sensation rather than pure intellect and validates imagination and tacitly held beliefs, which are as important as that which is rational and logical (Adler 2006, 491). This quest to understand the place of the imagination and the need to become aware of the role that symbols play in daily life have their roots in the early Enlightenment, especially in the writings of Giambattista Vico (1668–1744), who sought ways to integrate history and myth into understandings of reality; Alexander Gottlieb Baumgarten (1714–1762), who considered that human beings are primarily aesthetic beings; and Immanuel Kant (1724–1804), whose inquiries into the relationship between form and content are seminal to aesthetic inquiry (for a fuller exploration of these three philosophers, see Bathurst 2009).

Therefore, the aesthetic lens awakens the imagination in that it uses the symbolic to alert us to specific issues that have an impact on the way we live. This implies that the scientific and aesthetic become intertwined, with the ultimate goal being a "tendency towards social action" (Welsch 1997, 73) with an examination of taken-for-granted values and behaviors. It is this context of critiquing the Western Hemisphere's voracious appetite for consumable goods and the urgent need for social engagement that underpins our foray into aesthetics.

Aesthetics and Economics

According to the economist E. F. Schumacher (1977), instrumental rationality and the privileging of economics as the primary site of human endeavor has a deleterious effect on our existence. He argues that the scientific view that underpins contemporary economics is founded on Descartes' belief that humanity's goal to become "masters and possessors of nature" (Descartes, cited in Schumacher 1977, 19) has left us bereft of imagination. In further support of this view, Schumacher offers insights from the French philosopher and Cartesian critic Jacques Maritain, who claimed that, although reducing human life to numeric data could be useful at a technological level, it leaves unexamined the existential essence and meaning of that data.

Schumacher's (1973/1999) primary concern is that the notion of growth is detrimental to sustainable human existence and that Cartesian thinking is the root cause of modernity's flaws. However, critique alone is an insufficient change motivator. Hence, Schumacher offers an alternative epistemology based on lived experience. He claims that we interact with our world both internally and externally, and that there is a continuous reference to the Self and Other that can be summarized with the following questions: "What do I feel like? What do you feel like? What do I look like? What do you look like?" (Schumacher 1977, 74).

These four questions open the possibility for the kind of aesthetic engagement that is both self-reflexive and communitarian, thus establishing a cocreative climate of possibility that offers leaders a new way of guiding organizations. Schumacher's paired questions concerning feeling and seeing imply a way of interacting with the world that is beyond individual interior responses. Rather, there is an alterity about them, thus requiring a mutually constitutive embodied relationship between the Self and the Other.

Schumacher's questions stimulate "serial epiphanies" (Kester 2004, 1) because they necessitate an awareness of the Self's feelings and insights and an engagement with the feelings and insights of the Other. In summary, aesthetics invites the kind of emotional, sensate engagement that looks for ways in which we see and discern issues of concern for the Self and Other.

To explore the leadership potential that aesthetic engagement invites, we discuss the provocative power of the visual arts. Turning from art's decorative nature and its investment potential, we argue that art is confrontational and challenges the perceiver with a "catalytic jolt" (Bathurst and Edwards 2009, 120). To this end, O'Sullivan (2006) differentiates between *recognition* and *encounter*; the former implies habitual affirmation of the world as we know it, and the latter challenges our modes of existence and presents sometimes uncomfortable alternatives with which we must grapple.

How, though, might aesthetic encounters offer a mechanism for critiquing the economic crisis that confronts our world? In addressing this question, we argue that the painter is doing more than adding pigments to a canvas that appeal to our sense of order, or the musician is performing sounds that are more than just pleasing to the ear. Rather, each line, shape, dab, or chord is an "empirical pregnancy" (Merleau-Ponty 1968, 207) that brings to birth ideas and perceptions that offer the possibility of transformation.

Although the paint appears on the surface of the canvas, it implies a "surface of an inexhaustible depth" (Merleau-Ponty 1968, 143) that continuously invites deeper engagement. Thus, aesthetic encounter requires a response on our part that we can mine for the riches that it might yield only by taking time to stop. Seen through aesthetic eyes then, the collapse of the financial system is a gift that causes us to pause and engage beyond the presenting issues such as restoring order to the trading floors of the world's stock exchanges, thus encouraging us to go beneath the surface issues and probe deeper underlying causes and solutions.

To illustrate how this occurs, we first offer a method of encounter through the work of the artists Peter Robinson and Tyree Guyton; then we show how aesthetic engagement could be used as a mechanism of both critique and social revitalization.

Aesthetic Encounter

Art and Identity

Born in New Zealand in 1966, Peter Robinson held various residencies in Germany from 1995 to 2001. Describing his part-Maori ethnicity with the numeric value of 3.125 percent, Robinson uses this number as an ironic reference to his mixed-blood identity. He is both European and Maori, and in straddling both cultures, he seeks to provoke us, his viewers, into reflections of our own identities, asking us to grapple with the sometimes inherent absurdity in identifying as someone who is different from another and, by accident of birth, may be deemed either inferior or superior to other people.

Therefore, Robinson's work is replete with ironic references to colonization, in sometimes rough-drawn words in German and English. In the large 1997 mural painting *Strategic Plan: First We Take Manhattan*,[1] Robinson uses the traditional Maori colors of red, white, and black to critique the dominating and life-sapping effects of business. In the mural, statements situated around a central Maori tiki figure in the focal center are filled with sarcasm.[2] For example, in "Strategy 2" he writes, "Present the exotic and familiar simultaneously" and "Strategy 3 Cash in on fashionable dialogs such as globalization and post colonialism." In these assertions, Robinson confronts us with the perfunctory nature of strategic plans that offer the empty promise of growth and prosperity. Along with writing in German and English, he writes text in Maori, such as, "He pikitia kei runga I te pakitara. He aha kei roto I te pikitia," which can be translated as "The picture is on the wall. What is in the picture?" In another place, Robinson asks in Maori, "What is in my eye?" Here, there is an ironic reference to the biblical notion of hypocrisy in

Luke 6:41, where Jesus tells the joke of someone trying to take the speck out of someone else's eye when he has a log in his own! The discursive twist and ambiguity in the mural is deliberate and indicates that we critique not only corruption but also the sometimes trite aphorisms and mantras that businesses use to promote their services. Robinson's mural, *Strategic Plan: First We Take Manhattan*, based on the words of the Leonard Cohen song "First We Take Manhattan," is an audacious attack on the notions of taking and owning for one's own benefit at the expense of others, thus striking at the heart of the economics of consumption.

Robinson's other works that are particularly salient are his two installations in which he used discarded car crates that contained Japanese car parts imported to New Zealand (Burke and Weiermair 1995, 88–89). There was once a thriving car-assembly industry in New Zealand, but it was decimated in the 1990s through fierce offshore competition for cheaper labor and the costs of transportation. Robinson's painted boxes are similar in that they both have the front of the box removed, to reveal a white interior with a small sign "Sorry sold out" leaning against the back side. The outside, however, is covered in small rectangular shapes, some white and some black. Robinson has written various declamations inside each rectangle encouraging people to buy and consume. One of the boxes contains statements like "Trusted value," "Scoop deals inside," "Don't miss out," and "Sorry no credit" and reveals the crassness that is consumerism (Robinson 1994).[3] Another box is held in a private collection in Germany (Caughey and Gow 1997, 26–27) and contains images of structures like the Eiffel Tower and maps of countries such as the United Kingdom. All images, whether land or structures, are for sale and contain compelling taglines such as "Room with a view" for the Eiffel Tower and "So admit it you're dying for it" for the United Kingdom. The Leaning Tower of Pisa contains the ironic invitation "Handy man's dream"! In both of these car-crates-turned-works-of-art, Robinson declaims that ultimately we consumers have sold out to an economic system that privileges an elite group of individuals who have scant regard for the Other—both business stakeholders and the communities within which they operate. By walking around the boxes, the viewer is amused, titillated, and even entertained by the ironic juxtapositions. But as we walk to the open front with its stark white interior, perhaps it is us, the viewers, who have sold out to an economic system that takes but gives little in return.

It takes time to engage with Robinson's work. For instance, to fully absorb the ideas he explores in the car crates, one needs to slowly walk around the work, to pause and linger on the roughly drawn but subtle ideas. Confronting the viewer is a sense of dis-ease around the paradoxes of consumption and poverty, racial identity and the inequalities inherent within that identity, the propriety rights of land ownership, and the use and abuse of products such as motor vehicles. There are no soft edges to Robinson's works, and we the viewers are jolted out of our *comfort* and the fake security that our purchasing power offers. These themes of consumption and identity provoke existential questions that inquire into the meaning of human life that are also at the heart of the questions asked by Schumacher, urging us with courage to inquire into our own feelings and insights.

Robinson invites his viewers through his acerbic wit and criticism to consider the kinds of qualities that build community cohesion. Therefore, with insights into the cocreative relationship between the Self and the Other, illustrated by the mural and installation art of Peter Robinson, we turn to a discussion of the economic decline of the industrial heartland of the United States of America: the city of Detroit.

Detroit and the Heidelberg Project

The city of Detroit has endured a history punctuated by traumatic incidents since its first destruction in the major fire of 1805. At that time, a prominent local priest, Father Gabriel Richard, professed, "*Speramus meliora; resurget cinerbus.* We hope for better things; it will rise from its ashes" (Herron 2007, 7). This prophecy has proved its poignancy as the city has striven to maintain its identity over the years despite devastating fires, violent race riots, and more recently the ravaging effects of the economic recession.

As a reflection of its resilience, in 2010 *Time* magazine undertook a yearlong project to track the recovery of Detroit. For, as the magazine's editor John Huey (2009, 4) maintains, "The future of Detroit affects us all." Using the power of the photographer's lens, *Time* journalists reveal a city that is broken and destroyed. In his piece "*No*town," whose title contains the pun as an illusion to the famous Motown recording label that was founded in Detroit in 1960, Okrent (2009) includes a picture of the grand ballroom of the Lee Plaza Hotel. We see an ornate ceiling in desperate need of restoration, and as our eyes move to the foreground, we are confronted with broken furniture and a lidless grand piano tipped on its side. The hotel ballroom, the place of the rich and famous who gathered to celebrate the fruits of their labors, is desecrated. It is no more a valued site but rather an emblem of the brokenness that is Detroit.

Concerted efforts by the federal government to keep the recession from destroying an entire sector have allocated the Detroit automobile industry rescue packages valued in the millions. This has come in the face of leadership practices that have had scant regard for sustaining an industry in the face of more efficient manufacturing practices in Japan and Korea. However, other Detroit residents have been at work trying to restore the city for many years in spite of the city's decline. In particular, the artist Tyree Guyton has spent the past twenty years working at grassroots levels to raise the morale and profile of suburban Detroit.

Guyton was a high school dropout who returned to education as an adult, graduating in 1986 from the College of Creative Studies in Detroit. Although he could have sought a conventional artistic career in either New York or Los Angeles, upon graduating, Guyton decided to return to his home area in Detroit's eastern suburbs and Heidelberg Street. It was there that the Heidelberg Project was born: a community-based artistic program that involved members of that community in creating installation artworks that have become the focus of national attention. Along with his love for Detroit, Guyton's motivation was to raise his community's awareness of the violence and alienation that people in the Heidelberg area were experiencing. By taking discarded objects like vacuum cleaners, washing machines, and shoes, the installations demonstrated to the residents that objects that had become redundant and even useless in former times could take on profound significance as works of art.

The restive racial issues that lie close to the surface of suburban Detroit are central to Guyton's work. Heidelberg Street was the place of residence of Rosa Parks in her later life, and a decorated bus remains as a shrine to her activism and stands as testament to the courage of an individual who stood against the strident racial divisions of her youth. Like the New Zealander Peter Robinson, for Guyton these racial issues underpin his art and encourage engagement with the Other.

Guyton has responded to Detroit's decay by engineering what Kester (2004, 82) calls dialogic art: art that is "difficult" and designed to "thicken and complicate" rather than to simplify or comfort. The transformative potential of the installations Guyton has built, rebuilt, and continues to build are brightly colored, amorphous, collage-type, visual experiences utilizing found objects, from in, on, and around Heidelberg Street. The interactive nature of his artworks is reinforced by the inclusion of community members, especially families, who bring items that can be added to the installations. Hence, the Heidelberg Project is more than just Guyton's individual conception of the world; it involves the whole of the neighborhood in the collection of objects and the ongoing construction and reconstruction of the works.

Art installations of the kind at the Heidelberg Project are "socially produced spaces" (Kinloch 2009, 156) that challenge and provoke, and yet paradoxically build community. In particular, the Heidelberg Project is vibrant and chaotic and disturbs the neatness and comfort of the city elders, which in itself offers a mechanism for resistance by the members of the community in their desire to protect their creations. Numerous attempts to clear Heidelberg plots of their "junk" have been met by determined protest. For, as one young protester declared in her handcrafted sign "Heidelberg Project Is More Than Art" (Hoopes 2007, 89), the installations reveal a community that is increasing in solidarity and presence in a city that is often hostile to the community's collaborative efforts.

These installations and the engagement of the community are done with an intensity that is visceral. Kinloch (2009) writes of students from her language class at the local high school reporting their profound experience of viewing a memorial to victims of gun violence in 1994. Through their visceral encounters, students were able to "establish connections between the project and local politics" (Kinloch 2009, 169).

This same wrestling to make sense of, to discuss, and ultimately to construct the installations is also evident among commentators. For instance, Herron (1993, 199) provides a critical appraisal of Detroit's history that includes a discussion of the Heidelberg Project, and although his commentary is, at times, rather bleak, he paints a stunning visual image of the artworks: "[Guyton's] houses literally vomit forth the physical elements of domestic history; furniture, folds, televisions sets, signs, toilets, enema bottles, beds, tires, baby buggies come cascading out doors and windows and through holes in the roof, flowing down the outside walls and collecting in great heaps on the lawn, so that the whole looks like some sort of man-made lava flow. The magma of discarded lives; these visible tokens of a humiliated history."

Here is evidenced the contradictory construction of decay, an indication of a community that is itself discarded using its now-useless materials to reclaim its identity. What first appears on the surface to be chaotic vomit, on walking around the sites, visitors to the project develop awareness of the positive nature of the works, becoming caught up in the same transformative possibilities that the community also experienced. Hence, the vacant lots of art, as described by Nasar and Moffat (2004), provoke deeply felt emotional responses. However, the liminality of the space also invites engagement and activism, as the constant flow of visitors are confronted with "the harsh reality of the demise of the city, the decay of dreams and hopes, and Detroit's shame in its own history" (Jackson 2007, 30). Such experiences of pain arouse questions about the nature and meaning of existence.

In Guyton's world, everyday objects are commissioned for more serious purposes. For example, in *Soles of the Most High*, Guyton plays on the homonyms *soles* and *souls*, and he hangs old shoes in the highest branches of a tree in response to his grandfather's stories about the lynching of African American slaves. Nasar and Moffat (2004, 14) report that Guyton remembers his grandfather, Sam Mackey, telling him, "You couldn't see the people, but you could see the soles of their shoes."

Such raw images are likely to stir painful memories of past injustices, and this explains, in part, why Guyton's work has been described as providing "the signs of a past sickness" that many citizens would like to see erased (Sheridan 1999, 354). However, because art freezes images in time and space, it does not permit such erasure and provides a vehicle for self-reflection and transformation. Viewers walking around the Heidelberg Project are confronted with an uncomfortable and even distasteful history of racial division and prejudice, a history that viewers would rather forget. But this history is not geographically isolated in Detroit and the United States alone, for Guyton's vision is global.

For example, Walters (2001) describes other shoe installations, including *A Lot of Shoes*, in which vast numbers of old shoes are lined up along the sidewalk to symbolize the unemployed of the world queuing for work. Shoes are also chillingly utilized in an installation that consists of an enormous pile titled *The Oven*, as homage to those murdered in the Holocaust, and as a reminder to visitors that "the most mundane objects can testify to a buried history" (Walters 2001, 70). Through this work, Guyton seeks to engage with us, seemingly asking, "What history have *you* buried?" and "How will we reclaim *our* community?"

Another, more positive interpretation of the *Soles* work is provided by the children's author Linda McLean (2007, 4), who tells readers that "the tree of shoes is symbolic of adding life and newness to the community." Through this claim, McLean offers a process whereby renewal may occur: by confronting the ugliness and trauma of the past and by digging up and exposing our buried histories, we may find a way of walking toward recovery.

Guyton has painted some houses in brightly colored polka dots that are tangible evidence of the power to reclaim that which has been lost and forgotten. The *Dotty Wotty House* is the "centerpiece of the Heidelberg Project" (Walters 2001, 72) and provides an anchor for both community members and visitors. It offers a space at which to pause and reflect on the things that have disturbed and challenged; and its fame as a national work of art presents a site of pilgrimage for those seeking the courage to develop their own projects to revitalize their communities.

To this end, Guyton has also used shoe installations to push for peace in other community settings. For example, in 2006 he created *United We Walk* (McLean 2007) as part of a Dr. Martin Luther King Jr. Day celebration in West Bloomfield, Michigan. The community-building possibilities provided by Guyton's art underpin his description that it is "medicine of hope."[4] Ordinary shoes become the vehicles for profound experience. Although we may be different in ethnicity, beliefs, traditions, and political persuasion, shoes are our one unifying item. Guyton's art highlights this most mundane item—ordinary shoes, owned by everyone, worn daily—and makes it transformational. As we take our own shoes and begin to walk around and about, engaging in our communities aesthetically, we become cocreators with artists like Guyton, to bring hope in the midst of collapse and crisis.

Dialoging Aesthetically

We have argued that both Robinson's and Guyton's work invite dialogue, and we have appropriated Kester's (2004) term *dialogic art* to describe the complexities and sheer audacity of Guyton's works and the acerbic nature of Robinson's criticisms of colonial oppression and consumption. There is something of the carnivalesque in their works in that they are at once humorous and compellingly critical. Although Robinson's paintings are highly sought after and are displayed in public galleries and held in private collections, Guyton's art installations are public. Guyton has turned Heidelberg Street into a quasi public square, an open space that accommodates a carnival atmosphere, the kind of carnival that creates opportunity for ordinary folks to critique the power of ruling elites. Hence, in this regard, "Carnival is not a spectacle seen by the people; they *live* in it, and everyone participates because its very idea embraces all the people" (Bakhtin 1968, 7, emphasis added). It is not surprising, then, that ruling officials are wary of the carnival, for it contests, in the most public of spaces, epic narratives on which national identity is built (Hirschkop 1999, 296).

Inevitably, dialogic art is a public pursuit. Furthermore, its goal is not to achieve a unifying voice of a single logic as in John Dewey's idealized version of art as a unifying process. For Dewey (1934, 167), "there is unity only when the resistances create a suspension that is resolved through cooperative interaction of the opposed energies." Dewey's prescription of "resolved" differences where balance between competing ideologies is achieved belies the intentionality of artists like Robinson and Guyton who bring their critiques of unsustainable social practices to the fore, criticisms that sometimes offend. As Mattern (1999, 70–71) argues, "Perhaps Dewey's single most glaring political failure was his apparent inability to understand why people might turn to *confrontational* forms of political action such as opposition, resistance, and subterfuge."

It is the carnival of the public square with all the untidiness and chaos that is the ideal space for dialogue to occur. As Hirschkop (1999, 249) maintains, "The marvelously open expanses of the public square are not only literally but metaphorically spacious, allowing history a room for movement which it is denied in the bourgeois parlour or home." In summary, dialogic art is communitarian in its focus and provides for a wide range of responses and conversations that contest and critique official rhetoric.

Aesthetic Leadership

We began this chapter noting that the experience of crisis raises existential questions of ultimate meaning and concern, and that artists lead us as individuals into an encounter that is dialogic and potentially transformative. We have discussed how public art facilitates an encounter that often contradicts the ideologies of ruling elites. How, then, can leaders respond to the call to dialogue, and what are the implications to those charged with the responsibility of navigating the global economy out of its precarious position? To address these questions, we advocate for change in the way leaders interact with their communities.

Although there are those who will be held accountable for corrupt financial dealings that have caused suffering to entire communities, and some of these public figures may suffer the ignominy of court trials and imprisonment (Gandel 2010), we believe that there needs to be a reformation of the way leadership is understood and that aesthetics holds some of the clues as to how to proceed. We note with Stacey and Griffin (2005) that leaders can tend toward controlling and domineering behaviors, thereby stifling organizational life. They maintain that leaders need to act "with others in reflective and imaginative ways, aware of the politically destructive processes one may be caught up in" and that this may be at odds with traditional theories that see leaders as standing "outside the system, designing, manipulating variables and pulling levers in order to stay in control" (Stacey and Griffin 2005, 13).

The aesthetic encounter, we have noted, brings to the surface histories that have been buried and forgotten. Leaders may find, in response to the works of artists like Robinson and Guyton, that their own beliefs about how the world of organizations ought to operate are provoked. Aesthetic encounter involves becoming sensitive to richness and complexity, with the view to transformation at individual and societal levels. This sensitivity may include putting aside doctrinal theodicies about leadership practice and becoming more comfortable with the chaotic and disorderly without necessarily attempting to bring resolution, thereby embracing both beauty and order along with the ugly and confused.

Inevitably, recasting leadership beyond the individual hero-leader manifest in a reward structure based on a bonus culture, and called "obscene" by President Obama (Wiseman and Shell 2010, 1), requires that we look at alternative ways of leading. Furthermore, President Obama himself has made the overhaul of the financial system one of the defining goals of his presidency, declaring, "I did not run for office to be helping out a bunch of, you know, fat-cat bankers on Wall Street," but at the same time he stands accused by his opponents of playing at "political theatre" (Jackson 2009, 7). However, recasting leadership beyond the obscene privilege of which Obama speaks requires an aesthetic awareness that is sensitized both to ethical practice and to a keen responsiveness to the needs of revitalizing communities. For aesthetic engagement provokes awareness beyond self-driven ambition and offers the opportunity for a pause to examine existing practices.

Therefore, aesthetic engagement highlights several ideas that are transferable to leadership practice. The first, we offer, is the need for humility on the part of leaders. Although Collins (2001) advocates for humility as necessary for mature leaders (level 5 in Collins' parlance—people who are exemplary in their roles) as if this were something extraordinary, we believe that through aesthetic engagement all leaders are confronted at a visceral level with their humanity in all its ambiguity and frailty. This willingness to be unmasked and to stand emotionally naked before an artwork translates into leadership practice by understanding that admissions of weakness and of uncertainty about the next step to take are part of the aesthetic leader's normal habit of being. In summary, humility unmasks the illusion of control and allows for leaders to work *with*, in a collaborative manner, rather than *over* their staff, directing and dominating.

Such humility, according to Hammarskjöld (1964, 148), brings each individual back to a sense of the simple yet profound in our existence: "To have humility is to experience reality, not in relation to ourselves, but in its sacred independence. It is to see, judge, and act from the point of rest in ourselves. Then, how much disappears, and all that remains falls into place. In the point of rest at the centre of our being, we encounter a world where all things are at rest in the same way." This humility, as exemplified by one of the twentieth century's highly acclaimed leaders, offers us in the twenty-first century a guide as to how to lead aesthetically, being aware of the supreme importance of every individual person.

Second, we claim that the aesthetic leader asks, "Where are we going and what are our needs?" These questions arise out of the same questions that works of art ask of us. In response to the challenges and catalytic jolt that art provokes, we are required to turn to others in dialogue for solutions. Again, this dialogic habit translates into leadership practice in the daily conversations leaders have with staff and other stakeholders that continually question the meanings and intents of strategic decisions and policies. This dialogic approach is centrifugal and pulls away from a single monologic voice, having the effect of engaging people at all levels of the enterprise (Bathurst 2004). This requires that leaders allow for space to open in conversations in which new and unexpected ideas may emerge from others in the firm.

Finally, we think that aesthetic engagement eventually asks, "What can we do together to create a diverse community that respects, values, and celebrates difference?" Through dissonance, works of art challenge our sense of order, and our ideas of consonance and unity are confronted. So, too, leaders are challenged with the need to develop a diverse workplace that accepts, values, and welcomes people of difference. Rather than eliminating them through redundancies or redeployment, allowing for dissenting voices offers the opportunity to create a diverse workplace with all the difficulties of working together that this implies. As Mckay and Avery (2005) maintain, a diverse workplace is difficult to achieve, with minorities feeling welcome during their induction into a workplace but ultimately sidelined and ignored because they do not fit into the prevailing culture. This alienation leads to retention difficulties as organizations struggle to accept difference. However, aesthetic engagement confronts each of us with our underlying prejudices and asks how we will build solidarity within difference.

The aesthetic approach to leadership seeks to "bring together dramatic disruption and streetwise wisdom" through engagement with art "reconciling the exceptional with the everyday" (Eagleton 2003, 186). And this is the task that confronts both Ben Bernanke, chair of the Federal Reserve, and President Obama as they seek to mitigate the disastrous effects of the global economic meltdown. Therefore, we invite Bernanke and Obama to walk with us through the Heidelberg Project. This request should come as no surprise, given that Detroit is the home of Diego Rivera's dramatic mural painting *Detroit Industry*, commissioned by Edsel Ford, the son of legendary car manufacturer Henry Ford, in 1932. This painting, with its focus on industry and worker solidarity, offers a precedent with which to make our invitation to take this walk. As we walk around the Heidelberg Project, we would allow Guyton's art to guide our own discoveries and epiphanies. In the process, we may be confronted with our own emptiness and the intellectual and emotional defenses we have erected within ourselves against the accusation that we have sold out.

However, understanding art is not just a matter of private interpretation. As we take this least popular and more difficult road, we would converse with one another, discussing what we are feeling and seeing. We would then discuss how our responses to the artworks could provoke new policy directions and strategic changes. We would then affirm that leadership is not about an individual taking charge. Certainly, when it comes to the global economy, no single individual has sufficient insight or the political power necessary to determine the steps that must be taken to achieve recovery. Even though we note that *Time* magazine chose Bernanke as its Person of the Year in 2009, the aesthetics of leadership does not rely on one person to lead. What aesthetics opens for us is a communitarian approach that includes numerous voices in conversation and dialogue.

Hence, given this dialogic notion of leadership, in conversation with Bernanke and Obama, we are cognizant that both men come to the current economic crisis with an awareness of the harmful effects of poverty on community development. Bernanke's research as an economics scholar centered on the Great Depression of the 1930s, a fascination that went right back to his youth, listening to stories his grandparents told, especially of the troubles in Charlotte, North Carolina, which was "full of shoe factories that closed during the Depression, leaving the community so poor that its children went barefoot" (Grunwald 2009, 24).

This issue underpinned his academic career and helped shape his advocacy for a Keynesian interventionist approach, which characterizes his work as chair of the Federal Reserve Bank. This position that sees him grapple with complex economic questions of global importance comes with his many years of researching the effects of the Depression, and the potential for economic downturns to destroy communities and trap citizens in a cycle of poverty informs his current responses to the economic crisis.

President Obama began his working life as a community activist and organizer, becoming a director of the Developing Communities Project on Chicago's South Side in 1983, which included the troubled Altgeld Gardens. Described as the "worst community in Chicago" (Painter 2008, 93), Altgeld is notorious for its racial divisions. It is a poor community located near numerous manufacturing plants, former steel mills, waste dumps, and landfills. Each year, there are a number of locals who die from cancer and other diseases that may be related to polluted waterways from industry or asbestos in houses of the area. One of Obama's first jobs in taking up his position was to rid Altgeld Gardens of its asbestos.

In terms of its demographics, Altgeld Gardens is reminiscent of East Detroit, so Obama would certainly find many similarities between the poor neighborhoods of Chicago and Detroit. If President Obama were to respond to our invitation to visit the Heidelberg Project with us, we might expect that he would walk with us to the *Dotty Wotty House*, observe some of the installations, and actively engage with us in cocreative dialogue. As one who revealed "aspects of [him]self that resist conscious choice and that—on the surface, at least—contradict the world [he] now occupies" (Obama 2007, xiv), he has a unique ability to identify with the complexities of the U.S. citizenry (Steele 2008).

These complexities are not entirely racial in their makeup. Rather, as president, Obama is charged with making sense of the global economic crisis and the competing demands of the international need for interventionist policies that preserve the integrity of financial systems and, at the same time, reform those institutions. We note that, along with President Obama, there exists a gulf between the rampant greed of the Wall Street financial system and the struggling ordinary person on Main Street. However, as Sloan (2009, 62) astutely argues, the Wall Street–Main Street polarity between evil and good is a flawed analysis: "Without a doubt, the financial meltdown and its ensuing horrors began on Wall Street. However, Main Street is not a totally innocent lamb in all this. Yes, the greedheads tempted people with mortgages and other products they couldn't afford. But they could have said no, as many did. And they could have tried to live within their means or, better yet, below them, instead of falling prey to financial fantasies."

In response, as we walk around the Heidelberg Project with Bernanke and the president, remaining conscious of our complicity in the financial meltdown, we might unravel the complexities of the domestic and global economic issues that confront us in the presence of provocative art that leaves no history buried beneath the surface. We might, in our strolling conversation, assent to Smuts (2007, 72) in his belief that "a painful art experience is largely more desirable and easier to have than a painful emotional life experience." Obama could well value the safety of his encounter with Guyton's art and use it as a timely reminder of how the Self and the Other interplay in a cocreative space. Certainly, we can imagine that Bernanke and Obama, confronted with the installation *Soles of the Most High*, would contemplate their own shoes as they negotiate the pathways of the once-vibrant streets. Together our minds would grapple with our inescapable histories and seek out new paths to walk beyond the fine leather quality and comfort our shoes offer us. For, through Guyton, rejected soles may present a pathway to renewed souls, and out of the confrontation with his art are created stories capable of spurring political action in which we can all participate.

Political action is driven by our own conscience and our encounters with art. These encounters open space for us to develop the kind of humility needed to transform the conversation from the self-obsessed "I" to the communitarian "we" by which together we seek to become sensitized to the needs of our diverse communities and create space for all to participate. Hence, in this chapter we have maintained that economic transformation is neither solitary nor individual but necessarily involves cocreative social action. Artists like Robinson and Guyton have stimulated the artist within each one of us as we have taken time to linger and converse over their work. In that lingering, we can become the kind of aesthetic leaders required to solve the crises of this time.

Notes

1. For a reproduction, see the Web site of Collection FRAC Lorraine, at http://collection.fraclorraine.org/collection/show/467?lang=en.

2. A tiki is a Polynesian totemic figure and may be in the form of a large carving, as in the figures on Easter Island, or small enough to hang on a necklace. Small tikis are popular souvenirs for tourists.

3. See the Web site of the Dunedin Public Art, at http://www.dunedin.art
.museum/collection.asp?searchtype=.

4. See http://www.heidelberg.org.

References

Adler, N. J. 2006. The arts and leadership: Now that we can do anything, what will we
do? *Academy of Management Learning and Education* 5 (4): 486–99.

Aristotle. 350 BCE/1995. *Poetics*, translated by S. Halliwell. Cambridge, MA: Harvard
University Press.

Bakhtin, M. 1968. *Rabelais and his world*, translated by H. Iswolsky. Cambridge, MA:
Massachusetts Institute of Technology Press.

Bathurst, R. J. 2004. Dialogue and communication: Exploring the centrifugal force
metaphor. *Communication Journal of New Zealand* 5 (1): 22–40.

Bathurst, R. J. 2009. Enlivening management practice through aesthetic engagement:
Vico, Baumgarten and Kant. *Philosophy of Management* 7 (2): 61–76.

Bathurst, R. J., and M. F. Edwards. 2009. Developing a sustainability consciousness
through engagement with art. In *Management education for global sustainability*,
edited by J. A. F. Stoner and C. Wankel, 115–37. New York: Information Age Publishing.

Boal, A. 1979. *Theater of the oppressed*, translated by C. A. McBride and
M.-O. L. McBride. London: Pluto Press.

Broughton, P. D. 2008. *What they teach you at Harvard Business School: My two years
inside the cauldron of capitalism*. London: Viking.

Burke, G., and P. Weiermair. 1995. *Cultural safety: Contemporary art from New
Zealand*. Wellington: City Gallery, Wellington.

Caughey, E., and J. Gow. 1997. *Contemporary Art 1*. Auckland: David Bateman.

Collins, J. C. 2001. Level 5 leadership: The triumph of humility and fierce resolve.
Harvard Business Review 79 (1), 66–76.

Dewey, J. 1934. *Art as experience*. New York: Capricorn.

Eagleton, T. 2003. *Sweet violence: The idea of the tragic*. Malden, MA: Blackwell Publishing.

Gandel, S. 2010. The case against Goldman Sachs. *Time*, May 3, 16–21.

Grunwald, M. 2009. Ben Bernanke: The 2009 *Time* person of the year. *Time*, January
4, 20–33.

Hammarskjöld, D. 1964. *Markings*, translated by L. Sjoberg and W. H. Auden.
London: Faber and Faber.

Herron, J. 1993. *After culture: Detroit and the humiliation of history*. Detroit: Wayne
State University Press.

Herron, J. 2007. Getting to the Heidelberg Project. In *Connecting the dots: Tyree
Guyton's Heidelberg Project*, edited by T. Guyton, 1–9. Detroit: Wayne State University Press.

Hirschkop, K. 1999. *Mikhail Bakhtin: An aesthetic for democracy*. Oxford: Oxford
University Press.

Hoopes, D. S. 2007. Defending the Heidelberg Project. In *Connecting the dots: Tyree Guyton's Heidelberg Project*, edited by T. Guyton, 85–99. Detroit: Wayne State University Press.

Huey, J. 2009. Assignment Detroit. *Time*, October 5, 4.

Jackson, D. 2009. Obama: "Fat-cat" bankers owe help to U.S. taxpayers. *USA Today*, December 14, 7a.

Jackson, M. 2007. Trickster in the city. In *Connecting the dots: Tyree Guyton's Heidelberg Project*, edited by T. Guyton, 23–37. Detroit: Wayne State University Press.

Kester, G. H. 2004. *Conversation pieces: Community and communication in modern art*. Berkeley: University of California Press.

Kinloch, V. 2009. Suspicious spatial distinctions: Literacy research with students across school and community contexts. *Written Communication* 26 (2): 154–82.

Kort, E. D. 2008. What, after all, is leadership? "Leadership" and plural action. *Leadership Quarterly* 19 (4): 409–25.

Mattern, M. 1999. John Dewey, art and public life. *Journal of Politics* 61 (1): 54–75.

Mckay, P. F., and D. R. Avery. 2005. Warning! Diversity recruitment could backfire. *Journal of Management Inquiry* 14 (4): 330–36.

McLean, L. K. 2007. *The Heidelberg Project: A street of dreams*. Northville, MI: Nelson Publishing and Marketing.

Merleau-Ponty, M. 1968. *The visible and the invisible*, translated by A. Lingis. Evanston, IL: Northwestern University Press.

Nasar, J., and D. Moffat. 2004. The Heidelberg Project—Detroit, Michigan. *Places* 16 (3): 14–17.

Obama, B. 2007. *Dreams from my father: A story of race and inheritance*. Edinburgh: Canongate.

Okrent, D. 2009. *No*town. *Time*, October 5, 20–28.

O'Sullivan, S. 2006. *Art encounters Deleuze and Guattari: Thought beyond representation*. New York: Palgrave Macmillan.

Painter, A. 2008. *Barack Obama: The movement for change*. London: Arcadia Books.

Robinson, P. 1994. Untitled [crate]. Dunedin Public Art Gallery. http://www.dunedin.art.museum/collection.asp?searchtype=.

Robinson, P. 1997. Strategic plan—First we take Manhattan. Collection FRAC Lorraine. http://collection.fraclorraine.org/collection/show/467?lang=en.

Schumacher, E. F. 1973/1999. *Small is beautiful: Economics as if people mattered*. Point Roberts, WA: Hartley and Marks.

Schumacher, E. F. 1977. *A guide for the perplexed*. New York: Harper & Row.

Sheridan, D. M. 1999. Making sense of Detroit. *Michigan Quarterly Review* 38 (3): 321–53.

Sloan, A. 2009. What's *still* wrong with Wall Street. *Time*, October 29, 62–67.

Smuts, A. 2007. The paradox of painful art. *Journal of Aesthetic Education* 42 (3): 59–76.

Stacey, R. D., and D. Griffin. 2005. Introduction: Leading in a complex world. In *Complexity and the experience of leading organizations*, edited by D. Griffin and R. D. Stacey, 1–16. New York: Routledge.

Steele, S. 2008. *A bound man: Why we are excited about Obama and why he can't win.* New York: Free Press.

Walters, W. S. 2001. Turning the neighborhood inside out: Imagining a new Detroit in Tyree Guyton's Heidelberg Project. *Drama Review* 45 (4): 64–93.

Williams, R. 1988. *A vocabulary of culture and society.* London: Fontana Press.

Wiseman, P., and A. Shell. 2010. Obama takes on banks and their "obscene bonuses." *USA Today*, January 21, 1b.

Wright, R. 2005. *A short history of progress.* New York: Carroll and Graf.

3   Smashing Moneytheist Mirrors

How Artists Help Us Live with Financial Schizophrenia

Pierre Guillet de Monthoux

Before the crisis, we lived in global faith that value was all about economic exchange satisfactory mirrored by money. To constructively confront postcrises worlds, we must leave such "moneytheism" behind. While tracing the roots of "moneytheism" and warning of its fatal consequences, this chapter claims that art intuitively enlightens and broadens our perspectives. A performance at the Venice Biennale in 2009 by the Italian artist Michelangelo Pistoletto illustrates how this can happen.

Blurred Reflections

Subprime mortgage lenders force people out of their homes. Lehman Brothers files for bankruptcy. Public and private debt skyrockets. And almost simultaneously, all the problems of population, poverty, environment, morality, and social order cluster under one headline: "Financial Crisis!" At the outset, the crisis misleads us into believing that money is the cause and that political problems are the effect, and we soon become confident that the world can be reduced to matters that money can measure. The more the financial crisis dominates our minds, the more the world becomes a financial entity that money best mirrors. The crisis justifies our financial faith and converts us all to true believers in a moneytheist ideology.

In the precrisis United States, when 40 percent of corporate profit was derived from financial operations, finance was primarily considered a somewhat boring technical exercise that created wealth and provided a dull job for some highly paid Wall Street experts, who resorted to lap dances, luxury, and cocaine to get their pathetic kicks. We based our faith to manage whatever lurked beneath the surface on experts in shadow banking and architects of financial deals.

Faith in money as a mirror would seem obvious and unproblematic. To carry it to a more specific level, it also seems plausible that complex politics could be reflected in this mirror. As the crisis unfolds and narrow technical perspectives fade, we struggle to grasp how this mess of complex financial structures and opaque transactions affects our world. And what we see in the mirror grows blurry and distorted. Unnerved, we panic, for moneytheism has even blocked other ways of understanding the world. When money loses its meaning and we are robbed of our blind financial fundamentalism, we feel desperate, abandoned, and confused. In a worst-case scenario, we may even be dangerous to ourselves and to the world. We search for a solution. How do we treat moneytheism? Can it be set right? Is there a targeted therapy to eliminate the condition or at least to repair the damage?

The Artist Cure for Moneytheism

Putting an end to moneytheism requires fresh thinking and creativity, and when economists and financial experts can no longer suggest valid solutions, turning to art and the artist for a way out may be a wise alternative. This somewhat unorthodox idea was inspired by an event that happened in Geneva, Switzerland, in April 2009. Michelangelo Pistoletto, one of the most famous living visual artists and the grand old man of many Venice Biennales, as well as a pop and performance artist and initiator of *arte povera*, delivered a presentation at the Flux Laboratory, a select private art space backed by one of the oldest private banks in Geneva. His talk was about "socially responsible art," the motto for his own art foundation, Cittadellarte, in northern Italy. The audience was made up of Swiss bankers and financial professionals. After the reception, a small group of highly respected private bankers deeply concerned about the global financial situation gathered around the artist and engaged him in a three-hour conversation, which lasted long after the other guests had gone home. The conversation was intense and serious and had all the earmarks of a therapy session.

Without a doubt, it requires a special kind of artist to help bankers understand the ramifications of an art that is socially responsible. This kind of artist bears no resemblance to the classical image of the artist most of us

FIGURE 3.1 Michelangelo Pistoletto at Flux Laboratory, April 2009, Geneva

have. And the questions we pose reveal our very traditional assumptions: How does this new kind of artist operate? How might art have an impact on moneytheists?

Seeing Michelangelo Pistoletto in action in Geneva helps clarify the characteristics of the new artist-therapist and demonstrates what makes art and artists well suited to taking on a challenge like moneytheism. Furthermore, a performance by Pistoletto at the 2009 Venice Biennale held only two months after the Geneva encounter substantiates the therapeutic effect of art on moneytheism (Figure 3.1).

The New Insider Artist

The Städel Schule in Frankfurt, one of the most highly regarded art academies in Europe, recently published an overview of its teaching over the past decade.[1] Städel professors, many of whom are celebrated names in art markets, contributed articles to the publication, and its pages render a portrait of the contemporary artist that is far from the romantic cliché. The art critic Jan Verwoert writes about the outmoded "bad" Bohemian, who lacks social intuition and humor; who is "arrested in obtuse self-reference"; and who asserts "his own pose, with great seriousness, as the only authentic one against those of the others."[2] Old artists have to their credit their victories in the struggle for "artistic freedom," but new "good Bohemians" wage another battle for "good life." Art as a stage for solitary subjective expressions has given way to artists making art on the basis of their concern with environments and knowledge gained in social relationships. In art today, the era of subjectivity of single creative "outsiders" is old hat. Instead the frequent use of the term *singularity* signals a new insider artist, one who avoids the stiffly objective as well as the populist common sense while focusing on remaining critical though embedded in society.[3]

Art schools today help students navigate outside the blue lagoons of cozy art worlds and get used to swimming in deep water with real sharks. Städel's rector Daniel Birnbaum wants to make art schools connect to the real world from a new position between the monastic studios of old-fashioned solitary artists and the business bazaars of art fairs and biennials. Art thrives on knowledge that you cannot simply connect to with the right password.[4] Almost a century ago, John Dewey urged those looking at art to consider art as experience.[5] The encounter between the Swiss bankers and Pistoletto is a result of this new way of being an insider artist and still remaining critical.

Critique Inside Economies

How, then, do singular insider artists practice criticism? And further, how can this criticism make us think differently about global finance beyond moneytheism? The rector of Städel is a philosopher who frequently invites other philosophers to share their thoughts about the role of artists in practicing this new kind of criticism from within.[6] These invited lecturers are actually dealing with economic problems on a day-to-day basis, which makes them good coaches for young artists willing to take on active roles inside today's monetary muddles.

In talking with the students, Luc Boltanski notes that "artistic" criticism of societal problems within capitalism counts even more than "social" criticism did decades ago. Yesterday, managers and leaders talked to social scientists; today, they exchange ideas with artists. In his work *The New Spirit of Capitalism* with Eve Chiapello, a favorite read of art students, Boltanski ascribes contemporary artists an eminent role in judging the development of economy and management.[7] No one can ignore the singular insider artist's impact on opinion through the media when he or she captures and amplifies the negative indignation about social issues as efficiently as the old official artists celebrated the positive sides of the regimes whose servants they were.

To Paolo Virno, workers in contemporary economies are like artists. Some even claim that they form a new creative class that contributes to what is labeled "creative industry." In 2004, a similar argument from the managerial perspective became very popular when Daniel Pink published an article in *Harvard Business Review* titled "The MFA Is the New MBA." Focusing on performance artists and the way art today is more a process than a product, Virno claims that artists inherently have what it takes to find a place in the modern economy and work life.[8]

A third thinker attentive to the critical artist inside society is Jacques Ranciere.[9] The artist in Ranciere's argument is active as an aesthetic agent who clears the ground for new fields of attention. This is how new issues are given a voice and a treatment otherwise impossible because the issues tend to be vague and lack the form necessary to be granted a place on a political agenda.

Georgio Agamben addresses the question of what such aesthetic action involves. What action can bring new political issues to an agenda? To Agamben, actions of such a quality belong to a third category situated between instrumental and intentional action. They are neither about figuring out ends nor about using tools to reach them. Agamben calls this third kind of noninstrumental and even nonintentional action a "gesture."[10] A gesture creates a space for common communication within a formerly unexciting realm, and this is precisely what many artists are aiming for. When Nicolas Bourriaud finally declares art to be about relational aesthetics, his message, which is extremely popular among young artists, echoes both Immanuel Kant's view of the role of aesthetics in the shaping of a public realm and Joseph Beuys's conception of art as forming social sculpture.[11]

It is important to note that Bourriaud's aesthetics, as well as the aesthetics of many of the thinkers mentioned here, does not share the transcendental aspect of the Kantian third critique. What is shared is a focus on ways in which art is put to action for the opening up of a public space through the constitution of a sensus communis and, of course, a conviction that such phenomena are better understood as applied aesthetics. In that spirit, Pistoletto and other artists might contribute to debates like the one on global finance. The relational gesture is then a part of the therapy that artists provide as a cure for moneytheism—therapy that helps us consider what goes on outside the mirror of money. In that spirit, Städel Schule's rector Birnbaum, serving as the director of the Venice Biennale in 2009, invited Pistoletto to stage a performance,

FIGURE 3.2 Michelangelo Pistoletto and Daniel Birnbaum at Venice Biennale, June 2009

pictured at the end of this chapter, which put into action what Pistoletto had been talking with the Geneva bankers about: a piece of art with critical impact on moneytheism (Figure 3.2).

Exchange as Mirroring

To constructively debate the financial crisis with artists acting from positions of singularity as insiders akin to relational aesthetics in their exchange with society, some taken-for-granted fundamental concepts in the traditional moneytheist doctrine will have to change. For example, the idea of exchange has been a foundation in the constitution of political economy since the moral philosophy of enlightenment of Adam Smith. To exchange the surplus of a harvest for other goods was a basic economic action. Political economy further developed out of the cross-fertilization of the concept of exchange with that of equality. The postulate of equal exchange, implying a perfect mirroring, then became the platform from which both liberal and socialist doctrines emerged. The introduction of paper and book money made such theorizing far more problematic than in times when barter and metal currencies dominated trade and industry. Almost a century after metallic standards were dropped, careful economic analysis faces an increase of problems that makes equal exchange less of a convincing bedrock assumption on which to safely erect the elegant sets of equations of economic theory.

Artists can provide constructive criticism because the situation in economics has a clear parallel in visual arts. Money in the classical economy mirrored the goods and services it could buy, much as old mimetic art was a trustworthy rendering of something existing outside the frame of the artwork. Money stood for something other than itself in the same way that art mirrored its model or the landscape or the object depicted. Today, most art as nonfigurative as money is unrelated to real trade. The "outside" assumption is difficult to save from serious suspicion, for neither art nor money is an outside mirror.

Once equal exchange starts to wither under artistic critique, the concept of value becomes ambiguous as well. Economic socialism rests on analyzing profit by the unpaid value of objective work in factories. In a similar way, liberal economists account for monetary profit as mirroring the subjective value of the product to the individual consumer. Value, objective and subjective, is the cause of price, and the possibility of prices causing value is theoretically ruled out with the assumption of money neutrality. Taking for granted that changes in price reveal underlying changes in value by monetary measurement is again something art and artists question. Hanging out with contemporary artists weakens the link between price and value and provides the opportunity for a new discourse, especially if artists help us resist the temptation of utopia.

Utopia: Forcing Prices to Mirror Values

The disconnect between price and value creates a chasm between the world of nonmonetary values, where commodities are produced by means of commodities,[12] and the world of prices set by means of prices.[13] In the absence of an artist mentor, all this seems pretty intimidating to us poor folks brought up with a commonsense faith in strong, almost metaphysical, links connecting prices to values.[14] We cling to moneytheism to suppress what could be perceived as inconsistent logic.

Financial experts already accept this price–value dichotomy. Econometrics, which uses sophisticated mathematical methods to analyze prices in relation to prices, implicitly confines the meaning of finance to the domains of professional reports and scholarly articles. If economists and financial professionals stick to their assigned roles on global financial stages, they cannot voice anything but prices.[15]

Stretching the price–value connection continually weakens our common-sense, moneytheist faith. In desperation, we seek to make things plain and simple by just forcing prices back to values.[16] If this pressure doesn't work, and it never will, we may be seduced into turning our backs on money, prices, and markets. In the extreme case, we travel back to utopian thinking, with its roots in Plato's *Republic* and Moore's *Utopia*, where money and commerce were banned from the isolated state of eternal bliss. Liberals like Friedrich Hayek and Ludwig von Mises have eloquently warned against taking this first step down the slippery slope to serfdom.[17] Their argument unfortunately results in an inverted, equally blind faith in self-regulation.[18] And each temptation lurks in the wings of the center-stage financial crisis and can be avoided only if economists and managers pay attention to the artist, who has the gift to make us abandon our faith in moneytheism.

The Gift as Radically Different

Apart from the conviction that price will reflect value, a theory of Adam Smith, another conceptual obstacle blocks understanding the blindness of moneytheism.[19] This is a monetary doctrine on economic development, which claims its main support in Max Weber's thesis on Protestant ethics and the spirit of capitalism from 1905. Although Weber's analysis is limited, the doctrine preaches that exchange on markets by means of money and credit must overrule all other human interaction in the race to economic development. Based on Weber's description of Calvinist Geneva, this tenet is now widely diffused as the universal norm of economic success: moneytheism.

The financial crisis works as a flash of lightning, revealing a world totally incompatible with what went on in Geneva centuries ago. This is also the conclusion of philosopher Marcel Henaff when comparing Weber's findings on Calvinism with his own studies of Catholicism, a far more economically successful doctrine.[20] Although the sweeping generalization of Weber's local studies postulates that modern developing societies must by necessity turn human relations into economic exchanges, Henaff shows how the force of this ideology has blinded researchers to the fact that other successful cultures rarely abide by this credo. Fundamentalist moneytheism blocks our understanding of gifts as something radically different from exchange. The moneytheist argues that gifts are but exchanges in disguise, for all givers share the expectation of future reciprocity. Only the species of economic man is apt to survive. The moneytheist firmly believes that as societies progress, all exchanges will eventually be stripped of their disguises. To this, Henaff responds that no one can seriously believe that Catholic societies are general economic failures and that there is a rich articulate philosophy of giving the gift as a radically different but complementary alternative to exchange. Living out a capitalist schizophrenia is far less apt to lead to madness than stubbornly suppressing the condition. And so once again, it is time to turn to the artist for a recommended therapy for this affliction.

Giving Versus Exchanging

To imagine all human relations as economic exchange is as deranged as thinking that a defrocked monk named Calvin models successful development. What worked in a walled city in 1560 is not the same as what works globally today. The openness of the Swiss bankers to Pistoletto indicates that something happened—even in Weber's Geneva—for artists probably dwell more in the ethos of giving than of exchanging.[21] In his *Gift, Imagination and the Erotic Life of Property*, Lawrence Hyde explores the roots of an idea that may seem outmoded to calculating rationalists but nevertheless is central to the creative worker; it is the idea of genius.[22]

Books of art history and philosophy are plentiful, and many volumes include testimonies of artists who find it complicated to act as sellers on markets. Plato's classical attack on the Sophists could be read as an ideal example of this dilemma. Plato claims that selling philosophy for money by necessity spoils the purity of the philosophic idea, and marketing and marketers today are subject to much of the same criticism as Sophists in Plato's time.[23] Hyde provides us with an explanation. Ideas like those of philosophers or other creative people have long been considered dependent on individual talent. Talent is what makes the qualitative difference between arts and crafts, for example. Yet talent seems impossible to acquire by mere training. It is hard to define and can be recognized only when it is encountered. Furthermore, talent cannot be purchased on the open market. One of the difficulties in managing talented employees is that they view themselves as working in accordance with a higher calling and not just as earning an income.[24] Is the obvious incompatibility of calling and commerce comparable to the difference between giving and exchanging? In the final analysis, talent seems more a mystical or divine gift that deserves respect and recognition for what it is.

Art and Artists' Scrapping of Moneytheism

Some years ago, a book was published under the ironic title of *Turning the Back on Art.*[25] It was about corporate art patrons who brag about their expensive art collections and use them only as a backdrop for portrait photographs. On the night when the Swiss bankers met with Pistoletto, collectors who had accumulated art and capital suddenly turned to face the artist. A pioneer of the new breed of artists, Pistoletto had prepared for this discussion for decades.[26] More than thirty years ago, Andy Warhol as well as Joseph Beuys, both friends of Pistoletto, had engaged in conversations reconnecting art and business.[27] The opportunity provided by the financial crisis prompted Pistoletto to sit down with the real capitalists and begin a new conversation,[28] and this dialogue contained the promise of a new political economy and the scrapping of moneytheism.

The old political economy postulates equality between value and price. This shortcoming of old political economy is never solved but only circumnavigated in econometrics, which relates prices to prices.[29] Therefore, traditional financial discourse is a discourse without values. The financial crisis makes this brutally obvious and provokes myriad values lining up to reconnect economy to politics. Simple reconnection is unsatisfactory, however, as it would only bring back liberal-socialist mirroring. Endless bickering and faultfinding would displace creative debate. When Lord Keynes claimed that too little credit was the cause of the financial crash, for example, Friedrich Hayek, voicing the mirroring opposition, countered that too much credit was the real villain. Or when Republicans accused Democrats of creating a subprime crisis by granting irresponsibly generous housing credit to poor Americans, Democrats piled the blame back on Republicans for not having minted more credit and avoided bank failures in financial institutions like Lehman Brothers.

Artists are able to contribute because they are human beings who dwell in two radically different worlds: one of values and one of prices. They help us understand that the two worlds are parallel and can be connected in a multitude of ways. And herein lies the artistry economists refer to as entrepreneurship.[30] Nothing can be taken for granted; a boost of aggregate prices does not entail more total value, and much effort and talent is required to make values spill over into prices. Equilibrium can no longer be considered a built-in mechanism of balance, and Adam Smith's bold ambition to make economists into the Isaac Newtons of the social world must be abandoned.[31]

Smashing the Mirrors: The Therapy of Pistoletto's Performance

To recap, then, we have met with singular individuals—in this instance, artists—who would like to improve human relations. We visited an art school and found education focused on how art can survive inside a society and still be critical. We met philosophers helping artists to reflect on their work as relational change agents. Then we saw how art is connected to gifts and how artists can make us realize that societies can thrive and nations can increase their wealth through economic exchange and generous giving. Artists seem to be entrepreneurs living in both the world of prices and the world of value.[32] We stumbled on a definition of artistic work not as instrumental action, not as calculated intention, but as a gesture.

It is striking that this reorientation taking place in the art world seems to occur against a backdrop of overwhelming concern with what happens in the world economy. Reading a documentary account of new art education is like reading texts by anthropologists exploring conditions for human existence in contemporary capitalisms. Most art shows and performances offer surprising explorations of life under capitalistic rules. Few artists think that economic conditions unilaterally influence existence; the time of clear-cut Marxist or liberalist illustrations is long gone. Values-in-use cannot easily be singled out from values-in-exchange. Things are far more complex. We live not only in a world of money but also in a world of authentic life. Commerce blurs with creativity and only in a vulgar faith in moneytheism can the outmoded financial Calvinist worship one pure invisible God. There are so many worlds, but how do they connect?

A few weeks after his Geneva conversation, I saw Pistoletto at the opening of the Venice Biennale in June 2009. There in the Arsenale, I photographed his staging of a performance crushing a number of huge gold-framed mirrors. Soon the big representative screens were no longer. On the floor, thousands of small glittering pieces reflected flashes from an army of photographers. Is a financial crisis like the artist's gesture? Has it irreversibly smashed the mirrors of moneytheism? If so, what's next? (Figures 3.3–3.9).

FIGURE 3.3 Michelangelo Pistoletto, performance at the Venice Biennale, 2009

FIGURE 3.4 Michelangelo Pistoletto, performance at the Venice Biennale, 2009

FIGURE 3.5 Michelangelo Pistoletto, performance at the Venice Biennale, 2009

FIGURE 3.6 Michelangelo Pistoletto, performance at the Venice Biennale, 2009

FIGURE 3.7 Michelangelo Pistoletto, performance at the Venice Biennale, 2009

FIGURE 3.8 Michelangelo Pistoletto, performance at the Venice Biennale, 2009

FIGURE 3.9 Michelangelo Pistoletto, performance at the Venice Biennale, 2009

Notes

1. Heike Belzer and Daniel Birnbaum, eds., *Kunst lehren teaching art: Städelschule Frankfurt/Main* (Cologne: Walther König, 2007).

2. Jan Verwoert, "Free, We Are Already Free: What We Need Now Is Better Life," in Belzer and Birnbaum, *Kunst lehren teaching art*, 102.

3. Some still see art as outside society. Professor Edgar Schein claimed at the 2010 Conference of the American Academy of Management in Montreal that art and artistry were useful as an escape from social order. Even what is officially called outsider art is often the product of persons locked up inside institutions inside society.

4. Daniel Birnbaum, "Teaching Art: A Proposal from Frankfurt," in Belzer and Birnbaum, *Kunst lehren teaching art*.

5. John Dewey, *Art as Experience* (New York: Putnam, 1958).

6. See Daniel Birnbaum and Isabelle Graw, eds., *Under Pressure: Pictures, Subjects and the New Spirit of Capitalism* (Berlin: Sternberg Press, 2008).

7. Luc Boltanski and Eve Chiapello, *The New Spirit of Capitalism* (London: Verso, 2006).

8. Paolo Virno, *A Grammar of the Multitude* (New York: Semiotext(e), 2002).

9. Jacques Ranciere, *The Politics of Aesthetics* (London: Continuum, 2004).

10. Georgio Agamben, *Means without End* (Minneapolis: University of Minnesota Press, 2000), 49–62.

11. Nicholas Bourriaud, *Esthétique relationelle* (Paris: Les Presses du Réel, 2001); Nicholas Bourriaud, *The Critique of Judgment.* (Oxford: Clarendon Press, 1991).

12. Piero Sraffa, *Production of Commodities by Means of Commodities* (Cambridge: Cambridge University Press, 1975).

13. Brian Rotman, *Signifying Nothing: The Semiotics of Zero* (London: Macmillan, 1987).

14. This popular meaning is far from self-evident but rather is constructed by one century of political action resting on plausible theoretical assumptions.

15. See, for example, the almost schizophrenic abyss: Soros the speculator and Soros the debater or Stiglitz the Nobel Prize winner and Stiglitz the popular author.

16. This explains the nostalgia for the closed economies of socialism as well as the elevation of liberalism to a religion of the invisible hand.

17. Contemporary examples include the regime in North Korea and the Cambodian Khmer Rouge.

18. The utopian core of liberalism is made clear in its most vulgar offspring: libertarianism.

19. Smith said that although market prices might fluctuate, they will converge toward the natural price in the long run.

20. Marcel Henaff, *Le prix de la vérité* (Paris: Edition du Seuil, 2002), published in English as *The Price of Truth: Gift, Money, and Philosophy* (Stanford, CA: Stanford University Press).

21. Pistoletto, for instance, runs his own art academy financed by money he earns selling his artwork. He is careful to keep the two linked activities separate: he does

not display his work in the academy, and his spouse, Maria Pioppi Pistoletto, runs the business while Michelangelo takes care of the educational side. Giving and exchanging coexist but in separate worlds, and this is might be the key to his success as a pioneer of insider art.

22. Lawrence Hyde, *Gift, Imagination and the Erotic Life of Property* (New York: Vintage, 1983).

23. Roman Laufer and Catherine Paradeise, *Marketing Democracy: Public Opinion and Media Formation in Democratic Societies* (New Brunswick, NJ: Transaction Books, 1990).

24. Helle Hedegaard Hein, "Rutiner og rammer, kunst og kreativitet" [Routines and frames, art and creativity], in *De nye professionelle: Fremtidens roller for de veluddannede* [New professionals: Future roles for the well educated], edited by Bøje Larsen and Helle Hedegaard Hein (Copenhagen: Djøf / Jurist- og Økonomforbundet, 2007), 195–220.

25. Wolfgang Ullrich, *Mit dem Rücken zur Kunst* (Berlin: Verlag Klaus Wagenbac, 2000).

26. See Pierre Guillet de Monthoux, *The Art Firm* (Palo Alto, CA: Stanford University Press, 2004).

27. Remember Andy Warhol's concept of business art and Joseph Beuys's slogan "Kunst = Kapital."

28. "Real" in the sense that Swiss private bankers pride themselves on not running their businesses as limited stock companies. If the bank fails, so does the banker; he or she loses his or her entire fortune.

29. This tautology is obscured by the use of *cost* instead of *price* in the vocabulary of economists.

30. We are here interested in an entrepreneur active not just in the world of prices and the world of values—not in, for example, creators only operating in the universes of value or arbitrageurs only chasing differences in prices.

31. Maybe even thirty years after its publication, Janos Kornai's analysis of socialist economic crises is worth revisiting to deepen the debate about today's crises of global capitalism: *Anti-Equilibrium* (Amsterdam: North Holland Publishers, 1971).

32. The old political economists cannot actually see a place for entrepreneurs inside their system. They cannot accept someone in their theory who is neither a worker nor a capitalist. Keynes—who by the way was an art lover—realized that no development was possible without this third artist and gave him status in the political economy as an entrepreneur.

4   Hence God Exists

Skip McGoun

The quantification of risk began in the late nineteenth century, and until the middle of the twentieth century it was cautiously developed by scholars well aware of the limitations of the approach. But beginning in the 1930s, the process took a perverse turn, and by the 1950s a culture had emerged in economics and finance in which mathematics was no longer a functional tool but had become an end in itself. One's status was determined by one's computational skills, regardless of their practical efficacy. No one challenged the questionable underlying assumption that the financial world worked the same as the physical world and was subject to similar immutable, mathematical laws. In the financial world, it's time to acknowledge the quite reasonable ineffectiveness of mathematics. Our equations are not expressions of laws; they are metaphors. They express useful truths, but they are not themselves the truth.

Introduction

Invited by Catherine the Great to visit her Court, Diderot earned his keep by trying to convert the courtiers to atheism. Fed up, Catherine commissioned Euler to muzzle the windy philosopher. This was easy because all mathematics was Chinese to Diderot. De Morgan tells us what happened: "Diderot was informed that a learned mathematician was in possession of an algebraical

Parts of this chapter have been previously published as McGoun (1995a), McGoun (1995b), and McGoun and Zielonka (2006).

demonstration of the existence of God, and would give it before all the Court, if he desired to hear it. Diderot gladly consented. . . . Euler advanced toward Diderot, and said gravely, and in a tone of perfect conviction 'Sir, $(a + b^n)/n = x$, hence God exists; reply!' " It sounded like sense to Diderot. Humiliated by the unrestrained laughter which greeted his embarrassed silence, the poor man asked Catherine's permission to return at once to France. She graciously gave it. (Bell 1937, 146)

Wall Street's having seriously wounded the global financial system and not just the dignity of a single French philosopher would have impressed Euler, had it been intentional and not a consequence of its own ignorance. The quantification of risk began in the late nineteenth century, and until the middle of the twentieth century was cautiously developed by scholars well aware of the limitations of the approach. But beginning in the 1930s, the process took a perverse turn, and by the 1950s a culture had emerged in economics and finance in which mathematics was no longer a functional tool but had become an end in itself. One's status was determined by one's computational skills, regardless of their practical efficacy. No one challenged the questionable underlying assumption that the financial world worked the same as the physical world and was subject to similar immutable, mathematical laws.

And few are challenging it now, in spite of the catastrophic failure it has led to. Instead we rationalize that we were just using the wrong distributions of outcomes, and when we use the right ones, our equations will work just fine. In the physical world, Eugene Wigner marveled at "the unreasonable *effectiveness* of mathematics." In the financial world, it's time to acknowledge the quite reasonable ineffectiveness of mathematics. Our equations are not expressions of laws; they are metaphors. They express useful truths, but they are not themselves the truth. This chapter traces this history, from the skeptical origins of the mathematization of risk to the entrenchment of mathematics as a professional status symbol and the proliferation and misinterpretation of mathematical models in financial markets. If current finance practitioners were as careful as economists of a century before, it's quite possible that there would have been no economic crisis.

The Origins of Risk Measurement

Just before the beginning of the twentieth century, research programs in economics and mathematics came together. In economics, work on the theory of distribution had taken up the question of profit—specifically, whether profit is the return to the entrepreneur for bearing risk in the same manner as wages, interest, and rent are the returns to the laborer, capitalist, and landlord respectively (Clark 1893). It was natural for this discussion of risk and risk bearing in economics to include the role of insurance, which had used descriptive statistics for a number of years. And at the same time in applied mathematics, advances in inferential statistics were generating an interest in the subject that led some to seek other economic applications of statistics.

In one of the earliest articles, Edgeworth (1888) applied probability to historical cash flows to estimate cash reserve requirements. As expected, in a pioneering effort more than a century old, his methods now appear quaint, but his comments on the modest role of a formal mathematical language in this context provide an interesting counterpoint to the aggressive position that many would take more than a half century later: "The theorist must not pretend to wisdom, if he knows so little what he is about as to mistake his abstract formulae for rules immediately applicable to practice" (Edgeworth, 1888, 127). Edgeworth clearly had a normative view of quantification. To him, it was a way to sharpen intuition or to make heuristics more precise. Ironically, Markowitz (1952) and Sharpe (1964), who were largely responsible for the institutionalization of probabilistic measurement of risk in finance and were awarded Nobel prizes for their efforts in modern portfolio theory and the capital asset pricing model, shared this view in their earliest work.

Before the century was out, some authors had begun to explore the relationship between probability and risk, usually in the context of insurance. For insurance purposes, the usual measure of the risk of an event was the relative frequency with which the event had occurred in the past. A recurring theme in the work of Haynes (1895) was that, for many risks, such statistics are either unreliable or nonexistent. As risk is present even when statistics are not, risk and relative frequency probabilities must not be the same. Other authors struggled with this difference in different terms. Ross (1896) used the terms *variation* and *uncertainty*. *Variation* is descriptive of the possible outcomes, for which there are no historical relative frequencies or statistics, and *uncertainty*, the equivalent of *risk*, is a consequence of this variation.

By 1900, risk had become a very important topic in economics. There appeared to be opportunities for the use of new probabilistic methods to understand risk, yet no specific steps had been taken in this direction. From a historical standpoint, the legacy of the pre-1900 period is the point made by both Haynes (1895) and Ross (1896) that reverberates throughout later work—

for Haynes, that there are risks for which there are reliable statistics and those for which there are not; and for Ross, that it is unquantifiable variation that creates uncertainty. This is the reference-class problem—there are economically important circumstances that are perceived as risky but that are also without relevant historical precedent.

The noted economist Irving Fisher's (1906) underlying philosophy was that probability is a measure of ignorance. His words suggest a more subjective theory of probability than a relative frequency theory: "Chance exists only so far as ignorance exists; varies with different persons according to their comparative ignorance of the matter under consideration; and is in fact a measure of ignorance. Of course the actual statistical record may afford an important and sometimes the only basis for our degree of knowledge and ignorance. . . . But while statistics supply data for the forming of subjective estimates of chances, they do not, themselves, constitute chances" (Fisher 1906, 268). Other passages, though, indicate greater optimism regarding the use of relative frequencies and are impressively prescient regarding what life on Wall Street would become: "Nevertheless it is more than conceivable that the time may come when practical brokers will make use of probability computations in the same way that they now make use of bond tables" (Fisher 1906, 283).

Between 1906 and 1920, the idea of risk as the dispersion of a relative frequency distribution was at least made explicit, if not fully accepted. Lavington (1912, 398–99) wrote: "This condition may be represented by a curve of prospective net returns, which range, perhaps, from a large positive to a large negative amount. The 'spread' of this curve represents the amount of Uncertainty." Lavington attributes this idea to Pigou (1960, 774), who is himself somewhat vague about the relationship between the dispersion of the distribution and risk: "Within the symmetrical group we may distinguish curves which are spread out, like open umbrellas, and curves which are narrow, like closed umbrellas. The former sort represent schemes in which a wide divergence, the latter schemes in which only a small divergence, of the actual from the most probable return, is preferable."

By 1920 the dispersion of a relative frequency distribution had been clearly identified as risk. Terminology was still somewhat vague, and the philosophical considerations were not fully understood, but risk could be measured. It is peculiar, though, that despite the unrestrained optimism of Norton and the more cautious optimism of Fisher, no one actually attempted to measure risk and relate it to returns. Data were available, and there was no reluctance to make lengthy computations in other contexts—computations that were time-consuming without computers but not technically difficult. Yet specific measurements of risk were never made. Perhaps this was because the apparent enthusiasm for the measurement of risk as the dispersion of a relative frequency distribution was tempered by concern regarding the reference-class problem raised more than twenty years earlier. Risk was indeed something different or something more.

Frank Knight (1921) certainly believed that statistics could not be used to measure risk. His distinction between risk and uncertainty is the one idea from this pre-modern-finance period that is at least referenced (though not accepted) in the current literature. Although his definitions are not the same as those of earlier authors, he is concerned with the familiar reference-class problem that had been around for many years. His statement of the problem is nonetheless worth quoting in full for its unambiguous expression of the issue:

> It will appear that a measurable uncertainty, or "risk" proper, as we shall use the term, is so far different from an unmeasurable one that it is not in effect an uncertainty at all. We shall accordingly restrict the term "uncertainty" to cases of the non-quantitative type. . . . The economic relations of risk in the narrower sense of a measurable probability have been extensively dealt with in the literature of the subject and do not call for elaborate treatment here. Our main concern will be with the contrast between Risk as a known chance and true Uncertainty, and treatment of the former is incidental to this purpose. (Knight 1921, 20–21)[1]

And:

> Business decisions, for example, deal with situations which are far too unique, generally speaking, for any sort of statistical tabulation to have any value for guidance. The conception of an objectively measurable probability or chance is simply inapplicable. (Knight 1921, 231)

The early history concludes with a key work published by Irving Fisher (1930, 316) in which his position regarding the statistical measurement of risk was unambiguous:

> While it is possible to calculate mathematically risks of a certain type like those in games of chance (classical probability) or in property and life insurance where the chances are capable of accurate measurement (relative frequency probability), most economic risks are not so readily measured. To attempt to formulate mathematically in any useful, complete manner the laws determining

the rate of interest under the sway of chance would be like attempting to express completely the laws which determine the path of a projectile when affected by random gusts of wind. Such formulas would need to be either too general or too empirical to be of much value.

Thus, probabilistic measurement of risk had been soundly and unambiguously rejected by 1930. There are a number of possible explanations for this. It might have been because there was insufficient pressure for or insufficient interest in measuring risk, yet there was considerable interest in the stock exchange, an obvious target of statistical analysis, and volumes of data were readily available. Before computerization, the computations would have been tedious, but the mathematical techniques were well known, and the possibility of beating the market was a strong incentive to apply them. It might have been that an intuitive sense of risk was thought to be sufficient, but both Edgeworth (1888) and Norton (1904) spoke of the benefits of quantification. It might have been that the concept of probabilistic measurement of risk was not as well developed then as it appears in retrospect to have been, but authors from Fisher (1906) on are too explicit to be significantly misinterpreted, and there is ample evidence that the idea had been in gestation for a number of years before then. It also might have been that the accepted economic methodology of the time was antithetical to a probabilistic measurement of risk. This was, after all, the era of nonmathematical American institutionalism. However, a number of economists including Irving Fisher (1906) seem to have been willing in principle to make the simplifying assumptions common in neoclassical economics. The only realistic explanation for the rejection was a consensus conclusion that a probabilistic measure of risk was essentially inapplicable to economic activity.

Then things changed. Weintraub (1985) and Craver (1986) describe a virtual exodus of German and Austrian economists to the United States in the late 1930s. Many of these émigré economists had been mathematicians before they turned to economics, and they played a major role in the prewar explosion in the collection and analysis of economic statistics. Among them were Jacob Marschak, Gerhard Tintner, Paul Rosenstein-Rodan, and Oscar Lange, whose names are all associated with the probabilistic measurement of risk. The problems with measuring risk probabilistically were swept under the rug by appealing to the peculiar nature of economic theory with its necessary simplifications: "To [the objection that the acting man does not and cannot make exact calculations] I would answer that we know well that investors are not actuaries; nor are housewives accountants. Any chapter of economic theory starts from simplified and idealized behavior patterns and treats the results as mere approximations" (Marschak 1941, 52).

There was no empirical evidence suggesting that it was appropriate, and none of the fundamental problems had been dealt with in any way other than to cavalierly dismiss them. Without attempting to sort out the various methodological currents swirling about at the time, it appears as if Marschak and his colleagues viewed economic research from a much different perspective from that of Knight and Fisher. This might have been an outcome of their mathematical training. Instead of attempting to devise an original, effective way to model the risk present in most economic activities, they simply borrowed the mathematical probability calculus, about which Knight and Fisher had already expressed serious doubts.

Snooks (1993) believes that there might have been a shift in the perception of economic research at this time, contending that somewhere between the 1930s and 1940s there was a decline in concern for the reality content of econometric models. He quotes Morgan (1990) to the effect that data were no longer regarded as a creative source of ideas for building new models but simply as a means of testing a priori models. It mattered to Knight and Fisher whether people would have assessed risk probabilistically; otherwise, their theories could not have been explanatory. It did not matter to Marschak and his colleagues as long as probabilities provided data. Had their theories worked, then their simplifications must have been appropriate. Theirs was a sound, albeit optimistic, approach, if the attachment to relative frequency probabilities had not been so strong as to preclude its abandonment when it proved ineffective.

Mathematical Gamesmanship

At that time in the 1930s, mathematics was a tool, and still in the twenty-first century, economics and finance scholars think of it as the tool of their trade—so useful a tool that without it, one cannot practice the trade (Klamer and Colander 1990) And of course the more skill with which one wields the tool, the better one is at the trade. When Marschak and his colleagues were writing, though, economists' use of mathematics was not taken for granted, and the use of mathematics was often debated within the profession. In the late 1940s and early 1950s, there were a number of articles published addressing the issue, including an exchange in a 1954 issue of *Review of Economics and*

Statistics in which the editor himself confessed the embarrassment of "literary economists" in general and his own awe in particular:[2]

> This symposium clearly reveals that mathematical economists have a great faith in the potency of mathematics as a tool to be used in economics. Their willingness, even anxiety, to state their case, in itself is symptomatic. No similar enthusiasm was revealed by literary economists, perhaps because, like Pigou, they believe that "Objections from people innocent of mathematics are like objections to Chinese literature by people who cannot read Chinese. . . ." Even one so unlearned in mathematics as the present writer has been impressed by the contributions that can be made by the use of mathematics. (Harris 1954, 383)

Not all economists, however, were willing to be so easily disciplined. Novick (1954, 358) takes a defiant stance, consistent with the role of his article to provide a target for the defenders of mathematization: "Those of us who have only a limited training and a still more limited experience in mathematics are too often cowed by the symbols and are afraid to challenge them lest we be embarrassed by showing our ignorance. This is unfortunate since the use of mathematics as a form of communication provides no greater virility to the ideas than the verbalization which heretofore has been more typical of the social sciences."

The respondents to Novick were not hesitant to attack him, some more politely and subtly than others:

> Dr. Novick has added his voice to the swelling chorus of exasperated voices protesting in a variety of ways, in rhyme or with reason, the increasing use of formal mathematical language, constructs, and derivations in economic and statistical analysis. . . . There is nothing in the existing difficulties between "mathematical" and "non-mathematical" economists—illustrated by the substantive contents as well as by the emotional overtones of Dr. Novick's comments—that time and effort will not cure. (Koopmans 1954, 377)
>
> This it not to say that a practical budgeter like Mr. Novick need disturb his busy brain over this abstract matter. (Samuelson 1954b, 380)
>
> Mr. Novick approaches mathematical economics in the spirit in which many people approach modern art. He admits that he does not understand it, but he is sure he doesn't like it. (Duesenberry 1954, 361)
>
> But I can't help admiring [Novick's] straightforward advice to previously cowed and quivering literary economists: just dismiss mathematical economics as "esoterica." (English translation: anything I don't understand.) When it comes to mathematics, Novick agrees with Lady Bracknell in *The Importance of*

Being Earnest: he does not approve of anything which tampers with his natural ignorance. . . . Novick's contribution is to suggest that non-mathematicians should ignore mathematical economics, and that mathematical economists ought to do something about communicating. (I have often myself thought it rather dense of foreigners not to speak English, so I can understand his point of view.) (Solow 1954, 373)

The mathematical economists did not just direct their ad hominem comments at Novick:

One may detect traces of naiveté among social scientists, outside the field of economics. These uninitiated expect unreasonable results from the mere application of this powerful tool. The fact that they have been impressed beyond justification is not, however, an acceptable argument against the methodology. (Klein 1954, 360)

It would, of course, be difficult for a person without mathematical training to appreciate the full value of these results, but they are nevertheless powerful and within the grasp of all those students who will avail themselves of the opportunity of studying them. (Klein 1954, 360)

The author appears to have the choice of being completely unintelligible to the non-mathematician, or else making his article very long-winded, imprecise, and unnecessarily obscure to those with mathematical training. (Champernowne 1954, 371)

The difficulty in making $\Delta Y = S^{-1}(\Delta I)$ intelligible to persons who have not found time to learn about matrices is therefore a main obstacle in getting them to understand the ramifications of any change involving three or more interdependent variables. (Champernowne 1954, 372)

On the other hand it is sometimes forgotten that arguments against the most general types of mathematics are just arguments against science in general, i.e., against the assumption that we can understand connections between phenomena—in this case economic phenomena—in some general way. If determinacy—in whatever loose form—is not accepted at all, there is no economics: no mathematical economics and no literary economics. Perhaps there would remain economic novels; personally I would prefer other novels then. (Tinbergen 1954, 368)

The only real question is a question of fact: do mathematical methods have any power? That they do has been demonstrated repeatedly by the problems they have solved and by the muddled impasses which literary reasoning has not been able to break through. (Dorfman 1954, 377)

Survival in the literature is a test of fitness, if an imperfect one. If mathematical techniques continue to produce good economics then, still as a Darwinian, I predict that long before the appendix has disappeared from the human digestive tract most people interested in economic theory will as a matter of course learn some mathematics. (Solow 1954, 374)[3]

Some authors deny that mathematics is used for effect. Those who admit it claim that it does not occur often, and when it does, they are of course not the ones doing it:

Neither have I met any expounders of mathematical economic theories whose hopes have been to impress the gullible by wielding a tool to which supernatural powers are attributed. True, our culture past and present contains numerous examples of the use of esoteric symbols to impress instead of communicate—from the formulas of the medicine man to the use of Latin in religious observances. (Koopmans 1954, 378)

To some extent, Novick pictures the mathematical economist, or more generally social scientist, as a charlatan and dilettante. It is true that some may use mathematics to confuse, bewilder, or impress others, but it would be an extremely narrow viewpoint that overlooked the constructive efforts of those using the mathematical method. (Klein 1954, 359)

Subconsciously, however, I suspect that the power and intrinsic challenge of mathematics may have led some, if not to believe just that, at least to consider empirical work as a lower form of intellectual activity. And I think it is true that mathematical knowledge is sometimes used as a protective cover and a form of gamesmanship in winning arguments. And economists, being human, no doubt find it difficult sometimes to resist the temptation of displaying their mathematical knowledge when a simpler argument could be found. However, this can be greatly exaggerated. I do not believe that most mathematical economists deliberately engage in this type of activity, even though it may appear so. (Chipman 1954, 364)

There is also a certain amount of purely mathematical muscle-flexing that goes on. This is the inevitable reaction of the ex-ninety-pound-weakling. But there's really not much. (Solow 1954, 374)

A prospective economist of the time would have done well to follow Samuelson's avuncular advice:

In conclusion, ask yourself what advice you would have to give to a young man who steps into your office with the following surprisingly common story: "I am interested in economic theory. I know little mathematics. And when I look at the journals, I am greatly troubled. Must I give up hopes of being a theorist? Must I learn mathematics? If so, how much? I am already past twenty-one; am I past redemption. . . ?" I think a better answer might go somewhat as follows: Some of the most distinguished economic theorists past and present, have been innocent of mathematics. Some of the most distinguished theorists have known some degree of mathematics. Obviously, you can become a great theorist without knowing mathematics. Yet it is fair to say that you will have to be that much more clever and brilliant. . . . Moreover, without mathematics you run grave psychological risks. (Samuelson 1952, 65)

Samuelson does not specify how these "grave psychological risks" will manifest themselves in economics; rather, he quotes the incident between Euler and Diderot that opened this chapter and refers to Euler as a "charlatan," a characterization that is interesting. Earlier in the chapter from which this quotation was taken, Samuelson refers to Euler's Theorem, which must have been discovered by the mathematician during a pause in his chicanery. Apparently, Samuelson has no trouble recognizing one as quackery and one as serious mathematics, but it was not the same for Euler. To continue the anecdote regarding Euler and Diderot: "Not content with this masterpiece, Euler in all seriousness painted his lily with solemn proofs, in deadly earnest, that God exists and that the soul is not a material substance. It is reported that both proofs passed into the treatises on theology of his day" (Bell 1937, 147).

A common indication that mathematics is a weapon is the existence of a pecking order among economists based on the use of mathematics and not on the results of its use: "Much is being made of the widespread, nearly mandatory use of mathematics. . . Professional journals have opened wide their pages to papers written in mathematical language; colleges train aspiring young economists to use this language; graduate schools require its knowledge and reward its use. The mathematical model-building industry has grown into one of the most prestigious, possibly the most prestigious branch of economics" (Leontief 1971, 1).

The preceding quotations have shown that mathematics is a medium of disputation in economic and financial scholarship in which those skillful in its use can subdue those who are not, independent of any substantive economic meaning. The characterizations of nonmathematical economists as cowed and quivering, naive, uninitiated, muddled, and gullible and the references to power, survival, fitness, gamesmanship, and muscle flexing are too pointed to ignore, even though the terms are often used in denials that they apply. And as the academy had gone, so went Wall Street. So-called rocket scientists and quants are accorded the highest status. It doesn't matter whether the quantitative methods work, and in fact it is usually difficult or impossible to tell whether they do or don't, or just what *work* really means. What matters is that they look impressive and are intimidating to the less mathematically adept, who might not understand the mathematics but are still well equipped to challenge the assumptions on which the models were based, if they were open to their scrutiny.

This is not to say that mathematics is inappropriate in economics and finance or on Wall Street—just that it has its limitations. However, the believers who are adept at conjuring with mathematics have no interest in questioning the underpinnings. And the nonbelievers haven't bothered to acquire enough facility with mathematical jargon to lend their challenges credibility.

Models as Metaphors

Although mathematics has been used quite successfully in the natural sciences, no one quite knows why it works as well as it does. In fact, the noted physicist Eugene Wigner (1967) posed this very question in the title of a famous article: "The Unreasonable Effectiveness of Mathematics in the Natural Sciences." The universe just seems to be structured in such a way that mathematics describes it very precisely.

In contrast, the use of quantitative models such as the option pricing model (OPM) in finance, given that in the social sciences empirical successes have not been not been so striking as in the physical sciences, remains questionable. In science in general and finance in particular, there are figurative truths as well as literal truths; in effect, quantitative models in finance such as the OPM are best thought of as metaphors. They are not identities and cannot be applied literally, but they do provide us with figurative knowledge—an epistemologically meaningful form that might legitimately be called a useful framework.

Usually, a metaphor is thought of as a literary or rhetorical figure or trope. A metaphor explicitly states that something is something else, even though we know that it is not. Because of their palpable "falsity," metaphors might be considered unscientific, and in fact we usually regard them as somewhat dramatic. The metaphor "argument is war," for example, certainly offers us colorful ways of talking about arguments. Although we can "defend a position" and even "launch a counterattack" in an argument, no one will have to "receive emergency surgery in a field hospital." Some entailments of the metaphor of war apply to arguments (positions and counterattacks), others (field hospitals) do not. Arguments are war not in a literal sense but in a figurative sense. Metaphors are not identities; that is, something is not identical to something else. But some aspects of something are the same as for something else, some of which identical aspects may have suggested the metaphor and others of which are suggested by it.

The importance of metaphor in science has long been recognized. Hesse (1965) describes it as transferring associated ideas and implications from one system to another system by using the language of the one to describe the other. Lakoff and Johnson (1980) similarly define metaphors as ways of expressing one experience in terms of another. Something does not have to be something else to tell us something about it that helps us understand it. And when we think and speak about something as if it were something else, we are inclined to act in such as way that it actually becomes more like that something else. There is no doubt that the metaphor "argument is war" can help us understand why arguments are the way they are, as there must be similarities between arguments and war that enable us to use the same language to describe both. The metaphor enables us to perceive some of these similarities between arguments and war that we had not seen before, thereby deepening our understanding. And common use of the metaphor may in fact make our arguments more like wars.

Finance theories such as the OPM are metaphors similar to the metaphors we find in the natural sciences. Because the statement "market price is model price" rarely if ever has unequivocal empirical support, it is probably not an identity in any traditional "objective" scientific sense. Options are not, and need not be, literally priced in accordance with the OPM, for example. In the language of metaphor, specific option prices are not one of the entailments of the OPM. It is not a positive model (what prices are) or even a normative model (what prices ought to be) in the traditional economic uses of the terms. But it does tell us some things about option pricing that we did not know before and that help us to understand it. It is definitely a useful model, and it has far more scientific value than the somewhat derogatory adjective *useful* implies.

The first published appearance of the term *contingent claim* actually appears to have occurred in several articles in a 1976 issue of the *Journal of Financial Economics* by Smith (1976) and Cox and Ross (1976), as well as Ingersoll (1976). Smith's was a survey article on the state of the art in option pricing, which introduced the issue. He begins it with a paean to the OPM:

> Although much interest in option pricing has been generated from the development of new options markets, such as the Chicago Board Options Exchange, the recent rapid development of theory and the application of that theory can be traced to the path-breaking paper by Fischer Black and Myron Scholes (1973). In that paper, they provide the first explicit general equilibrium solution to the option pricing problem for simple puts and calls. They then suggest that this analysis could provide a basis for the general analysis of contingent claim assets, assets whose value is a non-proportional function of the value of another asset. (Smith 1976, 3)

Although Black and Scholes (1973) did describe in their article how their model might be used to value common stock and bonds, as the title "The Pricing of Options and *Corporate Liabilities*" (italics added) promised, they did not use the term *contingent claim* as Smith implies.

Even more interesting than the introduction of Smith's article is the conclusion. It ends with an provocative admission: "However, that the Black-Scholes analysis has generated substantial interest seems to derive more from its implications for a general theory of the valuation of contingent claims, than for its direct application to value simple puts and calls. Nevertheless, to date, the only example of empirical verification of this analysis which employs data other than that for put and call trading is by Ingersoll (1976). The potential benefits of empirical research in this area appear to be large" (Smith 1976, 47). In other words, the notoriety of the OPM was due to its creation of the category of "contingent claims" and not to its performance valuing them.

It appears that Brennan (1979, 55) is responsible for the massive broadening of the category "contingent claims" to its present dimensions: "The discrete time model, on the other hand, imposes no such requirements and hence extends the scope of option pricing principles to the relative valuation of a broad class of assets for which one or other of these assumptions (regarding stochastic processes and continuous trading) is not satisfied. . . . The opportunity of a firm to make profitable investments in the future, if that should prove profitable, is a contingent claim which is not traded." This extended the OPM to encompass Myers and Turnbull's (1977, 331) notion of the firm as "a portfolio of tangible and intangible assets. The tangible assets are units of productive capacity in place—real—assets and the intangible assets are

options to purchase additional units of productive capacity in future periods."
Hence, "real options" were born.

Derivative first appeared much later, in the *Journal of Financial Economics*
in the article "Comments on the Valuation of *Derivative Assets*" (Bick 1982,
italics added). The abstract begins with the following sentence using *derivative* to modify yet another noun: "This paper presents an alternative approach
to derive the Breeden-Litzenberger valuation formula, which expresses the
price of an arbitrary *derivative security* in terms of call option's prices" (Bick
1982, 331, italics added). Breeden and Litzenberger (1978) themselves did not
use the word *derivative* in their article. So it remains unclear exactly where it
came from, as Bick does not write as if he were introducing it for the first time.

The history of these terms poses something of a puzzle for the concept of a
derivative. What causes the puzzle is that the structural similarity that all derivatives share does not seem to have been recognized before anyone thought
to apply the OPM to them, as there was no special category of "derivatives" or
even "contingent claims" until several years after the publication of the OPM.
But without a glaringly obvious structural similarity sufficient to create a special category, what would have ever caused anyone to think that a complicated
equation such as the OPM could have been applied to all of those assets, instruments, products, or securities that eventually came to be derivatives? It
certainly wasn't any promising empirical successes, as Smith (1976) admitted
at the end of his survey article that very, very little testing had been done until
long after the extension of the OPM.

There is an old saying, "To a man with a hammer, everything is a nail."
Regarding the OPM, it is as if following the invention of this hammer, more
things were discovered to be nails than anyone had ever thought were nails.
In fact, the term *nails* itself was created specifically to encompass them. All
this occurred before anyone even tried to use the hammer on more than a
handful of what came to be called nails. And when anyone did, the hammer
didn't work very well, and the nails were often bent or didn't go all the way
into the wood. Nonetheless, the hammer quickly became the tool of choice
among carpenters.

The solution to this puzzle is that derivatives certainly do not share a glaringly obvious structural identity that permits the OPM to be literally applied
to them. Rather, they share a less dramatic structural similarity that figura-
tively entails certain logical implications of the OPM. The OPM is a metaphor ("market prices are model prices") that has explanatory power through
its revelation of a pattern that unifies a number of phenomena. It is not a

deterministic equation (market prices = model prices) that explains prices in a lawlike way; rather, it is a symbolic representation of what influences the pricing of assets that had not previously been seen as priced in a similar way.

Conclusion

Mathematics first entered economics very cautiously and deliberately, being used as a tool by scholars who were well aware of its limitations. Over time, in what is likely to have been an attempt by economists to emulate the success of physicists, its use overtook its usefulness. Mathematics became an end in itself, and the status of an economist came to be determined by the virtuosity with which mathematics was deployed rather than the results to which it led. This was the situation in the 1950s and 1960s when finance emerged as an academic discipline and quantitatively oriented MBAs flowed out of graduate programs into Wall Street. Asset-pricing models grew more and more complex, and their use more and more widespread as they were applied in more and more domains. The models also grew more and more distant from the assumptions on which they were based. It's not that this plethora of models with us today have no value; as metaphors, they can offer important insights into how markets work and what variables are relevant. But what the models can't do is tell us exactly what to do. And when the outputs from some models are used as the inputs into others, the problems are compounded. The financial crisis occurred for many reasons, but a fundamental one was the quite reasonable ineffectiveness in the financial world of the same mathematics that has been unreasonably effective in the natural one.

Notes

1. Here, Knight must be referring to insurance and actuarial computations. Outside of these, the literature regarding statistics and risk was not at all extensive.

2. "My dictionary defines 'literary economist' as 'euphemism for non-mathematical economist'" (Samuelson 1954a, 359).

3. Decades later, Solow (1990, 449, quoted in Shackelford 1992, 574) wrote: "Life seems to call much less for mathematics and even a bit less for analytics and much more for creativity, critical judgment, and the ability to communicate." Either economics is much different from life, or Solow's opinion regarding mathematics has changed.

References

Bell, E. T. 1937. *Men of mathematics*. New York: Simon & Schuster.

Bick, Avi. 1982. Comments on the valuation of derivative assets. *Journal of Financial Economics* 10 (3): 331–45.

Black, F., and M. Scholes. 1973. The pricing of options and corporate liabilities. *Journal of Political Economy* 81: 637–59.

Breeden, D. T., and R. H. Litzenberger. 1978. Prices of state-contingent claims implicit in option prices. *Journal of Business* 51: 621–51.

Brennan, M. J. 1979. The pricing of contingent claims in discrete time models. *Journal of Finance* 34 (1): 53–68.

Champernowne, D. G. 1954. On the use and misuse of mathematics in presenting economic theory. *Review of Economics and Statistics* 36 (4): 369–72.

Chipman, John S. 1954. Empirical testing and mathematical models. *Review of Economics and Statistics* 36 (4): 363–65.

Clark, J. B. 1893. Insurance and business profit. *Quarterly Journal of Economics* 7: 40–54.

Cox, John C., and Stephen A. Ross. 1976. A survey of some new results in financial option pricing theory. *Journal of Finance* 31 (2): 383–402.

Craver, Earlene. 1980. The emigration of the Austrian economists. *History of Political Economy* 18 (1): 1–32.

Dorfman, Robert. 1954. A catechism: Mathematics in social science. *Review of Economics and Statistics* 36 (4): 374–77.

Duesenberry, James S. 1954. The methodological basis of economic theory. *Review of Economics and Statistics* 36 (4): 361–63.

Edgeworth, F. Y. 1888. The mathematical theory of banking. *Journal of the Royal Statistical Society* 51: 113–27.

Fisher, Irving. 1906. *The nature of capital and interest.* New York: Macmillan.

Fisher, Irving. 1930. *The theory of interest.* New York: Macmillan.

Harris, Seymour. A postscript by the editor. *Review of Economics and Statistics* 36 (4): 382–86.

Haynes, John. 1895. Risk as an economic factor. *Quarterly Journal of Economics* 9: 409–49.

Hesse, M. 1965. The explanatory function of metaphor. In *Logic, Methodology, and Philosophy of Science,* edited by Y. Bar-Hillel, 249–59. Amsterdam: North-Holland Publishing.

Ingersoll, J. 1976. A theoretical and empirical investigation of the dual purpose funds: An application of contingent claims analysis. *Journal of Financial Economics* 3: 83–124.

Johnson, Mark. 1987. *The body in the mind: The bodily basis of meaning, imagination, and reason.* Chicago: University of Chicago Press.

Klamer, Arjo, and David Colander. 1990. *The making of an economist.* Boulder, CO: Westview Press.

Klein, L. R. 1954. The contribution of mathematics in economics. *Review of Economics and Statistics* 36 (4): 359–61.

Knight, Frank H. 1921. *Risk, uncertainty and profit.* Boston: Houghton Mifflin.

Koopmans, Tjalling C. 1954. On the use of mathematics in economics. *Review of Economics and Statistics* 36 (4): 377–79.

Lakoff, George, and Mark Johnson. 1980. *Metaphors we live by.* Chicago: University of Chicago Press.

Lavington, F. 1912. Uncertainty in its relation to the net rate of interest. *Economic Journal* 22: 398–409.

Leontief, Wassily. 1971. Theoretical assumptions and nonobserved facts. *American Economic Review* 61: 1–7.

Markowitz, Harry. 1952. Portfolio selection. *Journal of Finance* 7 (1): 77–91.

Marschak, Jakob. 1941. Lack of confidence. *Social Research* (February): 41–62.

McGoun, Elton G. 1995a. The history of risk "measurement." *Critical Perspectives on Accounting* 6: 511–32.

McGoun, Elton G. 1995b. Machomatics in egonomics. *International Review of Financial Analysis* 4 (2–3): 185–99.

McGoun, Elton G., and Piotr Zielonka. 2006. The Platonic foundations of finance and the interpretation of finance models. *Journal of Behavioral Finance* 7 (1): 43–57.

Morgan, M. S. 1990. *The history of econometric ideas.* Cambridge: Cambridge University Press.

Myers, Stewart C., and Stuart M. Turnbull. 1977. Capital budgeting and the capital asset pricing model: Good news and bad news. *Journal of Finance* 32 (2): 321–32.

Pigou, A. C. 1960. *The economics of welfare.* 4th ed. London: Macmillan.

Ross, Edward A. 1896. Uncertainty as a factor in production. *Annals of the American Academy of Political and Social Science* 8: 92–119.

Samuelson, Paul A. 1952. Economic theory and mathematics: An appraisal. *American Economic Review* 42 (2): 56–66.

Samuelson, Paul A. 1954a. Introduction: Mathematics in economics: No, no or yes, yes, yes? *Review of Economics and Statistics* 36 (4): 359.

Samuelson, Paul A. 1954b. Some psychological aspects of mathematics and economics. *Review of Economics and Statistics* 36 (4): 380–82.

Shackelford, Jean. 1992. Feminist pedagogy. *American Economic Review* (May): 570–76.

Sharpe, William F. 1964. Capital asset prices: A theory of market equilibrium under conditions of risk. *Journal of Finance* 19 (3): 425–42.

Smith, Clifford W., Jr. 1976. Option pricing: A review. *Journal of Financial Economics* 3: 3–51.

Snooks, G. D. 1993. *Economics without time.* Ann Arbor: University of Michigan Press.

Solow, Robert. 1954. The survival of mathematical economics. *Review of Economics and Statistics* 36 (4): 372–74.

Solow, Robert. 1990. Discussion: Comment on "Educating and training new economics Ph.D.'s." *American Economic Review* 81: 448–50.

Tinbergen J. 1954. The functions of mathematical treatment. *Review of Economics and Statistics* 36 (4): 365–69.

Weintraub, E. Roy. 1985. *General equilibrium analysis: Studies in appraisal.* Cambridge: Cambridge University Press, 1985.

Wigner, E. 1967. The unreasonable effectiveness of mathematics in the natural sciences. In *Symmetries and Reflections*, edited by E. Wigner. Bloomington: Indiana University Press.

Comments

5 The Art of Finance

Steven S. Taylor

> The art of accounting and finance is the art of using limited data to come as close as possible to an accurate description of how well a company is performing.
> —*Berman, Knight, and Case 2008*

Although financial data are presented as objective numbers, accounting and finance professionals know that finance is more art than science, in the sense that considerable, context-specific judgment is required to make a variety of choices that can result in very different numbers. The professional standards of accounting suggest that accountants try to represent the "truth" as best they can, much in the same way that a physician tries to do no harm. But you don't have to be a critical theorist to recognize that there are powerful forces pushing those same accountants to paint a particular portrait of the organization's performance and that there are many truths that can be told. However, it is not my intent to dive into the philosophic questions of truth and power but rather to take seriously the idea that finance is an art.

Following the work of Barry and Meisiek (2010), I suggest that the art of accounting and finance is more usefully thought of as the craft of accounting and finance. The distinction they make is that craft is about destinations and art is about departures. Craft applies a systematic set of skills in an established process to achieve a desired end result. For example, a wood worker carefully planes her pieces of wood, cuts out the dovetails for the joints, assembles, and then sands and finishes a chair. It is pretty much the chair the woodworker had in mind when she started making it. In contrast, art is about reaching the audience's imagination by engaging their senses and taking them someplace they haven't been before—a departure. For example, when I see a good play, I am transported into the world of that play, and I imagine all sorts of things about what that world is like and what it means for me to be in that world, if only as an observer.

It is in this sense—that craft is about destinations—that accounting and finance are a craft. They are trying to create numbers that accurately portray the financial position of the organization and provide a basis for managerial decision making. We generally aren't able to tell whether or not those numbers are well crafted; we must rely on a certified accountant to audit them and attest to their craftsmanship. There has also been an art of finance in recent years. There has been an art that is about departures, about taking us someplace new where we have never been before—namely derivatives. I use the term *derivatives* rather loosely in the popular sense to include all of the complex financial instruments that have been created in recent years, from credit default swaps to forward rate agreements and everything in between. This new genre of financial art played a key role in the financial disaster, one that might have been avoided if we had recognized it as art rather than accepting it as science.

As with many forms of art, the appreciation of derivatives requires specialist knowledge (Strati 1996). To really see the beauty in (or probably even understand) these financial instruments requires a great deal of mathematical expertise. But nonetheless, I think we can all appreciate the way in which they were an artistic exploration of the question of what might happen if we completely separated the abstract financial world from the material world in which we live.

Provocation is the domain of modern art. Organizations use theatrical performances to unfreeze (Taylor 2008) and provoke their own cultures. But in these cases, everyone knows that the art is art and that in the end we can all walk away, with only our minds having taken a hit. The financial artists seem to have drawn their inspiration from more modern forms of art. Improv Everywhere has become a genre executed all over the world, in which a semi-improvised mission is performed in ordinary settings. For example, the No Pants Subway Ride is now an annual event in New York City, in which thousands of people take off their pants and ride the subways at the same time. If you watch the videos on YouTube, you see that the unsuspecting audience members are surprised and generally amused. It's not clear whether this is more provocation or prank, but either way it is relatively harmless, which is not the case with the financial derivatives. If, like the No Pants subway riders, the financial artists had been making their art with their own money, then the derivatives would have been spectacular art—a morality play writ large for all to see. But they used other people's money and by extension other people's lives as the raw material of their art form, with the consequences we all know so well.

There are art forms that involve their audiences directly, such as theatrical improvisation. But these art forms have a well-developed set of craft skills that are meant to protect the nonartist audience members. The actors rehearse and prepare themselves for their encounter with the audience. Even for something as simple as a freeze improv, in which the actors are only required to freeze and hold their position for a few short minutes (usually in a busy public place such as New York's Grand Central Station or Banff's Banff Avenue), the actors will rehearse to prepare themselves, to learn what it feels like to hold a position for three minutes. The craft skills of art include staying in constant touch with the evidence of your senses (Springborg 2010), and this seems to be missing from the financial art of derivatives.

Young accountants learn part of the skills of their craft doing the grunt work of physical inventory in year-end audits. This keeps them in touch with the evidence of their senses and how the numbers relate to the physical reality—to the truth in its most physical and direct form. I think this may be where the financial derivatives artists went wrong—they lost touch with the craft of accounting. They lost touch with the craft skills of accounting, the need to constantly stay with your senses to keep the connection between the tangible physical world and the accounting numbers they are meant to represent.

If we had all recognized the financial derivatives as art—as something being created that takes us someplace new, as a departure—then we might have seen the lack of craft. We might have questioned the idea of using other people's money (and lives) as the stuff with which to make art. We might have critiqued it as the bad conceptual art it was. And if now, after the fact, we recognize it as art, we might learn from it, and we might let it raise serious questions about our modern financial system.

References

Barry, D., and S. Meisiek. 2010. The art of leadership and its fine art shadow. *Leadership* 6 (3): 331–49.

Berman, K., J. Knight, and J. Case. 2008. *Financial intelligence for IT professionals: What you really need to know about the numbers.* Boston: Harvard Business Press.

Springborg, C. 2010. Leadership as art: Leaders coming to their senses. *Leadership* 6 (3): 243–58.

Strati, A. 1996. Organizations viewed through the lens of aesthetics. *Organization* 3 (2): 209–18.

Taylor, S. S. 2008. Theatrical performance as unfreezing: Ties that bind at the Academy of Management. *Journal of Management Inquiry* 17 (4): 398–406.

6 The Play Ethic and the Financial Crisis

Pat Kane

For those of us whose topic is the cultural, psychological, and evolutionary reality of play in the human condition, the financial crash of 2008–2009 only confirms the ambiguous and paradoxical nature of our subject.

One can cite immediately the self-description of many financial agents in this environment as players in the financial game themselves, part of a long tradition of sportive and contestive metaphors in Western business culture.[1] The oeuvre of the journalist Michael Lewis, which moves effortlessly between casino capitalism and sports studies, is exemplary here.[2] In his classic writings on the organization man of midcentury America, William H. Whyte notes that when business uses sports metaphors, "the goal of sports activity is always unambiguous. . . . Participants do not come together to discuss or debate the ends for which the activity has been established, but rather take this end for granted and apply themselves in a single-minded fashion to the task of developing the most efficient means to achieve the predetermined, unchanging and noncontroversial end: winning."[3]

What's interesting in Whyte's quote is the implication that contestive, zero-sum games as a framework for finance are not the only way that participants in a marketplace might come together. Discussion or debate on "the ends for which the activity has been established"[4]—what mainland Europeans might easily call stakeholder capitalism or South East Asians the infinite game of the keiretsu—is not within the autotelic purview of the Anglo-American financial player.[5] They are focused on their own and/or their shareholders' pecuniary victories, with all other social externalities beyond the game simply imperceptible.

And "developing the most efficient means" to maximize shareholder and personal value is a delightfully moderate phrase to apply to the financial "innovations" that brought the transatlantic banking system to its knees. There are a few fascinating parallels between innovative processes in both sports and finance, conducted as finite games in which victory comes at any cost. In both spheres, there is a semicovert pursuit of biotechnical enhancement of human performance, which tests the existing regulatory structures to their limits.

In sports, we see subterranean regimes of chemical and surgical enhancements surfacing controversially in every other tournament—and even, with the disabled athlete Oscar Pistorius (known as the "Blade Runner"), a challenge to the very adequacy of the human skeleton.[6] In finance, we see the cognitive and cybernetic enhancements that the "quants" derive from their superpowered computers, which enable the algorithmic trading of minute fractions of debt and currency fluctuation, at speeds largely beyond human deliberation.[7] In both domains, we see the perversion that the theologian James Carse once predicted as the result of an "infinite game put at the service of a finite game"—that is, human possibility and ingenuity harnessed to the ends of supremacy-in-contest, a slip from the autotelic to the autistic.[8]

The perversion comes in the very collapse of the fair-play ideal inherent in both sportive and financial games. The relentless pursuit of personal performative advantage subverts the very regulations and refereeing that gives each game space its legitimacy—that which guarantees that the market or sporting field will be an open, viewable spectacle of evident strategy and meritable effort. Without referees or regulations, each zone of contestation would be a chaos of all against all.

Thus, we see a complex resurgence of the power of regulators in both sport and finance. The soccer referees empowered to penalize divers and fakers in match play themselves were taking advantage of the outlawing of particularly egregious and destructive tackling; the financial regulators across the developed West pressing for greater transparency in, and impedance of, trading—and like the soccer referees—were literally attempting to shape the rhythm and flow of financial transactions.

The subtle balance of the role of conscious regulation vis-à-vis free play in these arenas of transaction and interaction is interesting to note. There has been a strong intellectual alliance between free-market ideology and game-theoretic or complex adaptive systems science for quite a while now. Prepared by Hayek's idea of the market as a "game of catallaxy,"[9] which enables wealth growth as a consequence of the necessarily limited systemic knowledge of the market trader, much of the economic theory that accompanied the networked digital (or so-called new) economy of the 1990s and 2000s had a romance with an evolutionary context for enterprise.

These writings—exemplified by *Wired* magazine and its founding editor and lead theoretician, Kevin Kelly—saw the company as an survival-oriented organism in a ecosystem: relying on its own adaptive resilience and flexibility to progress, probing its niche until it established some local dominance, or otherwise expiring, but in any case excepting itself from wider "discussion or debate about the ends of [its] activity" as epistemologically impossible.[10] If the environment of finance is regarded as a teeming rain forest of biological diversity, rather than something more institutional (and thus regulable), then financial innovations of whatever kind become acceptable in the general creative destruction: a collateralized debt obligation or derivative is mere mulch falling healthily to the forest floor. Two years after the crash of 2008–2009, we know differently.

Yet if we are to think about the relationship between play theory and business or finance more progressively, it might be worthwhile to shift the terms of consilience between economics and biology away from game theory and complex adaptive systems thinking and toward the ethological and psychological studies of the ground of play being conducted by scholars like Stuart Brown, Brian Sutton-Smith, and Marc Bekoff[11]—that is, away from abstracted logics of interaction between entities in a network and toward the actual behaviors of embodied, materially potentiating complex mammals (like us). I would stress that, as an evolutionarily determined psychology, this is far from what behavioral economists describe as the *Homer [Simpson] economicus*, that easily governable human afflicted by short-term perspective and a fatal inability to regulate desire or mood.[12]

I am more interested in how the developmental moment of play in complex mammals, but particularly humans, constitutes our neoteny—that is, the way we extend the flexibilities, enthusiasms, and response abilities of the child at play throughout the span of our adult lives. What are the conditions that support and enable healthy, resilience-building play and instill a capacity for adaptive potentiation into humanity? And what might they tell us about the healthiest arrangement between the free play of financial speculation and the structure of financial regulation?

To begin, let me suggest that neoteny's generation of play and play forms throughout the human life span is homologous with the deeply constitutive processes shaping the design, functionality, and culture of the Internet. The Internet could represent an extension of the ground of play that we see across the higher complex mammals—that open but distantly monitored developmental zone of time, space, and resource in which potentiating risks are taken by explorative, energetic organisms, in conditions where scarcity is held at bay.

Lion cubs or chimps compelled to diversively play, risking injury and predation, but in a delimited zone with ultimate defenses; children at their local playground, enjoying their rough-and-tumble with solid equipment and open space, under some kind of municipal governance; all of us on the Internet, improvising our sociality and extending our conviviality with powerful communication tools, resting on a complex but (so far) resilient infrastructure— all of these can be cast as complex mammalian grounds of play. They share three conditions: (1) they are loosely but robustly governed; (2) a surplus of time, space, and materials is ensured; (3) failure, risk, and mess are treated as necessary for development.[13]

So the constitutive power of play in humanity—that neoteny-driven potentiation that excites both autonomists and sociobiologists—seems to also require a constitutional dimension: a protocol of governance securing certain material and emotional conditions, to enable a rich plurality of play forms. When Lawrence Lessig speaks of the Internet as an "innovation commons," the resonance with a sociobiological vision of the ground of play is clear.[14] His idea that the Internet represents an architecture of value is also homologous with these conditions for play: both are discernable zones of rough-and-tumble activity in which our social-ethical identities are forged.

Map this over to the tumult of computerized finance, however, and a certain blitheness appears in the presumption that a play ethic is implied by the operations of an end-to-end network like the Web. Tiziana Terranova has looked at how the Internet has come to be blamed for the uncontrollable nature of the financial crash of 2008. Specifically, she examines how the hyper-gossipy "echo chambers" of Web 2.0 had "contaminated" financial capital, scrambling any rational assessment of risk in a "fog of data," itself caused by a widening of financial agency to the everyday chattering traders of social media: "The internet would have therefore brought on an intolerable multiplication of the number of economic operators whose joint behaviour lacks that intrinsic rationality that permits the market to correctly assess commercial value. On the other hand, the ease with which it became possible to buy and sell shares exponentially multiplied the number of transactions that became practically untraceable and consequently increased market volatility."[15]

Terranova cites the famous *Newsweek* article that argues that a new, well-designed simple dashboard must be built to represent global financial transactions on the Internet—an interaction design composed from instantly comprehensible graphs and dials, governed by consistent color codes that can tell all of us, not just Bloomberg-literate traders, "what is currently working properly in financial markets, what isn't, what you should be terrified about."[16] As Karin Knorr Cetina has also noted, this is continuous with the already "visual and scopic" fetish of financial culture—the market "fully visible on screen" producing a "global inter-subjectivity," composed from traders' "immediate, synchronised and temporal continuity" with the activity on their terminals.[17]

But this desire for a visual, even haptic, clarity to financial information strikes me as consonant with the valences of play in the financial game space. Is it any surprise that the *Newsweek* device sounds like some new interactive kids toy by Fisher-Price? As an image for a tool that might enable the sensible regulation of finance trade, it looks like something well engineered for the kindergarten (or if you're an iPad-wielding knowledge worker, for the corner coffee shop with Wi-Fi)—something that's guaranteed as safe and consistent for use by responsible intermediaries.

Add to these toys whatever new raft of rules, impedances, and breakpoints that will result from new postcrash regulatory regimes and the new space of finance capital comes to resemble a developmentally aware kindergarten or early school:[18] where the irrational exuberance of the players is presumed but is forced to engage with standards of civil behavior, with participants (to quote Whyte again) "coming together to discuss or debate the ends for which the activity has been established."[19]

In the open Internet beyond finance, the most communally substantive of activities (i.e., the open-source developer community) self-consciously forges (or source forges, to adapt the title of one of their main institutions) the values that guide their practice. Their open play with code forms comes along with a play ethos that values creativity, participation, and adhered-to common standards and protocols, the rules of their game.[20] What might a comparable play ethic for the financial sector be? Is there a way for the necessary rough-and-tumble of capital markets to be an expression of healthy, diverse neoteny? Can there be a creative destruction that sustains and is sustained by a better-monitored financial system, rather than a perverse pathology of accumulation that unravels the very grounds of its operation?

So am I suggesting that stakeholder capitalism is what the Danes would call *leg godt*, "Lego," or "good play"?[21] Possibly. And it would surely be better than the toxic, testosteronal, autistic play of financialized capitalism that puts infinite invention into the service of finite, zero-sum pecuniary victory. Italian Marxists would say that all contemporary finance is parasitic rent seeking on the productive excess that a communicational society inherently generates, which defines Antonio Negri's "communism of capital" or "value beyond measure."[22] But that is another perspective, for another time, on the game of money under capitalism. For now, Yochai Benkler's parental injunction—and network theology—about "sharing nicely" will suffice.[23]

Notes

1. Micheal Oriard, "'The Game' in Business Fiction," in *Sporting with the Gods: The Rhetoric of Play and Game in American Culture* (Cambridge: Cambridge University Press, 1991); see also Francine Hardaway, "Foul Play: Sports Metaphors as Public Doublespeak," *College English* 38, no. 1 (1976): 78–82.

2. See Michael Lewis, "The End," *Portfolio*, November 11, 2008, http://www.portfolio.com/news-markets/national-news/portfolio/2008/11/11/The-End-of-Wall-Streets-Boom/index.html.

3. William H. Whyte Jr., "The Language of Business," in *Technological and Professional Writing*, edited by Herman A. Estrin (New York: Harcourt, Brace, and World, 1963), 83.

4. Ibid.

5. Gavin Kelly, Dominic Kelly, and Andrew Gamble, eds., *Stakeholder Capitalism* (New York: Macmillan, 1997); Charles Hampden-Turner and Fons Trompenaars, *Mastering the Infinite Game* (Chichester, U.K.: Capstone, 1997).

6. See Oscar Pistorius's Web site (http://www.oscarpistorius.com); see also "Oscar Pistorius Eyes London 2012 with New Personal Best," *BBC Sport*, March 24, 2011, http://news.bbc.co.uk/sport1/hi/other_sports/disability_sport/9434999.stm.

7. Rob Curran and Geoffrey Rogow, "Rise of the (Market) Machines," *Wall Street Journal*, June 19, 2009, http://blogs.wsj.com/marketbeat/2009/06/19/rise-of-the-market-machines/.

8. James Carse, *Finite and Infinite Games* (New York: Ballantine, 1976).

9. Friedrich Hayek, *Law, Legislation and Liberty* (Chicago: University of Chicago Press, 1978), 115, http://bit.ly/afhZoV (Google Books).

10. See Kevin Kelly, *New Rules for the New Economy* (London: Penguin Books, 1999), http://www.kk.org/newrules/contents.php.

11. Stuart Brown, *Play* (New York: Avery, 2009); Brian Sutton-Smith, *The Ambiguity of Play* (Cambridge, MA: Harvard University Press, 1997); Marc Bekoff, ed., *Animal Play: Evolutionary, Comparative and Ecological Perspectives* (Cambridge: Cambridge University Press, 1998).

12. Alan Wolfe, "Hedonic Man," *New Republic*, July 9, 2008, http://www.tnr .com/article/books/hedonic-man.

13. Pat Kane, "Play, Potentiality and the Constitution of the Net," *Play Ethic*, November 13, 2009, http://www.theplayethic.com/2009/11/play-potentiality-and-the-constitution-of-the-net.html (paper presented at the conference "Internet as Factory and Playground," New School, New York, November 12–14, 2009; available at http://digitallabor.org/speakers1/pat_kane).

14. Lawrence Lessig, *The Future of Ideas: The Fate of the Commons in a Connected World* (New York: Random House, 2001), 23.

15. Tiziana Terranova, "New Economy, Financialization and Social Production in Web 2.0," in *Crisis in the Global Economy*, edited by A. Fumagalli and S. Mezzadra (New York: Semiotext(e), 2010).

16. Paul Kedrosky, "The First Disaster of the Internet Age," *Newsweek*, October 18, 2008, http://www.newsweek.com/id/164588.

17. Karin Knorr Cetina, "The Market," *Theory Culture and Society* 23, nos. 2–3 (2006): 551–56.

18. Pat Kane, "Wisdom Lovers: An Education for Players," *The Play Ethic: A Manifesto for a Different Way of Living* (London: Macmillan, 2004), 183–216.

19. Whyte, "The Language of Business," 83.

20. John Markoff, *What the Dormouse Said* (New York: Viking, 2005); Fred Turner, *From Counterculture to Cyberculture* (Chicago: University of Chicago Press, 2006).

21. Richard Roberts and David Kynaston, "The Rout of the Stakeholders," *New Statesman*, September 17, 2001, http://www.newstatesman.com/200109170017.

22. Antonio Negri, "No New Deal Is Possible," *Radical Philosophy*, May–June 2009, http://www.radicalphilosophy.com/default.asp?channel_id=2187&editorial_id=27980.

23. Yochai Benkler, "'Sharing Nicely': On Shareable Goods and the Emergence of Sharing as a Modality of Economic Production," *Yale Law Journal* 114 (2004): 273.

7   Cassim's Law

Henrik Schrat

Fairy tales can be considered a basic narrative grammar of society. The way they unfold and relate the actors can be used as metaphorical key to unlock a different understanding of what is going on today. In this chapter, Ali Baba and the forty thieves is used as a template to look at the financial crisis.

Ali hides up a tree as the thieves get closer in the forest. Watching them as they open Mount Simeli, he hears the magic code: "Open, Sesame." After the thieves have left again, he tries his luck and takes a bit home from the stolen goods piling up inside the mountain. The story gathers up speed as Ali's brother Cassim comes into play with his greed. We will see later how it develops.

To say it up front: the comparisons are open, but they all seem to make sense and create a fertile metaphorical ground for reasoning—whether some bankers are the thieves or the greedy brother, or whether the state makes an appearance or the personal egoism of all of us. My text is the corresponding speech at table in a pub: unjust, arrogant, and with a lot of pleasure. Thus, it understands itself as part of the narrative social discourse that it is dealing with.

And, I might be forgiven, there are irony and cynicism at play.

The Merchant and His Story

How is the Ali Baba text embedded in the management literature? It focuses on cultural markers rather than on data and suggests using a narrative processor to make sense of what is going on in the global economy. Reinhardt

FIGURE 7.1 Henrik Schrat (2008), *Mount Simeli*, ink on paper, 40 × 60 cm.

and Rogoff, in examining quantitative data on crisis developments, have come to the conclusion that in developing an early-warning system for crisis, "the greatest barrier to success is the well-entrenched tendency of policy makers and market participants to treat the signals [of distress] as irrelevant archaic residuals of an out-dated framework, assuming that old rules of valuation no longer apply."[1] So we focus on this behavior and look on narrative ways to understand it.

It is clear to Karl Weick that a good story is an essential tool for making sense of what is going on in an organization.[2] Yiannis Gabriel even opens his book *Storytelling in Organizations* with the Grimm brothers, who told a version of the Ali Baba story in their collection of tales. The Grimm brothers collected and wrote the oral histories down, which ossified them in a way but also raised their mythical significance to stimulate the imagination, to offer reassurance, to justify, and to explain.[3]

That is how I suggest looking at them: by negotiating facts as metaphoric placeholders within a story space. In doing so, a different light falls on their mechanics, and a broader perspective on economic processes opens. They become stronger a part of an overall cultural system. In 1994 Pierre Guillet de Monthoux and Barbara Czarniawska already were leading the way in analyzing organizations through literature in *Good Novels, Better Management*,[4] but our Ali Baba is in a sense much simpler than a novel. The fairy tale operates as the bare bones of metaphorical mechanics, especially the Grimms' straightforward and short version of the tale. In narrative, according to Czarniawska later, understanding can be reconciled with explanation, and hermeneutics and semiotics can be combined in the same way that motives are reconciled with causes in an interpretation of human action.[5]

Chopped Cassim

In our fairy tale, there is one just and sympathetic character with whom we can identify: Ali. He hears the thieves coming, flees up a tree, and witnesses how the words "Open, Sesame" magically open the mountain where the thieves store their treasures. Later, his brother Cassim hears about the treasure. Cassim is already rich; but we know: the more there is, the more is asked for, also due to the imperative of counting, as we are going to hear. So he goes, too, to steal more of the thieves' stolen goods. He takes ten mules with him to carry the wealth.

At this point, there are several parallels to reality: one fellow leads the way, and another, possibly a little dumber, imitates him on a larger scale. With the help of the magic words, Cassim gains entrance to the mountain and starts to fill the cart he brought. However, he is so excited by all the treasure that he forgets the magic words and becomes trapped inside the mountain with all the treasure. The thieves return, kill Cassim, chop him into pieces, and display these as a deterrent to others. So, Cassim doesn't return home. Ali goes to look for him. There is not much to be done anymore: he brings the pieces of his brother back home. To bury his brother properly, Ali blindfolds a tailor, who sews Cassim together again. It was Marjaneh, a female slave, not Ali, who came up with the trick, and she has plenty more in store.

Greed Buried

At this point, I let the fairy tale rest for a moment and turn to happenings in the market that I wish to apply the tale to. Given the performance of the markets in 2009, the men and women who are partly responsible for the current crisis have been sewn back together, but unlike Cassim, they have not been buried. What in 2008, with everything racing downhill, was a different question, urges us now to change the metaphoric narrative: from Scheherazade to Mary Shelley. Frankenstein is the classic figure that stands in for a system that is botched back together from different body parts.

The will to execute political influence and the regained popularity of John Maynard Keynes's work is matched on the side of some market actors with this creepy activity: Cassim's law, or the automatism of turning larger wheels than one understands and for personal sake. Keynes wrote in the high times of modernism. A still-unbroken belief in an overarching metanarrative of growing civilization mediated by reason governed the view on social and economical development. Having this as a legitimation, the political class of the time had a more comfortable backbone available than it has today.

The balance between Milton Friedman's idea that the market is the best social program, and in the long run the market is the great leveler, and Keynes's idea that in the long run we will all be dead (so the state must intervene) is tending, once again, toward state intervention, thus putting economic issues in the political and public limelight. Demand for political personalities who are not mere clerks for the corporate site of the society has risen at once. Deregulation of the markets, which started with Margaret Thatcher and Ronald Reagan and the retreat of the state, has lost its appeal as a solution for society. Local communities that privatized and sold their water supply or waste management services have found themselves in deep trouble with bankrupt investors and owners on the other side of the globe. Cassim's law is not wise a decision in many situations. We basically knew it wasn't true, but we again believed, "This time is different." Every vessel has its limits. But have you ever heard somebody say, "No thanks, my bank account is already full"?

So it might be unfair to quote Blythe Masters, and by doing so bringing a face into this text. Masters—an employee of Goldman Sachs, which made credit default swaps popular and marketed them aggressively—said at the Security Industries and Financial Markets Association meeting on October 28, 2008, after the first major slide in the markets: "It's probably safe to say that the image of our industry is at an all-time low. . . . Last time we were dancing to Hootie and the Blowfish, but this time we will listen to the Harlem Boys Choir."[6] Of course it was not hard to see that the image of the finance industry was at an all-time low, but it is amusing to see the different cultural allocations. At the last meeting, they danced to Hootie and the Blowfish; now the time for the gospel choir from Harlem has come. Another year has passed by, and we are likely to have Hootie and the Blowfish back, given the resurgence of the market, or Marilyn Manson could be appropriate, too. Banking and finance administration are exciting jobs—the all-time low does not originate in the profession but in the empty way it was executed.

But back to wallowing in the mire of the crisis and opening up the focus to the general phenomena behind it. And I will be offering more parallels to the Ali Baba story. The step from deriding bankers to greed as such still has to be made, and from there, the step further to the dominance of consumerism and the order to pay. It comes as no surprise that everyone wants more if most socially relevant values are traced back to promises of payment. The Promised Land has been placed in a shop window. Every now and then a window cleaner comes by to wipe away the nose-shaped stains on the glass. Moses, too, was only permitted to view the Promised Land from Mount Nebo, not to enter. The enticement of consumerism behind the window panes is packaged at the bank counter: that is where the money is, or maybe not. In the face of the market, we are all equal—that is the great achievement of the market society. But by dint of nature, democracy stops at the bank counter.

And another legend comes to an end at this counter. The diversity of what is consumable is reduced to a binary code: to pay or not to pay. All the talk of the double role of the consumer as cultural decision maker is of little value here. Consumerism has produced the incredible cultural variety of twenty thousand kinds of training shoes. And of course economic processes are governed by symbolic processes and hence related to culture. But at the bank counter, all is countable: all heterogeneous objects are reduced by the market to quantity, and cultural differentiation will be driven by the market only where it can be turned into promise of payment. With *Mehr Geld*, Ralph Heidenreich and Stefan Heidenreich have, in my opinion, written one of the sagest books on the crisis, pinpointing the problem as the counting imperative that always goes up, and hence increases.[7] One, two, three, four—this cries out for a five-o'clock rock. And more! More!

As a rule, the open-sesame code has four digits and must be entered at the automatic teller machine. Ali Baba was the first who spied out pin codes. Why on earth did the thieves not speak in low voices? However, just knowing the code is still no guarantee for success. For one, the cave might be empty. Or, as was the case in the story, one might not be able to find the way out again. Entering the treasure chest is like taking a shot of heroin. People moralize about taking drugs with facial expressions laden with responsibility, but no one even mentions eight-by-ten-meter advertising billboards for cars or new phone contracts, in terms of the effect on people's minds nothing short of a drug. Is it all we have to offer from Western democracy than consumerism as capitalism's main argument toward other ideas? Greed as a weapon has turned against ourselves. The crisis might give us a chance to understand what makes people tick, people for whom consumerism is not everything and for whom religion or conviction might come first.

However, buying a car does not seem to jump off the list of desirable things to do. In 2009, you received 2,500 euros for buying a new car in Germany, and many countries had similar policies. This must surely go down as one of the more absurd, cynical ideas in history. If, at least, something meaningful had been subsidized with the money. But cars! I see it as a sort of crisis-welcoming money, like the one hundred welcome-to-the-West deutschmarks I received in 1989 when the Berlin Wall came down. This is the moment I cannot help but long for a specific quality of the GDR. Money played no role in the self-understanding of normal people. No one had much anyway, or, if you'd like, everyone had the same amount. I am of course not referring to the macroeconomic untenable nature of the state of things, nor to dictatorship and terror. This is about the mad feeling that money is of no importance. Not because one has too much or too little. The category itself was irrelevant—that is what was so inimitable and unbelievable, that it was outrageous. It was dangerous. Most of the values that the current crisis is questioning did not even exist in the minds of most East Germans back then.

The narrative form values take on in our minds is the way desire and energy are developed. Here lies the abyss. The credit default swap (CDS) constructions caused perception of the risks to disappear. As Bodo Kirchoff, a well-known German writer, remarked, the relabeling of *loans* as *securities* did not just involve giving them a new name but entailed far-reaching consequences. Such a renaming plays into the cultural sphere of society, and I am sorry to say that in this respect we had either amateurs or criminals at work who weren't capable of understanding the whole thing, not to mention their own constructions. Years earlier, Warren Buffett had called financial innovations of this kind means of mass destruction. Not too many companies are working in their backyards uncontrolled on H-bombs. In the case of repackaging loans, Cassim's law was paramount.

Ways to Look at It: About Smashing Gifts

Here, I introduce a few thoughts of Wilhelm Röpke and George Bataille to braid my approach into a broader history of economic thinking and ultimately pave a way to the final reflection.

Taking a look on how other thinkers have dealt with the subject can equip us with different tools to deal with the situation. It is beneficial to review the ideas of Wilhelm Röpke (1899–1966), an Austrian economist in the first part of the twentieth century. He viewed man as an embodied soul, not as the reductive figure of *Homo economicus*. The telling titles of his books *The Social Crisis of Our Time* (1942), *Civitas Humana* (1944), and *A Humane Economy* (1957) make him one of the forerunners of thinking about responsibility, downsizing, local factors, and civil society. They also make him one of the masterminds of the *Wirtschaftswunder* after World War II. Although Röpke believed in competition, he was aware of its power to call on the wolf's nature in human beings, and that it is eating into morality (German: *Moralzehrer*). To equate it, building up moral reserves in other parts of life like environment and family was one way for him to go. This might be a deeply romantic idea, but it introduces and links different spheres of social self-understanding to competition and financial gains.[8] "More than any other thinker in the twentieth century, it would be Röpke who helped to build a bridge between advocates of the free market on the one hand, and Christian humanists and conservatives on the other."[9]

Besides the renewed discussion on ethics, the crisis has another good side: destruction and waste. And that, yes, is culture. It is a gigantic celebration of potency, an orgiastic overspending. Why don't people finally stop complaining? It is pathetic. The globe winces. It remains to be seen whether the West has taken Viagra and will continue hammering away. Now, a year on, it seems, that the blue pill is in operation indeed. But it is still not clear that, not sleep, but grief and humility will follow. That, too, would be wonderful. Long-forgotten organs would have to be rediscovered to come to terms with the situation.

Georges Bataille, the French writer and philosopher, would have been thrilled. He surely is the patron of what is happening. To come to a close, I have to pay tribute to his ideas. His economic theory is one of the strangest, but surely one of the most inspiring and far-reaching thought buildings around the economic aspects of society. As laid out in his 1947 book *The Accursed Share*, he deliberately termed his subject matter *general economy* to mark a broader approach. Bataille takes off with the distinction between productive and unproductive expenditure. The ideal of utility says that activity is only of worth if it can be traced back "to the fundamental demands of production and preservation."[10] Unproductive expenditure, however, deals with the surplus that cannot be reinvested. Yet it is that part that defines us as cultural beings, for better or worse. It finds its way in art, luxury, mourning ceremonies, games—or it is destroyed in wars and catastrophic events, thus threatening the prevailing system. According to Bataille, the problem lies in the combination of (cosmic) excessive energy and limited growth: "The living organism . . . ordinarily receives more energy than is necessary for maintaining life; the excess energy (wealth) can be used for the growth of a system (e.g., an organism); if the system can no longer grow, or if the excess cannot be completely absorbed in its growth, it must necessarily be lost without profit; it must be spent, willingly or not, gloriously or catastrophically."[11]

Money born as credit can be produced ad infinitum; it has something of unlimited excessive energy about it in the uncoupling from growth—comparable to Bataille's wasteful cosmic energy.

Credit as cosmic energy—not bad. So remember next time, do not play with things like this! At least, get a priest into play, or someone whose ethical horizon is a bit wider than what we can deduce for a lot of economic actors who were in the driver's seat in the past years. Ethics is not just a manual for rewriting codes of conduct; it is a key for understanding complexities of cultural systems and economy as an essential part of it. Bataille asks for a Copernican turn in moving restricted economic thinking toward general economy, going along with a reversal in its ethical foundation. Big words for big problems.

He uses the metaphor of changing a tire to explain trying to fix the complex system. Changing a tire on a car is of limited use if there is no road. As long as we don't think about the roads and what they require, we should stay clear of building cars altogether.

We have witnessed this catastrophic event of destruction. The use of CDS is a war declaration against civil society, but let's grant its inventors access to another community. Salvation is at the doorstep. At this point I can—indeed, must—inform Blythe Masters that with CDS she created a performative artwork of the highest order. We might see it at the next Documenta. It is a fascinating construction but is executed in the wrong place.

To shed light on this claim, I have kept an image, which has strongly influenced Bataille, to the end. It is a custom attributed to the indigenous peoples of the islands off the Pacific Northwest of the United States, made known by Marcel Mauss's book *The Gift*.[12] The custom consists of symbolic trade between tribes. A tribe works on a present for a year, a present for a neighboring village. A finely carved, fragile object is forged over thousands and thousands of working hours. On the celebration day, the tribe makes its way to the neighboring village in a procession led by the chief carrying the delicate, precious present himself. The neighboring village is expecting them. The chiefs come face-to-face with each other, and the gifts are marveled at with many oohs and aahs. Then the one chief dashes the gift on the ground in front of the feet of the other chief. "Dash!" as Donald Duck, that great critic of capitalism, would put it—and he would have continued, "Better an end with horror, than horror without end."

So it is a grand gesture, this crisis. But is there any other village at all? At whose feet is all this being dashed? It is at our own feet. And this—yes, this— is true greatness. *Dash!*

Is there anything besides irony or nihilism in all that? Already that would be enough, if it gets our brains moving. But there is more to it. If parts of the financial system are dashed, the easiest way to open a route to progress is to relate the problem to the most-quoted economic paradigm, Schumpeter's destruction for making new things.[13] It's an ancient concept—something is smashed to pieces to give room to a new approach, to give way, to ease out and to let go. It hurts, mostly, hurts and helps. The way risk disappears in a construction like the CDS is ironically a good simile for delegated responsibilities—responsibility decreased as form of social coherence.

Personally accepted responsibilities do not only reduce the risk for societies at large but also give meaning to what one does. Beyond food and shelter, money does not have any meaning and cannot give us values. Most of us have learned that in school, I guess, but have long forgotten it. So keep an eye on Cassim's law, so watch out, if you are about to expand beyond the borders where you cannot control the impact, and where your personality disappears.

· · ·

Bit by bit I have introduced a fairy tale as a metaphorical springboard to an understanding of what happened in the crisis. On one hand, this is a creative technique for dissecting and rerelating the incidents in the market to achieve an enriched understanding. On the other hand, based on their deep origin in culture, tales offer eye-level access and suggest images of highly abstract processes. They open ways to meet the incidents on a level of personal responsibility. Transgressing deliberately the field of personal responsibility leads to what I have called Cassim's law. Greed, consumerism, and the counting imperative as pickets have helped to map the terrain. Ultimately, Wilhelm Röpke and George Bataille have been sketched out as connecting points to a broader, off-the-beaten-track history of thinking.

Who Are You?

To close the text, I return to Ali Baba. The Grimm brothers tell a much shorter version of the tale than that of Ali Baba in the Arabian Nights tales. The Grimms end with the greedy brother's head being chopped off by the thieves. The bad guy has lost every sense of proportion by his intoxication with money. Hence, he gets killed. Mission accomplished. In the Arabian Nights version, that is the moment when the real problem starts. What is essential is Ali's responsibility for a socially acceptable funeral. It is all to be negotiated against a backdrop of society including Allah. After the tailor has Cassim cobbled together, Cassim is buried. That is what Ali cares for. But the tailor's role triggers the next problem. The thieves come to town, and the tailor tells them that he had a strange job recently: he was blindfolded, brought to a house, and then sewed a chopped-off head back onto a body. But go and read the story yourself. It's worth it. And then try to find out who in the story represents the Securities and Exchange Commission, the rating agencies, the banks, and (foremost) you.

Notes

1. Carmen M. Reinhardt and Kenneth S. Rogoff, *This Time Is Different: Eight Centuries of Financial Folly* (Princeton, NJ: Princeton University Press, 2009).

2. Karl Weick, *Sensemaking in Organizations* (Thousand Oaks, CA: Sage Publications, 1995), 60–61.

3. Yiannis Gabriel, *Storytelling in Organizations: Facts, Fictions and Fantasies* (Oxford: Oxford University Press, 2000), 9.

4. Barbara Czarniawska and Pierre Guillet de Monthoux, eds., *Good Novels, Better Management* (Chur, Switzerland: Harwood Academic Publishers, 1994).

5. Barbara Czarniawska, *A Narrative Approach to Organization Studies* (London: Sage Publications, 1998), 4.

6. Blythe Masters, speech at the Security Industries and Financial Markets Association meeting, October 28, 2008, http://events.sifma.org/2008/292/event.aspx?id=8566.

7. Ralph Heidenreich and Stefan Heidenreich, *Mehr Geld* (Berlin: Merve, 2008).

8. Wilhelm Röpke, *Jenseits von Angebot und Nachfrage* (Düsseldorf: Verlagsanstalt Handwerk, 2009).

9. A well-written book on Wilhelm Röpke is John Zmirak, *Wilhelm Röpke: Swiss Localist, Global Economist* (Wilmington, DE: ISI Books, 2001).

10. Georges Bataille, *Die Aufhebung der Ökonomie* (Munich: Rogner and Bernhard, 1975), 10.

11. Georges Bataille, *The Accursed Share* (New York: Zone Books, 1998), 21.

12. Marcel Mauss, *The Gift* (London: Routledge, 2002).

13. Joseph Schumpeter, *Capitalism, Socialism and Democracy* (New York: Harper Perennial Modern Classics, 2008).

RELIABLY

8 Managing the Global Financial Crisis

Lessons from Technological Crisis Management

Paul Shrivastava, William Gruver,
and Matt Statler

This chapter applies lessons from technological crisis management to the current global financial crisis. We consider the antecedent conditions and causes of the crisis, and then examine and apply key lessons from the crisis management literature to reach a deeper understanding of these conditions. On the basis of this deeper understanding, we explore policy implications, including long-term planning for managing the crisis process, regulating risk and leverage, building surveillance systems, improving global communications, and redesigning a new sustainable global economic order. Finally, we offer a series of reflections on how the failure of the imagination can be addressed in the context of technological system design and risk management.

• • •

Since September 2008, the financial crisis that began in August 2007 in the subprime mortgage market had spread to all financial markets and engulfed all major economies. Stock markets lost 30 percent to 50 percent of their values. Major economies (e.g., United States, Germany) were formally in recession. National governments were investing trillions of dollars to stabilize markets and unfreeze credit. Within four months of the onset of the crisis, the U.S. government had committed $3.2 trillion, the European Union $2.5 trillion, and China almost $1.0 trillion to market stabilization and economic stimulus measures. But the crisis shows few signs of abatement. Most countries are expecting that their economies will get much worse before they get better. Although financial and political leaders are spouting messages of hope and recovery, they also acknowledge that this is the worst financial crisis since the Great Depression and will take years, if not decades, to recover.

Was this crisis unavoidable? How is it likely to evolve? How can it be managed? How can future crises be prevented? Traditional economists and financial experts are trotting out many short-term solutions aimed to shore up the existing system. It is amazing that, although there exists more than twenty-five years worth of research on crisis prevention and management, little of this knowledge was used to deal with the financial crisis.

The field of crisis and disaster management has studied a variety of crises, including technological disasters, product failures, computer network breakdowns, and natural disasters (e.g., earthquakes, floods, hurricanes, fires). Frameworks for understanding crises have developed for anticipating them, and prevention measure and crisis management techniques have been established (Siomkos 1990; Turner and Pidgeon 1997; Smith and Elliot 2006). But with the academic world's penchant for operating within its own narrow silos, this collective knowledge of crisis management has not permeated into the fields of economics or finance.

This chapter is an attempt to build a conversation between crisis management research and financial-economic crisis managers. We assume that cross-disciplinary dialogues are both feasible and desirable. By learning from past research in crisis management, we might develop robust solutions to the global financial crisis.

The chapter begins with a brief summary of the financial crisis and its antecedent conditions and causes. The next section examines some key lessons from the crisis management literature. In the third section, we apply these lessons to the global financial crisis to reach a deeper understanding of the crisis process and causes. We then explore policy implications, including long-term planning for managing the crisis process, regulating risk and leverage, building surveillance systems, improving global communications, and redesigning a new sustainable global economic order. Finally, we present a series of reflections on how the failure of imagination can be addressed through the practice of technological system design and management.

The Global Financial Crisis

The worldwide financial crisis that started in 2007 is the result of the bursting of the real estate bubble in the United States, the United Kingdom, and elsewhere. The collapse of this financial bubble has spread from real-estate-related assets to all other financial markets primarily for two reasons: (1) forced selling as leverage is reduced by financial institutions and (2) the loss of trust in counterparties and governments. The actions of finance ministers and central bankers in recent years seem to be making some progress in protecting the viability of the system and thereby establishing some trust, but even if the initiatives to date and those yet to come ultimately prove to have been successful, the system will have been saved only at an enormous cost that must be repaid by generations to come. If one looks earlier than August 2007 for events that may have foretold the economic trouble we were bringing on, two years appear particularly meaningful: 1977 and 1999.

As large as the government's response to date to the credit crisis might seem, it is already proving inadequate. When the Federal Reserve took over the world's largest insurance company, AIG, in September 2008, its capital infusion of $85 billion for an 80 percent ownership was judged to be more than adequate to prevent a systemic collapse. On October 9, after seeing the extent of AIG's problems more closely, the Federal Reserve had to inject another $38 billion. And on November 10, the Treasury restructured some of the key terms of the previous injections and agreed to add another $40 billion.

The crisis has spread beyond the financial sector. The $700 billion Troubled Asset Relief Program (TARP) authority given to the Treasury secretary by U.S. Congress on October 3, 2008, succumbed to political pressure and expanded to include two of the three major companies in the American automobile industry. Similarly, additional tranches of consumer relief also seemed inevitable. The $94 billion stimulus of $600 checks sent to Americans and announced in January 2008, with distribution to consumers in the spring of 2008, did little to spur the economy. The $787 billion American Recovery and Reinvestment Act that was signed into law in February 2009 is a classic example of Keynesian stimulus.

The government regulators were in uncharted waters, and they were reacting on the fly. Bear Stearns was saved from bankruptcy through its acquisition (with federal government assistance) by JPMorgan; Lehman Brothers was allowed to go into bankruptcy. First the TARP directly purchased toxic assets. Then it was used to make capital injections into troubled institutions. First, $85 billion would save AIG; then it was double that amount. Is it any wonder that investors are showing their lack of trust in the economy through the sinking stock market? Is it any wonder that voters showed their lack of trust in government by electing the least experienced candidate from either party's primaries to be their next president?

Antecedent Conditions of the Crisis

The Community Reinvestment Act (CRA) was signed into law by President Carter in 1977. It was created in response to national pressure to address the deteriorating conditions of American cities, particularly lower-income and minority neighborhoods. After amendments in 1989, 1992, 1994, and 1995, the act became the impetus behind the subprime mortgage market. The logic of the legislation was sound—some would say noble—expanding the American dream of home ownership to those less able to afford their own home would improve not only those individuals but also their neighborhoods. The legislation had its intended effect. In 2005, 20 percent of mortgage originations ($625 billion) were for subprime borrowers. The cumulative effect of allowing access to this new class of mortgage recipients was that over the previous thirty years, home ownership had grown to the point that in 2005 it reached a record level of 69 percent of the population. With Wall Street innovating its way into the mortgage market through securitization, the drop in housing prices that began in 2006 had a ripple effect that expanded far beyond the affected subprime homeowners and led to the current worldwide financial tsunami.

Two events that occurred in 1999, when considered together and in retrospect, have had unintended consequences that have proved nearly lethal to the financial system. On May 4, Goldman Sachs sold shares to the public for the first time in its 130-year history. Then, on November 12, President Clinton signed into law the Gramm-Leach-Bliley Financial Services Modernization Act. Both of these actions were intended to accomplish the same purpose: to make American financial institutions better able to compete in the global economy. Both actions were well intended and made eminent sense in the midst of worldwide stock market euphoria spawned by the Internet and dot-com mania.

Goldman Sachs was the last of the major Wall Street houses to go public (Donaldson, Lufkin, and Jenrette had been the first in 1969). Its partners had debated the merits of such a change for years, and even when the decision was made to go forward, the decision was reached only after vigorous debate and much disagreement.

What neither the firm's partners nor outside observers were able to foresee was the resulting change in the firm's risk tolerance. As of May 4, 1999, all of Wall Street was playing with other people's money (OPM). The acronym is interesting in that it is pronounced exactly the same as the drug opium and can have similar consequences that in the short term are euphoric but in the longer term can be lethal to the individual and the system as a whole. In the case of OPM, this short-term versus long-term dichotomy comes in the form of increased leverage that can become excessive. When Goldman was a private partnership, its partners faced unlimited personal liability when making capital allocation decisions; post–initial public offering (IPO), their much more limited liability was identical to that of any other senior executive in a public corporation. Human nature is such that one is much less risk averse when one's personal potential loss is lowered; ergo, the temptation to take on more risk when operating within the framework of a public corporation versus a private partnership. So, with Goldman's IPO, one of the largest market participants was prepared to play without the self-imposed restrictions that had been present in its earlier form.

The restrictions on Wall Street were not entirely self-imposed, however. After all, this was a regulated industry. In fact, until 1999 it was a very tightly circumscribed industry with its governing law being the Banking Act of 1933, the famous Glass-Steagall Act. And this is where the other seminal event of 1999 takes on importance. On November 12, the government in its wisdom abolished the law that had served the financial services industry so well for sixty-six years. Glass-Steagall had restricted riskier banking activities by separating investment banks from deposit-taking commercial banks, but with the passage of Gramm-Leach-Bliley, Glass-Steagall was gone and with it another restraining mechanism. The industry had lobbied hard for its abolition. With globalization beginning in financial services in the 1980s and accelerating in the 1990s, American banks increasingly found themselves at a disadvantage to the universal banks permitted in Europe and Asia. Many of the skills they needed to compete with these new competitors could not be developed in the home market because Glass-Steagall was prohibiting them from entering those businesses. The logic sounded compelling, and it was—to a point.

Gramm-Leach-Bliley changed the players to make them bigger and faster, but it didn't change the referees or improve their capabilities to keep up with the new, bigger, faster game. The regulators assigned to the industry in 1933 remained largely the same—smaller and narrower than the industry they were regulating. The Securities and Exchange Commission (SEC) regulated the investment-banking operations of the then-permitted universal banks, the Federal Reserve and the Federal Deposit Insurance Corporation (FDIC) regulated the deposit-taking banking operations, and the respective state insurance regulators were responsible for the insurance operations. No one regulator saw the whole picture. In an attempt to remedy this weakness, in 2004 the SEC agreed to abolish the net capital rule in return for broader oversight. Once again, however, what appeared to make sense at the time had extremely dangerous systemic consequences a few years later. Investment banks had been restricted to leverage ratios of 12:1 by the net capital rule. With its abolition, leverage ratios increased to more than 30:1 at firms like Bear Stearns and Lehman Brothers. At Goldman Sachs, this change along with the new ability to risk OPM rather than the partners' personal capital resulted in its leverage ratio increasing to 26:1.

If these leverage ratios seem high, it's because they are. Commercial banks, which as part of their regulation by the Fed are restricted in their leverage, typically have leverage ratios closer to 12:1 than to 30:1. The investment banks, however, were not alone in their infatuation with their newly empowered leverage. Government-sponsored enterprises (e.g., Fannie Mae, Freddie Mac), through a similar series of well-intended regulatory relaxations and encouragement by Congress to underwrite more subprime mortgages, were leveraged at ratios in excess of 50:1 at the time of their takeover by Federal Housing Finance Agency.

When residential housing prices began to fall in 2006–2007, it led to a devaluation of the securitized instruments that owned the underlying home mortgages; nearly all of Wall Street was forced into selling good assets (unrelated to the emerging subprime crisis) to meet capital calls brought on by the effect of the subprime crisis on the securitized mortgage-backed assets, for which there were no buyers. As firms began to disappear as a result of their inability to raise enough capital quickly enough, counterparty risk increased to the point that worldwide lending ground to a halt, thus resulting in the global credit crisis.

Excessive leverage was obviously present on Wall Street, but it was not alone in overreaching. Main Street was also part of the problem because it, too, was overleveraged. Before the availability of subprime mortgages, to be considered for a mortgage, an applicant had to post a substantial down payment (between 20 percent and 30 percent) and demonstrate an earnings history sufficient to support the principal and interest payments incumbent in the sought-after mortgage. The Community Reinvestment Act indirectly led to the reduction, or in many cases disappearance, of these standards. As a result, the new subprime homeowner often had little or no skin in the game. Home ownership leverage with a 20 percent down payment had been 5:1.

With a subprime mortgage and a token down payment, that could be increased to 100:1 or infinite with no down payment. When home prices began to slip in 2006–2007, homeowners were faced with the ugly side of leverage, but with no meaningful skin in the game it was easier for them to walk away from their ownership responsibilities rather than face the consequences of high leverage in a market where asset values were slipping. The mortgage holders then quickly sold their properties without regard to price, and the asset values of neighboring homeowners deteriorated further. The race to the bottom was off and running.

Subprime mortgages were not the only leverage held by Main Street. Credit cards (and their high-interest debt) are currently seen as the next wave of deleveraging for consumers with consequences that could be as lethal as subprime mortgages. Outstanding credit cards in the United States amount to an average of five per every American older than the age of eighteen. The average amount owed on each of those cards is $1,000, so each American on average owes double-digit interest rates on $5,000 of credit card debt. If measured by households, each American holds $8,500, or 120 percent of annual disposable income, in credit card debt.

Much like subprime mortgages, much of this credit card debt has been securitized in an effort to diffuse the risk of the issuers (many of the Wall Street banks already hard hit by the subprime crisis). Also, much like the subprime assets, Wall Street owns a lot of the securitized assets, but so also (because of securitization) do institutions around the world. As credit card defaults increase, will these asset-backed securities (this time with credit cards) force another wave of asset devaluations to the already-fragile capital bases of Wall Street? With events like this on the horizon, is it any surprise that the banks, having lost trust in their counterparties, are still not robustly lending, even after the recent government support interventions?

Lessons from the Field of Crisis Management

More than two decades of research on industrial and technological crises cannot be summarized in a short chapter. We know that crises are caused by failures in technology, human decision processes, and organizational policies. Additionally, the U.S. Federal 9/11 Commission Report (2004, 339) cited "failure of imagination" as one factor contributing to the lack of preparedness for the terrorist attacks on the Pentagon and the World Trade Center. More recently, a number of plank-walking financial industry executives have claimed that systemic risks in the financial system were previously unimaginable. In both of these instances, the failure of imagination did not occur everywhere all at once. The scenario of using planes as weapons to attack the World Trade Center had been gamed (Komarow and Squitieri 2004), and certain prominent investors had been pointing out the instability of the housing market for years (Paumgarten 2009). Widespread and repeated failures of imagination instead occurred among multiple groups of strategic decision makers working within and across various organizations, all of whom were then surprised when the towers fell and the markets crashed. How are such systemic failures of imagination possible, and what can be done to avoid them in the future? In this segment, we selectively present key lessons from the crisis management literature.

• • •

First, crises occur within systems that are sociotechnically complex and opaque. These systems are tightly coupled and interdependent with other similar complex systems. Technical complexity of the system is a function of the large number of parts, subsystems, operating procedures, equipment and materials, organizational policies, and human interventions that go into creating modern systems (Perrow 1984). Whether it is a chemical plant, an oil tanker, a space vehicle, the educational system, the financial market system, or the economy, each one of those systems is complex beyond the comprehension of a single individual or even groups of experts.

Technical complexity allows high-quality services to be delivered, but it is also a source of system opacity. Not everyone understands these systems. System metrics are often recorded and tracked, but only a few experts can make sense of them. This opacity makes it hard for even seasoned observers of the system to diagnose trouble in the system. Opacity makes it difficult to track errors propagating through the system. The Financial Stability Oversight Council, established by the Dodd-Frank Act, is an attempt to deal with this opacity (Rosenthal, Charles, and t'Hart 1990).

Second, crises are "processes" spread over space and time. They are initiated by a triggering event—an event of seminal and symbolic significance in terms of damages and impacts. In the technological world, a triggering event could be an industrial accident, a product injury, an executive kidnapping, or a plant sabotage of bombing. Triggering events are usually preceded by antecedent conditions that make the system prone to crisis. These conditions could take the form of poor maintenance, reduction of surveillance staff, lack of regulation of hazards, and risks (Shrivastava et al. 1988).

A triggering event defines the onset of the crisis. In the current crisis, many cite the decision of the U.S. government to allow Lehman Brothers to enter bankruptcy as the trigger to the worldwide crisis. This is followed by the stage of expanding damages. Damages expand in the physical, medical, financial, reputational, and public-image domains. Damages spread over space and time and engulf more victims, organizations, and agencies. Sometimes damages can spread over time to several years and may become intergenerational.

The third stage of the crisis process is rescue, relief, rehabilitation, and recovery. It starts soon after the onset of crisis and can last for many years, depending on resources parlayed into dealing with the crisis.

The fourth stage of the crisis process is return to normalization. Organizations implicated in the crisis have to recover by adjusting their products and production systems and by restructuring. Communities, too, return to some sense of normal operation by restoring disrupted routines and practices (Kasperson and Kasperson 1988).

Third, crisis causes include simultaneous and interacting failures inside organizations (human, organizational, and technological failures) and in their external environment (regulatory, infrastructure, and preparedness failures). Internal failures occur in the technological core, in organizational context, and in human interactions with the technology. The technological core includes hardware, software, equipment, materials, and procedures used in operations of industrial facilities or systems. This core is surrounded by an organizational context consisting of culture, systems, structure, procedures, and policies. Human interactions with the technology take the form of operator and managerial judgments and decisions. External failures contribute to crises by expanding their impacts. These failures include poor or inadequate regulations, insufficient safety infrastructure, and lack of community preparedness to deal with crises (Shrivastava 1993; Smith and Elliot 2006)

Fourth, crisis processes have several characteristics. The first important characteristic of crises is surprise. No matter how well managers understand the normal operations of their businesses, they are never ready to face a crisis. Even if managers have been in similar crises (or near misses) before, they fail to recognize the coming of the next one. There is deep emotional denial that a crisis can occur, even when there are obvious early warning signs. Thus, crises represent novel situations for which managers are not prepared (Morin 1993). Being unprepared, managers are forced to make crisis decisions with imperfect information. Crises often occur suddenly and involve events that managers have not analyzed previously. There is a tremendous pressure to act quickly. Delays or inaction can further escalate damages. During crisis, many variables that are normally under the control of managers become out of reach. Additionally, many new, uncontrollable variables become salient to the crisis. Different things go wrong even before any remedial actions are taken, and sometimes remedial actions themselves exacerbate different aspects of the crisis. Like falling dominoes, the events cumulatively build up the seriousness of damages and the scope of their effects. Information available for making decisions in crisis is incomplete, contradictory, subjective, undocumented, and in the form of opinions. Managers have little time available to verify the correctness of information or to analyze it.

Fifth, technological crises are invariably accompanied with critical scrutiny and investigations from the outside and breakdown of governance. The media, regulatory agencies, politicians, and community leaders seek information on the crisis and investigate its causes. If the crisis is serious enough, a presidential-level inquiry is instituted. In addition, other specialized inquires may focus on technological causes, legal liabilities, social and environmental impacts, rescue and relief needs, and financial solutions.

The media are hypercritical. Media reports take on a negative tone, and there is an ongoing search for blame and culprits, particularly among top management. The board of directors and top management are often thrown into confusion. A confused board representing different constituencies and stakeholders pulls the company in different directions. Confusion occurs among top managers because responsibilities are not always clear. Robert Rubin's role at Citigroup, for instance, was vague until the very day of his resignation. Yet he is now often named as the initiator of Citigroup's aggressive move into what are now toxic assets. Was he responsible? What are the responsibilities of a senior counselor and chair of the executive committee?

Sixth, crises impose severe financial and emotional stresses on implicated organizations. For corporations, they result in a decline in stock prices. Crises are a source of heightened uncertainty and unknowable financial consequences. This causes investors to overreact. Stable, long-term investors tend to abandon companies associated with such open-ended uncertainties. The increased uncertainty invites short sellers to slam the company's stock. Such trading may put the troubled company in play and vulnerable to corporate takeover.

The emotional stress on managers comes from the loss of control. Managers panic and are overcome by a feeling of helplessness. They perceive themselves as under attack from all sides and besieged. This mentality provokes unproductive protectionist measures. They try to protect organizational resources at all costs. They put up legal defenses. They shut down internal communications. They stonewall the media. They downplay effects of the event. They try to blame a single individual or people outside the firm for causing the crisis. Under such stressful conditions, decisions get focused on the short term. They deal with symptoms instead of fundamental causes. These unprepared responses deepen the crisis for the firm (Pauchant and Mitroff 1992).

Seventh, crises are preceded by smaller errors and near misses, which can serve as early-warning signs. Crisis prevention needs vigilance and surveillance over key components of the system, as well as risk decision processes. An important determinant of surveillance mechanisms is the regulatory infrastructure in place. Weak regulations allow unwarranted risks into communities and unwarranted risk taking by managers (Luhmann 1990).

Early-warning signals are sometimes ignored by managers, because of production pressures, errors in judgment, a lack of clarity and uncertainty of the signal, or organizational communication barriers. Value at risk (VAR)—the state-of-the-art risk management analytic developed by JPMorgan, and by the time of the crisis employed by nearly all major Wall Street firms—was clearly signaling the increased risks to each individual firm. Competitive pressures, not the least of which was meeting the quarterly expectations of the investment community, resulted in none of the major firms responding to the alarm that VAR was sounding. To prevent crises, organizations should establish early-warning systems in technical plants and facilities and in administrative processes. These systems serve as the eyes and ears of the organization and identify potential sources of crises in advance. Warnings must reach top management so that they can inform strategic decisions.

Eighth, successful crisis management focuses on structuring the crisis, crisis communication, emergency management, rescue and relief, and conflict resolution. Crisis management begins with the organization's preparation for crises and prevention planning. Preparation involves ensuring adequate safety policies and equipment. Preventative planning should assume that theoretically any type of crisis can affect the corporation, but real crisis potential depends on types of technologies in use, the hazards inherent in their products, and the safety infrastructure of their external environment. The

FIGURE 8.1 A model of corporate crisis management

next step is to establish crisis management and damage-control systems at both the corporate and business unit levels. These systems include emergency management, stakeholder communications programs, and conflict resolution mechanisms. Once the immediate impacts of the crisis are addressed, companies must embark on business recovery. Long-term recovery should focus on changes in products, production systems, and the business model. This model of crisis management depicted in Figure 8.1 includes an organizational-learning element that allows the company to continually maintain vigilance and improve its operations.

Applying Lessons of Crisis Management to the Global Financial Crisis

This section explores how some of the key elements that we have distilled from the technological crisis literature were manifested in the global financial crisis.

• • •

First, we know from crisis experiences at Bhopal, Three Mile Island, Exxon *Valdez*, and with the NASA Challenger that crises occur in complex and opaque systems. The global financial system is both complex and opaque. There are many rules, regulations, national and international standards, product and service features, and technological systems that contribute to the complexity of financial systems. These systems are overseen partly by private companies, partly by federal agencies, partly by state agencies, and partly by self-regulatory organizations (SROs)—government-authorized industry regulators, such as the Financial Industry Regulatory Authority (FINRA). Accountability and responsibility rules are not always clear. Most important, however, a central overseer is often lacking—one who is not limited to a particular silo and thus sees across the various aspects of these complex systems. The ability of third-party analysts and observers to gauge what is happening inside markets and companies is weak because of a lack of transparency. Even where a third party has transparency (as in the case of independent auditors), the observer is not sufficiently knowledgeable to know what a problem looks like.

The connectedness and interdependence of systems has created a financial miasma that no one fully understands. In fact, even within a single company or government agency, one department or manager may not fully know what another department or manager is doing or seeing.

Second, crises are caused by simultaneous interacting failures inside and outside organizations. The subprime lending that is at the heart of the global financial crisis exhibits both internal and external failures. Countrywide, Washington Mutual, and others lent money to unqualified buyers, who had little or no equity in the asset they were buying. The buyers, therefore, had no skin in the game, so that when asset prices deteriorated, their rational response was to walk away from the loans and give up the asset that was being held as collateral. The lenders, however, also kept no skin in the game, in that they sold the risky loans to investment banks or GSEs (Fannie Mae or Freddie Mac), which in turn securitized the loans and sold them to investors. Credit-rating agencies assigned ratings to the resulting pooled securities that, in hindsight, were naive, wildly optimistic, or both. Regulatory agencies responsible for monitoring such lending and securitization failed to see the risks in these practices.

Third, technological crisis literature is replete with examples of managers missing or ignoring early-warning signals. At the Union Carbide Bhopal plant, the managers ignored their own internal audit report conducted by the headquarters staff that identified eighty different safety breaches in the plant. At Exxon Shipping, the drunk captain of the Exxon *Valdez* was known to have drinking problems, as evidenced by his suspended driver's license. But the company failed to notice it and let him command the oil tanker. At Enron, numerous attempts by lower-level employees to warn upper management of the illegal practices were deliberately ignored. And for years, Bernard Madoff got away with a $50 billion Ponzi scheme until he turned himself in and confessed to authorities in December 2008. Even after receiving tips that Madoff's performance could not be real, the SEC found nothing wrong because it was locked into the silo of his brokerage business, not his investment advisory business.

In the financial crisis, there were both internal and external early-warning signs. Internally, by the mid-2000s, the aforementioned risk metric used by Wall Street (VAR) was telling management that its risk profile was increasing to dangerous levels. Externally, both the administration and its congressional counterparts saw risks to the financial system. Unfortunately, the polarization in Washington that began in the 1990s had become so strident by the mid-2000s that each side heard the other crying wolf, with the result that no consensus could be reached. In 2003, when the administration sought to increase federal oversight and standards for the GSEs, Representative Barney Frank, speaking for congressional Democrats who were the strongest supporters of subsidized housing, objected: "The more people, in my judgment, exaggerate a threat of safety and soundness, the more people conjure up the possibility of serious financial losses to the Treasury, which I do not see. I think we see entities that are fundamentally sound financially." In contrast, in 2005 when regulators proposed higher standards for no-money-down, interest-only mortgages, the Republican administration and the Federal Reserve, fearing that unnecessary excessive regulation would slow down economic growth, objected and did nothing to tighten the standards.

Fourth, crises lead companies into defensive postures and a siege mentality. In the financial crisis, this is manifested in banks losing trust in their counterparties and investors losing trust in their banks. Even when the Treasury injects capital into the banks to make them more solvent, they continue to hunker down and not lend money. Even when investors see stock and bond prices driven down to a quarter or half of their value over one or two years previous, they hoard their money in zero-interest Treasury securities. And countries often implement beggar-thy-neighbor policies like trade barriers or currency devaluation. The buy-American provision in the bailout bill passed by the U.S. House of Representatives in January 2009 is eerily reminiscent of the Smoot-Hawley Tariff Act of the 1930s, which most observers now cite as a contributor to the Great Depression.

Fifth, crises throw top managers and leaders into confusion. Faced by novel situations, no programmed responses, and lack of preparedness, managers and board members alike are bewildered. Their responses are disorderly and internally conflicting, often worsening the crisis. Leaders are also embarrassed and seek quick, short-term solutions that can get them out of the hole quickly. The September 2008 bankruptcy of Lehman Brothers and the sale of Merrill Lynch threw financial and political leaders into a panic. Treasury Secretary Henry Paulson hurriedly proposed a bailout plan worth $700 billion on three pages of paper. Within a week, leaders of both parties in the U.S. Congress, the Bush administration, and the two presidential candidates were all eagerly proposing that Congress pass that package. The public was outraged and vehemently opposed to the plan. It failed on first vote. But political leaders eventually developed the idea further and in a week passed the plan. Such hurried solutions to deep and complex problems are invariably inadequate. No wonder that even three months after passing the bailout bill, the credit markets remained illiquid.

Policy Implications

What are the policy implications of the crisis management literature for the current global financial crisis? Financial systems are like technological systems with respect to their complexity, interdependence, opacity, managerial control, and many other features. The causes of the current global financial crisis, like the causes of technological disasters, are rooted in human, organizational, and technological failures within financial companies, coupled with regulatory, infrastructure, and prepared failures in their environments. We explore below some preliminary policy implications in two categories of crisis prevention and crisis management.

Surveilling Risk and Leverage

In hindsight it is clear that there was massive failure in the pricing and regulation of risk. Historically, the U.S. financial system has done a good job of regulating risk. However, in the past three decades, a deep deregulatory ideology has permeated the country. Americans are historically and naturally suspicious of government. They learned with the New Deal banking and securities legislation that worked successfully for sixty-five years that effective, efficient regulation is a necessary precursor to establishing the trust that lies at the heart of all financial markets. It is not simply a need for more oversight. The system has become too large, too fast, and too complex for regulators to keep up.

For instance, currently, the SEC conducts backward-looking audits, searching for past transgressions. In addition, federal regulators should focus on guiding companies, helping them to adhere to sound principles of risk management and to avoid imprudent business practices.

The remedy is not to simply regulate the system and stymie its ability to be creative and innovative. Instead, we need surveillance systems that can monitor risk and leverage on a systemwide (global) level. Yes, this will mean some additional regulation. But this sort of regulation is different in three ways. First, it is directed toward reducing opacity and enhancing transparency and accountability. Its goal is not to tell companies what to do and what not to do in dealing with risk. Instead, its goal is to make clear to investors, analysts, observers, auditors, credit-rating agencies, and regulators what companies are in fact doing. Second, it is principles based instead of the whack-a-mole current system, which excessively focuses on past transgressions. It is designed to help organizations address the weaknesses of their internal risk management systems. For instance, in the Citigroup case, if a senior counselor was in fact responsible for the company increasing its risk profile, why was he or she not in the chain of command with clearly defined responsibilities and accountability? Third, it must be integrated. The SEC cannot give the Madoff broker-dealer an A-OK and completely miss the fraud he or she was perpetrating on investment clients. It is not single country or single market based, but systemwide—global. Because of the interdependencies between banks, and the ability to transfer funds electronically across national boundaries, the top financial institutions around the world need to be brought under a surveillance system in which regulators in all of the countries in which they operate see the findings of other country regulators on a real-time basis to coordinate their inquiries and responses.

Redesigning a Sustainable Economic System
Regulating the existing system is not sufficient. A key lesson of crisis management is in reconsidering the design of the entire system (e.g., products, operations, financial and managerial structures, control systems). The current financial system has a number of unsustainable features. It is heavily focused on fulfilling needs of the investment community while ignoring the needs of other stakeholders. If we simply restore the financial system of its past form, it will continue to erode its own social usefulness and the natural environment. Sophisticated securities markets might not be the proper investment arena for many small investors. Redesign of the global financial system should make it socially responsive and ecologically sustainable. This means questioning the

role of consumerism (and credit); reassessing resource-intensive production, packaging, and logistics; and reconsidering the nature and design of labor or work.

The U.S. tax code currently encourages home ownership through leverage by treating mortgage interest as a tax deduction. Having now seen the effects of leverage on our financial system, should the deductibility be eliminated and treated the same as any other interest payment on a loan? Rather than using the tax code to encourage home buying, should the code be rewritten to encourage education for twenty-first century jobs by making interest payments on educational loans deductible?

Long-Term Plan for Crisis Management
Crises are processes spread over time and space. They are not single events. The process of global financial crisis is starting to unfold. The impacts of this crisis are likely to last for many years, perhaps decades, to come. This calls for establishing a long-term crisis management plan and team that will manage the process through its expansion and normalization phases. The goal of crisis management is not to restore the financial system to its original form and structure. Instead, there needs to be a clear vision of a sustainable global economy that can serve the needs of a global population of 9 billion (by 2042) under known constraints of carbon accumulation and ecosystem limits.

Who should be on the crisis management team is another critical aspect of dealing with this crisis. Clearly, it cannot be the same people—financial and political leadership who let the crisis emerge in the first place. The old leadership with its ideas and authoritarian personalities needs to be replaced with a new team with a vision of sustainable economic growth, supported by ecological-economic development ideas and policies. Most important, we need to broaden economic policy making to include cultural, social, and ecological considerations.

The crisis plan must address the root causes of the crisis—homeowners' inability to meet their mortgage payments and the resulting toxic assets on the balance sheets of our financial institutions. Other elements should include, at a minimum, an emergency economic stimulus, long-term job recovery of high-value-added and creative jobs, balanced taxation and budgets, and a focus on eco-friendly and renewable energy technologies. The idea of the emergency economic stimulus is to jump-start basic aspects of the economy such as the credit freeze and to ameliorate job losses.

Global Stakeholder Communications

The current crisis has highlighted the need for the global coordination of crisis responses. The financial system is a tightly coupled and highly interdependent global system. Participants, decision makers, and stakeholders reside in many nations. In a crisis, they all need information simultaneously. Varying transparency standards and lack of communications exacerbate the crisis. There was no global coordination for the first year of the subprime crisis. It was not until the fall of Lehman Brothers in September 2008 that other countries began to grasp the extent of their vulnerability to the current crisis. There then was a flurry of international coordination activities between treasury officials from the United States, Europe, and China. However, these were short lived, and in a few weeks each country went back to handling its own internal mess. Managing a global crisis requires information be available to decision makers and markets across the world. A communication system that delivers information to decision makers and stakeholders would have to include uniform corporate financial transparency standards and common accounting standards. The reach of the communication system should go beyond information systems for specialists (analysts and financial professionals) to include the entire investing public.

Bold Actions to Get Ahead of the Curve

The most common way of acting in a crisis is to react to its daily evolving vagaries. This may sound realistic and prudent, but it is self-defeating. In a reactive mode, managers can never get ahead of the evolving events to stop them. Instead, we propose a set of bold proactive measures early in the crisis, to get ahead of the emerging events. These actions must be anchored in a grand vision of how things can be. Carter Glass, first a congressman and later a U.S. senator from Virginia, had such a vision in the twentieth century when he authored first the legislation that created the Federal Reserve in 1913 and later in 1933 the aforementioned legislation that separated investment from commercial banks for sixty-six years. In twenty-first-century Washington, however, no similar politician has risen above the polarization with a vision to see through the blame game with a vision for tomorrow. The vision must encompass at least some of the key variables that are at the root of the crisis. In the current crisis, this means we need a fresh vision of appropriate levels of credit and leverage, requirements of ownership of real estate assets, role of the securities and derivative products and stock markets, production and consumption, and jobs. The bold action should take the country well beyond a minimal level needed to survive the crisis. So, for example, if before the crisis we were at 5 percent unemployment and during the crisis we are close to 10 percent unemployment, the vision for job creation should not be just to manage the economy back to the 5 percent rate. Instead, a bold approach could be to reach the structurally lowest levels of unemployment with new types of jobs that are financially rewarding as well as stretching and fulfilling. The types of jobs created is as important as (if not more important than) the numbers of jobs. Instead of low-end service jobs or standard construction-type jobs, the focus should be on creative and high-technology, high-value-added jobs that will be in demand in the future and retain robust wages. For example, rather than simply repairing bridges and highways, perhaps it would be additionally appropriate to restructure the electricity grid and create a nationwide electronic medical record.

Such actions, and choices about how to put such policies into action, require a great deal of imagination and creativity. Thus, in the final section of this chapter, we offer a series of reflections about how to address the failure of imagination in the practice of technological system design and management.

Addressing the Failure of Imagination in Practice

We suggest that failures of imagination take place in practice, using this term technically to refer to "embodied, materially mediated arrays of human activity centrally organized around shared practical understanding" (Schatzki 2001, 2). From a practice-oriented perspective, surprises are not exclusively cognitive, psychological phenomena; they also have social, emotional, embodied, and material dimensions.

It would require perhaps several dissertations to trace out these dimensions of the current global financial crisis, but as a broadside point for critical reflection, it is fair to point out that today's strategic decision makers and crisis managers have precious few occasions in which they can engage in the kinds of activities that have historically been associated with developing imaginative responses to surprise events. Play and the arts have served Western civilization since ancient Greece as activities through which imagination may be developed in practice. Today, although these activities may occur frequently in Montessori schools, they remain fairly uncommon in the boardroom, and when they surface, it is often only as a diversion.

To ground the notion that crisis managers should play more to avoid future failures of imagination, we can trace various contemporary dynamics within the business environment, examining the ways in which risk is commonly conceptualized and managed in practice, and identify play and the arts as "technologies of foolishness" (March 1979; Jacobs and Statler 2005) that can complement the technologies of reason typically employed in the practice of crisis management.

Managing Risks in Practice

Organizations operating in a global environment are exposed to a broader spectrum of potential disruptions. Meanwhile, the trend of catastrophic natural disasters appears to be rising around the world. Organizations additionally face increased political risks, including everything from nonstate actors such as Al-Qaeda to the expansion of the European Union. These risk factors are compounded and intensified by the market dynamics identified here.

In this context, complexity and contingency are accepted among strategy makers as ontological features of the environment. And yet the risks associated with these features cannot be considered exclusively as neutral, objectively verifiable facts. As noted above, there are other important dimensions of any crisis, including psychological, sociological, cultural, and embodied phenomena. These intersubjective, human dimensions are also historical, following specific trajectories of evolution that coalesce into organizational practices and institutional fields of practice. In turn, these practices frame the very concepts of complexity, contingency, and risk (Power 2007).

In practice, the opacity of these reciprocal relationships makes it difficult to trace and predict causality across a sequence of events. Although the expansion of computational capacity provides increased support to management decision making with regard to large-scale risks, such as climate change or influenza pandemics, there is no vacuum in which these complex relationships and interdependencies can be comprehensively modeled. By selecting the variables and the parameters that constitute the model, risk managers make a series of assumptions about the interdependent relationships between and among various entities or agents. Viewed topologically (Statler and Richardson 2008), these interdependencies are the conditions under which the organization can sustain itself. If these conditions happen to change, as often occurs with antagonistic, competitive threats as well as systemic threats such as market failures, then the utility of the model is constrained, and it becomes difficult to predict the effectiveness of any risk mitigation strategy.

Hedging against these constraints, many large organizations have invested in human capabilities to manage risks associated with crisis events.

The risk-related management disciplines have blossomed in recent years, nourished by resources expended in response to extraordinary events (e.g., 9/11, Katrina, the Indian Ocean tsunami) as well as banal circumstances (e.g., increased reliance on global communications and supply networks). Through the early 2000s, an observer of the field could differentiate organizational functions such as disaster recovery, emergency management, business continuity planning, physical security, and risk management (a catchall category that, for many financial institutions, includes operational risk, credit risk, market risk, currency risk, and strategic risk). These functions could be differentiated in terms of their respective strategic objectives: information technology data security, emergency preparedness and employee safety, resilience of (especially revenue-generating) business operations, long-term strategic advantage. These functions could also be differentiated in terms of their tools and techniques, standards of practice, professional associations, and governance structures.

However, more recently, these organizational silos are breaking down, and formerly distinct fields of practice are often merging. Integrative concepts such as enterprise risk management seek to provide all-encompassing frameworks, and indeed, the competitive consulting marketplace is awash in acronyms and service offerings that promise seamlessly profitable operations no matter what hazards may arise. Guided by such concepts, the various risk-oriented disciplines are increasingly consolidated, reporting up to central committee-level chief risk officers. These individuals often strive to look holistically at the long-term sustainability of the firm, its stakeholders, and the environment (Anderson 2006).

As we noted above, the risk-oriented disciplines have largely not yet been integrated with other management functions, including finance, marketing, and human resources. Like these other functions, risk management often appears on the balance sheet as a cost center, so in times of a global financial crisis, many risk management professionals can find themselves with a sudden windfall surplus of labor capacity. Meanwhile, the functions they had performed before being laid off are being temporarily abandoned in many organizations or left—as often occurs in matrix reporting structures—to be fulfilled by someone who allocates only a small percentage of time to the effort.

Leaders (in management and on governance boards) are left with hard choices. Viewed holistically, risks are up and available risk management resources are down. What is worse, the emergent character of threats in a global system means that crisis managers cannot ever be certain to what extent current investments in training people and developing systems will prove effective, for example, in an avian-flu pandemic with 30 percent mortality rates. In this context, crisis managers seeking to take actions that effectively sustain the firm must make difficult decisions about what is the right thing to do and about how much is enough.

Imagination in Practice: Play and the Arts

As noted above, crises invariably come as a surprise, and decisions made in response to crises are accompanied with critical scrutiny and investigations from the outside. These two aspects of crisis situations are not coincidentally related—in response to any surprise, a basic ethical question arises: what is the right thing to do? This question must always be answered anew by the people managing the risks associated with that surprising crisis event. In turn, stakeholders will reflect on, and likely debate, how well or poorly those individuals and organizations managed those risks.

In this respect, crisis management involves what Werhane (1999) has referred to as moral imagination. Moral principles and ethical values shape how people acting with incomplete information make decisions. Because this enacted, ethical dimension of crisis management remains difficult to quantify, it can hardly be programmed into a machine. Because it remains open to the uncertainty of the future, it remains difficult to circumscribe through regulations or other governance practices. Instead, it must be imagined in the moment of response, enacted by the people who are managing the crisis. In this sense, crisis management occurs at the juncture where ethics and economics converge in aesthetics, in the imagination of possible futures-embodied practice. How, then, can this practice be improved to prevent future failures of imagination, moral or otherwise?

Thus, in addition to the macrolevel policy recommendations articulated above, we suggest that the global financial crisis signals a need for reflection on the specific activities that can provide people in organizations with opportunities to cultivate imagination in practice.

In the *Republic*, Plato describes a situation in which a stranger comes to the door and the guard dog must decide whether to bite or to wag its tail. For leaders who, like the dog, must improve their capabilities to decide the right thing to do on the basis of incomplete information, Plato advocates music and gymnastics as the appropriate pedagogical methods. It may sound strange, but any executive who has participated in an outdoor leadership development course or provided corporate sponsorship for a community cultural event has had some experience with this mode of learning.

Behind such familiar experiences, there is a deep, well-established tradition that runs from ancient Greece through the pairing of arts with sciences in the modern university curriculum. This tradition looks to play and the arts pedagogically as sources of instruction that can balance the knowledge gained through the empirical sciences with a measure of judgment. From this perspective, play and the arts appear as practices that may enable the development of a more imaginative, holistic, and embodied approach to crisis events.

James March (1979) famously signaled a need for "technologies of foolishness" (see also Jacobs and Statler 2005) to complement the technologies of reason commonly used by managers. Recent research supports the notion that a playful mode of intentionality can improve the quality of strategy-making processes by integrating cognitive, social, and emotional levels of experience (Roos, Victor, and Statler 2003); enabling the development of embodied metaphors that shape group sensemaking processes (Heracleous and Jacobs 2008); and supporting the development of shared organizational identity (Oliver and Roos 2006). Similarly, there is support for the notion that arts-based processes can more generally support management learning (Taylor and Ladkin 2009) and leadership development (Adler 2006) by enabling new insights and knowledge (Meisiek and Barry 2007); improving skills and behaviors (Cowan 2007); intensifying emotional experiences (Grisham 2006); and even improving overall firm performance (Styhre and Eriksson 2008).

With respect to crisis management, play and the arts may introduce a greater qualitative diversity of considerations and experiences (including ethical values and aesthetic judgments alongside economic factors) that cannot be easily measured or quantified but remain crucial to the future sustainability of the organization. Following Socrates' argument about the dog, music (i.e., the arts) and gymnastics (i.e., play) may provide crisis managers with a practical means of exercising the imagination that has failed rather too often in the recent past.

From an organizational design perspective, the challenge involves framing play- or arts-based experiences in relationship to existing organizational practices, integrating them where appropriate. In some cases, it may be best to frame them as completely separate, distinct activities—such as an off-site retreat or a skunk works. In other cases, it may be more appropriate to present play as a new perspective or attitude toward existing tasks, a mode of intentionality (Roos et al. 2003) that involves openness to emergent change.

From a management control perspective, either of these design options requires a degree of slack and an investment of resources. Some organizations build in slack as a business process focused on strategic innovation (Hayes 2008), whereas others seek it periodically as a support to strategy-making and organizational development processes. In any case, the market currently supports a range of often customizable options to pursue arts-based and alternative forms of management learning, including off-site retreats, custom executive education programs, organizational change process, executive coaching and leadership development, and so on (Wankel and DeFillippi 2007).

For crisis managers, large-scale emergency simulation exercises (much like the Department of Defense's war-game simulations in crafting national security strategy) may be one particularly amenable context for integrating arts- or play-based components. These events can involve a diverse range of public- and private-sector emergency response and recovery functions in a specific region or industry. Recent anecdotal evidence suggests that the success of such exercises depends on the development of trust among exercise participants and on maintaining a safe space to fail; both are outcomes associated with play- or arts-based learning (Grisham 2006; Oliver and Roos 2007).

In closing, it may be useful for skeptics as well as curious readers of this chapter to note where such technologies of foolishness are already present in the field of crisis management. For example, participants in simulations and exercises such as those referenced above usually agree to play, and senior leaders consult Carl von Clausewitz's *Vom Kriege* or Sun Tzu's classic *The Art of War* for strategic guidance. In this light, crisis managers may already be relying on play and the arts in limited but important ways. If such playful and artistic practices are cultivated, they may help sustain the design and management of organizational systems in the face of future crisis events.

References

Adler, N. J. 2006. The arts and leadership: Now that we can do anything, what will we do? *Academy of Management Learning and Education* 5 (4): 486–99.

Anderson, D. 2006. The critical importance of sustainability risk management. *Risk Management* 53 (4): 66–74.

Apuzzo, Matt. 2008. Under pressure, US eased lending rules. *The Guardian*, December 1. http://www.guardian.co.uk/uslatest/story/0,,-8105585,00.html.

Burgi, P. T., C. D. Jacobs, and J. Roos. 2005. From metaphor to practice in the crafting of strategy. *Journal of Management Inquiry* 14 (1): 78–94.

Cowan, D. A. 2007. Artistic undertones of humanistic leadership education. *Journal of Management Education* 31 (2): 156–80.

Enrich, David. 2009. Rubin departs Citi. *Wall Street Journal*, January 10.

Grisham, T. 2006. Metaphor, poetry, storytelling and cross-cultural leadership. *Management Decision* 44 (4): 486–503.

Gruver, W. R. 2008. Big regulator for the little investor. *New York Times*, September 13.

Habermas, J. 1975. *Legitimation crisis*. Boston: Beacon Press.

Hayes, Erin. 2008. Google's 20 percent factor: How adding 20 percent free time could make corporate America more productive. *ABCNEWS Online*, May 12. http://abc-news.go.com/Technology/story?id=4839327&page=1.

Jacobs, C., and L. Th. Heracleous. 2006. Constructing shared understanding: The role of embodied metaphors in organization development. *Journal of Applied Behavioral Science* 42 (2): 207–26.

Jacobs, C., and M. Statler. 2006. Toward a technology of foolishness: Developing scenarios through serious play. *International Studies of Management and Organization* 36 (3): 77–92.

Kasperson, R. E., and J. X. Kasperson. 1988. Emergency planning for industrial crises: An overview. *Industrial Crisis Quarterly* 2 (2): 81–88.

Kemeney, J. 1979. *The Presidential Commission Report on the Three Mile Island accident*. Washington, D.C.: Government Printing Office.

Komarow S., and T. Squitieri. 2004. NORAD had drills of jets as weapons. *USA Today*, April 18. http://www.usatoday.com/news/washington/2004-04-18-norad_x.htm.

Kreps, G. 1989. *Social structure and disaster*. Newark: University of Delaware Press.

Luhmann, N. 1990. Technology, environment and social risk: A systems perspective. *Industrial Crisis Quarterly* 4 (3): 223–32.

March, J. G. 1979. The technology of foolishness. In *Ambiguity and choice in organizations*, edited by J. G. March and J. P. Olsen, 69–81. Bergen, Norway: Universitetsforlaget.

Mitroff, Ian I. 2005. *Why some companies emerge stronger and better from a crisis: Seven essential lessons for surviving disaster*. New York: AMACOM Books.

Mitroff, I., and T. Pauchant. 1990. *We are so big and powerful nothing bad can happen to us*. New York: Carol Publishing.

Morin, E. 1993. For a crisiology. *Industrial and Environmental Crisis Quarterly* 7 (1): 5–22.

Nanda, A., M. Salter, B. Groysberg, and S. Matthews. 2006. The Goldman Sachs IPO. Harvard Business School Paper No. 9-800-016, April 14, Harvard Business School, Cambridge, MA.

9–11 Commission Report. 2004. National Commission on Terrorist Attacks upon the United States. http://www.9-11commission.gov/report/911Report_Ch11.pdf.

Nocera, Joe. 2009. Risk mismanagement. *New York Times*, January 4.

O'Connor, J. 1989. *The meaning of crisis*. London: Basil Blackwell.

Oliver, D., and J. Roos. 2007. Beyond text: Constructing organizational identity multimodally. *British Journal of Management* 18 (4): 342–58.

Pauchant, T., and I. Mitroff. 1992. *Transforming the crisis prone organization*. San Francisco: Jossey-Bass.

Paumgarten, N. 2009. The death of kings. *New Yorker*, May 18, 40–57.

Perrow, C. 1984. *Normal accidents: Living with high-risk technologies*. New York: Basic Books.

Plato. 1968. *The Republic of Plato*, translated and edited by Allan Bloom. New York: Basic Books.

Power, M. 2007. *Organized uncertainty: Designing a world of risk management*. Oxford: Oxford University Press.

Roos, J., B. Victor, and M. Statler. 2004. Playing seriously with strategy. *Long Range Planning* 37 (6): 549–68.

Rosenthal, U., M. T. Charles, and P. t'Hart. 1990. *Coping with crises: The management of disasters, riots and terrorism*. Springfield, IL: Charles C. Thomas Publishers.

Schatzki, T. 2001. Introduction: Practice theory. In *The practice turn in contemporary theory*, edited by T. Schatzki, K. Knorr-Cetina, and E. von Savigny, 1–14. London: Routledge.

Shrivastava, P. 1993. Crisis theory/practice: Towards a sustainable future. *Industrial and Environmental Crisis Quarterly* 7 (1): 23–42.

Shrivastava, P. 1994. *Greening business: Towards sustainable corporations*. Cincinnati, OH: Thompson Executive Press.

Shrivastava, P., I. I. Mitroff, D. Miller, and A. Miglani. 1988. Understanding industrial crises. *Journal of Management Studies* 25 (4): 285–304.

Siomkos, G. 1989. Managing product harm crises. *Industrial Crisis Quarterly* 3 (1): 41–60.

Smith, Denis, and D. Elliot. 2006. *Key readings in crisis management: Systems and structures for prevention and recovery*. New York: Routledge.

Statler, M., and R. Richardson. 2008. Aesthetics and the topology of risk. *Management Online Review*. http://www.morexpertise.com.

Styhre, A., and M. Eriksson. 2008. Bring in the arts and get the creativity for free: A study of the artists in residence project. *Creativity and Innovation Management* 17 (1): 47–57.

Taylor, S. S., and D. Ladkin. 2009. Understanding arts-based methods in managerial development. *Academy of Management Learning and Education* 8 (1): 55–69.

Turner, Barry, and Nick Pidgeon. 1997. *Man-made disaster*. London: Butterworth Heineman.

Wankel, C., and R. DeFillippi. 2007. *University and corporate innovations in lifetime learning*. Charlotte, NC: Information Age Publishing.

Werhane P. 1999. *Moral imagination and management decision making*. New York: Oxford University Press.

World Commission on Environment and Development. 1987. *Our common future*. New York: Oxford University Press.

9 Failures of High Reliability in Finance

Nathaniel I. Bush, Peter F. Martelli, and Karlene H. Roberts

The recent failures and resulting crisis related to mortgage-backed securities and derivatives are symptomatic of deeper organizational problems in the global financial services sector. Both the culture and tools of high finance produce conditions that are inconsistent with high reliability outside a narrow set of system parameters. Using perspectives from high-reliability organizing theory, we review critical features of firm-level and system-level behavior in financial services that reduced overall system tolerance and yielded catastrophic consequences. We assert that overspecialization, control and conformity, insensitivity to unknown risks, and lack of flexibility in response contributed to systemic failure. We analyze industry character to reveal how organizations institutionalized critical design flaws. Moreover, we examine how similar failures within most financial organizations compounded as a result of the highly interconnected nature of the system. Finally, we offer a short list of prescriptions that would improve reliability in the future.

Introduction

> It is difficult to get a man to understand something when his salary
> depends upon his not understanding it.
> —*Upton Sinclair*

This work was partially supported by National Science Foundation Grant No. CMMI 0624296.

In the final days of summer 2008, devastating blows were dealt to the confidence of the American economy. Fannie Mae and Freddie Mac were taken over by the government in early September, and Lehman Brothers filed for bankruptcy protection by the middle of the month. By that point, the S&P 500 had fallen 20 percent from its all-time peak; it would fall an additional six hundred points (nearly half its value at the time) in the following six months, with most of that decline coming within one month of the Lehman bankruptcy. Worse yet, the credit markets froze during the subsequent period, despite the passage of comprehensive bailout legislation and the injection of hundreds of billions of dollars into the financial system.

Although the first public signs of the subprime crisis dated back to the demise of Bear Stearns in March, the period starting in September 2008 marked the beginning of more widespread economic problems. The subprime mortgage crisis had finally infected the rest of the nation. Nevertheless, these events, and the crisis of confidence they triggered, were only symptoms of a long-standing ailment. The seeds of all these events had been slowly sown over many earlier years, with the effect of making the so-called Great Recession an inevitable event. As with so many other catastrophes, by the time people were widely aware of the problem, halting the consequences became nearly impossible.

Similar to other types of man-made catastrophes, the causes of the financial crisis accumulated slowly over time, and the results should have been predictable to those in the financial industry; however, although many people were aware of certain components of the hazard, most of them were ignorant as to the severity of what was about to happen. This ignorance came in a variety of flavors: those who did not understand the complex financial instruments their organizations were involved with and were therefore unaware of potential systemic risks; those who were true believers in the perfection of deregulated "free markets" and their ability to root out fraud, and in the perfection of their models; and those who understood the risks but for whom the cognitive dissonance associated with acknowledging those risks was too great to bear. This ignorance, coupled with a lack of regulatory oversight and strong perverse incentives, allowed the massive escalation of leverage and risk that made a crisis inevitable. It also allowed a set of behaviors inconsistent with reliable long-term functioning of complex institutions, both within and between firms. Finally, among those who were not ignorant of the flaws in the financial system, there was a strong tendency toward exploitation of those problems rather than efforts to root them out.

Individually and collectively, financial institutions violated the core principles associated with operating in a high-reliability manner. These violations stemmed both from the incentive structures at work at the firm and system levels, and from the attributes that convey legitimacy at those same levels. They also led to positive feedback loops between factors conveying legitimacy and incentives at both levels. Behaving as one's incentives would dictate (e.g., maximizing profits and bonuses) signals competence, value, and prestige, and thereby conveys legitimacy; attributes that convey legitimacy (e.g., sophisticated quantitative modeling and high work volume) lead to higher short-term profits, thus fueling incentives. Moreover, the same mechanisms translated the within-firm attributes to the within-system level, and vice versa (e.g., profitable leveraging practices at one firm were adopted by the industry broadly, while the homogenization of the industry and resulting narrow margins required higher leverage to maintain expected levels of profit). These relationships suggest behavioral interactions consistent with both the component and the combinatorial complexity that many high-risk systems often face, where *component complexity* refers to the number of potential interactions between units dependent on one another and *combinatorial complexity* to the existence of feedback loops and partially or completely delayed effects from decisions.

All of this took place within a dissolving regulatory framework that enabled these developments. The form reregulation should take has been the subject of much debate since the onset of the crisis, but one thing we believe is that part of the solution is creating a culture consistent with high-reliability principles. This must be done in concert with properly aligning incentives in the industry. The financial system is every bit as vital to our modern world as flight operations, space launches, firefighting, and industrial operations (all classic territory for high-reliability organizational, or HRO, studies), and it is necessary that constituent firms begin to behave in a high-reliability manner.

We are at a crossroads that will determine the future of our economic system. We can either take measures to reduce the likelihood of similar catastrophes in the future, or we can continue to be plagued by destructive boom-and-bust cycles that misallocate resources and in turn wither public confidence. The rest of this chapter focuses on the ways the financial system and firms failed to behave in a high-reliability fashion, their reasons for doing so, and how HRO processes could have altered their behavior and helped prevent some of the worst impacts of the crisis. Revisiting the framework presented in Weick and Sutcliffe's instant classic *Managing the Unexpected*, we discuss the performance of finance in the context of each of their five characteristics. We conclude by tying together threads from each principle to form a cohesive assessment of the application of high-reliability theory to the financial system, and we generate a number of recommendations for systemic change.

Preoccupation with Failure

> HROs encourage reporting of errors, they elaborate experiences of a near miss for what can be learned, and they are wary of the potential liabilities of success, including *complacency*, the temptation to *reduce margins of safety*, and the drift into *automatic processing.*"[1]
> —Weick and Sutcliffe, Managing the Unexpected, 10–11

While constantly seeking more sophisticated and predictive numerical models throughout the past two decades, financial organizations exhibited complacency by maintaining a dogmatic belief in historical trends and relationships. A long uptrend in housing prices was interpreted as evidence that this behavior would continue and that prices could not fall. Although this seems ludicrous in retrospect, it is worth remembering that many credible sources agreed with this reasoning at the time. As late as 2007, luminaries such as Alan Greenspan and Ben Bernanke contended that housing prices were not unsustainably high.

Seemingly stable historical trends, even when they are relatively short term when viewed in retrospect, were responsible for many of the financial crises of the past. From the first recorded speculative bubble, the Dutch tulip mania that peaked in 1637, to the failure of Long-Term Capital Management (LTCM) in 1998, to the technology stock bubble that burst three years later, belief in the continuation of trends was vital to the creation of the disaster. In the case of LTCM, the firm's confidence in the stability of the spread between yield rates of various bonds emboldened it to accept leverage ratios well outside of safe margins—ratios often in excess of 50 to 1. When these supposedly stable relationships reversed during the Russian and Brazilian bond defaults, the firm was rapidly wiped out by its derivatives exposure. Because of its large number of contracts with other financial firms, the collapse threatened the stability of Wall Street as a whole, and the Federal Reserve orchestrated a buyout of LTCM by a consortium of fourteen other firms.

As with LTCM, financial institutions (including and especially hedge funds) decreased safety margins by going after increasingly tenuous statistical relationships and ever thinner profit margins to increase returns. To make these profitable at a level acceptable to investors and management, they used leverage (borrowed money) to increase the multiples on the marginal returns, thereby further decreasing safety margins. The high leverage ratios that were once only the territory of high-risk hedge funds became commonplace on Wall Street during the height of the mortgage-backed security boom. The average leverage ratio grew to 30 to 1, meaning that firms only needed to lose approximately 3.33 percent on their underlying securities to become insolvent. In downturns, these high leverage ratios can create positive-feedback cycles, thus accelerating losses and exacerbating the declines. Moreover, they can act to cause price declines in seemingly unrelated markets. Robert Pozen writes:

> Excess leverage was a key factor in aggravating the financial crisis in general and pushing down stock prices in particular. The ratio of average assets to capital rose significantly between 2004 and 2008 at large banks, investment houses and hedge funds. . . . As the financial crisis continued, credit became scarce and collateral requirements increased . . . as financial institutions experienced heavy losses related to home mortgages, they were forced to sell assets to maintain leverage ratios set by their regulators. As these institutions sold assets, prices declined in response to increased supply, creating further losses and triggering additional asset sales. This cycle can easily spread from weak institutions to healthy ones, as widespread selling creates price declines in all asset categories.[2]

The instability generated by high leverage ratios was exacerbated by growth in the derivatives markets. Because the value of derivatives is based on the change in value of an underlying security, they are intrinsically more volatile. Complex methods of hedging out this volatility—through instruments such as the use of spreads, other derivatives and insurance contracts, and so on—were developed to mitigate this; however, these are usually again subject to the stability of delicate relationships across different underlying securities. At the onset of a crisis, market behavior becomes more erratic, and the dependability of those relationships is uncertain. Given the peak of nearly $673 trillion in notional value of the over-the-counter (OTC) derivatives markets that existed in June 2008, the impact of derivatives' volatility eradicated the safety margins that existed.[3]

In order to explore and exploit those correlations between various financial instruments that produced the reliable-seeming—yet razor thin—profit margins, financial firms have become almost totally reliant on computer trading algorithms and financial models. Trading programs have existed since the late 1980s, and were in fact a major factor in the 1987 market crash known as Black Monday. In that event, portfolio insurance had become a widespread service offered by institutional investors. They guaranteed their clients against losses over a given level by using a combination of derivatives and programs that automatically sold securities into a market downturn. For an individual investor, this system made sense. However, when this practice became widespread, the behavior of all market participants became highly correlated, and a positive-feedback cycle was established. A small downturn after a long bull market triggered selling and exercising of put options, which in turn triggered deeper negative moves, which triggered more selling, and so on. Unsurprisingly, in retrospect, when everyone wants to get out of the market simultaneously, liquidity becomes a problem. For long stretches of time on the morning of the crash, some securities saw no trading at all. Everyone wanted to sell, and there was no one buying. This created large discontinuities in stock prices, with sharp instantaneous-seeming drops in price rather than a smooth, downward curve. These drops violated assumptions used to model stock prices and volatility. Some regulation of portfolio insurance pertaining to market liquidity was put into place after Black Monday, but the era of computerized trading had only begun, and the risks associated with it became more opaque after the rise of hedge funds, with their hidden methods and transactions.

The use of computer models in trading, however, may actually be less important to the stability of the markets than the use of computer modeling to discover arbitrage opportunities. These are the aforementioned razor-thin profits that can be obtained by exploiting small market inefficiencies in the relationships between securities. The relationships are now typically discovered through the use of complex models that examine historical statistical variations between said securities. Statistical extrapolations from these models are the source of what we believe to be preposterous assertions made by financial modelers, such as, "Losing more than X percent of the fund's value is a *ten-sigma* event"; that is, the loss should not happen even once in the history of the universe.

Finally, high leverage and a huge derivatives market taken together resulted in an explosion of counterparty risk—the risk that contractual partners will not be able to uphold their end of a bargain—as well as systemic risk from the interconnections in the financial markets. With so many trillions of dollars in notional value, the failure of one institution has the capacity to impose massive costs and losses (or even just the specter of such costs and losses) on other institutions, thus driving them to failure as well. Moreover, without barriers between types of financial institutions (e.g., Glass-Steagall), the high volume of buying and selling enabled by soaring leverage permitted all financial institutions to become involved in all markets. Institutions did this both in an effort to diversify their investments, and thereby actually decrease risk, and in an effort to exploit new arbitrage opportunities. However, these conditions taken together created a domino-like situation, where the failure of one part risks the security of the whole.

The LTCM incident appears to have been a dress rehearsal for the recent financial crisis. All the same elements were there: high leverage, belief in the continuity of a trend, near-total reliance on computer models of markets, highly interconnected counterparty risk, and tremendous use of derivatives. (In an ironic twist, Bear Stearns refused to participate in the consortium of financial firms that took over LTCM, and it was also the first Wall Street firm to fail in the recent crisis.)

Within each element discussed here, there was a failure on the part of financial institutions to be mindful of risk—they were simply not preoccupied with failure but were focused on the siren song of immediate success. Their attention was on opportunities for growth, on successful exploitation of new financial instruments and markets, and on options created by deregulation. Investors failed to attend to either the elements of the unfolding crisis or to the causes and lessons of previous crises. In fact, the principle causes of disasters such as Black Monday and the collapse of LTCM were subsequently embraced by the larger financial community as ingenious and profitable innovations. Financial crises were not considered terribly unusual or even something to necessarily worry about. James Dimon, chairman and chief executive officer of JPMorgan Chase testified before the Financial Crisis Inquiry Commission in January 2010, saying, "Not to be funny about it, but my daughter asked me when she came home from school, 'What's a financial crisis?' and I said, 'Well it's something that happens every five to seven years.'" Nor were the specific risks a total mystery. Dimon also said, "One of the surprising things about all these things, a lot of these problems with mortgages, derivatives . . . they were known."[4]

This lack of preoccupation with failure demonstrated by the financial sector is not malicious but rather is an outgrowth of the incentives fostered by existing corporate and regulatory structures. In the conclusion and recommendations sections, we discuss how to better incentivize participants to achieve high-reliability characteristics.

Reluctance to Simplify Interpretations

> HROs take deliberate steps to create more complete and nuanced
> pictures. They simplify less and see more. Knowing that the world they
> face is complex, unstable, unknowable, and unpredictable, they position
> themselves to see as much as possible. They encourage *boundary span-*
> *ners* who have *diverse experience, skepticism toward received wisdom*, and
> negotiating tactics that *reconcile differences of opinion without destroying*
> *the nuances* that diverse people detect.
>
> —*Weick and Sutcliffe*, Managing the Unexpected, *11–12*

While mathematical models employed in the financial sector have increased
in complexity over the past two decades, overall attention to complexity and
nuance has declined. Reluctance to simplify has little to do with the opacity or complexity of the computing or procedural technology used; it has
everything to do with the perspectives and robustness of cognitive models
and interpretations of the reality of the situation. Experts with real-world experience in the industries in which they trade securities were replaced with
computer programmers and statisticians. Moreover, decision making is less
receptive to diverse information and more likely to be dominated by quarter-
to-quarter profit orientation, which homogenizes behavior and leaves little
room for skeptics in an organization.

Chuck Prince, the former CEO of Citigroup, in an interview with the *Fi-*
nancial Times in July 2007, infamously stated, "When the music stops, in terms
of liquidity, things will be complicated. . . . But as long as the music is playing,
you've got to get up and dance. We're still dancing."[5] He made this statement
to describe why Citigroup was still involved with subprime-mortgage-backed
securities when it was becoming obvious to everyone that they had turned
"toxic." Although Prince received scorn for this statement, his basic argument
is sound. In an interview with Charlie Rose, the finance author Michael Lewis
pointed out, "If you're the CEO of a publicly traded Wall Street firm, and everyone else is making a profit quarter-to-quarter from this racket known as the
subprime mortgage bond market, and you don't participate, you get fired. So
the pressures and incentives are all wrong. In a way, they couldn't not do it."[6]

At the heart of this issue is the homogeneity that developed in finance
during the past twenty to thirty years, a homogeneity that reflects oversimplification. Instead of taking a diverse set of approaches to investing, thereby
decreasing systemic risk, increasingly there is only one right answer to the
question of how to invest—put your money in the hottest stock or sector,

just like everyone else. To do any less in an age of seemingly near-perfect and instantaneous data access is to invite replacement. This has extended to the point that some mutual fund managers spend much of the quarter (up to a few days before the reporting deadline) invested in securities that are outside of the official securities categories their fund declared to investors that it will use. This is done in an effort to replicate results in higher-yielding sectors and thereby attract money, or at least not lose it to those same sectors. Homogeneity, even when officially forbidden, now rules.

This type of homogeneity needs to be distinguished from following best practices, where reliability is typically increased by propagating effective techniques through an industry. Unlike with best practices, the type of homogeneity prevalent in the financial sector was not developed through scientific investigations of what promotes stability and long-term sustainability. Instead, this homogeneity developed as a result of short-term trend following and decision making. If best practices are akin to good nutrition, then mimicry in the financial sector has been like a fad diet.

Ultimately, the financial world has provided no incentives to avoid oversimplification, because the traders and executives in finance learned that they will not be held responsible for major losses. Nassim Taleb, author of *The Black Swan*, said in testimony before Congress in 2009, "I was a trader for 21 years, and every time I said, 'What if we blow up?' they said, 'Who cares, the government bails us out.' I've heard that so many times throughout my career, '[D]on't worry about extreme risk . . . worry about going down five or ten percent, don't worry about extreme risk. . . . That's not our problem anymore.'"[7] These beliefs were validated in the eyes of those inside and outside finance by the recent bailouts of most of the largest financial institutions in the nation with Troubled Asset Relief Program funding. By eliminating an entire set of extreme outcomes that finance insiders should be concerned with, bailouts create a simplified set of motivations, interpretations of risk, and decision-making systems. It is worth noting again that if some actors did not embrace this simplification, they would fail to perform up to expectations during periods of growth and would simply be replaced by those who were willing to avoid such complexity.

Sensitivity to Operations

Latent failures are "loopholes in the system's defenses, barriers and safeguards whose potential existed for some time prior to the onset of

the accident sequence, though usually without any obvious bad effect."
These loopholes consist of imperfections in features such as supervision, reporting of defects, engineered safety procedures, safety training,
briefings, certification, and hazard identification. . . . People who refuse
to speak up out of fear enact a system that knows less than it needs to
know to remain effective."

—*Weick and Sutcliffe*, Managing the Unexpected, 13

Finance is a sector with low sensitivity to operations as a result of the semi-
independent nature of much of the trading activity and a high number of
latent failures that persist for long periods without detection. The boom-and-
bust nature of the recent decades allowed these failures to persist for extended
stretches, particularly because of the duration of each market phase. In the
case of each cycle, a long boom or growth period ended with a rapid unwinding. During the growth phase, excessive risk taking rarely creates losses, un-
sanctioned transactions are easy to hide or ignore when they are profitable,
and losses are easy to lie about because they are both unexpected and easily
hidden with opaque transactions and complex bookkeeping in the labyrin-
thine web of a large modern financial institution. The subsequent unwinding
then reveals the excessive risk taking, and sometimes outright fraud, that occurred during the boom. As Warren Buffett famously said, "It's only when the
tide goes out that you learn who's been swimming naked."[8]

The most dramatic examples are cases of "rogue" traders who operated for
extended stretches without detection. In 2008, Jerome Kerviel generated a $7
billion loss for Société Générale by trading more than $70 billion in deriva-
tives in excess of his official limit. His positions were losing money and were
rapidly sold off when discovered. This rapid liquidation drove prices down
and was responsible for much of the eventual loss. When questioned, Kerviel
claimed that taking larger-than-permitted positions was common practice at
the firm and that management turned a blind eye so long as the trades were
profitable.

Similarly, Toshihide Iguchi generated $1.1 billion in losses for Daiwa Bank
over eleven years with an estimated thirty thousand unauthorized trades. He
finally confessed to the losses in 1995 when he feared discovery. *Time* magazine reported, "Interviewed in jail, Iguchi said he had seen his earlier actions
as merely a violation of internal rules. 'I think all traders have a tendency
to fall into the same trap. You always have a way of recovering the loss.'"[9]
Similarly, the 1995 bankruptcy of Barings was the result of three years of

unauthorized and highly speculative trading by Nick Leeson in Singapore, in one of the bank's "error" accounts, eventually generating more than $1.4 billion in losses.

There are dozens more examples of such illicit behavior, including many simple cases of insider trading, where the typical punishment is a fine less than the profits gleaned, some minimum-security prison time, and then a move to CNBC as a financial commentator. There are also an unknown number of cases in which traders successfully recouped their losses and thereby avoided detection. There is little incentive to dissuade such deviance when it is profitable, especially when opacity of the financial institutions makes it difficult to detect dangerous deviance from lucrative, but safe, activities.

Sometimes, even after irregular activities are discovered, it is unclear whether they were criminal or just foolish; if they were sanctioned or merely overlooked. A prime example is the Repo 105 operations at Lehman Brothers, where executives moved as much as $50 billion in securities off Lehman's books before the reporting periods to decrease the appearance of leverage, only to repurchase those securities immediately after reporting.

Ultimately, these examples of a lack of sensitivity to internal operations return us to issues of regulation and incentives. With the prospect of bailouts during systemic collapse, and a lack of government insistence on fine-grained oversight of trading activities, the firms have little reason to interfere in the behavior of their star workers. As discussed in the previous section, quarter-to-quarter profitability is the dominant incentive. When the methods used to achieve that goal do not stand up to close scrutiny, it will be the scrutiny that is in short supply, unless it is mandated.

Commitment to Resilience

> HROs develop capabilities to detect, contain, and bounce back from those inevitable errors that are part of an indeterminate world. The signature of an HRO is not that it is error-free, but that errors don't disable it. Resilience is a combination of keeping errors small and of improvising workarounds that keep the system functioning. . . . HROs put a premium on experts; personnel with deep experience, skills of recombination, and training.
>
> —*Weick and Sutcliffe,* Managing the Unexpected, *14–15*

The previously articulated failures had the cumulative effect of dramatically decreasing resilience in finance. High leverage, coupled with oversimplified goals and information, and low awareness of operations, led to high volatility and frequent crashes. Recovery occurred only after heavy subsidization by governments. In fact, government is essentially the sole source of resilience—and even then, only resilience back to the system that produced the very errors that led to the crisis.

The financial industry failed to incorporate lessons from previous meltdowns: LTCM and the 1987 crash should have been instructive, but the industry took the very practices that led to those previous crises and employed them throughout the sector. However, the problems with generating resilience in finance may run deeper than the individual characteristics of, or violations by, corporate finance personnel. The current foundations of financial culture, both in the means of advancement and in level of compensation, may be antithetical to creating the resilience requisite to high reliability.

The financial industry is dominated by an up-or-out culture, where failure is little tolerated at the lower levels of operation. Because those individuals who experience failure (and near misses) are rarely promoted, experience with errors is minimally present at the upper levels of financial organizations. We see this lack of experience as a critical impediment to creating a resilient and learning organization. Attraction of the "quants," selection of aggressive financial engineers, and attrition of those unable or unwilling to adopt the ethos of short-term performance enforced a systemically myopic culture. Experience with failure, or at the very least organizational memory via strict procedures, is critical to the long-term welfare and resilience of the sector.

Moreover, we suggest that the existence of very high salaries and bonuses in the financial sector may be directly in opposition to the creation of resilience. With the recent public outcry about high bonuses at floundering institutions, as well as in finance generally, a common retort among industry insiders is that high compensation is necessary to retain talent. Beyond the now-banal observation that the industry would be better off without the type of "talent" that created the recent financial crisis, we also find it apparent that high compensation actually reduces resilience by reducing commitment to the industry and its institutions. When a typical new investment-banking recruit can expect to receive more money in the first four to five years than the cumulative lifetime earnings of the average American, he or she cannot reasonably be expected to care about the long-term health of the industry.

Moreover, high turnover further encourages a short-term mentality, thus resulting in annual bonuses becoming the main motivation among bankers. In his March 18, 2010, article in the *New York Times*, William Cohen put it succinctly: "For goodness sake, what other business on the face of the earth, aside from Wall Street, pays out between 50 percent and 60 percent of each dollar of revenue generated to employees in the form of compensation!"[10] Indeed, even in the first quarter of 2010, amid a still-depressed job market and recovering economy, Goldman Sachs contributed more than $5 billion to its bonus pool while its gross profits stood at $11.8 billion. This represents 43 percent of gross profit dedicated to bonuses, which is only slightly down from the firm's historical average of between 49 percent and 50 percent. One might imagine this was only because of its strong return to profitability in 2010; however, it paid 55 percent of gross profits out in bonuses in 2009, and its 2008 bonuses exceeded profits by more than $8 billion. Other financial institutions show a similar pattern: Morgan Stanley paid out 57 percent of gross revenues in 2009 despite a net loss, and Bank of America paid approximately $4.4 billion in 2009 bonuses to its investment-banking employees while netting only $6.3 billion in profits.

Even with some newly instituted three-year vesting periods, the types of payouts that yield hundreds of thousands of dollars for the typical investment banker cannot help but cultivate a get-it-while-you-can mentality. Unlike industries in which individuals need to commit thirty or more years to their work to earn a comfortable retirement, many investment bankers expect this in less than a decade. This creates a systematic disconnect between the enduring health of a financial firm and the future well-being of the decision makers in that firm. Furthermore, this is another situation in which within-firm and within-system attributes reinforce each other: risk taking in the industry leads to periodic financial crises, which leads to individual incentives to take outsized risks and earn outsized profits before the next collapse.

Deference to Expertise

> HROs cultivate diversity, not just because it helps them notice more in complex environments, but also because it helps them do more with the complexities they spot. Rigid hierarchies have their own special vulnerability to error. Errors at higher levels tend to pick up and combine with errors at lower levels, thereby making the resulting problem bigger, harder to comprehend, and more prone to escalation. . . . Decisions are

> made on the front line, and authority migrates to the people with the
> most expertise, regardless of their rank. . . . HROs differentiate between
> normal times, high-tempo times, and emergencies and clearly signal
> which mode they are operating in. Decisions come from the top when it
> is normal, they migrate during high-tempo operations, and a predefined
> emergency structure kicks in when there is danger.
> —*Weick and Sutcliffe*, Managing the Unexpected, 16–17

At first glance, having "deference to expertise" seems to be one of the few ways financial organizations operate like high-reliability organizations. However, the type of expertise they employ and the metamorphosis of the command structure, both within and between financial institutions, during the recent crisis reveal failures here, too.

Financial institutions do respect expertise—but not a diverse form of expertise. As noted above, wages and legitimacy are tied to the ability to produce and interpret the complex and opaque statistical instruments of finance, and it is that expertise to which the sector particularly defers. The heavy quantification of the financial sector allowed institutions to arbitrage increasingly narrow inefficiencies, both removing slack from the system and making them heavily dependent on, and attentive to, expertise in statistical modeling. We take the high prevalence of math, physics, and statistics Ph.D.'s on Wall Street (along with the occasional finance degree) as evidence to this effect. Rather, industry experts—those who have actually worked in some meaningful and concrete way in a particular sector—have more qualitative, fine-grained, hard-to-transfer knowledge of the sector and its attributes. This form of local knowledge garners them little respect or attention, but we suggest that is exactly the sort of expertise that leads an organization to be sensitive to early signs of trouble. Bankers who had personal experience working in the real estate sector would be more circumspect about the dangers of purchasing obligations based heavily on subprime mortgages, as they would have understood the propensity for defaults and foreclosures to affect other properties, and the recent changes in the quality of mortgages being granted.

In addition, the migration of authority during a crisis in the financial sector is almost perfectly inverse of that in an HRO. During the profitable and freewheeling times before a crisis, decision making in financial institutions tends to be highly diffused, with individual traders given extreme degrees of latitude to commit money and increase leverage. This is part of the reason many rogue traders over the years were able to rack up billions in losses without the knowledge of their superiors. At the onset of a crisis, decision making tends to become centralized in the executive team. This migration of authority also led to the recently exposed unethical accounting methods employed by Lehman Brothers. The Repo 105 transactions began only after the onset of the financial crisis and the centralization of authority at the investment bank. A group of top executives established the contracts, not a lower-level set of traders. In a system with more diffuse authority and ground-level expertise during a crisis, such large-scale deception would be difficult to coordinate and nearly impossible to hide for so long.

Finally, we suggest that centralizing decision authority during the crisis generated a deeper systemic shock than would likely have occurred otherwise. When the crisis began, instead of authority moving from strong central control toward experts, the executives in each institution, along with the heads of the Treasury Department and the Federal Reserve, sharply and suddenly centralized decision making. If this had not happened, it is unlikely that we would have witnessed the level of credit paralysis that occurred during the months following the bankruptcy of Lehman. Executives in each institution quashed lending in an effort to insulate themselves from the toxic assets they were afraid of acquiring. Not only did this stop the transfer of the intended securities, but it had two perverse side effects: it tightened credit on solvent institutions, encouraging emergency measures such as rapid layoffs and buying freezes; and it prevented the very market functions and transactions that would have appropriately valued the toxic assets themselves. With the lending freeze in effect, troubled securities could not lose value in an orderly fashion, but instead they became pariahs, with their market values plummeting to well below appropriate levels, as there was no market for them at all.

Devolution of lending authority to industry experts, regional offices, and local branches (in the case of the commercial banks) might have buffered the crisis rather than exacerbating it. Experts would have responded to attractive asset prices, stimulating buying as values fell, while local lenders would have been able to better distinguish between businesses and sectors that were creditworthy and those that would be destroyed by a recession. Using local knowledge to guide lending could have averted a substantial number of layoffs and much of the decrease in commerce that the nation experienced, as stable and collateral-rich firms would have retained credit access, thereby enabling them to modulate their activities to fit the new economic climate rather than treating the situation as a worst-case scenario.

Conclusions

Lloyd Blankfein, chairman and chief executive officer of Goldman Sachs Group Inc., told the Financial Crisis Inquiry Commission about the executives' state of awareness in fall of 2008, saying, "I know it's become part of the narrative that people knew what was going to happen at any minute. We never knew what was happening at any minute."[11] We assert that everyone should have known the financial crisis was a possibility, and that many would have seen the warning signs if the finance culture had a preoccupation with failure and a reluctance to simplify interpretations. Those who were aware of the risks but were unwilling or unable to voice their concerns because of the structure of the system and its incentives might have been able and encouraged to speak up if the culture were committed to resilience and sensitive to operations. Those who did voice concerns might have been listened to if the culture had greater diversity and more deference to expertise. Finally, we argue that these attributes, coupled with greater transparency, individual liability, and a long-term focus, might have decreased the excessive risk taking and leverage so prevalent throughout the system.

It is essential to note that high-reliability organizing is a continual process, not an end result that can be achieved and then no longer attended to. In any dynamic system, the underlying conditions are constantly changing and require continual mindfulness, creativity, and reflection to address them. These facts are antagonistic to the present short-term profit orientation of the financial industry. Current ownership structures, compensation incentives, and modeling methods focus attention and incentives on maximizing the next quarter's or year's profits. Beyond the component failures of individual errors or violations, the large number of semi-independent, yet highly mutually reliant components yields a system particularly prone to unexpected interactions and vulnerable to the resulting consequences. Too often, short-term profit-maximizing behavior decreases resilience in the long term by removing buffering slack from the system, thus causing a cascade of results: high levels of mimicry between firms, expanded variance and volatility in the market, increased covariance between asset classes, and systemic risk arising from the entire financial industry behaving as if it were one large firm.

In no way do we suggest that high-reliability measures absent of economic and policy changes are sufficient to change finance—only a strategy combining firm-level with system-level reliability measures is bound to succeed. We suggest that, together with incentive realignment and some base-level rules of the game enforced through regulation, building a sensitive and resilient system requires incorporating long-term focus through training on safety margins in leveraging instruments, instilling attention to different perspectives and appreciation of sector expertise, and promoting a strong culture of long-term institutional success.

Recommendations

In the context of regulation, the finance industry would benefit from being introduced to high-reliability processes and provided with incentives to embrace them. Many managers have found the following five processes useful in improving their organization's reliability. We use these guidelines to suggest firm- and industry-level recommendations.[12]

Process auditing enhances reliability by establishing systems for ongoing checks and balances designed to identify expected as well as unexpected problems; follow-ups on problems identified by previous audits are critical. In engineering sectors, process auditing includes safety drills and equipment testing. With respect to the financial sector, we see the Barings breakdown as an example of the failure of process auditing. In that case, Barings was willing to forgo its standard supervision mechanisms because of a rogue trader's perceived short-term profitability. Regulatory oversight needs to include occasional risk audits that respond dynamically—increasing the level of oversight and stringency as risks rise, and demanding that internal risk monitoring and prevention procedures be strictly enforced.

The reward system is the payoff an individual or organization receives for behaving in an expected way. Organizational reward systems have powerful influences on the behavior of individuals in them. Every organization needs to assess whether it rewards the behavior it desires—for reference, we point to a classic study in organizational science addressing the fallacy of rewarding behavior A while hoping for behavior B.[13] The correspondence between incentives and legitimacy-conveying attributes in the financial industry caused those firms to adopt risky behaviors to maximize short-term rewards. This was a product not only of economic forces but also of a legitimization of risky behaviors, as noted above. Keying individual-level rewards to long-term organizational performance is vital, such as with bonuses that vest over decades or as retirement benefits, and are subject to possible clawbacks.

The potential for quality degradation has to be monitored constantly. One way to monitor quality is to identify a referent organization generally considered of the highest quality in the industry. In this case, we equate quality less with absolute return than with sustainable operations and reliable returns over time. We suggest a financial rating institution that models risk, including systemic fragility and behavioral risk, with periodic stress tests (as Treasury Secretary Timothy Geithner recently performed), with an eye to sustainability and giving ratings accordingly. As with the Japanese Top Runner program, in which the most energy-efficient appliances set the new standard for the industry, the practices of the highest-rated institutions would be promulgated as part of a suite of risk management options.

Failure to adequately perceive and assess risk is the proverbial elephant in the room. The attraction to complex, statistical models at the expense of safety margins and broad-based local knowledge led industry executives to be wildly overconfident in their ability to arbitrage at the edges of safe performance. There are two elements of risk perception: whether knowledge exists about the risk the organization faces and whether the organization does anything about it. A multifaceted approach is warranted here. In order to create internal incentives to perceive and mitigate risk, the aforementioned long-term-oriented reward system will be useful; however, it will be insufficient on its own. Additional, even contradictory, perspectives are necessary to perceive a diverse and dynamic set of risks. These perspectives should include those from outside the institutions, offering a spectrum of response and mitigation options that evolve with increasing risk levels. This would make use of the rating organization and tests discussed in the previous paragraphs, along with industry experts who would serve as an independent panel of advisers. The panel would provide input on the construction of stress tests to the ratings organization and would generate crisis and response scenarios for both the rating organization and the financial institutions. Moreover, it should be deliberately diverse, including former institutional insiders, former regulators, and the often-ignored industry critics (e.g., Nassim Taleb, Nouriel Roubini). Generated scenarios should be similarly diverse, not limited to the worst cases previously experienced, but projecting even larger disruptions and disjunctions to reflect the empirically observed nature of market volatility.

Finally, we suggest integrating some command-and-control mechanisms into human resource operations. Because high reliability is often concerned with high-tempo environments (e.g., landing aircrafts on carrier decks), we think that some of the usual HRO recommendations do not quite fit in this case. Instead, we focus on recommending redundancy of both people and

hardware as a built-in auditing system and incorporating training on reliability and long-term focus both at the firm level and in MBA programs.

The benefits of employing high-reliability principles in finance would not
only accrue in the financial sector. In a recent *New York Times* article, David
Leonhardt writes:

> The obvious reason to re-regulate finance is to prevent the next crisis or at
> least to make it less damaging. But there are other potential benefits to reform.
> Consider what has happened to the American economy over the last three de-
> cades. Highly leveraged financial firms have become a dominant part of the
> economy. Their profits allowed the firms to recruit many of the country's most
> sought-after employees—mathematicians, scientists, top college graduates and
> top former government officials. Yet many of those profits turned out to be
> ephemeral. So some of the best minds were devoted to devising ever-more-
> complex means of creating money out of thin air, the proceeds of which then
> drew in even more talent.[14]

However, the problem turns out to be even worse than that when the results are traced further. The fruits of these talented individuals' labor were
not merely ephemeral; they were poisonous. Creating the illusion of low-risk
securities out of diced-up risky loans drove an enormous amount of capital
into the real estate industry—far more than would have otherwise entered.
That same illusion of safety encouraged stunning leverage ratios, often in
excess of 30 to 1, which amplified the impact of the crisis just as they were
intended to amplify the size of the profits. Taken together, these factors generated a massive misallocation of capital, wasting not only the minds involved
but also the resources of the nation. The worst part of this bust—as with tech
stocks, railroads, and tulips before—isn't just the current problems but the
revelation that the boom was actually a counterproductive fantasy.

Insofar as they can help buffer out volatility in organizational and systemic performance, use of high-reliability principles not only reduces the oc-
currence of catastrophes but also helps ensure that episodes of growth and
success are genuinely beneficial. Systems with sustainable, well-founded, and
low-volatility growth are unlikely to commit resources frivolously or excessively. To avoid the bust, they also avoid the explosive boom, which is the
ultimate source of misallocation. As John Stewart Mill wrote, "Panics do
not destroy capital; they merely reveal the extent to which it has been previously destroyed by its betrayal into hopelessly unproductive works." High-
reliability principles applied in finance will likely yield a return to the days of

"boring" banking, but that kind of boredom would surely come as a relief to almost everyone now.

Postscript

In early 2011, as we submit the final formatted text of this chapter for publication, circumstances have reverted to something like business as usual: investment banks have returned to handing out record-breaking bonuses; the bankers have returned to conspicuous displays of wealth; the S&P 500 is back above 1,300 and making new fifty-two-week highs regularly (returning to within 14 percent of its all-time high); and financial practitioners have renamed some of their investment strategies and are applying them to new industries and asset classes (often in opaque off-book transactions). While all this occurs, the official U.S. rate of unemployment remains above 9 percent, possible sovereign defaults loom, new bubbles continue to inflate, only a fraction of necessary reregulating legislation has been proposed and passed, and financial executives remain almost entirely ignorant of HRO principles and practices. Although it is foolish to predict a specific date or triggering event, it seems that the seeds of the next financial crisis are already being sown.

Notes

1. Karl E. Weick and Kathleen M. Sutcliffe, *Managing the Unexpected: Assuring High Performance in an Age of Complexity* (San Francisco: Jossey-Bass, 2007), 10–17.

2. Robert Pozen, *Too Big to Save? How to Fix the U.S. Financial System* (Hoboken, NJ: John Wiley & Sons, 2010), 127.

3. Bank for International Settlements, "Semiannual OTC Derivatives Markets' Statistics," February 23, 2011, http://www.bis.org/statistics/otcder/dt1920a.pdf.

4. James Dimon, testimony before the Financial Crisis Inquiry Commission, First Public Hearing, Panel 1, January 13, 2010, http://fcic.law.stanford.edu/videos/view/17 (at approximately minute 134).

5. Michiyo Nakamoto and David Wighton, "Citigroup Chief Stays Bullish on Buy-Outs," *Financial Times*, July 9, 2007.

6. Michael Lewis, interview on *Charlie Rose*, March 16, 2010, http://www.charli erose.com/view/interview/10911.

7. Nassim Taleb, testimony before the U.S. Congress Committee on Science and Technology, September 10, 2009.

8. Warren Buffett, as quoted in "Indecent Exposure," *Economist*, August 5, 2007.

9. Toshihide Iguchi, as interviewed in "I Didn't Set Out to Rob a Bank," *Time*, February 10, 1997.

10. William Cohen, "Lehman's Demise, Dissected," *New York Times*, March 18, 2010, http://opinionator.blogs.nytimes.com/2010/03/18/lehmans-demise-dissected/.

11. Lloyd Blankfein, testimony before the Financial Crisis Inquiry Commission, First Public Hearing, Panel 1, January 13, 2010, http://fcic.law.stanford.edu/videos/view/17 (at approximately minute 183).

12. Carolyn B. Libuser, "Organizational Structure and Risk Mitigation" (Ph.D. dissertation, University of California, Los Angeles, 1994).

13. Steven Kerr, "On the Folly of Rewarding A While Hoping for B," *Academy of Management Journal* 18 (1975): 769–83.

14. David Leonhardt, "Heading Off the Next Financial Crisis," *New York Times*, March 22, 2010.

10 Wrong Assumptions and Risk Cultures

Deeper Causes of the Global Financial Crisis

Ian I. Mitroff and Can M. Alpaslan

The causes of the global financial crisis are not merely financial. The crisis did not happen merely because we failed to understand the technical aspects or the economic implications of financial products and innovations. The deeper causes lie within us and within the institutions we create.

In the following sections, we analyze two contributing factors to the global financial crisis: (1) the economics and finance departments in business schools and universities and (2) Wall Street. Specifically, we look at a set of assumptions that constitute the deepest inner core of these institutions. By definition, assumptions are not easily visible to those outside of an institution or industry. In fact, because assumptions are taken for granted, they are often invisible to those on the inside as well. As a result, they are largely unconscious and difficult to question. Nonetheless, their effects can be devastating. That is why we believe it is imperative that, before jumping to any conclusions about the causes or remedies of the current global financial crisis, scholars examine in depth the cultures of these two institutions and the validity of their assumptions.

A Risky Definition of Risk

We turn our focus first to some of the fundamental assumptions held by economics and finance departments (EFDs) and the way they define risk.

This chapter is based on *Swans, Swines, and Swindlers: Coping with the Growing Threat of Mega-Crises and Mega-Messes* (Stanford, CA: Stanford University Press, 2011).

We believe that the culture of most EFDs is characterized by a reductionistic mind-set. For instance, the EFDs assume generally that human motivation, a complex phenomenon with many facets, can be reduced to self-interest,[1] human emotion to fear and greed,[2] all available information about asset values to market prices,[3] and all information about the riskiness of assets to asset price volatility.[4] In fact, their obsession with reductionism lies at the heart of their flawed approach to defining and measuring risk.

In their research programs and curricula, EFDs put heavy emphasis on measurement, quantification, and precision. Thus, historically, for the EFDs, risk has been a complex issue to define and measure. But when the EFDs were finally able to reduce risk to asset price volatility, risk was no longer a vague concept. Equipped with the tools of math and statistics, the EFDs began to model risk as if it were measurable and thus more real. Of course, such a big reductionistic move was supported by the EFDs' reductionistic assumptions about human nature and markets.

Unfortunately, it was not easy for outsiders, or even insiders to the economics profession, to question the EFDs' questionable assumptions or to present disconfirming evidence against them.[5] Their assumptions were held by a great number of scholars and Nobel Prize winners, and some of the most reputable journals, such as the *Journal of Finance*, were dominated by these scholars. Questioning the dominant culture also meant lowering one's chances of publishing in top journals and getting tenured. One may argue that the culture of the academic tenure system was another factor that had contributed to the global financial crisis and must be included in an attempt to understand it.

In summary, the EFDs' culture of reductionism and quantification—with the help of the tenure system—turned the fuzzy concept of risk into a precise measure. These developments started affecting the global financial system and the global economy when Wall Street not only accepted the academic conceptualization and measurement of risk, but also began to use it to quantify risk, portfolio diversification, performance of money managers, and so on.

Wall Street: A Culture of Risk

The academic definition of risk, which failed to account for unknown unknowns, had two more flaws: it assumed that the past is a perfect indicator of the future and that investors are rational.[6] Although some academics warned Wall Street that the risk models it created were inaccurate, Wall Street didn't care much. After all, the academics' definition of risk was useful: it allowed Wall Street to quantify risk and to create financial products (e.g., index funds, exchange-traded funds, derivatives, securitization, collateralized debt obligations, collateralized mortgage obligations) that could be easily sold to the global economy. As these financial tools spread risk around the globe and allowed Wall Street to leverage its gains, they also increased the correlation among various asset classes. Over time, these financial products became more complex, and world markets became more tightly coupled.

True, the complexity of the financial instruments involved and the lack of proper regulation of the industry are certainly key factors in understanding the current financial crisis. But one of the most important underlying causes of the crisis was the general assumptions of those at the top the finance industry and the culture they promoted and rewarded.[7]

Since the global financial crisis started to unfold, the first author has had repeated conversations with a friend—call him Adam Smith (which is not his real name or necessarily indicative of gender; in fact, Adam is a composite of several people)—who works for a major bank. Adam has uncovered a set of primary assumptions and beliefs that were at the heart of the financial industry. The assumptions and beliefs that he has exposed result from hours of interviews and conversations that Adam has conducted with some of the top analysts, managers, and executives of Wall Street. They are also the result of his analyzing countless books, reports, and articles. They derive as well from Adam's many hours of working among and thus observing at firsthand the behavior of the "natives."

The following set of assumptions or beliefs Adam observed not only tell us about the dominant culture on Wall Street but also reveal the dark side of Wall Street:

- We are the masters of the universe; we can manipulate anything and anybody to our advantage; we can game the numbers and the system to serve our needs.

- We're smarter than anyone else; unless you are as smart as us, you can't possibly understand the complicated financial instruments we've invented.[8]

- We don't need controls and regulations. We have been selected for our unique skills and talents. As a result, we know what's best for us.

- We bet and play with others' money. It's a high-risk, high-reward environment. It's not for everyone.

- We are entitled to the huge amounts of money we make because of the value of the huge deals that we bring to market.[9]
- We don't fail—period! We're too big and important to fail. Indeed, the world cannot allow us to fail because we are essential to the functioning of the world's capital markets.[10]
- Because numbers are the only things that really matter, we can manage risk by reducing it to a mathematical equation.[11]
- You are only as good as your last kill, that is, big deal. If you are not producing, then you are not valued.[12]
- To succeed, you have to make difficult decisions. There is no room for bleeding hearts. If to get ahead you have to fire your best friend, then don't think twice about doing it.[13]
- We can't control the markets. We just pay attention to today and to the transactions immediately in front of us that are within our control.
- If you're standing still, then you're moving backward.
- We are a culture based on performance. We are constantly grading and weeding out the weak and underperforming.[14]

All of the preceding assumptions and beliefs reflect the narrow-mindedness and insularity of Wall Street. They express a deep sense of entitlement and narcissism, as well as an inability and/or unwillingness to self-regulate. In fact, these assumptions and beliefs constitute a self-sealing and perpetuating system. In many ways, they are defense mechanisms.

Table 10.1 shows how the set of assumptions and beliefs identified above reinforced one another and has led, as a whole, to dangerous Freudian defense mechanisms that we were able to observe on Wall Street.[15] The first column of Table 10.1 gives the traditional form of a particular defense mechanism as it was first discovered. The second column of Table 10.1 provides an example.

The Silent Majority: Victims, Villains, or Both?

Obviously, not everyone in the industry subscribes fully to these beliefs, but the majority either overlooked or tolerated these assumptions and beliefs to a great degree. In fact, a great number of stakeholders both inside and outside of Wall Street mostly remained silent and enjoyed the ride. Here is a partial list of those stakeholders:

TABLE 10.1 Freudian defense mechanisms on Wall Street

Defense Mechanism	Example
Disavowal: Impacts are negligible! We are in control!	Bernanke said in March 2007 to Congress's Joint Economic Committee, "The impact on the broader economy and financial markets of the problems in the subprime markets seems likely to be contained."[a]
Idealization: We don't have problems!	Before the financial crisis, Wall Street was extremely confident that its risk management models worked well.[b]
Denial: We are not wrong!	Most finance and economics departments insisted for many years that the efficient market hypothesis was correct and that the markets were rational and efficient.[c]
Grandiosity: We're big, powerful, and important!	Several large financial institutions and companies believed that they were too big to fail.
Projection: We are the victims! They are to blame!	AIG blamed the "perfect financial storm" for its woes.[d]
Intellectualization: The probability something big will happen is small!	Long-Term Capital Management collapsed as a result of a low-probability event that its risk models ignored.[e]
Compartmentalization: It can't affect the whole system!	A small London branch office (with a dozen or so staff) brought down AIG.[f]

[a] "Mortgage Problems Aren't Spreading to Economy," *Minneapolis Star Tribune*, March 28, 2007, http://www.startribune.com/business/11216636.html?elr=KarksUUUodey3lGdiO7aiU.

[b] Emily Thornton, "Inside Wall Street's Culture of Risk," *Bloomberg Businessweek*, June 12, 2006, http://www.businessweek.com/magazine/content/06_24/b3988004.htm.

[c] Justin Fox, *The Myth of the Rational Market* (New York: HarperBusiness, 2009).

[d] Al Bawaba, "AIG Blames 'Perfect Financial Storm' for Its Woes," August 6, 2009, ProQuest, ABI/INFORM Trade and Industry (1819062511).

[e] Roger Lowerstein, *When Genius Failed: The Rise and Fall of Long-Term Capital Management* (New York: Random House, 2001)

[f] Peter Koeing, "AIG Trail Leads to London Casino," *London Telegraph*, October 18, 2008, http://www.telegraph.co.uk/finance/financialcrisis/3225213/AIG-trail-leads-to-London-casino.html.

- Fannie Mae and Freddie Mac, which relaxed their underwriting standards
- Politicians who forced Fannie and Freddie to do so
- Home buyers who borrowed too much to pay for a house they could not afford
- Credit-rating agencies that, without appropriate statistical or otherwise analyses, gave AAA ratings to risky mortgage-backed securities

- Home builders who built excessively
- Suppliers of construction materials, manufacturers of automobiles, furniture, appliances, and televisions who produced excessively
- States that happily collected property taxes on new home sales

To put it mildly, something is wrong with this picture. It is, in fact, inherently unethical. The silent majority dutifully and silently played its role, and assumed (and hoped) that home prices would continue to skyrocket while money remained cheap. Some believed that they would be able to sell their overpriced homes later to a bigger fool. Thus, everyone took their increasing home values and gambled with them, doubling down with each win but playing with the "house" money. When the roll was over, when the house of cards collapsed, all parties stood up, stunned, beaten, their assumptions shattered.

Are the aforementioned players victims or villains? Have they contributed to the financial crisis, or were they merely its victims? Or are they both at once?

It is the experience of being both a victim and a villain, greedy and taken advantage of all at once, that makes the financial crisis existential. In the end, once the crisis had struck and shattered shared, collective assumptions, the players dutifully got into a firing line of their own making, except the line became a circle. And the global financial crisis became a crisis of confidence. It became an unwillingness to believe in one another, as parties saw the face of greed and shortsightedness deeply grounded not only in Wall Street's culture but also in the global collective consciousness.

The real cause of the financial crisis is simply our unquestioned assumptions and beliefs, and the institutions we create.

To avoid triggering defense mechanisms such as the ones we identified earlier in the chapter, and their devastating effects, the now-global financial system must be able to question and change its assumptions and beliefs. It must move away from a culture of selfishness and narcissism and toward a culture of trust.

A Culture of Trust

A financial system is basically a trust-based system. No financial system can operate effectively without trust.

Even after the financial crisis, most of us still have to assume that our financial system is trustworthy. For instance, we still trust that money is a valid form of payment and assume that others do as well. We trust that the banks will be there tomorrow. We trust that our pension funds, insurance companies, and investment advisers have our best interests at heart. We trust policy makers. We trust the Fed chair's monetary policies. In short, trust is the central assumption in any financial system.

Thus, we offer a set of counterassumptions or beliefs that a trust-enhancing financial system would have:

- We are the moral masters of the universe; we never manipulate anything or anybody to our advantage.
- We have been selected for our unique moral values. Although we can self-regulate, we also want controls and regulations.
- We never bet with your money. We don't take unnecessary risks with your money that we wouldn't take with ours. We know what's best for you and all of us.
- We are not entitled to the amounts of money we make unless we do so responsibly.
- We make mistakes! We know we are essential to the functioning of the world's capital markets. That is why we will not get too big to fail.
- Moral values matter. We manage risk but never reduce it to a mathematical equation.
- We are only as moral as our last action. If we are not acting morally, then we ought not to be valued.
- To succeed, we have to make difficult decisions. But there is no room for machismo. We try to make the best decisions, and we never put aside our values and emotions.
- We can't control the markets. But we do our best to pay attention to the future.
- We are a culture based on trust. We are constantly grading and weeding out the untrustworthy.

Summary

The primary purpose of this chapter has been to identify one of the main causes of the global financial crisis: the assumptions, beliefs, and cultures of Wall Street and EFDs.

We first focused on the role of academia. Specifically, we argued that the EFDs played an important role in contributing to the current financial crisis. Next, we focused on another influential factor: Wall Street's culture of risk.

We also emphasized that many stakeholders remained silent and kept dancing while the music was on. We could have looked at the deep-seated assumptions and beliefs of these stakeholders and many others, including the Fed, the Securities and Exchange Commission, or the Treasury Department, to improve our understanding of the global financial crisis. By no means is our analysis complete. But the key point is this: the main cause or the remedy of the global financial crisis is not merely financial; it is also cultural. The financial system needs to move from a culture of selfishness and narcissism to a culture of trust.

Notes

1. Richard Thaler, "From *Homo economicus* to *Homo sapiens*," *Journal of Economic Perspectives* 14, no. 1 (2000): 133–41; Jane J. Mansbridge, ed., *Beyond Self-Interest* (Chicago: University of Chicago Press, 1990).

2. Jocelyn Pixley, *Emotions in Finance* (Cambridge: Cambridge University Press, 2004).

3. Justin Fox, *The Myth of the Rational Market* (New York: HarperBusiness, 2009).

4. Ibid.

5. Ibid.

6. Donald Mackenzie, "Long-Term Capital Management and the Sociology of Arbitrage," *Economy and Society* 32, no. 3 (2003): 349–80.

7. For an in-depth treatment of many of these same assumptions that constitute the culture of Wall Street, see Karen Ho, *Liquidated: An Ethnography of Wall Street* (Durham, NC: Duke University Press, 2009). See also Sim B. Sitkin and Amy L. Pablo, "Reconceptualizing the Determinants of Risk Behavior," *Academy of Management Review* 17 (1992): 21–22.

8. Bethany McLean and Peter Elkind, *Smartest Guys in the Room: The Amazing Rise and Scandalous Fall of Enron* (New York: Penguin, 2003).

9. James Stewart, *Den of Thieves* (New York: Simon & Schuster, 1992).

10. Andrew Ross Sorkin, *Too Big to Fail: The Inside Story of How Wall Street and Washington Fought to Save the Financial System—and Themselves* (New York: Penguin, 2009).

11. Roger Lowenstein, *When Genius Failed: The Rise and Fall of Long-Term Capital Management* (New York: Random House, 2000).

12. Ho, *Liquidated.*

13. Ibid.

14. McLean and Elkind, *Smartest Guys in the Room.*

15. Anna Freud, *The Ego and the Mechanisms of Defense* (New York: International Universities Press, 1967).

Comments

11 A Busy Decade

Lessons Learned from Crisis Planning and Response from 1999 to 2009

Michael Berkowitz

As we enter the second decade of the twenty-first century, crisis managers and executives are faced with more uncertainty than ever. On the hazard front, myriad threats loom: political instability and terrorism; continued public health threats; an increasingly interconnected and complex, though not necessarily more resilient, utility infrastructure; and annually increasing death, damage, and disruption associated with extreme weather events.

Additionally, for private-sector planners, two other factors make crisis planning more challenging and more important. First, the business and political worlds are more interconnected, and following the economic crisis of 2008–2009, regulators and governments are taking a greater interest in the risk management of the firms operating in their jurisdictions. Second, as globalization expands the geographic footprint of many organizations, operating strategies are evolving in ways that make risk and crisis management more complex.

In such an environment, planners would do well to look to crises of the past ten years and take stock of what worked and didn't during an exceptionally busy decade globally for crisis managers. And it's possible the lessons learned by managers responsible for business continuity and crisis management may have broader relevance for managers of other types of crises, including for executives and economists concerned with the management of financial crisis.

In my mind, three lessons are the importance of both all hazards and hazard-specific planning, using crisis management processes and systems frequently and for small events to build capacity, and focusing on communications to stakeholders. I explore those lessons in more detail later.

In the late twentieth century, before the attacks of September 11, emergency planners in New York City did consider terrorism a significant threat. They used federal funds to run exercises focusing on scenarios of weapons of mass destruction, created the country's first chemical- and biological-terrorism response plans, and regularly engaged federal law enforcement and response agencies on the subject of terrorism response and recovery.

Even so, over the late 1990s, New York City emergency planners did significant and detailed work around hurricane preparedness, because the city is significantly at risk to rare but catastrophic hurricane impact.[1] Over those years, planners worked on debris management protocols (examining, for example, where to move the huge amount of debris generated from a hurricane landfall and which agencies had trucks, loaders, and other equipment), did damage assessment planning (identifying the structural engineers and looking at how to integrate their data), and planned for mass evacuation and sheltering operations.

None of those actions was undertaken with a 9/11 (or for that matter any terrorist) scenario in mind. Following the collapse of the towers, much of that work paid off. Although plans were in various states of completion and many had to be modified to better fit the unique circumstances of the 9/11 incident (e.g., much of this debris pile was on fire for days and weeks following the collapse), the hurricane response planning did help city, state, and federal responders and contractors respond quickly and efficiently.

In the years following 2001, New York City planners reevaluated preparedness efforts to more explicitly account for all hazards. They created generic debris management, damage assessment, communications, and other functional plans so that the applicability during all types of events was more apparent.

The most generic of all plans, the Citywide Incident Management System (CIMS) is modeled on the federal government's National Incident Management System (NIMS). It considers the most basic and generic elements of a response effort: which agencies and personnel have what responsibility during emergencies. Following criticism of its incident management during 9/11, New York City spent significant time on its incident management system leading up to the unveiling of CIMS in 2004. The protocols, though not perfect, have been used in plane crashes, steam explosions, and building collapses, to name a few types of events.

Although broad, flexible plans are important, crisis managers would also be wise to carefully consider specific disaster scenarios and account for unique response needs generated by such events. The kind of mass prophylaxis required by a large-scale clandestine anthrax release requires certain medical stockpiles, response systems, and personnel that will be used only in such an incident. If planners believe that such an attack is likely—as they did in the United States in the late 1990s—then specific hazard planning must follow.

In that effort, New York City planners worked on a very specific scenario: a clandestine release of anthrax, requiring the prophylaxis on all 8 million New York City residents in thirty-six to forty-eight hours. The plan that emerged (using schools and untrained workers to quickly distribute antibiotics) has virtually no application for any other scenario.

Indeed, when several institutions (including NBC News) received anthrax letters in October 2001, the evaluation and prophylaxis of those at risk was undertaken in a much different and controlled manner. Nevertheless, recognizing the specific needs of an identified risk scenario (in this case, the clandestine, large-scale release of anthrax) is essential no matter how broad and all-hazards-applicable we are tempted to make our plans.

This dichotomy is an important lesson as planners prepare for a new generation of paradigm-shifting events (make sure your plans are broad and widely applicable) as well as predictable but disruptive disasters (develop specific addenda or separate plans to account for high-risk events).

In 1996, after he created the Mayor's Office of Emergency Management (OEM) in New York City, Mayor Giuliani asked OEM to respond to myriad small-scale emergencies that befall a city of that size every day. The OEM personnel would respond to large house fires, water main breaks, and small building collapses. Additionally, OEM would activate the city's emergency operations center (EOC) for relatively small-scale heat and power emergencies and for predictions of moderate snowfall. Such activity and attention by an emergency management agency went beyond the scope of most such agencies nationally at that time, which were (and to a large degree still are) built to respond to significant or catastrophic incidents and coordinate recovery and rebuilding operations. Although the response to 9/11 has its share of well-chronicled problems,[2] its successes are partly owed to the emphasis and attention that Mayor Giuliani paid to emergency planning and response, and the frequency with which the city used those personnel and systems. Such frequency ensured that the major players in the response and recovery efforts were largely familiar with one another and with the systems and processes that were used over the following six months.

This model can be implemented on a smaller scale. Over 2008, Deutsche Bank used its crisis management system for ninety-two separate incidents in Asia alone. This was no accident and is not a statement about the exceptionally risky environment in which Deutsche Bank Asia operates. Instead, it is part of a conscious effort on the part of the bank's management to handle various low-level incidents using a crisis management terminology and structure. In 2008, most of those incidents were relatively minor events—small typhoons, telecom outages, labor unrest, and political demonstrations—that could have been handled by the business-as-usual silos and escalation procedures. But Deutsche Bank employed its crisis management process to instill the process of convening tactical managers and strategic decision makers and of distributing updates and information to a broad range of internal stakeholders.

When the Mumbai terrorist attacks happened in late November of that year, the bank had a lot of practice with crisis management, and although any rapidly unfolding event can cause decision-making and information-sharing issues, the incident was largely handled well by the bank, due in no small part to the practice that the managers had.

In nearly every significant crisis of the past ten years, communication—about the current situation, the prognosis, and how stakeholders and others should react to it and feel about it—has been an essential part of the successful resolution of the situation. This is particularly true in public health emergencies, during which people have complex relationships with the hazard itself, but it is essentially true during all disasters.

Given its importance as a part of our efforts to prepare for, respond to, and recover from incidents, it is surprising that crisis management organizations in both the public and the private sectors aren't more attuned to communications challenges. Often, crisis managers and planners are from tactical response units and don't have either the inclination or skills to handle the critical, challenging, and vast communications challenges that emergencies and disasters pose.

Additionally, as technology develops, the window of opportunity for crisis managers gets smaller.[3] This is particularly true at an investment bank where thousands of important internal stakeholders (i.e., traders) are wired to several live news feeds, viewing as many as eight computer screens at once and instant messaging with their friends at colleagues at client and competitor organizations. In such an environment, word travels fast and crisis managers must communicate quickly or risk letting the incident take on a life of its own.

The solution to this problem might seem counterintuitive. Traditionally, crisis managers (and for that matter executives) have eschewed any type of speculative communication, preferring to release only fully vetted and verified information, even to internal stakeholders. Unfortunately, this is impossible during most crises. Crisis managers must be prepared to speculate but to do so responsibly.[4] They must be clear and transparent about their speculation, so that it's possible for them to correct themselves when the facts become clearer. One good example of this is hurricane forecasters, who publish average error data and engage in long discussions about the various factors that influenced their forecast and what might change their analysis in the near term. At Deutsche Bank, we routinely speculate (at least to internal stakeholders) about causes, impacts, and other aspects of emerging incidents. But we do it responsibly, so that we clearly say what we don't know and what we're doing to find out.

Given the importance of communications, crisis management and communications organizations should be more closely linked in planning, exercising, and responding to such incidents.

. . .

Clearly, it has been a busy decade for planners and responders, and these are but three lessons that can be learned. It is unclear whether the coming ten years will be as busy as the past ten, but we should continue to learn from our successes and failures so as to make us better prepared for what is to come. Also, whether or not as of this writing the financial crisis that started in 2008 is over, crisis managers from that event and those in the fields of operational risk planning, preparedness, and response could learn from one another so that we can more effectively handle the next event, whatever its cause. In the words of President Obama's former chief of staff Rahm Emanuel: "Don't let a good disaster go to waste."

Notes

1. New York City is one of the country's most at-risk cities to catastrophic hurricane damage.

2. Reports on the New York police and fire departments by management consultant firm McKinsey and Company provide comprehensive, if not particularly nuanced, accounts of issues related to the 9/11 response.

3. Nic Gowing, *Skyful of Lies and Black Swans: The New Tyranny of Shifting Information Power in Crises* (Oxford: Oxford University Press, 2010).

4. Much of my thinking on this originates with Peter Sandman, a crisis communications expert. For more information, see his Web site at http://www.psandman .com.

12 A Critique of Managing the Global Financial Crisis

Lessons from Technological Crisis Management

Brett Messing

Analyzing the recent global financial crisis through the prism of technological crisis management is a particularly timely exercise and yields interesting insights into how to better understand and prevent financial crises. However, the massive complexity and interconnected nature of the financial system differentiates it in many important ways from technological breakdowns, product failures, and natural disasters. As the managing partner of GPS Partners, an energy-focused hedge fund that managed more than $2 billion at the onset of the recent financial meltdown, I had a front-row seat for the unprecedented events that began in earnest in 2007.

The chapter outlines the unintended consequences of certain landmark events that ultimately played a key role in triggering the recent financial collapse such as the Community Reinvestment Act, the Gramm-Leach-Bliley Financial Services Modernization Act, and the abolishment of the net capital requirement for investment banks. This failure of lawmakers and regulators to understand how these various events could and would interact to trigger the largest financial meltdown since the Great Depression demonstrates the dangerous combination of politics, a balkanized regulatory system, and an increasingly complicated financial system.

Additionally, I particularly like the use of Goldman Sachs's initial public offering as a metaphor for a financial system in which incentives are asymmetrical. Market participants in a multitude of roles, ranging from bank chief executive officers to hedge-fund managers and lending officers and investment bankers, are extremely well compensated for strong short-term results and bear, on a relative basis, little exposure to transactions that ultimately fail. This incentive structure leads to excessive use of leverage, a focus on the number of transactions rather than the quality of the transactions, and increasing opacity and complexity of products. To expound on this last point, product complexity has led to a real challenge in price discovery. This problem often results in the creators of products determining market prices, and by extension their bonuses, because there is not a robust trading market for highly structured products. There were many, many situations over the past financial meltdown in which market participants attempted to sell securities that had been marked to market at eighty only to find that the buyers were only willing to pay in the thirties.

I concur with the authors of the chapter, who focus on the complexity of the financial system as a root cause for its meltdown. A number of trading businesses, particularly debt securitization and derivatives, have evolved in complexity beyond the understanding of risk managers and, more important, bank chief executive officers. William D. Cohan's *House of Cards: A Tale of Hubris and Wretched Excess on Wall Street* chronicles the collapse of Bear Stearns and makes it clear, in no uncertain terms, that former Chief Executive Officer Jimmy Cayne was ill equipped to lead the company. Cayne was a stockbroker who had deftly climbed the political walls of Bear Stearns to ascend to its corner office. His shallow understanding of the complex mortgage securities traded and owned by Bear Stearns left him helpless to navigate the firm through the recent financial meltdown. A reader of Cohan's book is left more surprised that Bear Stearns survived for as many years as it did rather than shocked by its demise. Merrill Lynch's chief executive officer, Stanley O'Neil, and Citicorp's chief executive officer, Chuck Prince, both seemed to be similarly ill equipped to manage complex trading businesses. It is no surprise that Goldman Sachs, the only major firm run by a chief executive officer with significant trading experience, Lloyd Blankfein, emerged from the financial meltdown in a strong position.

Anecdotally, in my capacity as managing partner of GPS Partners, I regularly interacted with our firm's counterparties regarding financing matters and swap transactions. Given the importance of a counterparty creditworthiness, our trading partners are the largest financial firms in the world. As the financial meltdown accelerated, I increasingly interacted with more senior personnel at these various institutions as they endeavored to assess their counterparty risk. Almost to a firm, I observed that the sophistication level of the personnel was inversely related to their seniority in the firm. If commercial banks continue to derive the majority of their profits from trading businesses, it is incumbent on them to ensure that senior management has significant experience and knowledge about these businesses. Otherwise, the financial collapse of 2008 will surely repeat itself again and again in the coming decades.

I agree with the chapter authors' contention that crises are processes that are spread over space and time, but I am less comfortable with their assertion that there is an initiating triggering event of seminal and symbolic importance. Rather, financial crises seem to be unique in that there are a series of interconnected events that fuel a downward spiral. For example, I date the financial meltdown of 2008 to a series of events that occurred in 2007, including the bankruptcy of New Century Financial Corporation, a leading originator of subprime mortgages; the bankruptcy of two Bear Stearns hedge funds; the virtual collapse of a number of large quantitative hedge funds, culminating in the bailout of Goldman Sachs's Global Equity Opportunities Fund; and the fire sale of Countrywide Financial to Bank of America. Each of these events, listed in chronological order, was unlikely to occur without the preceding event. This daisy chain of events can be carried throughout 2008, including the Bear Stearns and Lehman bankruptcies and the shotgun merger of Merrill Lynch and Bank of America. Although many have sought to identify the U.S. government's decision to allow Lehman Brothers to fail as the triggering event of the financial meltdown, from the position of a market participant, the cow had been out of the barn for more than a year.

The chapter authors highlight three important elements of crises: surprise, speed, and the need for managers to make critical decisions with imperfect information. In retrospect, it seems difficult to understand why the financial meltdown was a surprise given all the facts that we know today. However, as eloquently expressed by the *New York Times* columnist Thomas L. Friedman in a column on May 19, 2002, "The failure to prevent Sept. 11 was not a failure of intelligence or coordination. It was a failure of imagination." Similarly, the financial meltdown of 2008 was caused by a failure of imagination.

Throughout 2006 and 2007, Monday mornings were transformed into merger Mondays as larger and larger private equity acquisitions were announced. The term *private equity deal* was really just a newer, nicer way of describing a leveraged buyout. These highly leveraged transactions were fueled by the securitization boom, which enabled bankers to dice and slice different parts of the capital structure. The markets were so accommodating that

Bloomberg News ran an article on April 2, 2007, titled "Bankers Mull $100 Billion LBO in Year of Record Deals."

The excess liquidity flowing through the financial system became evident to GPS Partners shortly after our launch. Our objective had been to raise $500 million and generate annualized returns between 10 percent and 12 percent. However, within eighteen months, we were managing more than $2 billion and generating returns of more than 30 percent. Additionally, although we did not use much leverage in the management of assets, investment and commercial banks were falling over one another for our business, with most offering four to five times leverage on equity securities. In summary, there were warning signs to market participants that suggested that the prevailing trends were unsustainable, but few, including us, imagined just how bad things could get.

The financial meltdown forced management teams to not just make decisions with imperfect information but to act. Doing nothing was not a realistic alternative. The pressure from various constituencies, including employees, shareholders, board members, regulators, and the media, was immense. Trying to publicly minimize the problem or convey a level of control that did not exist can create legal liabilities and undermine confidence. Additionally, in the aftermath of the WorldCom fraud in which the directors of the company's board settled with plaintiffs by agreeing to pay 20 percent of their personal net worths as restitution, supportive directors can turn on management quite quickly. In some cases, this newfound engagement on the part of directors can be a good thing for companies, whereas in other cases it can lead to action for action's sake. It is not surprising that most of the chief executive officers of the leading investment and commercial banks were forced to resign as the financial tsunami hit their respective companies. In time, historians will evaluate whether these management changes were wise or added greater instability to crisis situations. Nevertheless, they demonstrate the tremendous internal and external pressure on organizations to do something.

Clearly, the surveillance systems at almost every firm broke down or were ignored. It would be a worthwhile exercise to study whether this breakdown occurred because of technological weaknesses and limitations in risk management systems or because of human error. Although most institutions were completely unprepared for the financial meltdown, a handful prospered and others were able to manage through it. Paulson and Co., a $7 billion hedge fund, generated returns in excess of 500 percent by presciently positioning itself for the subprime meltdown. Goldman Sachs put in place a bearish hedge on the subprime market in late 2006 after losing money daily for two consecutive weeks on the firm's mortgage portfolio. The anomalous profit and loss performance of the firm's mortgage portfolio was brought to the attention of the firm's chief financial officer, David Viniar, who encouraged the firm's traders to aggressively hedge its significant exposure to the mortgage market, collateralized debt obligations, and other complex securities. It would be interesting to understand whether Paulson and Co. and Goldman Sachs got lucky or whether their surveillance systems were better constructed and better employed by senior management.

Making decisions with limited information likely results in a dispersion of outcomes that is particularly broad. Moreover, financial collapses are somewhat unique in that market participants are focused entirely on survival. Consequently, it is imperative that actions by market participants, regulators, and the government be designed to instill confidence. The U.S. Treasury Department's management of the Troubled Asset Relief Program did little to calm market participants as the government's indecision on its strategy undermined the very confidence that the program was intended to restore. By contrast, U.S. Treasury Secretary Robert Rubin's creative response to the 1994 Mexican peso crisis stabilized currency markets and likely prevented a regional economic slowdown.

The challenges faced by the financial system in its recovery stage are exacerbated by a lack of knowledge about the rules of the game, the regulatory framework, and the landscape of customers and competitors. For example, there have been a number of bankruptcy cases, such as Chrysler, General Growth Properties, and the Yellowstone Club, that raise questions about the sanctity of senior creditor status and bankruptcy remote entities. Without clarity about the rules of the game, investors will be unwilling to commit fresh capital and the recovery stage will stagnate. At the same time, a financial system that relies on rational economic behavior must have rules and regulations that recast risk-taking incentives by distributing the downside associated with risk more evenly across market participants. In March 2009, the California Public Employees' Retirement System (CalPERS), the largest public pension fund in the United States, began to ask its hedge-fund managers to agree to a clawback in incentive fees. This revised fee structure would result in hedge-fund managers being compensated for rolling three-year periods rather than individual one-year periods. The stated objective of CalPERS is to better align its managers' interests with its own interests.

The chapter authors' suggestion for principle-based regulations could not be more on the money. The existing regulatory landscape unintentionally encourages market participants to develop transactions that comply with the letter of the law while not necessarily embracing the spirit of the law. Additionally, as further suggested by the authors, greater transparency and reduced opacity will go a long way to solving this problem by providing investors with information necessary to make prudent decisions. For example, it was exceedingly difficult, even for sophisticated investors, to evaluate the balance sheets of major investment banks and understand that most of them were more than twenty-five times leveraged. If market participants understood the amount of leverage being employed by investment banks, it is quite possible that these companies would have been valued differently (i.e., lower), thus resulting in a higher cost of capital. The higher cost of capital might have encouraged management teams to lower leverage in return for a higher multiple and a lower cost of capital. Said differently, transparency into the balance sheets of investment banks might have led to a more optimal capital structure that would have been better equipped to handle the market meltdown. Although these conclusions are somewhat speculative, there are numerous analogous situations in which transparency has allowed market forces to operate more efficiently. Given the critical importance of free-flowing capital to our nation's economy, this solution seems very worthy of being given a chance.

The authors suggest that one potential solution to the balkanized regulatory system is to consolidate regulatory power in one global regulator. It is quite possible the financial markets have grown too large, too global, and too complex for one regulator. Consequently, the answer may lie in placing limitations on the size of financial institutions, so that the financial system does not become exposed to the too-big-to-fail problem again. Clearly, there are issues associated with global competitiveness that may make this solution unworkable. However, the events of 2008 clearly demonstrate how interconnected the world's markets are, and thus there may be more of an appetite for a global solution.

In summary, the chapter is particularly timely and provides a novel prism through which to evaluate the recent events in the financial markets. I agree strongly with the authors' observation that it is critical to develop regulations and surveillance systems to break the boom-and-bust cycle that has characterized U.S. financial markets for the last century. The future of our financial markets and our economy may, in fact, depend on it.

SUSTAINABLY

13 Green Financing After the Global Financial Crisis

Perry Sadorsky

Financial investment in new sustainable energy has grown very rapidly over the past few years with a compound average annual growth rate of 29 percent between 2004 and 2009. This growth rate is very impressive, given that 2008 marked the largest decline in global economic activity since the Great Depression of the 1930s. As the global economy recovers from the recession of 2008–2009, questions arise as to what the economic recovery will look like and how the economic recovery will affect green financing. This chapter looks at four economic recovery scenarios (U-shaped recovery, V-shaped recovery, stagflation, deflation) and the impacts that each of these scenarios will have on the future of green financing. Some suggestions are also presented as to which economic indicators to follow for signs of which of these scenarios is most likely to unfold.

$$\bullet \quad \bullet \quad \bullet$$

The global recession of 2008 came at a precipitant time for green financing. After several years of double-digit growth, green financing, described in this chapter as new investment in global sustainable energy, slowed considerably between 2008 and 2009. In 2009, investment in the new global sustainable energy market reached $162 billion, but this was 7 percent lower than the year earlier (New Energy Finance 2010). This number includes government and corporate research and development (R&D) spending and financial (equity, bond, and venture capital) investments. The global economic recession has

I thank Paul Shrivastava, Matt Statler, and Irene Henriques for their very helpful comments.

clearly had an impact on green financing. Given the severity of the global economic recession and the impact the recession has had on green financing, it is important to offer some insight and scenarios as to what the future of green financing will look like as economies around the world begin to recover.

The basic drivers behind sustainable energy, like climate change, energy security issues, resource depletion, and new technology are still intact. In addition, the government stimulus packages associated with the economic recovery have created a new driver, as the governments of the world's major economies have pledged a combined $183 billion toward sustainable energy (New Energy Finance 2009). These drivers can provide a powerful incentive for the development of more sustainable energy.

Climate change is now an undeniable fact that current and future societies will have to live with (Intergovernmental Panel on Climate Change 2007; Stern 2009; *Economist* 2009). The burning of fossil fuels emits greenhouse gases into the atmosphere, and since the Industrial Revolution, greenhouse-gas emissions have been growing faster than the earth's natural ability to absorb them. These gases trap the sun's heat as it is radiated back from the earth and cause global warming. Global warming leads to climate changes like drought, floods, rising sea levels, and volatile and unpredictable weather patterns, and each of these climate changes has the potential to seriously disrupt economic and social activity as we know it (Stern 2009). The consensus is that the amount of greenhouse gases currently in the atmosphere is around 430 parts per million (ppm) of carbon dioxide equivalent (Stern 2009). Holding the concentration of carbon dioxide equivalent at 450 ppm is very desirable, because this will limit average global temperature increases to around 2 degrees Celsius—an amount that will still cause climate change but climate change that can be managed (Stern 2009). Higher concentrations of carbon dioxide in the atmosphere will lead to greater effects of climate change, such as the permanent displacement of millions of people from low-lying regions and radically altered agriculture crop production cycles. Limiting the amount of carbon dioxide in the atmosphere requires a shift toward a low-carbon world, and a low-carbon world is one with a reduced usage of fossil fuels and an increased usage of renewable energy and green financing. The concentration of carbon dioxide equivalent is growing at 2.5 ppm per year, and as a result, the 450 ppm threshold will soon be upon us (Stern 2009). There is, therefore, a sense of urgency when dealing with climate-change issues. The International Energy Agency (IEA 2008) has looked into the amount of money that needs to be invested globally to stabilize greenhouse-gas emissions. Under the IEA's reference scenario (business as usual), there needs to be US$26.3 trillion of new energy investment between 2007 and 2030.[1] This includes a cumulative renewable energy investment of $5.5 trillion. Stabilizing greenhouse-gas emissions at 550 ppm would require a cumulative investment in clean energy of $9.7 trillion (World Economic Forum 2009).[2] Stabilizing greenhouse-gas emission at 450 ppm would require a cumulative investment in clean energy of approximately $14.8 trillion (World Economic Forum 2009). Given that global gross domestic product (GDP) in 2007 was US$54 trillion, this amounts to approximately 1 percent of global GDP per year. One could argue that a price of 1 percent of global GDP is not too high of a price to pay to build a cleaner, greener, and more sustainable future.

A nation's energy security issues arise from its reliance on imported energy products, particularly oil, to fuel economic growth. The major oil-consuming countries, for example, are not the countries with the largest reserves of oil. In 2008, the four largest oil-consuming countries, the United States, China, Japan, and India, collectively accounted for approximately 41 percent of global oil consumption (BP 2009). The United States, in particular, stands out for consuming 23 percent of the global total. By comparison, four countries, Saudi Arabia, Iran, Iraq, and Kuwait, collectively account for approximately 50 percent of the world's proven conventional oil reserves.[3] Oil-importing countries like the United States, China, Japan, and India are increasingly at risk of supply disruptions (due to terrorist attacks, inadequate infrastructure, or capacity to produce oil) that are either directed at countries that have large oil reserves or supply disruptions (due to terrorist attacks or monopoly pricing power) that affect the transport of oil to oil-importing countries. A greater reliance on domestically produced renewable energy by oil-importing countries would reduce their dependence on imported energy products and increase their own energy security. Green financing can therefore be thought of as financing energy security.

Energy use and economic growth are intrinsically linked together along a country's path to prosperity. The current economic recession may have temporarily weakened demand for energy, but once the global economy recovers, demand for energy will quickly pick up. Primary world demand for energy is projected to grow by 50 percent between 2004 and 2030, and the cost of meeting this increase in demand is projected to be US$20 trillion in 2006 dollars (International Energy Agency 2006). Moreover, the renewable energy category comprising geothermal, solar, wind, tidal, and wave energy is projected to be the fastest-growing energy source to 2030, with an average annual growth rate of 6.6 percent (IEA 2006). This presents an enormous opportunity for economies to expand their usage of renewable energy. How the renewable energy sector expands will depend in part on what pathway the global economy takes once a recovery is under way.

The year 2008 will go down in history as the year that individuals all over the world learned the meaning of new terms such as *subprime mortgages*, *credit-default swaps*, and *quantitative easing*. Subprime mortgages and credit-default swaps are now identified as major contributors to the worst economic downturn in sixty years. A problem that originated in the United States has spread to every corner of the world, the impacts of which are very unpleasant. According to the International Monetary Fund (IMF 2010, Table 1.1), economic growth (measured as percentage change in GDP) in 2009 declined by 2.6 percent in the United States, 4.1 percent in the Eurozone, and 5.2 percent in Japan. In 2009 the global economy shrunk by 0.6 percent, marking the first time the global economy has contracted since World War II. World trade volumes shrunk by 11 percent in 2009. Slumping global growth and falling trade volumes mean fewer jobs for people in both developed and emerging countries. The current economic recession is referred to as the Great Recession because of how widespread and deep it is. This chapter argues that, although the financial crisis contributed to the current global recession, it was really rising oil prices that drove interest rates up so quickly and created the financial crisis in the first place (Rubin 2009). Rising oil prices have preceded every recession since World War II (Blanchard and Gali 2007; Hamilton 2003, 2009). A shift away from petroleum-based energy products to renewable energy sources would lessen the impact that changes in oil prices have on an economy.

Given that the global economy has recorded the first year of negative economic growth since World War II and that central banks around the world have lowered key benchmark interest rates to close to zero, where do we go from here, and how does this affect the future of green financing? As the global economy starts to grow and recover from the current recession, interest rates will eventually have to rise. Rising interest rates increase the cost of borrowing money, which will impact green financing. There are four reasonable alternative scenarios. A quick turnaround is identified with a V-shaped economic economy, so named because GDP growth recovers fairly quickly after the recession. A moderate recovery (U shaped), one in which economic growth slowly returns to its prerecession values is a possibility. Stagflation, a combination of high inflation and low economic growth, is a possible scenario and was most recently experienced in the United States in the 1970s

(Mankiw and Scarth 2008). Deflation is a particularly nasty economic scenario in which economywide prices fall over a long period of time. Deflation was prominent in the 1930s and is currently a concern in Japan (Mankiw and Scarth 2008). In this chapter, each one of these scenarios and the implications for green finance is explored. Some suggestions are also provided to help determine in which direction the economy will go.

Green Energy and the Stages of Green Financing

According to REN21 (2008), renewable energy accounted for 18 percent of global final energy consumption in 2006, compared to fossil fuels, which accounted for 79 percent of the global total. Traditional biomass, at 13 percent of global final energy demand, was by far the largest component of the renewable energy sector. Large hydropower was the next largest component, with a 3 percent share of global final energy demand. Solar and wind energy, both of which are growing very rapidly, currently, however, make up a very small fraction of world primary energy demand.

The basic drivers behind sustainable energy are climate change, energy security issues, resource depletion, and new technology (New Energy Finance 2009). Rising oil prices, which are energy market price signals resulting from climate change, energy security issues, and resource depletion, are often considered an important driver behind the development of renewable energy. However, Henriques and Sadorsky (2008), using simulation analysis, have found that shocks to oil prices do not have as large an effect on the financial performance of alternative energy companies as do shocks to technology.[4] Publicly traded renewable energy companies tend to be viewed by investors as more like technology companies than energy companies. This creates a problem for renewable energy companies. Whereas new consumer electronics products can catch on with consumers fairly rapidly even when they command a premium price (e.g., the Apple iPhone, or more generally, any new product from Apple), renewable energy products generally do not experience this type of trajectory because, for most consumers, energy is a commodity input into the usage of other products rather than an end product in itself. In a study of renewable energy consumption in the Group of 7 countries (Canada, France, Germany, Italy, Japan, United Kingdom, United States), Sadorsky (2009) finds that oil price movements do not affect renewable energy consumption as much as per capita income or per capita carbon dioxide emissions. These results indicate that rising incomes and government policies aimed to curb carbon dioxide emissions will each have a bigger impact on the adoption of renewable energy than will rising oil prices. What makes the sustainable energy sector different from other economic sectors is that sustainable energy is influenced to a high degree by government regulation (Burer and Wustenhagen 2009). This parallels the conventional fossil-fuel energy sector, which is characterized as a mature and essential economic sector but as one that tends to be fairly heavily regulated. Without some strong drivers like climate-change and energy security issues, there is no great inertia to change the way energy is produced, delivered, and consumed. Government policies toward energy security and climate change, for example, will have direct effects on the sustainable energy sector (Lipp 2007). Governments that are looking for ways to reduce their country's dependence on imported oil may find the increased usage of renewable energy an attractive alternative. Countries aiming to meet their emission reductions under the Kyoto protocol will find that the increased usage of renewable energy or increased energy-efficient useful prospects in meeting their obligations (Labatt and White 2007).

For companies in the sustainable energy sector, it is informative to think of the drivers of green energy as being broadly classified as either technology push or market pull drivers (Burer and Wustenhagen 2009). Technology push drivers or policies are technology innovation policies like government-sponsored research and development programs aimed to increase the supply of sustainable energy. Market pull policies focus on increasing the demand for these new technologies. Examples of market pull policies include production tax credits, job-training programs, low-cost loans for business producing the new technologies or consumers adopting the new technologies, feed-in tariffs, government purchasing agreements for the new technologies, regulations on old or existing dirty technologies, and consumer cash-back incentives for early adopters of the new technology. Carbon taxes and carbon cap-and-trade mechanisms are also powerful market pull policies for increasing the adoption of sustainable energy, as these mechanisms, if correctly designed, induce consumers to switch from carbon-intensive energy uses to less carbon-intensive energy products. Government policy can thus be directed at both technology push and market pull. From a pure financing perspective, however, governments usually limit their role to funding early stage research and development. The manufacturing and rollout phases are usually financed with nongovernmental-sponsored funds.

According to New Energy Finance (2009), green energy product development passes through four distinct stages: technology research, technology development, manufacturing scale-up, and the rollout of new products. Associated with each of these stages is a funding source or sources. Government funding, for example, is used solely for technology research. Venture capital and private equity are used for later-stage technology research, technology development, and early-stage manufacturing scale-up. Public equity markets and mergers and acquisitions are used for manufacturing scale-up and the rollout of new products. Credit (debt) markets and carbon finance are used to fund the last stage, rollout. All of these sources of funding—government, private equity, public equity markets, and debt markets—are directly affected by current and future economic conditions.

Trends in Green Financing

Since 2004, investment in sustainable energy initiatives, which are often referred to as clean or green, has been growing very rapidly.[5] In 2007, for example, investment in the global sustainable energy market was $157 billion (New Energy Finance 2010). This represents a 44 percent increase over the previous year (Table 13.1).

The year 2008 saw a small increase as investment in the global sustainable energy market reached $174 billion (Table 13.1).[6] After rapidly growing for many years (by as much as 50 percent in some years), investment in the global sustainable energy market grew at just 10 percent between 2007 and 2008. Between 2008 and 2009, investment in the global sustainable energy market shrank by 7 percent. This slower growth rate between 2007 and 2008 and negative growth rate between 2008 and 2009 reflect the impact of the global recession.

TABLE 13.1 Global new investment trends in sustainable energy (US$ billions)

Units	2004	2005	2006	2007	2008	2009
Financial investment	18	41	76	116	130	119
S/RP, corporate R&D, gov't R&D	28	31	33	42	44	43
Total	46	72	109	157	174	162
Growth (%)	—	56	52	44	10	−7

SOURCE: New Energy Finance (2010), UN Environmental Programme.
NOTES: S/RP = small and/or residential projects. New investment volume adjusts for reinvested equity. Total values include estimates for undisclosed deals.

Financial new investment, with a total value of $130 billion, which does not include government R&D or corporate R&D, made up the bulk of the $174 billion invested in clean energy in 2008. The quarterly numbers for new financial investment are particularly revealing because they show just how dramatically the global recession affected the clean-energy sector in the last half of 2008 (Figure 13.1). Large drops in financial new investment in sustainable energy were observed in the first quarter of 2008 and the first quarter of 2009. Notice that the fourth quarter of 2007 was the strongest quarter on record and illustrative of the strong trend in green financing that was well under way before the 2008 recession. Since the second quarter of 2009, green financing has been fairly steady at approximately $33 billion per quarter.

When looking at financing by technology, since 2007 two technologies, wind and solar, have accounted for most of the new financing (Table 13.2). Not only did these technologies account for the bulk of new financing but also the same two technologies had some of the highest compound annual growth rates (CAGR) over the period 2004–2009. With an eye-popping 107 percent CAGR, solar stands out as a particularly impressive technology in which to invest.

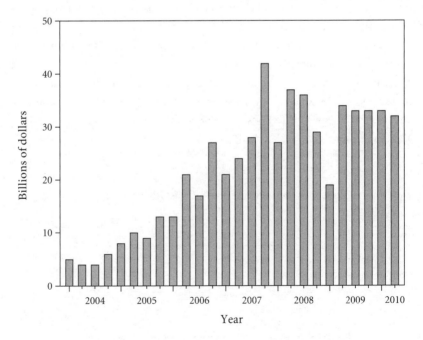

FIGURE 13.1 Financial investment in new sustainable energy
SOURCE: New Energy Finance (2010).

TABLE 13.2 Global trends in sustainable energy investment, by technology and region (US$ billions)

	2004	2005	2006	2007	2008	2009	2008–2009 %	2004–2009 CAGR %
Technology								
Wind	11.0	20.6	29.9	51.9	58.8	67.3	14	44
Solar	0.6	3.2	10.3	21.9	33.0	24.3	−27	107
Biofuels	1.5	6.0	19.7	19.7	18.4	6.9	−62	36
Biomass and waste	2.4	6.2	9.0	11.5	9.4	10.8	14	35
Energy-smart technologies	1.3	1.8	2.9	3.9	3.2	4.4	34	28
Small hydro	0.5	1.9	2.0	3.5	4.2	3.8	−9	46
Geothermal	0.8	0.4	1.2	1.6	2.2	1.5	—	—
Low-carbon services	0.0	0.6	0.7	1.3	0.4	0.3	−41	46
Marine	0.0	0.0	0.5	0.4	0.1	0.2	110	66
Total	18	41	76	116	130	119	−8	46
Geography								
Europe	9.2	18.7	28.1	48.4	48.4	43.7	−10	37
North America	4.6	11.3	27.1	32.9	33.3	20.7	−38	35
South America	0.5	2.8	4.5	8.0	14.6	11.6	−21	91
Asia & Oceania	3.7	7.9	14.9	24.4	31.3	40.8	30	61
Middle East & Africa	0.2	0.2	1.5	2.0	2.1	2.5	20	61
Total	18	41	76	116	130	119	−8	46

SOURCE: New Energy Finance (2010), UN Environmental Programme.

On a regional basis, North America and Europe tend to be where much of the new investment in sustainable energy goes. North America and Europe are not, however, the fastest-growing regions for new green financing. South America (91 percent), Asia and Oceania (61 percent), and the Middle East and Africa (61 percent) have the highest CAGRs.

Trends for Green-Energy Investors

Until the start of the most recent economic recession, investors in publicly traded clean-energy companies were being well rewarded for their investments. Figure 13.2 shows the performance of the WilderHill New Energy

Global Innovation Index (NEX) over the five-year period December 2005–December 2009. This index consists of approximately ninety clean-energy companies drawn from different sectors and regions of the world. Figure 13.2 compares the performance of the NEX with the Amex oil index (XOI), the Nasdaq (IXIC), and the S&P 500 (GSPC). At the end of 2007, the NEX was up a little more than 150 percent since December 2005. The effect of the global recession can be seen as all of the gains, and then some, were erased by early 2009. In general, investing in clean-energy companies tends to be quite risky. Henriques and Sadorsky (2008) find, for example, that clean energy companies, as a group, are approximately twice as risky, as measured by beta, as the S&P 500. For example, a 1 percent increase in the returns on the S&P 500 translates into a 2 percent increase in the returns of stock prices of clean-energy companies. In terms of risk, this puts clean-energy companies more on par with technology companies than with other energy companies (which tend to have beta values of less than one).

Over the period December 2008–December 2009, the stock market recorded an impressive rebound, with clean energy leading the way. The WilderHill New

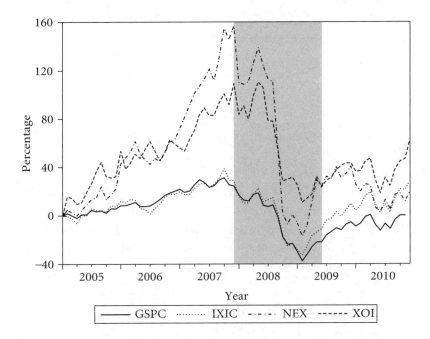

FIGURE 13.2 Performance of clean energy and other major stock market indices, January 2005–December 2010

NOTE: Shaded area indicates U.S. recession. Data from Yahoo! Finance.

Energy Global Index and the Nasdaq both outpaced the Amex oil index and the S&P 500 (Figure 13.3).

In addition to directly investing in clean-energy companies, the past few years have seen an outpouring of other green financial products (e.g., green exchange-traded funds, or ETFs; green exchange-traded notes, or ETNs; green bonds). There is even an ETN that invests in carbon emissions credits.

One such carbon product is the iPath Global Carbon ETN (GRN), which began trading on July 8, 2009. The GRN is linked to the Barclays Capital Global Carbon Index. The index tracks the European Union Emission Trading Scheme (EU ETS) and the United Nation's Kyoto protocol Clean Development Mechanism (CDM). The EU ETS and CDM are the two largest carbon emission markets (Labatt and White 2007). The development of this product means that individuals, companies, and organizations can add a direct carbon-finance product to their investment portfolios.

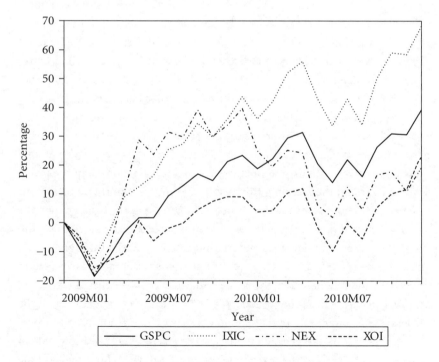

FIGURE 13.3 Performance of clean energy and other major stock market indices, December 2008–December 2010
SOURCE: Data from Yahoo! Finance.
NOTE: M = month.

In addition to green equity investments, there are some green fixed-income products. Green bonds offer an attractive alternative to finance sustainable value creation, particularly within the renewable energy sector. A green bond is a government-backed financial instrument designed to raise financial capital for the purposes of expanding renewable energy production. Currently, the European Climate Awareness Bond is active, and in Canada there is a proposed Canadian Green Bond.[7] The offerings of these new green products mean that it is now possible for an individual investor to design a completely green investment portfolio consisting of green equity, carbon equity, and green bonds.

The Making of the Great Recession

The origins of the Great Recession can be traced back to early 2001, when the U.S. economy was just coming off the bursting of the technology stock market bubble (which in itself is a remarkable story of foolish investor behavior).[8] The U.S. economy peaked in March 2001 and reached a trough in November 2001. To stimulate the economy, the U.S. Federal Reserve lowered interest rates (in particular the benchmark federal funds rate, the rate at which banks borrow and lend money to one another). The average American consumer does not pay interest rates as low as the federal funds rate, but mortgage rates are in part based on the federal funds rate. Prime interest rates, the rate that banks charge their best customers to borrow money, are, for example, usually 3 percent above the federal funds rate. The rates on a thirty-year conventional mortgage are priced fairly competitively and fluctuate more than the prime rate. As a result, the rate on a thirty-year conventional mortgage may be either slightly above or below the prime rate (Figure 13.4). In January 2001, the federal funds target rate was lowered from 6 percent to 5.5 percent (Figure 13.4). The federal funds target rate continued to be lowered throughout 2001 and into 2002. On June 25, 2003, the Federal Funds target rate was lowered to 1 percent, and it remained at this value until June 30, 2004 (when it was raised to 1.25 percent). After June 30, 2004, the Federal Reserve gradually raised the federal funds target rate over the following several years. On June 29, 2006, the federal funds target rate stood at 5.25 percent. The ultra-low federal funds rate of 1 percent that existed for almost a full year (June 2003 to June 2004) translated into lower borrowing costs for consumers. Even subprime borrowers, individuals whose creditworthiness was deemed to be less than prime, found borrowing attractive. At a federal funds target rate of 1 percent,

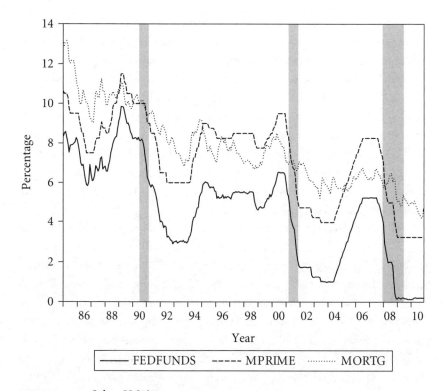

FIGURE 13.4 Select U.S. interest rates

SOURCE: Data from Federal Reserve Economic Data database, Federal Reserve Bank of St. Louis.

NOTE: Shaded areas indicate U.S. recessions. FEDFUNDS = effective federal funds rate, MPRIME = bank prime load rate, and MORTG = thirty-year conventional mortgage rate.

prime interest rates were 4 percent. During this period, a typical subprime mortgage came with a twenty-four-month interest-free period. In essence, people who did not have money, assets, or a steady stream of reliable income were allowed to borrow money to buy a house.[9] At the end of the two-year introductory-offer period, subprime mortgages were refinanced at much higher interest rates (partly because the interest-free period was over and partly because new financing costs were based on the federal funds rate, which had risen from 1 percent in May 2004 to 5 percent in May of 2006), which prompted many borrowers to walk away from their mortgage obligations. Prime interest rates in May 2006 were close to 8 percent, and a subprime mortgage holder was sure to pay a lot more than 8 percent. This created a vicious cycle as financial services companies that had approved the loans were suddenly short of cash as borrowers stopped (or in some cases never started) making interest payments. As defaults in the subprime mortgage increased, so, too, did the financial derivative products tied to subprime mortgages, with the result that the financial services companies that defaulted on their derivative obligations were forced to take on more debt. The financial derivatives products with a tie to the U.S. subprime mortgage market were sold all over the world, and in some cases to unsuspecting buyers who did not even know that the derivative was, at least in part, dependent on the U.S. subprime mortgage market. Financial services companies found themselves taking on greater losses, and some even declared bankruptcy. Credit-default swaps started entering the news media as some companies started recording enormous losses from these products.

A credit-default swap (CDS) is actually a pretty clever and useful financial product for spreading risk, which unfortunately can lead to huge losses for some of the participants. In its simplest form, a CDS is a bet on the creditworthiness of a company (Partnoy 2003). Consider, as an example, individual A who thinks that company XYZ is likely to have credit problems in the future that may lead to its defaulting on its loans. Individual A would like to place a bet on the possibility of a credit default occurring to company XYZ. Individual B thinks that company XYZ is financially solid and is very unlikely to have credit default problems. Individuals A and B enter into a CDS contract where individual A is the buyer of the contract and individual B is the seller of the contract. The specifics (e.g., duration, cost of premium, payout) of the CDS are written out in the contract. The seller of the contract, individual B, receives a premium up-front from individual A. If company XYZ has no credit-default problems, individual B makes money through the selling of the contract. In fact, individual B may be willing to write many different CDS contracts on companies that individual B believes are very creditworthy. Individual B receives a steady stream of income from writing the contracts and, as long as there are no defaults, does not have to pay any money out. If, however, company XYZ does default in a way that affects the CDS contract, individual B ends up owing individual A a whole lot of money, because the payout in the event of default is highly leveraged and many, many times greater than the amount of money individual B collected through the premium. The defaults resulting from the subprime mortgage crisis triggered a large amount of CDS contracts for which money had to be paid out.

Bankrupt financial services companies, massive losses from CDS contracts, and lack of trust between lenders and borrowers raised the costs of borrowing. The collapse in September 2008 of Lehman Brothers, in particular, sent shock waves through the global banking sector and accelerated the number of bankruptcies. Central banks can lower key benchmark lending rates, but if companies won't pass the low rates on to consumers, economic activity starts to collapse. People can't borrow money cheaply to buy new houses and cars, and business cannot borrow money cheaply to build new plants or buy new machinery and equipment. The end result is a global financial crisis resulting from a global credit crunch.

According to the National Bureau of Economic Research (NBER), the most recent U.S. recession started in December 2007 and ended in June 2009 (http://www.nber.org/cycles.html). The most recent economic recession is already longer and deeper than most postwar recessions. The effects are staggering. In 2008, the losses in American household wealth were a staggering $11 trillion ($8.5 trillion in financial assets and $2.5 trillion in housing assets; IMF 2009). The expected write-down on U.S.-based assets by all financial institutions over the period 2007–2010 is expected to be $2.7 trillion. The total expected losses on global assets over the period 2007–2010 is expected to reach $4 trillion.

Although low interest rates that fuel a property market bubble are the usual starting point to understanding the origins of the financial crisis and the Great Recession, in reality, the Great Recession, like other postwar recessions, was caused by rising oil prices. After all, the real question is, What caused interest rates to start rising in the second half of 2004?

Oil prices exert a tremendous influence over our economies (e.g., Blanchard and Gali 2007; Gately and Huntington 2002; Hamilton 2003, 2009; Jones, Leiby, and Paik 2004; Sadorsky 2008). Oil is used in the production or transportation of approximately 98 percent of everything we buy. Cheap oil, combined with free-trade agreements, has spurred globalization. After all, if transportation costs were high, it would not matter much how low labor costs were on the other side of the world. The savings from cheaper labor would be eroded by the higher costs of transportation (Rubin 2009).

Figure 13.5 shows a time-series plot of monthly spot-market U.S. oil prices as measured in U.S. dollars per barrel.[10] As Figure 13.5 shows, oil prices tend to rise just before or in the very early stages of a recession. Oil prices closed out 1998 at $11.28 per barrel. Oil prices gradually rose over the following few years, reaching a high of $34.40 in November 2000. Oil prices then trended downward to $19.33 in December 2001. Oil prices rose slowly through 2002 and 2003 before really taking off in 2004 and eventually reaching a high of $133.93 per

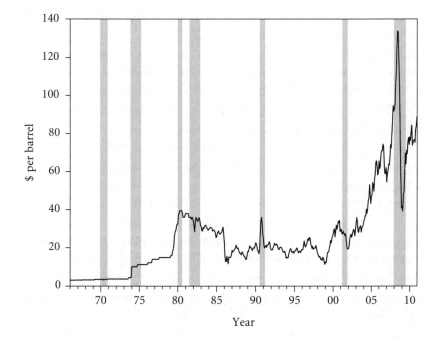

FIGURE 13.5 U.S. spot-market oil prices
SOURCE: Data from Federal Reserve Economic Data database, Federal Reserve Bank of St. Louis.
NOTE: Shaded areas indicate U.S. recessions.

barrel in July 2008. As Figure 13.5 shows, oil prices have become considerably more volatile after 2001.

Green Financing as Part of the Economic Stimulus Package

In response to the global economic recession, countries around the world have announced ambitious new fiscal stimulus packages for green energy. According to New Energy Finance (2009), there are three reasons for these green stimulus spending packages. First, the Great Recession of 2008 has pushed world leaders to find new ways to create jobs. Investing in green energy is one way to create job growth in the face of a crumbling domestic manufacturing sector. Second, record-high oil prices in 2008 and natural gas supply disruptions in Europe made it clear that energy security issues are a top priority in the economic and political arenas. Stimulus spending aimed to increase energy efficiency and use more renewable energy is an important way to increase energy security. Third, as world leaders grapple with the reality that climate-change issues need to be addressed, stimuli spending on clean energy helps countries reduce their greenhouse-gas emissions.

The governments of the world's major economies have pledged a combined US$183 billion toward sustainable energy (New Energy Finance 2009). Of this money, approximately 74 percent is to be spent by just two countries, the United States ($67.8 billion) and China ($67.2 billion; Figure 13.6). In the United States, the sustainable energy spending of $67.8 billion is just 0.47 percent of the $14.44 trillion economy in 2008, or just 8.6 percent of the most recent $787 billion U.S. fiscal stimulus spending package. On a proportional basis, green stimulus spending is not that large. Notice also that India, a country often mentioned along with China as one of the fastest-growing economies, has pledged nothing for green stimulus spending.

Although most countries have devoted a fairly small percentage of their economic stimulus recovery packages to renewable energy projects, one country, South Korea, is an exception. South Korea has devoted 20 percent

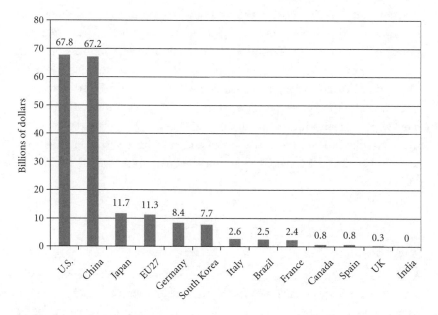

FIGURE 13.6 Green stimulus allocations to sustainable energy, by country, April 2009
SOURCE: New Energy Finance (2009).
NOTE: EU refers to the twenty-seven countries in the European Union.

of its overall stimulus spending to environmental measures, and thus has the greenest fiscal stimulus package (New Energy Finance 2009).

At a sector level of analysis, energy efficiency, accounting for $62 billion of the $183 billion package, has attracted the most amount of money. Grid development received the second-largest amount of money ($48.7 billion), and renewable energy received the third-largest amount ($34 billion). One thing to keep in mind, however, is that it is going to take some time for the green stimulus spending to actually have an economic impact. Determining a definitive timeline for the spending is difficult. New Energy Finance (2009) estimates that only about $40 billion of the $183 billion total pledged is scheduled to be spent in 2009. Approximately $75 billion will be spent in 2010, and the remainder spent after 2010.

So what do these green fiscal spending packages mean for sustainable energy? One thing that has become apparent is that in the face of energy security issues, climate change, and the worst economic slowdown since the Great Depression, concerned governments around the world are willing to, at least in principle, pledge government money to further increase energy efficiency and the adoption of renewable energy, which is good for the development of a cleaner energy world. For most countries, the amount of money devoted to green stimulus spending is, except for the case of South Korea, not that large in relation to the total amount of stimulus spending. This means that other nongreen sectors will receive larger amounts of money. Thus, although green stimulus spending will provide a further increase to green financing and green business, other less-green sectors could grow more quickly. New green stimulus monies are welcome, but they should not be considered a substitute for more established and ongoing government initiatives (e.g., feed-in tariffs, R&D credits, production credits) to promote sustainable energy use.

Economic Recovery Scenarios and the Impacts on Green Financing

As has been stated earlier, the basic drivers behind renewable energy, like climate change, energy security issues, resource depletion, and new technology, are still intact. As a result, one view could be that green financing should be relatively unaffected by economic business cycles. Green financing to build a sustainable future is a long-term concept, whereas business-cycle fluctuations are short term in nature (Shrivastava 1995). The problem is that the development of clean, sustainable energy depends on a combination of government support policies and green financing from the private sector, and private-sector business decisions are very much affected by business-cycle fluctuations. Moreover, in a global economy weakened by recession, energy consumption and resulting greenhouse-gas emissions fall and government priorities may change from promoting a sustainable economy to promoting a recovering economy with government policies aimed at short-term job creation.

Given that, in 2008, the global economy has recorded the first year of negative economic growth since World War II and central banks around the world have lowered key benchmark interest rates to close to zero, where do we go from here, and how does this affect the future of green financing? As Figure 13.7 shows, after growing rapidly for several years, green financing trended downward in 2009. Looking to the future, the questions are: What will the trend in green financing look like? Will the trend continue downward and gradually level off? Will the trend level off with a gradual increase? Or, will the trend turn from down to up fairly quickly before resuming a strong upward increase? The answer to these questions depends on the type of economic policies that governments choose and how effective those policies are at generating economic growth. Before the global economic recession, New Energy Finance had predicted that investment in clean technology would reach US$450 billion annually by 2012 and rise to US$600 billion by 2020 (World Economic Forum 2009). Whether these predictions remain accurate depends on what recovery path the global economy follows.

Between 2004 and 2008, total new investment in sustainable energy closely followed a linear trend (Figure 13.7). Estimating a linear trend over the years 2004 to 2009 shows that along the linear trend line, new investment in clean energy grows at a constant value of $26.7 billion per year. Using this linear trend line to predict future total new investment yields values of $186 billion for 2009 and $213 billion for 2010. The trend line predicts total new investment values in clean energy of $267 billion for 2012 and $480 billion for 2020.[11] The linear trend line prediction of $480 billion for 2020 is well below New Energy Finance's prediction of $600 billion. In comparison, estimating a linear trend line for total new investment in sustainable energy over the period 2004–2007 predicts a value of $632 billion in 2020.

The traditional way that central banks stimulate the economy through monetary policy is by lowering key lending rates. Low lending rates lower the cost of borrowing money, which makes it cheaper for consumers to buy goods

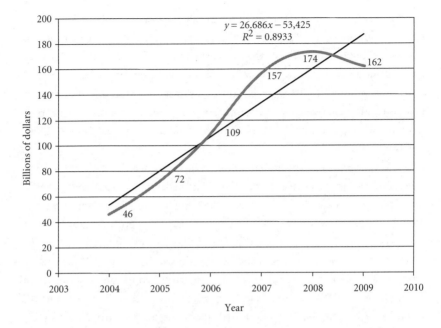

FIGURE 13.7 Linear trend fit of total new investments in sustainable energy

and services and business to build new plants and factories (and thereby employ more people). Once interest rates get close to zero, a liquidity trap develops whereby either interest rates cannot be lowered any further (nominal interest rates cannot go below 0 percent) or any further small reductions in interest rates have little or no effect in stimulating the economy. In this case, banks turn to quantitative easing, a term used to describe the actions of central banks that start to directly buy distressed assets and their own treasury bonds. The U.S. Federal Reserve currently has a plan to purchase $1.450 billion of mortgage-related securities and $300 billion of Treasury bonds. But as the global economy starts to grow and recover from the current recession, interest rates will eventually have to rise. Rising interest rates increase the cost of borrowing money. There are four reasonable alternative economic scenarios to the future, and each one of these has different implications for the financing of sustainable energy.

One possible scenario is for the global economy to start slowly growing again. Banks will lend money at low rates, consumers will start buying goods and services, and businesses will start producing more output and thus hire more workers. The economy will grow relatively slowly over a long period of time. Economic growth will trace out a U-shaped path. Economic growth will not be fast enough to generate inflationary pressures, so central banks can leave interest rates unchanged for some time and then gradually raise interest rates if inflation becomes a problem. The most recent U-shaped recovery in the United States occurred in 1975 (Figure 13.8A). This is a reasonably optimistic view for global economic recovery. This scenario would undoubtedly be good for green financing, as low interest rates and low risk premiums create favorable conditions for sustainable energy companies to borrow money. As previously discussed, green financing did very well in the years leading up to the global recession and a return to those prerecession years would greatly boost the amounts of money going into green financing. In this scenario, new investment in clean energy would eventually return to the trend line.

Another possible scenario is for the global economy to grow again but faster than many expected. The idea here is that because the global economy crashed as quickly as it did, perhaps there is the possibility that the recovery

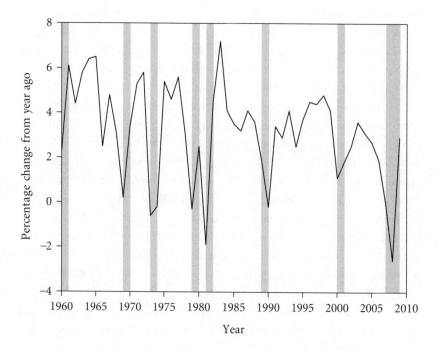

FIGURE 13.8A U.S. real GDP percentage change on previous year, 1960–2009
NOTE: Shaded areas indicate U.S. recessions. Data sourced from the Federal Reserve Economic Data database, Federal Reserve Bank of St. Louis.

will be faster than expected. This is what is known as the V-shaped economic recovery. Given the massive amount of fiscal and monetary stimulus being conducted around the globe by the world's largest economies, there is the possibility that all of this stimulus will stimulate economic growth sooner and faster than previously expected. Consumer spending and business investment will bounce back to prerecession values very quickly. This is really a best-case scenario for the global economic recovery, and green financing would benefit greatly from such a strong recovery. Future new investment would probably return to the trend line in the near term and eventually move onto a new steeper-sloped upward trend (Figure 13.7). The second most recent V-shaped recovery was the 1990–1991 U.S. recession (Figure 13.8A), also one that was brought on by trouble in the banking sector. The difference between 2008 and 1990 is primarily in the magnitude of the recession. Whereas the 1990 recession did impact the United States and some of its trading partners, the 2008 recession affected the entire global economy. Given that the most recent U.S. recession lasted for more than eighteen months (December 2007–June 2009), this type of quick economic recovery and a return to an average increase in total new investment in sustainable energy of $27 billion a year, however, seems unlikely.[12]

A third possible scenario is for the global economy to experience stagflation (inflation with low economic growth). In this scenario, economic growth remains sluggish, but the prices of oil and other commodities start to rise quickly, most likely as a result of strong economic growth in Asia and other emerging economies, thus resulting in widespread inflation. This scenario would be reminiscent of the 1970s. Economic policy makers, however, would be reluctant to let this happen again. Wringing stagflation out of an economy calls for a massive dose of monetary tightening, which reduces the money supply and pushes interest rates up (Mankiw and Scarth 2008). Rising interest rates slow consumption and business fixed investment even more and throw the economy into a recession. This can lead to the W-shaped economic recovery, most recently experienced in the United States in the early 1980s (Figure 13.8A). Although the 1970s were not a particularly good decade for economic growth and prosperity, the rising oil prices of that decade did bring about some much-needed government policy and stimulus to encourage the greater use of renewable energy. Germany, for example, a country that is now considered a leader in renewable energy, can trace its success today in renewable energy to government policies enacted in the late 1970s and early

1980s in response to the two oil-price shocks of the 1970s (Lipp 2007). Although stagflation would not be good for the overall economy, it is likely that, given past experience from the 1970s, this scenario would provide a stimulus to clean energy and green financing that would be above the trend line (Figure 13.7).

A fourth possible scenario is that the global economy experiences deflation and the global economic recession continues and even worsens. Consumers, having experienced large drops in property values and the prices of durable goods, would continue to postpone expenditures in the hopes of getting even lower prices in the future. After all, why buy a new car now when you expect the prices to fall even further in the near future? Companies, unable to sell existing inventories, slash prices in hopes of spurring sales. Weak sales force companies to lay off more workers and postpone investment and expansion. This type of scenario would be very bad news for the economy and green financing. Economic growth in this scenario resembles an L shape. The economy contracts and remains sluggish for many years. Examples of this kind of recovery include the United States in the 1930s (Figure 13.8B) and Japan in the 1990s. Nominal interest rates in the United States were less than 1 percent in the second half of the 1930s, and Japanese interest rates were less than 1 percent in the latter part of the 1990s. In normal situations, monetary policy works to expand the economy by reducing interest rates, and lower interest rates stimulate investment spending and consumption. When interest rates get close to zero, however, there isn't much room left for further decrease in interest rates, and this type of monetary policy becomes ineffective. This type of situation is often referred to as a liquidity trap. Aggregate demand, production, and employment get trapped at low levels. Slumping economic demand would reduce the demand for energy and energy-related products. Emissions of greenhouse gases would fall as economic activity fell. A drop in energy demand and greenhouse-gas emissions would weaken two of the main drivers behind green financing. This would not be a good scenario for green financing, and future green financing would probably be well below the trend line (Figure 13.7) for many years.

The four scenarios outlined above and their implications for new clean-energy investment are based on a business-as-usual assumption and are best thought of as representing the lower range of likely outcomes in the absence of any new strong government policy to curb greenhouse-gas emissions. A strong government-backed commitment in heavily greenhouse-gas-emitting

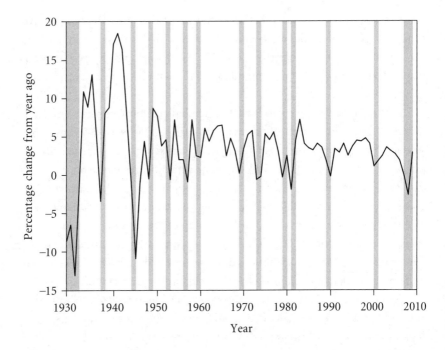

FIGURE 13.8B U.S. real GDP percentage change on previous year, 1930–2009
NOTE: Shaded areas indicate U.S. recessions. Data sourced from the Federal Reserve Economic Data database, Federal Reserve Bank of St. Louis.

countries like China and the United States to seriously address climate-change issues through cap-and-trade or carbon taxes would provide a much needed boost to the clean energy sector and ultimately help increase investment in clean energy. The ultimate boost to clean energy would come through a global initiative to combat greenhouse-gas emissions. Such a strong global initiative seems, at least for the time being, unlikely given that participants at the December 2009 Conference of the Parties meeting in Copenhagen failed to agree on a successor to the Kyoto protocol.[13]

Indicators of Future Scenarios

In the previous section, four different scenarios for the future of green financing were defined and described. A natural question to ask is: Are there any economic indicators that might be useful for predicting which future scenario is most likely to unfold? Predicting future economic growth and the direction of financial markets is fraught with difficulty because of the inherent uncertainty and dynamics involved. The U.S. government, through its various statistical agencies, publishes somewhere on the order of three hundred economic indicators every quarter. Although each of these indicators is useful for helping to understand the sector or subsector of the economy that it is designed to represent, the question arises, If one had to choose just one economic indicator to forecast future economic growth, which indicator would it be? According to the latest research from the field of financial economics, the yield curve would be the best choice (see, e.g., Wheelock and Wohar 2009, and references therein).[14] The yield curve is defined as the difference in yields between bonds of different maturity. Typically, the yield curve is defined as the yield on a ten-year government bond minus the yield on a three-month government Treasury bill. Under normal conditions, the yield curve has positive slope. Longer-dated government bonds have higher yields than short-term government bonds because there is more risk associated with holding longer-dated bonds and because investors need to be compensated with higher yields for taking on this extra risk. Now suppose that a consensus develops in the bond market that the economy is going to slow. A slowing economy means that the central bank will lower interest rates to stimulate economic activity. Bondholders rebalance their portfolios by buying longer-dated maturities and locking in the higher yields before the central bank lowers interest rates. Bond prices and bond yields are inversely related to each other. Investors sell short-term bonds and buy long-term bonds. As investors buy longer-dated bonds, the price of long bonds rises and the yield to long bonds falls. As investors sell short-term bonds, the price of short bonds falls and the yield to short bonds rises. Thus, the yield curve inverts (has negative slope). An inverted yield curve is thus an indication of an approaching recession. Harvey (1988) uses post–World War II data for the United States and finds that a yield-curve inversion leads an economic recession by five quarters.[15] These results have been supported by later work by Wheelock and Wohar (2009) and Mehl (2006). It is also important to know that the 1990–1991, 2001, and 2007–2009 recessions could all have been predicted from the inversion of the yield curve.

In addition to predicting recessions, the yield curve can also be used to predict values for future real GDP. The prediction model is a linear regression model that uses the current quarter's value for the yield curve to predict real GDP growth five quarters into the future. The accuracy of the yield curve in predicting GDP growth has deteriorated somewhat in recent years, but the yield curve is still a good predictor of economic recessions (Wheelock and Wohar 2009).[16] Green-financing enthusiasts, along with investors in general, need to keep watching the yield curve for signs of economic recession or prosperity. As of the first quarter of 2011, the yield curve had a positive slope, indicating no recession in the United States over the next five quarters.

An interesting question to ask is: Is the yield curve a valid economic predictor for other countries? There are two ways to answer this question. One approach is to determine whether the yield curve works in other countries. Another approach is to determine whether the U.S. yield curve has predictive power for other countries.

Although there has been considerable work published on investigating the yield curve–GDP connection in developed economies, there is not very much known about the relationship in emerging economies.[17] A European Central Bank research paper by Mehl (2006) attempts to rectify this. Mehl (2006) uses data from fourteen emerging economies to test the usefulness of the yield curve in predicting economic growth. The sample includes Brazil and India but excludes China and Russia. For almost all of the countries studied, the yield curve is a useful predictor of economic growth (as measured by real GDP). Moreover, the U.S. yield curve is found to be a useful predictor of economic growth in almost all of the emerging countries studied.

Is Economic Decoupling Between the U.S. and Large Emerging Economies Possible? If So, What Are the Implications for Green Financing?

The finding that the U.S. yield curve helps predict output growth in other countries, especially emerging economies, is important in helping understand the integration of world financial markets. As economies grow and prosper, they do more trade. As trade in goods and financial products increases, economies become more interconnected to one another. The prevailing fact over the past fifty years has been that the United States was the dominant economy in terms of economic output and financial markets. As of the first quarter of 2010, the U.S. economy, for example, accounts for approximately 25 percent of global GDP and 40 percent of world stock markets. These values are down somewhat from the start of this century when U.S. economic output accounted for almost 30 percent of world output and U.S. equity markets represented 50 percent of global equity markets. The importance of the U.S. equity market in affecting other developed equity markets has been a topic of study for some time. Dahlquist and Harvey (2001), found, for example, that equity performance in other developed economies tends to correlate relatively highly with equity performance in the United States. Higher (lower) equity returns in the United States correlate with higher (lower) equity returns in most developed economies. The relationship is also asymmetric. Stock market volatility in developed markets tends to be higher when the U.S. economy is contracting than when it is expanding. The equity markets of developed economies tend to perform much better when the U.S. yield curve is normal than when the U.S. yield curve is inverted.

Looking ahead, an interesting question to ask is: Could there be a decoupling between the United States and other large emerging economies like China and India? The answer to this question is one part yes and one part no. In general, as economic development proceeds, financial integration increases. Thus, one expectation is that across time, the emerging economies (which are often characterized by various types of segregation) should find their economies and financial markets more closely correlating with those of the developed economies, and in particular the United States. Trade statistics from the U.S. Census Bureau show that, although the U.S. and China are fairly connected through trade, India and the United States are not that closely connected. For 2009, U.S. imports of goods from China topped $296.4 billion, making China the number-one source of imports (19 percent of total U.S. imports). Canada (14 percent of total U.S. imports) and Mexico (11 percent of total U.S. imports) were the sources of the second and third most U.S. imports.[18] India was ranked number fifteen and supplied just 1.4 percent of U.S. imports in 2009. On a historical basis, trade between China and the United States has been rising over the past ten years, whereas trade between India and the United States has been fairly stagnant.

One thing that works in favor of decoupling is the existence of a large domestic marketplace. If China and India continue to develop their middle classes, then economic growth and development will likely depend more on their respective domestic market places rather than the United States. We have already seen an example of this in the most recently ended recession. The year 2009 saw most developed economies and the world economy slide into a recession (defined as two quarters of negative economic growth). This did not happen in China and India, where economies slowed but did not enter a recession. One advantage for fast-growing economies is that when economic growth is recorded at between 6 percent and 10 percent per year, even a slowdown of 2 percent or 3 percent is not enough to create a recession.[19]

One possibility is that emerging economies like Brazil, China, India, and Russia will become more integrated with developed economies and in particular the United States and the European Union, although the speed of integration may slow. Green financing, which depends on a mix of economic growth and energy policy, may become less coupled with what is going on economically and financially in developed economies. When it comes to energy supply, Brazil, China, and India (but not Russia) are more likely to employ and enjoy the benefits of leapfrog technology. Many emerging economies are not locked into existing energy infrastructures that rely solely on fossil fuels in the same way that developed economies are. For emerging economies, the need for energy is so great and the economic and politic barriers to renewable energy not so firmly entrenched as to block out the development and widespread adoption of renewable energy sources. Consequently, it is very likely that green financing may actually grow faster in emerging economies than in developed economies.

Conclusions

The year 2008 marked the largest decline in global economic activity since the Great Depression of the 1930s. As the global economy recovers from the Great Recession of 2008–2009, questions arise as to what the economic recovery will look like and how the recovery will affect green financing. This chapter looks at four economic recovery scenarios and the impacts that each of these scenarios will have on the future of green financing.

In the first scenario, a modest recovery, the global economy takes several years (two to five) to recover to its postrecession growth rates, and green financing takes approximately the same length of time to return to its trend line. The second scenario, a quick turnaround, envisions economic growth very quickly (less than two years) returning to postrecession values. A quick recovery will probably usher in a new era of green financing along a steeper-sloped trend line. This is the most optimistic scenario for both economic growth and green financing, but one that is unlikely to occur given the length of the most recent recession. The third scenario, stagflation, is a situation in which the global economy experiences high inflation as a result of rising commodity prices but sluggish economic growth. Previous experience with stagflation indicates that it can take between five to ten years to wring stagflation out of the economy. The slower economic growth depresses the investing climate for clean energy, but the higher prices for commodities, and in particular oil, would encourage governments to enact new energy policies aimed to promote greater usage of renewable energy. On the basis of previous experience from the 1970s, this scenario, though not good for economic growth as a whole, can, if dominated by rising energy prices, actually be beneficial to the renewable energy sector. The last scenario is deflation. This is a bad situation, as economic growth remains depressed for many years (five to ten), and green financing suffers along with it. Economic policy focuses on short-term job creation, and other important policy issues like renewable energy tend to suffer. This is the most pessimistic scenario for both economic growth and green financing. Predicting which of these scenarios is most likely to occur is difficult, but the yield curve can provide some clues. As of the first quarter of 2011, the U.S. yield curve is positively sloped, indicating no U.S. recession over the coming five quarters. A U-shaped recovery is the most likely scenario.

It is important to realize that each of these scenarios was developed under the assumption of no major climate-change policies (regional or international). Large greenhouse-gas-emitting countries, like the United States and China, could pass their own climate-change legislation that will effectively put a price on carbon emissions either through cap-and-trade or a carbon tax. In a larger context, world leaders may eventually be able to enact global climate-change initiatives and create an efficient and transparent successor to the Kyoto protocol. Either of these two events would give green financing a big boost.

Notes

1. Values are measured in 2007 U.S. dollars.

2. These values include renewable energy and energy efficiency but exclude nuclear power and large hydro projects.

3. Natural gas reserves are even more concentrated. Just three countries, Russia, Iran, and Qatar, account for 53 percent of the world's proven natural gas reserves (BP 2009).

4. The relationship between oil prices and renewable energy is complicated by the fact that oil price changes result from global demand and supply conditions in the international market for oil, institutional pressures (from the Organization of Petroleum Exporting Countries), political issues, and speculation.

5. The terms *clean energy, green energy, renewable energy*, and *sustainable energy* tend to be used interchangeably when discussing green financing.

6. According to New Energy Finance (2009), the following renewable energy projects are included: all biomass, geothermal, and wind generation projects of more than 1 megawatt (MW); all hydro projects between 0.5 and 50 MW; all solar projects of more than 0.3 MW, all marine energy projects, and all biofuels projects with a

capacity of 1 million liters or more per year. The $155 billion value can be broken down by types of investment (venture capital, government R&D, corporate R&D, private equity, public equity, asset financing) in the value chain (New Energy Finance 2009, figure 4).

7. "Green Bonds: A Public Policy Proposal" (http://www.greenbonds.ca/GB_Policy.pdf), prepared by Tom Rand of Action Canada.

8. In general, for bubbles to form, there must be something that people, en masse, all want to have, and there must be easy access to money or credit to facilitate purchases of bubble items.

9. One of the more astonishing examples of this is how a California strawberry picker earning $15,000 a year was able to qualify for a loan of $720,000 (Carol Lloyd, "Minorities Are the Emerging Face of the Subprime Crisis," April 13, 2007, *SF Gate*, http://articles.sfgate.com/2007-04-13/entertainment/17238073_1_mortgage-rates-zero-down-mortgage-american-dream).

10. The figure shows monthly closing prices for spot-market oil. Intramonth prices can be higher or lower than the monthly closing prices.

11. Linear trend lines are useful for prediction as long as the factors that generated the trend continue to do so into the future.

12. U.S. recessions are dated by the National Bureau of Economic Research (see http://research.stlouisfed.org/fred2/help-faq/#graph_recessions).

13. As of February 2011, Intrade Prediction Markets is currently reporting that there is a 35 percent probability of a U.S. cap-and-trade system for emissions trading to be established before midnight on December 31, 2013 (see http://www.intrade.com/jsp/intrade/contractSearch/).

14. There has been a lot of academic research done on studying the usefulness of the yield curve for predicting economic growth. The article by Wheelock and Wohar (2009) is a recent and readable survey of the literature.

15. Harvey (1988) defines the yield curve as the yield on a five-year government bond minus the yield on a three-month Treasury bill.

16. To see what the U.S. yield curve has looked like from March 1977 until the present, visit the Smart Money Web site (http://www.smartmoney.com/investing/bonds/the-living-yield-curve-7923/). Notice that the current U.S. recession, which began in December 2007 and ended in June 2009, could be predicted by the inversion of the yield curve that occurred five quarters previous.

17. As documented in Wheelock and Wohar (2009), there is some evidence that the yield curve predicts output growth in Belgium, Denmark, Canada, Germany, and the United Kingdom. Little evidence is found that the yield curve is a useful predictor of economic growth for Japan. In general, the results vary by country and time period studied. There is fairly strong evidence that the yield curve is useful at predicting recessions in developing countries (including Japan) as well as the Eurozone as a whole.

18. Foreign trade statistics from the U.S. Census Bureau, http://www.census.gov/foreign-trade/statistics/highlights/top/top0912yr.html#imports.

19. Tempering this possibility is the fact that China, in particular, has used export-driven economic growth strategies to enhance its own economic prosperity.

Currently, however, China has a comparative advantage in labor and the United States has a comparative advantage in capital (machinery, equipment, and human capital). These advantages, which form the basis of economic trade between the two countries, are not going to change for a long time. Moreover, as the Chinese economy continues to grow and expand, it is uncertain over how many more years economic growth can continue to average 8 percent to 10 percent per year.

References

Blanchard, Oliver J., and Jordi Gali. 2007. The macroeconomic effects of oil price shocks: Why are the 2000s so different from the 1970s? Massachusetts Institute of Technology Department of Economics Working Paper No. 07-21, August 18, Cambridge, MA.

BP. 2009. *Statistical review of world energy 2009*. http://www.bp.com/sectionbodycopy.do?categoryId=7500&contentId=7068481.

Burer, Mary Jean, and Rolf Wustenhagen. 2009. Which renewable energy policy is a venture capitalist's best friend? Empirical evidence from a survey of international cleantech investors. *Energy Policy* 37: 4997–5006.

Dahlquist, Magnus, and Campbell R. Harvey. 2001. Global tactical asset allocation. Working Paper, Fuqua School of Business, Duke University, Durham, NC. http://papers.ssrn.com/sol3/papers.cfm?abstract_id=795376.

The Economist. 2009. Getting warmer: A special report on climate change and the carbon economy, December 5–11, 1–14.

Gately, Dermot, and Hillard G. Huntington. 2002. The asymmetric effects of changes in price and income on energy and oil demand. *Energy Journal* 23: 19–55.

Hamilton, James D. 2003. What is an oil shock? *Journal of Econometrics* 113: 363–98.

Hamilton, James D. 2009. Causes and consequences of the oil shock of 2007–08. Working Paper No. 15002, May, National Bureau of Economic Research, Cambridge, MA.

Harvey, Campbell R. 1988. The real term structure and consumption growth. *Journal of Financial Economics* 22: 305–34.

Henriques, Irene, and Perry Sadorsky. 2008. Oil prices and the stock prices of alternative energy companies. *Energy Economics* 30: 998–1010.

International Energy Agency. 2006. *World economic outlook.* Paris: Organization of Economic Co-operation and Development and International Energy Agency.

International Energy Agency. 2008. *World economic outlook.* Paris: Organization of Economic Co-operation and Development and International Energy Agency.

International Energy Agency. 2009. The impact of the financial and economic crisis on global energy investment. Paris: Organization of Economic Co-operation and Development and International Energy Agency.

International Monetary Fund. 2009. *World economic outlook, crisis and recovery.* April. International Monetary Fund, Washington, D.C.

Intergovernmental Panel on Climate Change. 2007. *Climate change 2007: Synthesis report; Contribution of Working Groups I, II, and III to the Fourth Assessment of the*

Intergovernmental Panel on Climate Change. Geneva: Intergovernmental Panel on Climate Change. http://www.ipcc.ch/ipccreports/ar4-syr.htm.

Jones, Donald W., Paul N. Leiby, and Inja K. Paik. 2004. Oil price shocks and the macroeconomy: What has been learned since 1986. *Energy Journal* 25: 1–32.

Labatt, Sonia, and Rodney R. White. 2007. *Carbon finance: The financial implications of climate change.* Hoboken, NJ: Wiley.

Lipp, Judith. 2007. Lessons for effective renewable electricity policy from Denmark, Germany and the United Kingdom. *Energy Policy* 35: 5481–95.

Mankiw, N. Gregg, and William Scarth. 2008. *Macroeconomics: Third Canadian edition.* New York: Worth Publishers.

Mehl, Arnaud. 2006. The yield curve as a predictor and emerging economies. Working Paper No. 691, European Central Bank, Frankfurt, Germany. http://ssrn.com/abstract_id=940644.

New Energy Finance. 2009. *Global trends in sustainable energy investment 2009.* London: UN Environment Program and New Energy Finance, 2009.

New Energy Finance. 2010. *Global trends in sustainable energy investment 2010.* London: UN Environment Program and New Energy Finance.

Partnoy, Frank. 2003. *Infectious greed: How deceit and risk corrupted the financial markets.* New York: Owl Books, Henry Holt.

REN 21. 2008. *Renewables 2007 global status report.* Paris: REN21 Secretariat; Washington, D.C.: Worldwatch Institute.

Rubin, Jeffrey. 2009. *Why your world is about to get a whole lot smaller.* Toronto: Random House Canada.

Sadorsky, Perry. 2008. Assessing the impact of oil prices on firms of different sizes: It's tough being in the middle. *Energy Policy* 36: 3854–61.

Sadorsky, Perry. 2009. Renewable energy consumption, CO_2 emissions and oil prices in the G7 countries. *Energy Economics* 31: 456–62.

Shrivastava, Paul. 1995. Ecocentric management for a risk society. *Academy of Management Review* 20: 118–37.

Stern, Nicholas. 2009. *The global deal.* New York: Public Affairs.

Wheelock, D. C., and M. E. Wohar. 2009. Can the term spread predict output growth and recessions? A survey of the literature. *Federal Reserve Bank of St. Louis Review,* September–October, 419–440. http://research.stlouisfed.org/publications/review/09/09/part1/Wheelock.pdf.

World Economic Forum. 2009. *Green investing: Towards a clean energy infrastructure.* Geneva: World Economic Forum. http://www.weforum.org/pdf/climate/Green.pdf.

14 Leveraging Ourselves out of Crisis—Again!

Aida Sy and Tony Tinker

Few professions can claim to have instigated—almost single-handedly—a world-wide recession. Yet the breakdown in accounting controls and financial reporting are primary constituents of the current economic meltdown. The housing-market bubble involved the excessive use of leverage finance. These high-risk practices could have been prevented by the proper application of accounting controls and financial reporting. Yet it would be a mistake to reduce the crisis to a technical accounting failure. Rather, the context of this failure "necessitated" the accounting failures. The relevant antecedents lie in a conjunction of three contradictions of capitalism: a profitability, a realization, and concentration and centralization crisis. Only when contemporary accounting practices are located in this institutional, social, and historical context does it become clear why accounting practices failed. The basic ingredients of the present crisis are not new. Leveraged speculation began before, during the crash of 1929, and has reappeared several times in different guises—aided and abetted by lax audit and financial reporting practices. Today's "remedies" are mere palliatives that are not adequate to solve the problem. The current restructuring of the financial institutions is only a short-term displacement of the problem. It merely defers and transforms the present crisis into new institutional forms that may be too big to save.

• • •

There is a time-honored banking maxim: "Never borrow short to lend long." For banks, borrowing short involves using low-cost, immediately withdrawable deposits. Lending long means committing to long-term, not-so-easily-liquidated, high-risk, high-return investments. There is no problem in this, provided that the value of a bank's investment portfolio remains unimpaired. Indeed, problems diminish as long as asset values inflate in inflationary times (or in a speculative bubble). So it was with the housing market for several years. Then, the high returns from a growing investment portfolio exceeded the cost of financing from cheap depositor funds. Depositors remain safe as long as inflationary conditions pertain.

Deposits are the time bomb on a bank's balance sheet. Their contractual status entitles them to repayment of principle and payment of interest. Failure to comply with such payments authorizes depositors to sue for payment, and ultimately file for a winding-up and/or bankruptcy of the delinquent bank.

Financial reporting supposedly provides the public with advanced warning of pending leverage risk. Accounting controls can be designed to block high-risk transactions and to red flag such transactions if they occur. This chapter explores how and why these safeguards were compromised and the efficacy of the institutional restructuring aimed to resolve the current financial crisis.

Dialectical Contradictions of Capitalism

Capitalism is founded on expropriative social relations that underpin all historical moments of this social order. Political intervention at specific historical moments is always possible (Marcuse 1986;[1] Gramsci 1971[2]). However, because of capitalism's unstable social foundations, dialectical movements are simply negation of negations (Adorno 1973). The result is not closure, or a synthesis with permanent stability, but an unstable remainder with difference that contains within it the seeds of future crises. Problems are never solved; they are simply deferred and transformed.

The present financial crisis is composed of the conjunction of three contradictions that jeopardize the capital accumulation process (Gamble 1976):

1. The falling rate of profit
2. The realization crisis, or the disposal of overproduction
3. Concentration and centralization of capital

The Falling Rate of Profit

Banking and stock market work has undergone fundamental, technological change in recent years. Trading has fallen to what Karl Marx termed the "real" sub-subsumption of labor, where professional and craft work are radically transformed into low-cost, machine-minding, semiskilled work. Trading and banking transactions are now conducted electronically, at hyperspeed, with little or no human intervention. Instantaneous trading transcends time and space—it is performed on a global stage, twenty-four hours a day, seven days a week. Wall Street is now a tourist exhibit, preserved for its nostalgic resonance with a medieval corn market. Brokers and jobbers are obsolete. They have been replaced by software and electronic assemblies (COMEX, the European partner of the New York Stock Exchange, is a largely automated exchange).

The competitive effects of deskilling in banking contribute to the "falling rate of profit."[3] To counteract these market pressures, institutions and individuals have resorted to more exotic, high-risk and high-return financial instruments. These unstable circumstances persist to this day.

The Realization Crisis: The Disposal of Overproduction

The competitive drive for greater efficiency results in shedding high-cost labor and replacing it with (fewer) cheaper workers. The consequence is greater production with fewer workers and a commensurate reduction in the level of effective demand. Hence, capitalism has a chronic tendency toward overproduction and difficulty in disposing of surplus production. Credit—in its many forms—is an attempt to bolster demand to absorb surplus production. This is the negation that capitalism uses to counter the perennial problem of overproduction.

Home loans and mortgages are a form of credit that has sustained activity in the building and housing sector. Market pressures in the form of commissions to banks and real estate brokers have sustained a level of lending, often well beyond the capacity of borrowers to repay.[4] Second mortgages and reverse mortgages are additional lines of credit funded by property as collateral. The concealment of the leverage risk by brokers and bank salespeople is well documented.

Concentration and Centralization of Capital

Although elements of the two previous contradictions linger to this day, the concentration and centralization of capital presents the greatest instability because it is in this arena that today's solutions will become tomorrow's problems. Many of the institutional rearrangements, aimed to restore stability, have destroyed the firewalls that would have localized banking failures. The creation of entities that are now too big to save is an important focus of the following sections. Before proceeding, however, it is important to review the dialectical movements of instabilities that preceded the present crisis. This history is not merely a procession of events, but movements that dialectically connect the past to the present to the future.

Accounting Practices for Disguising Leverage

Leverage Ratios and Financial Risk

Auditor firms are charged under the 1933–1934 Securities Acts, and more recently under the Sarbanes-Oxley legislation of 2002, with certifying the accounts of publicly quoted companies. This charge extends to assessing a firm's system of internal controls, including those of the banks that were selling subprime loans to poorly informed borrowers. Hence, "the auditor is required to attest to management's assessment of internal control over financial reporting."[5]

Why did bank managers, auditors, and the regulators (the Securities and Exchange Commission and the Public Company Accounting Oversight Board) fail to comply with this legal obligation? The root lies in the compromised circumstances of these institutions. Auditors are paid by the corporations they are required to audit.[6] Notwithstanding additional safeguards introduced by the 2002 Sarbanes-Oxley legislation, this basic contradiction remains in the form of pressure to please the client.[7]

This willingness to accommodate the client was evident from the financial reporting practices of Enron, where the auditors (and regulators) allowed the firm to disguise its high-risk practices. The practice is known as off-balance-sheeting the risk. The manner in which this was accomplished can be shown with a series of examples. Table 14.1 shows the balance sheet of a "normal" firm, with a tolerable risk profile.

The important measures of risk are shown in Table 14.1: the proportions of equity ($60 billion) to depositors and loans ($40 billion; figures are presented as percentages to simplify the comparisons). The 60:40 ratio means that depositors have a cushion of $6 for every $4 of exposure (or a 3:2 ratio). If the

TABLE 14.1 Normal Inc.

Assets	SB	Claims	$ (billions)
Investments	85	Equity	60
Cash	15	Deposits, loans, etc.	40
Total	100	Total	100

TABLE 14.2 Bear Stearns, Lehman Brothers, Fannie Mae, Freddie Mac, UBC, Citi

Assets	$ (billions)	Claims	$ (billions)
Mortgages	97	Equity 4	4
Cash	3	Deposits, loans, etc.	96
Total	100	Total	100

investments fall in value (e.g., in a bad trading year, with a fall in the value of an investment portfolio, with a poor real estate investment), then asset value can drop by $25 billion before the depositor's claims are in jeopardy. Such a massive decline in investment values is unlikely, which confirms the adequacy of the size of the cushion for depositors. The 60:40 leverage ratio (also called a gearing ratio or a coverage ratio) is a reassuring statistic for depositors.

Table 14.2 shows the balance sheet of a typical bank—banks are, in general, high-risk enterprises. Table 14.2 shows a leverage ratio of 4:96, compared with a safe leverage ratio of 3:2 in Table 14.1. A mere 10 percent decline in the mortgage asset (of $9.7 billion) would wipe out the cushion of $4 billion and put a bank in a state of technical insolvency. However, as long as inflationary conditions pertain (i.e., mortgage and other assets increase in value), depositors are safe. But the recent dramatic decline in mortgage asset values has eclipsed the equity value of many financial institutions. The bubble has burst.

The Transitory Nature of the Accounting Sign

Accounting can re-present balance sheet values to minimize the appearance of financial risk. In terms of Tables 14.1 and 14.2, this involves inflating the equity value and deflating the depositor value, thus resulting in a safer leverage statistic than a firm really deserves. Better leverage statistics give greater assurance to existing and potential lenders (i.e., depositors). Lowering the risk profile increases the willingness of lenders and depositors to lend at lower interest rates. We can use Enron as a case study to show how a high-risk entity can be transformed into a low-risk business.

The two balance sheets in Table 14.3 show amounts in percentages to simplify the explanation. The left-hand balance sheet is for Enron alone, and it shows a reasonable risk profile: a leverage ratio of 5:5. Enron preserved this relatively healthy appearance in two ways:

1. The equity value (of 50 percent) was inflated by issuing shares that were not really shares. They should have been classified as debt

TABLE 14.3 Balance sheets for Enron and its unconsolidated subsidiary in the Dominican Republic

Enron U.S.				Enron Subsidiary: Dominican Republic			
Assets ($, billions)		*Claims ($, billions)*		*Assets ($, billions)*		*Claims ($, billions)*	
Dot-com	90%	Equity	50%	Elec. plant	100%	Equity	5%
Cash	10%	Liabilities	50%			U.S. government loan	95%
Total	100%	Total	100%	Total	100%	Total	100%

(liabilities). These shares paid interest (not dividends), and this was accepted as such by the Internal Revenue Service (IRS). In this sense, the IRS compounded the fabrication.

2. Enron's liability figure was deflated because Enron was not required to add to its 50 percent liabilities the U.S. government loan on its subsidiary's balance sheet.

Enron avoided consolidating the two balance sheets (and thus was able to present a rosy risk picture) by invoking a little known 5 percent rule. Created for special-purpose entities (SPEs), the rule was originally developed for an entirely different set of circumstances.[8] Invoking this rule allowed Enron to evade consolidation. The Dominican Republic was one of some twenty-seven poor countries where Enron, using lender financing from the U.S. government, entered into agreements (often by bribing an local elite) to privatize basic utilities (e.g., electricity, gas, water).[9] In all cases, the debt financing was kept off Enron's balance sheet.

Amalgamating Enron's balance sheet with its Dominican subsidiary provides a glimpse of what Enron was trying to hide. Table 14.4—again showing percentages—presents Enron's consolidated balance sheet.

Margin Trading and Margin Calls

Corporations never have cash on hand to pay immediate expenses, such as payroll and short-term creditors. Rather, firms like Enron borrow on the short-term money market. When investors discovered the extent of Enron's leverage, and therefore its leverage risk, they refused to accept Enron's paper or notes. Enron's liquidity thus dried up, and the firm was forced to file for bankruptcy.

TABLE 14.4 Enron's consolidated balance sheet: Parent company and subsidiary in the Dominican Republic

Assets (billions $)		Claims (billions $)	
Dot-com	45%	Equity	27%
Elec. plant	50%	U.S. government loan	48%
Cash	5%	Liability	25%
Total	100%		100%

This pattern of behavior—from high-risk leverage financing in an investment bubble to the bursting of the bubble, the withdrawal of credit, and bankruptcy—is a familiar pattern. The investment object of the bubble investment may differ: it could be real estate, it could be stocks and shares, or it could be tulips. The details are irrelevant, but the pattern is important. Consider, for instance, speculation in the recent subprime market.

In Table 14.5, a $2 million property is purchased with a down payment of $200,000 and a mortgage of $1.8 million. The house price increases to $3 million, and the buyer uses the increased value as security for a second mortgage loan of $1 million to invest in the stock market. When property values fall from $4 million to $2 million, the bank will make a margin call of $600,000 to cover the balance of the loan. As the initial deposit was merely $200,000, it is unlikely that the borrower would be able to make the margin call. Thus, the property would be placed in foreclosure, and the borrower would be forced to file for bankruptcy.

TABLE 14.5 Borrowing on margin and margin calls

	Initial cash down payment	Price of house or securities	Loan or mortgage from the bank
Original house purchase	$0.2M	$3M	$1.8M
Increase in property value		$1M	
Second bank loan to purchase securities		$1M	$1M
Property price falls to		$2M	
Bank makes margin call		$2.8M – $2M – $0.2M = $0.6M	

TABLE 14.6 Crises, regulation, and deregulation

Date	Crises, Regulation, and Deregulation
1920s	Florida real estate market boom
1929 crash	Syndicates and pools
1933	Glass-Steagall Act, FDIC
1933–34	Securities acts (audit and disclosure)
1980	Reagan repeals Glass-Steagall (Depository Institutions Deregulation and Monetary Control Act)
1980s	Savings-and-loan crisis: Resolution Trust MK1: $150, Total - 500B est.
1990s	Dot-com meltdown, $2 trillion–$3 trillion
1999	Gramm-Leach-Bliley Act (Financial Services Modernization Act), partial repeal of Glass-Steagall to remove firewalls between insurance companies' commercial and investment banks
2001	Enron default, $8 billion
2002	Sarbanes-Oxley
2002	WorldCom default, $12 billion
2008	Bear Stearns, $29 billion (JPMorgan); Fannie Mae and Freddie Mac, $200 billion; AIG, $85 billion; Lehman Brothers, $129 billion; Merrill Lynch, $130 billion (Bank of America), Morgan Stanley, Goldman Sachs Resolution Trust Mark ll: $700 billion
2008 and beyond	Northern Rock (U.K.) Bradford and Bingley (U.K.) Wachovia to Wells Fargo Washington Mutual to Bank of America Morgan Stanley to Mitsubishi UFJ Fortis to Belgium and France Dextor to France, Holland, and Belgium Kaupthing Bank to Iceland to Russia Kaupthing Edge to ING (Holland) Kaupthing Singer & Friedlander (U.K.) to U.K. Kaupthing (Austria) to Austria

The pattern repeats itself: borrowing on margin, a burst of the speculative bubble, margin calls, and bankruptcy. Consider Table 14.6.

Table 14.6 shows a timeline of the pattern of leverage borrowing, bubble speculation, crisis, margin call, and regulation. As Galbraith (1954) argues, the Florida real estate market was boom and bust, fueled by leveraged borrowing. The early 1920s Florida debacle was a rehearsal for the 1929 crash. Each case relied on margin borrowing to fuel a boom, followed by a crash and subsequent margin call and then default. The Florida bust and the 1929 crash differed only in that, in one case, the object of speculation was real estate and in the other it was margin borrowing to buy stocks and shares.

Table 14.6 shows that, because the inherent contradictory social relations of capitalism, legal, and other solutions to each crisis are never permanent, they merely defer and transform problems (Adorno 1973). The 1933 Glass-Steagall Act established the Federal Deposit Insurance Corporation (FDIC) to restore depositor and lender confidence in commercial banks. But this solution only set the stage for the free-rider, or moral-hazard, problem.[10] The availability of federally insured deposits was an invitation to reckless, speculative, and even fraudulent behavior. Speculators and managers knew that the state would cover their bets. The FDIC insurance set the stage for the crisis of the 1980s. Many savings-and-loan entities engaged in reckless conduct (Lincoln Savings and Loan being one of the most notorious).[11] Drexel Burnham Lambert's Michael Milken bragged about using federally insured funds, which Drexel bundled into $100,000 packets, to invest in junk bonds and high-risk real estate ventures.[12]

The 1930s also set in place contradictions that would continue to erupt into later years. The 1933–1934 Securities Acts created the Securities and Exchange Commission (SEC), which was given oversight powers over publicly quoted companies. The 1934 act required corporations to publish a prospectus and an annual report, which were examined and certified by a certified public accountant. The SEC was empowered to set standards for financial reporting; however, it immediately off-loaded this responsibility to the accounting profession. The problem then, and now, is that the auditor is paid by the corporations it is auditing. There is always a temptation to please the client. As a consequence, there was a parade of audit and financial failures, including Paramount Pictures, Reliance Insurance, National Student Marketing, Enron, ESM, BCCI, WorldCom, ZZZZ Best, OPM, Waste Management, Regina Vacuum Cleaner, and the list goes on (Briloff 1970, 1972). These contradictions were accentuated with the defunding of regulatory agencies (on entering office, Ronald Reagan cut the SEC's budget by 30 percent).

There has been the increasing assimilation of the polity by lobbying (O'Conner 1973). Politics is now an extension of the corporate market, as are advertising expenses (Stigler 1946; Peltzman 1976; Tinker 1984). The Lincoln Savings and Loan and Enron affairs (though twenty years apart) both involved aggressive lobbying in Congress to delay regulatory intervention and to compromise improvements in financial reporting. In the Lincoln case, the six-month delay cost several billion dollars. In the Enron case, executive remuneration with stock options remains, to this day, largely off the books thanks to heavy congressional lobbying. The result was not just the misstating of corporate income but also opening up of the floodgates to a bonanza in executive compensation.

Contradictions for the Present and Future

The 1999 Gramm-Leach-Bliley Act (the Financial Services Modernization Act) partially repealed the Glass-Steagall Act. It removed the firewalls between insurance companies and commercial and investment banks. The purpose of Gramm-Leach-Bliley was to expand profit opportunities of banks, but in doing so, it removed the protective barriers between different lines of business. By allowing banks to expand into different states, and beyond states into different countries, the impact of a failure in one sector would no longer be confined to that sector but could engulf the entire entity. Similarly, once upon a time, an insurance failure stayed in the insurance sector. Today, an insurance failure could envelop the FDIC side of a business. And most important, commercial banks that use FDIC deposits are, as a result of the recent government-approved mergers, now exposed to high-risk investment banking.

The list of time bombs has grown. Bear Stearns (an investment bank) was bought by JPMorgan (a commercial bank with federally insured deposits). AIG was a provider of regular insurance but is known to be deeply involved in credit swaps. The investment bank Merrill Lynch was assimilated by a grateful Bank of America (an FDIC-insured commercial bank).

Morgan Stanley and Goldman Sachs are investment banks that have both been granted the status of FDIC-insured commercial banks. Recent events involving these two banks foreshadow the future. In Romania, these banks are under investigation for short selling the Romania leu against the euro. So in this new era, federally insured U.S. deposits are exposed to overseas speculative ventures. National boundaries no longer provide a firewall. A meltdown in one country could ricochet into another. When Iceland nationalized its failing banks, its deposit insurance scheme was not extended to its bank's U.K. customers. The U.K. government assumed the liability and sued Iceland for compensation. In short, many of the 2008 bank takeovers, mergers, consolidations, holding-company formations, nonbank and bank ventures, and other aspects of the bailout have destroyed firewalls between different financial products, as well as the firewalls between different geographical and legal jurisdictions. The result is that meltdowns can no longer be localized— systemic risk has increased.

Wall Street: Too Big to Fail? Too Big to Save?

In the 1980s, the U.S. government stepped in to save Continental Illinois, the fourth-largest bank in the United States, with assets of $64 billion. The rationale for this unprecedented intervention was that the bank was too big to fail. Its collapse might have triggered a systemic meltdown of the entire banking system.

Today, regulators and the state face a new quandary: are some banks too big to save? Iceland provided a glimpse of what was coming. Iceland bailed out its banks (Kaupthing) and in doing so exhausted its foreign currency reserves. This placed the bankrupted nation in receivership with the International Monetary Fund (IMF). In exchange for IMF support, the IMF required the national bank to raise interest rates to 18 percent to stem the exodus out of the krona. An 18 percent cost of capital pushed Iceland's economy toward acute recession, as internal investment had ground to a standstill. By the same token, Fortis was too big for its host country, Belgium, to rescue—France had to lend a hand. Table 14.7 provides a too-big-to-save index.

Table 14.7 shows the total leverage of each of the top fifteen largest banks in the world, as a percentage of the host country's gross domestic product (GDP). For instance, the leverage of Switzerland's two largest banks, expressed as a percentage of that country's GDP, is 595 percent. Given the fragile nature of banks and national economies, it is difficult to know which time bomb listed in Table 14.7 will explode first.

Main Street: Too Big to Save?

The struggle in Washington was whether the $170 billion fund created by the 2008 Emergency Economic Stabilization Act (EESA) should be limited to bailing out Wall Street or whether the fund should be extended to rescuing Main Street. The claims from Main Street were compelling, large, and growing. General Motors, Ford, and Daimler-Chrysler headed the queue, with requests for a total of $25 billion. Not far behind were the airlines, numerous states facing massive deficits, and others.

Implications

In November 18, 2008, banking industry representatives appeared before the House Banking Committee to request that the government expedite the processing of bank applications for holding-company status. The aim was

TABLE 14.7 Too-big-to-save index: Top fifteen banks'
leverage as percentage of country GDP

Country	Leverage
Switzerland	595.32
Netherlands	336.86
Belgium	318.84
United Kingdom	206.21
France	198.07
Hong Kong	154.74
Spain	107.77
Japan	102.16
Sweden	82.96
Australia	82.07
Italy	70.32
China	63.26
Germany	49.88
United States	44.19
Canada	28.80

SOURCE: EUROBANK, http://www.euromoney.com/
Article/1961042/Worlds-largest-banks-2007-Global-bank-
rankings-Top-20-global-free-to-access.html; EUROMONEY,
http://www.euromoney.com/Article/1533691/Worlds-largest-
banks-Global-bank-rankings-Top-50-by-shareholder-equity-
free-to-access.html.

to expand the range of financial products that banks would be permitted
to offer, thereby alleviating their lackluster profits. Once again, longer-term
stability was being sacrificed to short-term expedients. Highly leveraged institutions would expand beyond the firewalls that previously were set to local-
ize risk. Geographical and product expansion by highly leveraged institutions
was creating a time bomb for the future.

The scenario is familiar. Faced with the savings-and-loan crisis in the
early 1980s, Ronald Reagan signed the Depository Institutions Deregulation and Monetary Control Act. He repealed parts of the 1933 Glass-Steagall
Act and allowed savings and loans to use federally insured deposits to move
beyond home loans into real estate, junk bonds, and other high-risk ventures. The savings-and-loan crisis cost the government's Resolution Trust

Corporation an estimated $150 billion and private individuals several hundred billion more. Current moves to anoint banks with holding-company status set the stage for a new savings-and-loan disaster.

Nor can we expect financial reporting by accountants to laser in on emergent corporate collapses. On the contrary, the big accounting firms and their banking industry clients lobbied successfully to insert a poisonous accounting provision into the 2008 EESA. Under this provision, banks are permitted to hide their impaired subprime assets from public view, by listing on their balance sheets subprime mortgage assets at their original contracted cost rather than their current depreciated value. Thus, a mortgage loan by a bank of $1 million that is now uncollectible and worthless is still shown on the bank's balance sheet as worth $1 million, thus allowing the bank to continue to appear more profitable and safer than it really is. This accounting legerdemain prevents investors and institutions from being able to distinguish between failing and healthy banks. It is an accounting ploy that perpetuates the caution that has frozen lending in the capital markets.

Notes

1. "All Marxian concepts extend . . . first . . . the complex of given social relations, and second, the complex of elements inherent in the social reality that make for the transformation into a free social order."

2. "The philosophy of praxis is a reform and a development of Hegelianism. . . . [I]t is consciousness full of contradictions, in which the philosopher understood . . . individually and as an entire social group, not only grasp the contradictions, but posits himself as an element of the contradiction and elevates this element to a principle of knowledge and therefore action."

3. Some recently laid-off Wall Street workers have interviewed with Southeast Asian banks. Salary offers are between a quarter and one-third of previous pay rates.

4. The predatory lending practices that led to the subprime crisis are reminiscent of those deployed by savings and loans in the 1980s. When FDIC-insured certificates of deposit (CDs) matured for Lincoln Savings and Loan, the owners were contacted by bank "salespeople" to flip their CDs into another investment. Customers were misled about the absence of FDIC insurance for the new product. The sales literature encouraged salespeople to target "the old, the meek and infirm." Florida retirees were especially hard hit by this fraud. Most of them died before any legal redress was secured.

5. Final Rule: Management's Report on Internal Control over Financial Reporting and Certification of Disclosure in Exchange Act Periodic Reports, *Securities and Exchange Commission,* 17 CFR 210, 228, 229, 240, 249, 270, and 274 (release nos. 33-8238; 34-47986; IC-26068; file nos. S7-40-02; S7-06-03), RIN 3235-AI66 and 3235-AI79.

6. The system is akin to schoolchildren paying their teachers. If schoolchildren paid their teachers, all children would get As. When auditors are paid by their client, the client is likely to receive a clean audit report.

7. For an accounting firm, the retention of a client is worth more than one year's audit fee. It is a series of fees—the present value of an annuity—plus any additional fees that may be extracted from the client by selling additional financial services. There are enormous pressures on audit partners to keep and please the client. Partners frequently receive commissions for new business and loss of income, and/or their jobs, if they lose a client.

8. The 5 percent rule was originally developed for automobile manufacturers who had developed credit subsidiaries to help customers buy vehicles on credit. GM Credit and Chrysler Credit were two such entities. If the auto manufacturers had consolidated or combined their banking subsidiaries and their own balance sheets, their leverage or financial risk ratios would be alarmingly high, and the auto firms' cost of raising money would become prohibitive. For this reason, automobile firms were exempt from consolidating balance sheets, as long as 5 percent or more of the subsidiary equity was held by outside parties. Enron used this loophole to escape consolidation.

9. Enron not only was engaged in massive off-balance-sheeting of its leverage but also was engaged in bully tactics against poor countries. In the Dominican Republic, for example, Enron secured the monopoly contract to upgrade the public electrical supply from an existing productive capacity of 11 megawatts (MW) to 15 MW. Once in charge, Enron reduced supply to 8 MW, causing widespread blackouts and endangering the lives and health of many citizens. It then argued that only a price increase would allow the company to finance the improvements needed to restore capacity. Riots ensued in many countries (sometimes put down by Enron police). Some rioters died. Not until Enron pulled the same stunt with the Californian electrical supply did Americans begin to question the Enron miracle.

10. Free riders are those who consume more than their fair share of a resource or shoulder less than a fair share of the costs of its production. This is closely related to the moral-hazard problem: the prospect that a party insulated from risk may behave differently than if it were fully exposed to the risk. Moral hazard arises because an individual or institution does not bear the full consequences of its actions, and therefore has a tendency to act less carefully than it otherwise would, leaving another party to bear some responsibility for the consequences of those actions. For example, an individual with insurance against automobile theft may be less vigilant about locking his or her car because the negative consequences of automobile theft are (partially) borne by the insurance company.

11. The unintended consequence of FDIC insurance eventually cost taxpayers $150 billion and an estimated $350 billion to private individuals.

12. Drexel Burnham Lambert eventually collapsed, and Milken was sentenced to eighteen months in a so-called country-club jail and fined $750 million (half of his net worth).

References

Adorno, T. 1973. *Negative dialectics*, translated by B. Ashton. New York: Seabury Press.

Briloff, A. J. 1970. Accounting practices and the merger movement. Testimony to the U.S. Senate Subcommittee on Antitrust and Monopoly of the Committee of the Judiciary, February.

Briloff, A. J. 1972. *Unaccountable accounting*. New York: Harper & Row.

Galbraith, John Kenneth. 1954. *The great crash*. Boston: Houghton Mifflin.

Gamble, Andrew, and Paul Walton. 1976. *Capitalism in crisis: Inflation and the state*. London: Macmillan.

Gramsci, A. 1971. *Selections from the Prison Notebooks*. London: Lawrence and Wishart.

Marcuse, H. 1986. *Reason and revolution*. London: Routledge Kegan Paul.

O'Connor, James. 1973. *The fiscal crisis of the state*. New York: St. Martin's Press.

Peltzman, Sam. 1976. Toward a more general theory of regulation. *Journal of Law and Economics* 19 (2): 211–48.

Stigler, G. J. 1946. *Production and distribution theories*. New York: Agathon Press.

Tinker, A. M. 1984. Theories of the state and the state of accounting: Economic reductionism and political voluntarism in accounting regulation theory. *Journal of Accounting and Public Policy* 3: 55–74.

15 The Normative Foundation of Finance

*How Misunderstanding the Role of Financial Theories
Distorts the Way We Think About the Responsibility
of Financial Economists*

Andreas Georg Scherer and Emilio Marti

The financial crisis has fueled a heated debate about the responsibility of financial economists. Critics such as Paul Krugman, Robert Shiller, and David Colander argue that financial economists have developed useless or even harmful theories. This is an important debate, but it suffers from the fact that the role of financial theories remains unclear. In this chapter, we enter the field of philosophy of science to clarify this issue. In particular, we emphasize the research interests and the various philosophical assumptions of three alternative views on financial theories. We analyze the widespread positivistic conception of financial theories and contrast it with a postmodern perspective. We conclude that both positions have limitations. As an alternative, we outline a constructivist conception of financial theories. In the final section, we use these insights from philosophy of science to clarify the responsibility of financial economists. Financial economists have to critically reflect the problems in practice that need to be addressed and to keep their theories closely tied to these original problems. We show how, in the case of the efficient market hypothesis, the misunderstanding of the role of financial theories led financial economists to neglect this responsibility.

We thank Paul Shrivastava for his helpful comments on an earlier draft and Ann Nelson (Zurich) for her kind help with the English language. For financial support, we are grateful to the University Priority Research Program Ethics at the University of Zurich.

Why We Need Clarity About the Role of Financial Theories

"Why did no one see the crisis coming?" Queen Elizabeth reportedly asked Professor Luis Garicano, director of research at the London School of Economics' management department during her visit to the school in November 2008 (Skidelsky 2009). The British Academy held a seminar on the subject and responded to this concern in an open letter to Her Majesty. The academy concluded that "the failure to foresee the timing, extent and severity of the crisis and to head it off, while it had many causes, was principally a failure of the collective imagination of many bright people, both in this country and internationally, to understand the risks to the system as a whole" (British Academy 2009, 3).

In fact, most financial economists failed to warn the public of the possibility of a financial crisis and of its severe consequences. And once the financial crisis was in full swing, the available financial theories could not offer sufficient advice to policy and law makers on how to handle the situation (Colander et al. 2009). Critics, such as Nobel laureate Paul Krugman (2009), therefore conclude that the theories developed by financial economists are useless for guiding practice because economists are "mistaking beauty for truth." Economists normally focus on the sophisticated mathematical modeling of financial markets and favor rigor over relevance, which finally leads to a loss of reality. Furthermore, the theories of finance encouraged banks and other financial companies to develop risky financial products (e.g., mortgage-backed securities, credit default swaps) and to support their lobbying strategies against the governmental regulation of financial markets. All this brought global financial markets to the brink of collapse (Eichengreen 2009). Eichengreen (2009) and others therefore argue that the theories of finance have not just been useless but also harmful to the public (see also Colander et al. 2009).

This fueled a heated debate within financial economics about the responsibility of financial economists. Some argue that financial economists "have to face up to the inconvenient reality that financial markets fall far short of perfection" (Krugman 2009) and should take into account "animal spirits" (Akerlof and Shiller 2009) or fat tails (Sornette 2009). Others suggest that financial economists "have an ethical responsibility to communicate the limitations of their models and the potential misuses of their research" (Colander et al. 2009, 4) or point to shortcomings in the education of future financial professionals (Chesney 2009, 2010). Still other financial economists see no need to change the way financial research is done. They argue, as Myron Scholes is quoted in the *Economist* (2009), that "much of the blame for the recent woe should be pinned not on economists' theories and models but on those on Wall Street and in the City who pushed them too far in practice."

This is an important debate in which many significant arguments have been made. At the same time, it is hard to balance these different arguments against each other. For example, it seems plausible that financial economists should make their theories more realistic by including animal spirits or fat tails. However, isn't it the very essence of financial theories that these are abstract simplifications of reality that neglect some of its complexity? Likewise, it seems plausible that financial economists should think about possible societal consequences when they develop and teach financial theories. Yet how can this be reconciled with the aspiration to offer value-free explanations of the "pervasive market forces" (Miller 1986, S467)? And to whom are financial economists finally accountable? Is it to investors, to shareholders, banking managers, or to the wider public?

In this chapter, we argue that we can answer these fundamental questions about the responsibility of financial economists only on the basis of a clear understanding of the role of financial theories. Thus, to clarify the responsibility of financial economists, we have to enter the field of philosophy of science and reflect on the foundations of finance on a meta level of analysis (Scherer 2003). This inquiry is the main objective of this chapter.

As we will see, there are alternative perspectives on the role of theories (McGoun and Zielonka 2006). We distinguish three different perspectives and discuss their contributions and limitations: positivistic, postmodern, and constructive perspectives on financial theories. We first present the most widespread conception of finance and financial theories. Positivistic finance defines theories as tools that help predict and control financial markets. We show that this conception has limitations. Some economists therefore endorse a postmodern perspective on finance as an alternative (postmodern finance). Postmodern finance conceives of theories as social conventions that improve mutual understanding between the powerful market players. Again, this perspective has its limitations, and it allows us to conclude that it is not one that is convincing. We therefore then outline an alternative perspective of what we call constructivist finance. Here, theories are considered linguistic devices that support the creation of justified financial markets. We then focus on the initial question about the responsibility of financial economists. On the basis of a constructivist conception of finance, we systematically develop a theoretical perspective on the responsibility that financial economists have.

Positivistic Finance: Theories Grasp the Essence of Financial Markets

Positivistic finance predominates within the finance discipline.[1] Adherents of this perspective claim that financial theories (models and hypotheses) look beyond the great variety of everyday financial phenomena and grasp what is essential for financial markets. Positivistic finance considers phenomena as ontologically given to the observer (i.e., the researcher) and suggests a structural similarity (or even identity) between financial models and hypotheses and the financial markets that they describe. Following this perspective, financial economists explore the deep structures of cause-and-effect relationships that hold financial markets together. In the literature, several explicit or implicit variants of positivistic finance are found: positive finance, normative finance, and foundational/aesthetic finance. For these distinctions, we build on an article by Elton McGoun and Piotr Zielonka (2006).

"Positive finance" (McGoun and Zielonka 2006, 49) is the most widespread variant of positivistic finance. According to positive finance, a model or hypothesis "is true if it corresponds to what people are doing" (McGoun and Zielonka 2006, 49). To empirically test the validity of a model or hypothesis, one has to compare predictions that are logically deduced from the model or hypothesis with descriptions of observable phenomena. If the predictions do not correspond with the descriptions of observable phenomena, the model or hypothesis has been falsified. According to positive finance, what is essential for financial markets can be empirically observed. Following this perspective, the empirical evidence speaks for itself.

Within positive finance, on the one hand, some scholars claim that every part of a good model or hypothesis has to correspond to reality (e.g., Spremann 2008). They stress that good models and hypotheses are based on realistic assumptions. On the other hand, Milton Friedman (1964, 14) famously argued that the assumptions of theories have to be unrealistic: "Truly important and significant hypotheses will be found to have 'assumptions' that are wildly inaccurate descriptive representations of reality, and, in general, the more significant the theory, the more unrealistic the assumptions (in this sense)." According to Friedman, good theories have to make significant and useful predictions. If they manage to do so, a correspondence between the theory and reality has been established.

The other two variants of positivistic finance assume that what is essential for financial markets cannot be observed empirically. Instead, adherents of these positions assume that the essentials of financial markets can be deduced analytically and have to cohere with more fundamental principles.

"Normative finance" (McGoun and Zielonka 2006, 49) is the second variant of positivistic finance. It assumes that human rationality is the fundamental principle from which one has to deduce what is essential for financial markets. According to normative finance, a model or hypothesis "is true if it corresponds to what people should [rationally] be doing" (McGoun and Zielonka 2006, 49). Models are conceived of as normative ideals and reconstruct what actions would be rational. The idea seems to be that rationality is the principle that holds financial markets together. Rationality is the essence of financial markets. Therefore, models and hypotheses can correspond to reality only if they make rationality their key assumption.

"Foundational/aesthetic finance" (McGoun and Zielonka 2006, 49) is the third variant of positivistic finance. It claims that a model or hypothesis is "true if it is a necessary consequence of a set of assumptions" (McGoun and Zielonka 2006, 49). Here, models and hypotheses are used to coherently describe an ideal world in which free interaction leads to market equilibrium. This means that market equilibrium is thought to be the fundamental principle that is essential for financial markets. William Sharpe argues this in his famous article on the capital asset pricing model (CAPM). Sharpe (1964, 434) suggests that "the proper test of a theory is . . . the acceptability of its implications." And because his model leads to "equilibrium conditions which form a major part of classical financial doctrine, it is far from clear that this formulation should be rejected—especially in view of the dearth of alternative models leading to similar results" (Sharpe 1964, 434). Sharpe seems to suggest that models (and hypotheses) can correspond to reality only if they are coherent with classical financial doctrine. Figure 15.1 illustrates these different variants of positivistic finance.

Despite these differences, all variants of positivistic finance share common features. To analyze them systematically, we should clarify both their ends and their means. This refers to the two fundamental questions of the philosophy of science (Burrell and Morgan 1979; Scherer 2003): (1) What is the purpose of research? and (2) By what means can this purpose be achieved?

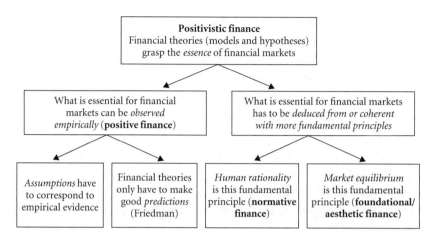

FIGURE 15.1 Variants of positivistic finance

The Purpose of Positivistic Finance

The work of the philosopher Jürgen Habermas is an ideal starting point for thinking about the purpose of theory. His theory of cognitive research interests has been applied to organization and management studies (see, e.g., Scherer 2003, 2009; Steffy and Grimes 1986; Willmott 2003). Habermas (1971) distinguishes three cognitive research interests: technical, practical, and emancipatory. The purpose of the technical cognitive interest is to enhance prediction and control. It focuses on the identification of cause-and-effect relationships and manipulation of variables, so that certain aims, such as enhancing efficiency or maximizing profitability, can be achieved. The practical cognitive interest aims to improve mutual understanding. Here the focus is on the interpretation of symbolic communication. The purpose of the emancipatory cognitive interest is to develop more rational social institutions and relations and to free human beings from dependency, subordination, and suppression, and to support the self-actualization of humans. To achieve this goal, this perspective seeks to identify patterns of domination and exploitation and "to discover which (if any) theoretical statements express unchangeable laws of social action and which, though they express relations of dependence because they are ideologically fixed, are in principle subject to change" (Habermas 1966, 294). Each of these three cognitive interests leads to a different kind of knowledge. Habermas argues that we need all three cognitive interests to advance knowledge and to further develop social conditions.

By contrast, positivistic finance (in all its variants) restricts itself to the technical cognitive interest. With its theories, it tries to enhance prediction and control. This is most straightforward in the case of positive finance (the first variant of positivistic finance). Here, models and hypotheses aspire to uncover the deep structures and cause-and-effect relationships that are constitutive for the way financial markets work. This knowledge can then be used by individuals, groups, or societies. It may serve hedge funds to predict and control returns or national banks to predict and control inflation.

For the other two variants of positivistic finance, it is less obvious that prediction and control is their purpose. The theories of normative finance cannot directly be used for prediction and control. This is because irrational behavior and other disruptive factors exist. Even though these phenomena are considered inessential to how financial markets work, they limit the ability of normative theories to predict and control. Normative models and hypotheses enhance our ability to predict and control indirectly. They tell us how to create the conditions for more rational (i.e., more efficient) financial markets that could be better predicted and controlled.

Within foundational/aesthetic finance, this indirect contribution to prediction and control becomes more pronounced. Here, theories are thought to coherently describe an ideal world in which free interaction leads to market equilibrium. Obviously, this knowledge cannot be used directly to predict and control the real world. But the models and hypotheses tell us that if certain preconditions are met, then we can predict and control the consequences. The models and hypotheses of foundational/aesthetic finance therefore tell us how to create more predictable and controllable financial markets (McGoun and Zielonka 2006). Again, the technical cognitive interest reigns supreme.

The Means of Positivistic Finance

Positivistic finance strives to develop models and hypotheses that enhance prediction and control. But what are the means with which it tries to live up to this purpose? What assumptions does it make to develop financial theories that help to predict and control? To think about the means of theories, we refer to Gibson Burrell and Gareth Morgan (1979), who argue that every theory has ontological assumptions, epistemological assumptions, assumptions about human nature, and methodological assumptions. Furthermore, we refer to Maurice Landry's (1995) distinction among three conceptions of problems. The analysis and resolution of problems is a main concern of research and practice in finance. In our view, these distinctions offer a good conceptual framework to think systematically about the means of positivistic finance.

The ontological assumptions result from a debate on whether reality is given independently of the perspectives of individuals (realism) or a product of social or individual construction (nominalism). Does the structure of the social world exist irrespective of our concepts and labels, or are our concepts and labels constitutive for this structure? As positivistic finance (in all its variants) claims that theories grasp the essence of financial markets, it obviously sides with realism.

The epistemological assumptions determine how knowledge about human actions can be obtained. Can actions be explained from outside, through observation (positivism), or can they be understood only from inside, by participating in the underlying practice and understanding the meaning of actions and utterances from the subjective view of the focal actor (antipositivism)? Positivistic finance clearly purports that the former is true. In all its variants, the subjective view from inside plays no role.

The assumptions on human nature depend on whether humans are considered to be determined by their environment (determinism) or whether the ability to make free decisions is ascribed to them (voluntarism). Positivistic finance assumes the former. It models humans as profit-maximizing agents. Their actions, however, are nothing but reactions to incentives and thus mere behavior.

The methodological assumptions refer to the question of whether social sciences should use the quantitative and experimental methods of the natural sciences (nomothetic theory) or whether they should rely on a qualitative and interpretive analysis of the humanities (ideographic theory). Positivistic finance asserts that the former is true. Because of this, many economists like to compare their theories to those of natural scientists. The economist David Levine (2009), for instance, suggests that "economic models are like models of photons going through slits."

What does this all mean for the concept of problems? Maurice Landry (1995) distinguishes an objectivist, a subjectivist, and a constructivist conception of problems. The objectivist conception conceives of problems as a part of the external reality. Their existence "does not depend on any subject's knowledge, although someone must be aware of their existence if they are to be called problems" (Landry 1995, 321). The subjectivist conception assumes that problems are created by subjective interpretation and structuring. A problem "results from a subject's attempts at structuring incoming perceptions and making them fit with both previously accumulated perceptions and with personal, moral, rational, or aesthetic values" (Landry 1995, 325). The constructivist conception of problems takes a middle ground: "problems have no existence on their own but are nevertheless grounded in some objective reality" (Landry 1995, 328). Problems are conceived of as pragmatic devices that help individuals adapt to reality.

Positivistic finance clearly has an objectivist conception of problems. A problem is considered a given entity of external reality that certain individuals judge as negative and that they want to change (Landry 1995, 316). To do this, they can use financial theories that help them to predict and control aspects of external reality. Theories can be used to overcome problems. It is important, however, to see that these models and hypotheses (that are supposed to grasp the essence of financial markets) do not depend on what individuals consider a problem. If people would start to see different problems, this would (as long as no new facts are discovered) not lead to other financial theories. The same models and hypotheses would be used to overcome these new problems. With its objectivist conception of problems, positivist finance makes sure that the problems humans face in financial markets have no influence on the theories about financial markets.

Limitations of Positivistic Finance

Positivistic finance conceives of financial theories as tools that help predict and control financial markets. We see two limitations of this conception of finance and its theories. Both have to do with the relation between theory and praxis.

The first limitation of positivistic finance is that it neglects the influence of praxis on theory. As just explored, positivist finance assumes that financial models and hypotheses are not influenced by the problems humans face in financial markets. Or formulated more abstractly, theory is supposed to be completely independent of the praxis of financial markets and the problems with which we are confronted in this praxis.[2] But this is not plausible. Empirical data always result from certain questions that are asked. The philosopher Peter Janich (1989, 264) maintains: "Not one single piece of data is 'given' in a strict sense but is rather the result of a specific question within the framework of the system of distinctions formed by the language in which the question ... is formulated. The unavoidable *linguistic* fixation of scientific findings depend[s] on normative presuppositions which cannot be replaced by experience." Janich points out that knowledge inevitably has a linguistic form and that language—like all human artifacts—is always influenced by human needs, preferences, and values and by the problems humans are faced with.[3] As a result, theory cannot be independent of praxis, and the problems we face in the praxis of financial markets will have an influence on the way we theorize. Here, philosophers such as Friedrich Kambartel (1976, 1979, 1985) argue that economics is not possible as a purely empirical-analytic science. He stresses that the praxis of (financial) markets and problems we encounter therein are constitutive for economics (Kambartel 1976). They are the normative foundation of economics. We will elaborate on this in the section "Constructivist Finance."

The second limitation of positivistic finance (at least for its positive variant) is that it furthermore neglects the influence of theory on praxis. Social sciences are in a different position than natural sciences because human beings can know what science writes about them and they can, by intention, change their actions accordingly. This is especially relevant in the field of finance. Here, most practitioners are aware of the findings of academic finance, and they keep themselves well informed (McGoun and Zielonka 2006). The influence of theory on praxis takes many forms. Fabrizio Ferraro, Jeffrey Pfeffer, and Robert Sutton (2005) argue that the models of finance might become—at least temporarily—self-fulfilling prophecies. They distinguish three ways in which theories influence the behavior they describe.

First, theories create social norms. If a theory (say the Black-Scholes model) has been established, people feel pressured to act according to it (read: value options with the criteria that are important according to the Black-Scholes model). Otherwise they will have to justify their deviation from the norm. Second, theories influence our language. They influence the meaning of words and may create new ones. For instance, in the 1980s the Black-Scholes model made it seem like the implied volatility is the only relevant thing when talking about options (MacKenzie 2006). Third, theories influence the institutional design. For instance, after 1986 the commonly used Autoquote software calculated the stock prices that according to the Black-Scholes model would be compatible with the displayed option prices (MacKenzie 2006). In these three ways, theories influence the way people behave with the result that their descriptions come true.[4]

Because of this influence, it appears to be naive to argue that the theories of finance are nothing but an objectification. It rather seems that they are constitutive for the financial markets they describe. This is mainly a challenge for positivistic finance (McGoun and Zielonka 2006). For the other variants of positivistic finance—normative finance and foundational/aesthetic finance—it is just an elimination of some of the disruptive factors if the praxis becomes more like the theory that describes it.

Postmodern Finance: Theories as Socially Created Conventions

After positivistic finance has been discarded, postmodern finance might seem the only alternative. Postmodern finance views theories as socially created conventions. It presents a completely different view of the relation between theory and praxis. McGoun and Zielonka distinguish two variants of postmodern finance.

"Social constructive finance" argues that a theory "is true if we agree it is true" (McGoun and Zielonka 2006, 49). Here the theories of finance are inseparably linked to the praxis of financial markets: as a cause or as a consequence (or as both). Either financial theories cause a certain praxis of financial markets insofar as they convince opinion leaders (and through this, the rest of the market participants) to "act in accordance with them," or financial theories are a consequence of the praxis of financial markets in that they are nothing but "a sophisticated confirmation of what we already believe to be true" (McGoun and Zielonka 2006, 53). In both cases, theories become the rules of a game called financial markets. There is no independent "there" left out there (McGoun and Zielonka 2006, 53). All is a convention. McGoun (1997) elaborates this further when he argues (with Baudrillard) that financial markets have become a hyperreality. Financial markets are considered a "post-modern game" (McGoun 1997, 98) of a societal elite.

Within "cultural finance," truth plays no role (McGoun and Zielonka 2006, 49). The creation of theories is considered an intellectual contest within a scientific community. With complicated—even beautiful (McGoun 1995)—theories, one may win prizes and professorships. The conventions are the result of a self-referential academic game (see Kieser and Leiner 2009). Financial markets are considered completely independent of theory. This builds on the postmodern idea that one cannot know anything about the world (the financial markets). Figure 15.2 shows these two variants of postmodern finance.

To think systematically about postmodern finance, we again want to analyze the purpose and means that postmodern financial economists ascribe to the theories of finance.

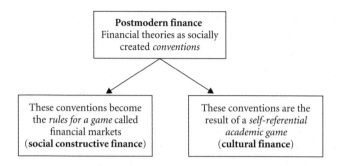

FIGURE 15.2 Variants of postmodern finance

The Purpose of Postmodern Finance

As elaborated in the previous section, Habermas distinguishes among a technical cognitive research interest, a practical cognitive interest, and an emancipatory cognitive interest. What purpose does postmodern finance ascribe to the theories of finance?

According to postmodern finance, theories cannot have a technical cognitive interest. This would require that they grasp something about how financial markets work. But postmodern financial economists deny that this is possible. Furthermore, according to postmodern finance, financial theories cannot have an emancipatory cognitive interest. This would require a standpoint for critical evaluation. One cannot uncover illegitimate power structures without knowing when power is used adequately and when it is abused. Because of their epistemological and ethical relativism, postmodern financial economists have to deny the possibility of a technical or emancipatory cognitive interest.

Instead, postmodern finance sees the purpose of financial theories in a practical cognitive interest that tries to improve "mutual understanding" (Willmott 2003, 95)—not among all members of society but only among the most powerful. Theories are viewed as conventions that improve mutual understanding between the powerful. This can be found in both variants of postmodern finance.

According to the social constructive perspective on finance, the powerful market players use theories to establish a view of financial markets that helps them stabilize or even increase their power. The creation of theories is understood as a process in which different viewpoints are compared and those that best serve the powerful win. For this process, the internal perspectives of the powerful market players are relevant. Their view of the world decides whether a theory is good or bad.

According to the cultural perspective on finance, theories help powerful individuals and schools within academia to dominate the field. By improving mutual understanding, financial theories help establish standards with which the powerful can discard some financial theories as lacking. McGoun (1995), for instance, argues that mathematical models set standards that facilitate exclusion. "Mathematics, like medieval Latin, is a medium of disputation in economics wherein those skillful in its use can subdue those who are not, independent of any substantive economic meaning" (McGoun 1995, 185; see also McGoun's elaborations in chapter 4 of this book).

The Means of Postmodern Finance
Postmodern finance sees the purpose of financial theories as improving mutual understanding among the powerful market players. But with what means can financial theories live up to this purpose? What assumptions are necessary to explain that financial theories can improve mutual understanding? Let us first discuss the four assumptions identified by Burrell and Morgan (1979).

Concerning the ontological assumptions, postmodern finance denies that the social world (including financial markets) has a structure that is independent of our concepts and labels (realism). Instead, postmodern finance argues that the concepts and labels created by the powerful are constitutive for the structure of financial markets (nominalism).

With its epistemological assumptions, postmodern finance rejects the idea that human actions can be explained from the outside through observation (positivism). The only thing postmodern finance deems possible is understanding human actions from inside, through experience and participation in actual practices and by considering the subjective views of the focal actors (antipositivism). But with this kind of subjective knowledge, we cannot aspire to validity or even objectivity beyond the language game we are in.

With its assumptions on human nature, postmodern finance takes a similar stand to that of positivistic finance. Positivistic finance assumes that humans are determined by their environment (determinism) and denies the possibility of free decisions (voluntarism). Similarly, postmodern finance argues that the powerful force their view of the world on everybody else. As a consequence, humans are determined by the institutional and intellectual structures established by the powerful. Only the powerful (who create new vocabularies) may be capable of free decisions.

Regarding its methodological assumptions, postmodern finance again takes a contra position to positivistic finance. It argues that it makes no sense for the social sciences to use the methods of the natural sciences (nomothetic theory). Instead, social sciences should focus on a qualitative and interpretive analysis of the worldview of the powerful to understand how they influence the concepts and labels we use (ideographic theory).

Again, these assumptions have important implications for the way postmodern finance addresses and analyzes problems in theory and practice. As explained already, Landry (1995) distinguishes an objectivist, a subjectivist, and a constructivist conception of problems. Postmodern finance has a subjectivist conception of problems. It assumes that problems "do not exist by themselves" (Landry 1995, 324) but rather result from our interpretation and structuring. Ultimately, the concepts and labels we use determine what we perceive as problems. As the powerful form our vocabulary, they also influence our perception of problems.

Limitations of Postmodern Finance

Postmodern finance argues that improving mutual understanding among the powerful is the sole point of financial theories. We think that this conception of financial theories has two limitations. As in the case of positivistic finance, these limitations result from a failure to adequately understand the relation between theory and praxis.

According to postmodern finance, the praxis of financial markets is constituted through the theories we develop about financial markets. This is most obvious in the case of social constructive finance. McGoun (1997) points out that the stock market crash of 1929 had massive implications for the real economy, whereas the stock market crash of 1987 had hardly any consequences. He sees this as evidence that financial markets have become "hyperreal" (McGoun 1997, 110). "What if financial transactions are not moves in an economic (real) game but moves in a non-economic (hyperreal) game? In a post-modern society, the traditional economic (real) role of finance has been marginalized. To understand finance and to develop effective public policy regarding financial markets, one must acknowledge its more cultural (hyperreal) role" (McGoun 1997, 97). If this were true, financial markets would be whatever we think they are. This would mean that the praxis of financial markets (external reality) could not set any limits to the theories about financial markets.

We think that the recent financial crisis shows that postmodern finance overestimates the influence of theory on praxis, while underestimating the influence of praxis on theory. As long as everything is working in the financial markets, people may indeed believe in financial theories and act according to them. During such times, theories are performative (MacKenzie 2006). Financial markets will come closer to the way they are described by financial theories. But we must not forget that actions that are led by financial theories may also fail. If they fail, people will start to rethink the financial theories and look for new ways to overcome the problems they face in the praxis of financial markets. Philosophers such as Kambartel and Janich stress that if actions fail, this prompts us to think systematically about the problems we face, and this may lead to new theories.

This shows two things about the relation between theory and praxis. First, contrary to what postmodern finance assumes, the praxis of financial markets has some influence on theory. The praxis of financial markets in this sense is an external reality that sets certain limits to the theories we develop and has an influence on whether theories succeed or fail when applied in practice. Second, the influence of theory on praxis is not as absolute as postmodern finance suggests. Consequently, the powerful cannot force society to adopt just any theory. Financial theories are not mere social conventions.

The same is true for cultural finance (the other variant of postmodern finance). If finance were nothing but a self-referential academic game, the praxis of financial markets could not set any limits to financial theories; however, since the financial crisis, academic finance has been under a lot of pressure to legitimize the way it is doing research. This pressure comes from groups and institutions (e.g., investors, regulators) that expect guidance from academic finance on how to overcome the problems faced in the praxis of financial markets. If their actions (that are led by financial theories) fail, they will ask academic finance to rethink its theories. We again see that the praxis of financial markets sets some limits to the theories about financial markets. Finance, therefore, cannot be a self-referential academic game.

Constructivist Finance: Theories Help Create Justified Financial Markets

Constructivist finance takes a middle ground between positivistic and postmodern finance. We have seen that the praxis of financial markets cannot—as positivistic finance suggests—force theories on us (as impartial observers). But this does not mean that the powerful can—as postmodern finance assumes—decide arbitrarily what theories societies should adopt. Actions that are led by theories can fail in the praxis of financial markets. This may prompt us (as beings interested in overcoming problems) to search for new theoretical advice. Constructivist finance starts from the insight that actions can be successful, or that they may fail, and that this sets some limits to the theories we create and apply to the resolution of problems. To start thinking about what constructivist finance could look like, we refer to the last two of the seven conceptions of finance distinguished by McGoun and Zielonka (2006).

According to "instrumental/pragmatic finance," a theory "is true if it corresponds to what would be useful for what people are doing" (McGoun and Zielonka 2006, 49). Theories are supposed to help overcome problems. McGoun and Zielonka seem to refer to individual problems. For instance, a hedge fund may use a model to limit its risk exposure. If actions based on this model succeed in limiting the risk, the model can be considered a good theory. There is, however, also another interpretation. A theory may also be called good if it helps us overcome societal problems. According to this interpretation, a theory is good if it helps us create financial markets that are justified from a societal perspective.

We think that the latter interpretation of instrumental/pragmatic finance is more convincing. But this raises the question, When exactly are financial markets justified? Positivism and postmodernism argue that what is justified can be determined only by the individual (subjectivism) or by society (relativism). We disagree with this ethical noncognitivism. Of course, there are no eternal metaphysical truths to be found about what is justified. But, as the philosopher Martha Nussbaum (1992, 212–13) points out, "When we get rid of the hope of a transcendent metaphysical grounding for our evaluative judgments—about the human being as about anything else—we are not left with the abyss. We have everything that we always had all along: the exchange of reasons and arguments by human beings within history, in which, for reasons that are historical and human but not the worse for that, we hold some things to be good and others bad, some arguments to be sound and others not sound." In such a deliberative process, we can evaluate what things are essential for us as human beings (Kambartel 1991; Scherer and Patzer 2011). Through this, we may find out what adds to the justification of financial markets and what makes them less justified. For instance, financial markets should enhance productivity and thereby help people step out of poverty. Financial markets have to be stable, as financially induced economic crises hinder millions of people to lead a decent human life. Furthermore, financial markets should be inclusive, as access to financial services is a prerequisite for self-development in a modern society. We therefore believe that there is no reason to be agnostic about what adds to the justification of financial markets and what makes them less justified. A discourse about these questions, in which some reasons will be found to be more convincing than others, is possible.

Now it remains to be answered how exactly theories can support the creation of justified financial markets. Here, the last of the seven conceptions of finance that McGoun and Zielonka (2006) distinguish becomes important. According to "rhetorical/metaphorical finance," a theory "communicates truth" (McGoun and Zielonka 2006, 49). This truth is communicated in a metaphorical way. "The essence of metaphor is understanding and experiencing one kind of thing in terms of another" (Lakoff and Johnson 1980, 5). We speak metaphorically if we say that atoms bounce together as if they were billiard balls. We use the everyday concept of a billiard ball to describe a much more complex phenomenon. According to rhetorical/metaphorical finance, the theories of finance offer us concepts to speak, metaphorically, about the much more complex phenomena occurring in financial markets. Theories would therefore say nothing about what financial markets are or how they should be. "They cannot predict anything with the precision we would like them to, but they can explain things by pointing out figurative similarities that enable us to live more comfortably in the financial world" (McGoun 2003, 432; see also McGoun's elaborations in chapter 4 of this book). This means that theories help us overcome the problems we face in the praxis of financial markets and through this, "enable us to live more comfortably in the financial world" (McGoun 2003, 432).[5]

In this spirit, we want to think of theories as "linguistic devices" (Lorenzen 1987, 118; see also Scherer 1995; Scherer and Dowling 1995). The purpose of linguistic devices is to facilitate the analysis and discussion of complex phenomena and thereby to help overcome problems we face in praxis. Depending on the problem situations, different linguistic devices (theories) are needed. Therefore, we cannot rely on models and hypotheses alone (as positivistic finance used to do). Here we distinguish between structured and unstructured problem situations. Unstructured problems are complex, uncertain, and they attract many conflicts. To overcome such "messy" (Mitroff and Mason 1980) problems, we require little formalized linguistic devices that are able to accommodate different interpretations, such as "frameworks" (Porter 1991, 98) or "abstract linguistic devices" (Scherer 1995, 293). With structured problems, however, it is possible to see which factors are relevant, what their influence is, and how they are interconnected (Scherer 1995). To overcome such problems, we need highly formalized linguistic devices, such as models and hypotheses. Models and hypotheses focus on a few variables and the interrelation between them. They lead to unambiguous analytic solutions that tell us clearly what to do (Scherer 1995).

By combining insights from instrumental/pragmatic finance with insights from rhetorical/metaphorical finance, we can outline what constructivist finance could be. Constructivist finance views theories as linguistic devices that support the creation of justified financial markets. Figure 15.3 illustrates this.

To think systematically about what constructivist finance could be, we have to come back to our thoughts about the purpose and the means of theory.

The Purpose of Constructivist Finance

What cognitive interests are required if finance is there to support the creation of justified financial markets? We think that Habermas is right in arguing that all three cognitive interests—technical, practical, and emancipatory—are necessary.

It is obvious that we need a technical cognitive interest. As positivistic finance stresses, it is indispensable to predict and control how financial markets work to overcome certain problems we encounter in the praxis of financial markets. A technical cognitive interest is required, for instance, to understand

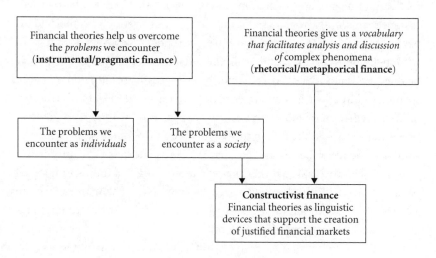

FIGURE 15.3 Constitutive elements of constructivist finance

how the interest rate influences inflation or how a market for emission allowances would work. Such knowledge is necessary for central banks to predict and control the inflation rate and for the European Union to create an efficient emissions-trading scheme. In such ways, a technical cognitive interest can help create justified financial markets.

At the same time, postmodern finance is right in emphasizing that finance needs to improve mutual understanding. This is because in many cases it is unclear what exactly the problems are that need to be overcome. In such cases, a practical cognitive interest is required to understand how the people involved see the problem and to improve the mutual understanding between them. However, there is an important difference between constructivist and postmodern finance. Postmodern finance argues that language games are ultimately determined by power relations and that reasons cannot play an essential role. As a result, postmodern finance resigns in the assumption that a mutual understanding will be only possible among the powerful market players. Contrary to this, constructivist finance assumes that in a deliberative process some reasons will be found to be more convincing than others. Therefore, a mutual understanding between all persons affected by financial markets can (at least theoretically) be reached, and constructivist finance argues that this should be the goal of the practical cognitive interest.

However, the technical and practical cognitive interests have their difficulties. With regards to the technical cognitive interest, it may be difficult to know whether connections between phenomena are parts of the world that cannot be changed or manmade institutions that can be changed. For instance, an empirical analysis of the bankers' motivation and their bonus payments may lead to a model that states that bankers can only be motivated with high bonuses. This relationship (between motivation and bonuses) may be due to human nature (that cannot be changed) or result from a certain corporate culture within banks (that can be changed). If the latter is true, the model's prediction that low bonuses will necessarily destroy bankers' motivation is not valid. With regard to the practical cognitive interest, we encounter similar difficulties. Let us assume that the corporate culture within banks plays a crucial role and that there exists a mutual understanding (among all persons concerned) that big bonus payments are legitimate. Again, we have to ask whether this mutual understanding results from emancipated individuals who have a clear understanding of the world or whether they are influenced by deep forces that let them misunderstand their own interests (see, e.g., Scherer 2009; Marcuse 1964).

We are confronted with the difficulty that the relationships we recognize (with our technical cognitive interest) and the mutual understandings we improve (with our practical cognitive interest) may be distorted by the interests of the powerful. Habermas therefore stresses the need for an emancipatory cognitive interest. Its goal is to unveil how deep forces influence the way we see the world and to identify whose interests are served by this. It exposes patterns of domination and exploitation to develop more rational and just social institutions and relations (Willmott 2003). The emancipatory cognitive interest is needed to analyze the findings of the technical as well as the practical cognitive interest. It has to be analyzed whose interests are served by the models developed with a technical cognitive interest; and it has to make sure that the internal viewpoints uncovered by the practical cognitive interest are not the product of domination or exploitation.

The Means of Constructivist Finance

Let us now analyze the means of the constructivist perspective on finance in the conceptual frameworks developed by Burrell and Morgan (1979) and by Landry (1995). With some important reservations, constructivist finance is closer to postmodern than to positivistic finance.

Regarding the ontological assumptions, constructivist finance agrees with postmodern finance that the structure of financial markets is not given, irrespective of our concepts and labels (nominalism). This does not mean, however, that we can represent the world in whatever way we please. We have to recognize that our theories about the world can lead to actions that fail and that these failures may prompt us to reconsider our theories about the world.

With its epistemological assumptions, constructivist finance assumes that human actions can be understood only from inside, through experience (antipositivism). Here, postmodern and constructivist finance agree completely.

Concerning human nature, constructivist finance assumes that free decisions are possible (voluntarism). At the same time, constructivist finance is aware that the viewpoints of humans may be distorted by domination and exploitation. To uncover this, an emancipatory cognitive interest is needed.

With its methodological assumptions, constructivist finance takes the view that social sciences should first and foremost rely on a qualitative analysis of people's point of view (ideographic theory). This is needed to understand how people see the world from their point of view. But to uncover domination and exploitation, it might make sense to use the quantitative and experimental methods of the natural sciences as well (nomothetic theory).

These assumptions correspond with a certain way of seeing problems. The constructivist perspective on finance is built on a constructivist conception of problems—instead of an objectivist or subjectivist one (Landry 1995). It assumes that "problems have no existence on their own but are nevertheless grounded in some objective reality" (Landry 1995, 328). They have no existence on their own because reality—as the ontological assumptions make clear—is not given, irrespective of our concepts and labels. The way we see problems is influenced by our needs, preferences, and values. Nonetheless, problems are grounded in some objective reality because the way we see problems leads to certain theories and they in turn lead to certain actions, and these actions can succeed or fail in overcoming problems (see, e.g., Habermas 2003). If our actions fail, this might prompt us to rethink our theories as well as the way we see problems. Constructivist finance views problems as pragmatic devices that help individuals to adapt to reality (Landry 1995, 328).

Strong Points of Constructivist Finance

The constructivist conception of problems makes clear that the praxis of financial markets plays a double role for our theories about financial markets. First, the praxis of financial markets initiates all our theorizing. Here we encounter problems that need to be overcome with the help of theory. Because of this, the praxis of financial markets is constitutive for theory. This is what positivistic finance fails to see: our theories are not independent of the praxis of financial markets and the problems we face therein.

Second, the praxis of financial markets sets limits to our theories. It is in the praxis of financial markets that actions that are led by theories succeed or fail. This limits the influence of theory on the way we see the world. Contrary to postmodern finance, we cannot conceptualize the world in completely arbitrary ways.

With its systematic orientation toward actions that may succeed or fail, we think that a constructivist perspective on finance circumvents the limitations of positivistic and postmodern finance. It succeeds in understanding the relation between theory and praxis adequately. Table 15.1 summarizes the key aspects of the three perspectives on finance.

The Responsibility of Financial Economists

After these meta-reflections from the philosophy of science, we want to focus on the initial question about the responsibility of financial economists. What

TABLE 15.1 Three perspectives on finance

		Positivistic Finance	Postmodern Finance	Constructivist Finance
Purpose	**Classification** (according to McGoun and Zielonka 2006)	Variants: • Positive finance • Normative finance • Foundational/ aesthetic finance	Variants: • Social constructive finance • Cultural finance	Constitutive elements: • Instrumentalistic/ pragmatic finance • Rhetorical/ metaphorical finance
	Cognitive interest(s)	Technical cognitive interest	Practical cognitive interest	Technical, practical, and emancipatory cognitive interest
Means	**Ontological assumptions**	The structure of financial markets is given irrespective of our concepts and labels (realism)	Our concepts and labels are constitutive for the structure of financial markets (nominalism)	Nominalism, but failed actions can prompt us to reconsider the theories that lead our actions
	Epistemological assumptions	Human actions can be explained from outside, through observation (positivism)	Human actions can be understood only from inside, through experience and participation (antipositivism)	Antipositivism
	Assumptions on human nature	Humans are determined by their environment (determinism)	Humans are determined by the institutional and intellectual structures that the powerful establish (determinism)	Free decisions are possible (voluntarism), but views may be distorted by domination and exploitation
	Methodological assumptions	Social sciences should use the methods of the natural sciences (nomothetic theory)	Social sciences should try to understand the subjective viewpoints of the people involved following the interpretive approach of the humanities (ideographic theory)	Ideographic theory, but nomothetic theory might help uncover domination and exploitation
	Concept of problems	Problems are a part of external reality (objectivist conception)	Problems are created by subjective interpretation and structuring (subjectivist conception)	Problems do not exist on their own but are nevertheless grounded in some objective reality (constructivist conception)
Conclusion	**How should we understand financial theories?**	As tools that help to predict and control financial markets	As social conventions that improve mutual understanding among the powerful market players	As linguistic devices that support the creation of justified financial markets

do our inquiries in the field of philosophy of science mean for the responsibility of financial economists?

Ontological, Epistemological, and Ethical Issues That Financial Economists Should Think About

First, financial economists have the responsibility to recognize that different groups face different problems in and with financial markets. Let us compare two groups and the problems they are confronted with. On the one hand, we have investors and the optimization problems they face. In their daily investment activities, they are confronted with questions such as, In which assets should we invest? How much risk should we incur and how can we measure this risk? and How can we measure the performance of traders and investment funds? On the other hand, we have politicians and civil servants and the regulation problems they face. They are confronted with a completely different set of questions: Which new financial products should be allowed? Should a tax on all transactions be imposed to reduce speculation? What should be done with failed banks in case of a crisis? Financial economists should critically reflect which problems constitute the starting point of their theoretical endeavors. Otherwise, they risk developing theories that either help overcome the problems of some illegitimate special-interest groups or that help overcome problems that nobody faces (Kambartel 1976).[6]

Second, financial economists have to think about what knowledge is required to overcome these problems. As optimization problems differ substantially from regulation problems, we need different knowledge to overcome these problems. Our knowledge, for instance, needs a different focus because different aspects of reality are relevant to overcome different problems. Similarly, a different form will be required, depending on how we use this knowledge. For instance, to overcome optimization problems, investors might want to focus exclusively on relative prices. This is because they can hardly make the overall price level part of their investment strategy. Even if an investor knew exactly that he or she is in a bubble, he or she could often not make any money with this information. This has to do with reserve requirements as well as with institutional and psychological reasons (Shleifer and Vishny 1997; Cassidy 2009). Investors cannot do much about bubbles. For this reason, it makes a lot of sense for theories that try to help investors overcome their problems to focus exclusively on relative prices. To overcome regulation problems, however, we will need a different focus. Here, bubbles are crucial. This brings us to the form of knowledge. Investors, for instance, often need precise knowledge, if it is to be any help at all in overcoming optimization problems. As mentioned, knowledge about a bubble could be used only if the investor knew exactly when a bubble is at which stage. To overcome regulation problems, however, one does not need this precision. If politicians and civil servants think, for example, about reducing speculation through a tax on all transactions, they only need to know whether bubbles exist and why. They do not need to know precisely at which stage the bubble is.[7]

Third, financial economists have to choose those theories that are best fit to deliver the required knowledge. Here we have to acknowledge, for instance, that "mathematical deductivist models" (Lawson 2009, 759) presuppose that financial markets work in a certain way. As Tony Lawson (2009, 764) elaborates, such models presuppose "that (i) empirical regularities . . . are ubiquitous, and (ii) social reality is constituted by sets of isolated atoms." One could argue that to assume that financial markets work this way is appropriate to get the precise knowledge that investors need for their daily investment decisions. This would mean that the theories of neoclassical finance are useful to overcome optimization problems. When it comes to regulation problems, however, ubiquitous empirical regularities and isolated atoms become problematic assumptions. During financial crises, empirical regularities break down—also known as "twenty-five standard deviation moves, several days in a row" (Larsen 2007, 25). Furthermore, in bubbles as well as in panics, we see clearly that "we are all of us inescapably socially situated and formed" (Lawson 2009, 765). The dynamics we encounter can be understood only in relation to "social relations, rules, positions, power structures and so forth" (Lawson 2009, 765). What interests us when we think about regulation problems is constantly in transformation and cannot be decomposed into isolated atoms. This raises serious doubts about whether mathematical deductivist models can deliver us the knowledge we need to overcome regulation problems.

What Can Happen if Financial Economists
Neglect Their Responsibility

If financial economists do not think about these ontological, epistemological, and ethical issues, theories can go terribly astray. Let us illustrate this with the efficient market hypothesis as an example. This theory states that prices in financial markets always "fully reflect" (Fama 1970, 383) available information. It is therefore not possible that assets that are known (from historical data or publicly available information) to have a similar performance (e.g., risk, return) are traded at different prices.

Investors have to decide which assets they buy and which money managers they employ. Eugene Fama (1970) makes these optimization problems the starting point of his theoretical endeavors. This determines, among other things, the focus and the form of his efficient market hypothesis. Fama develops his theory by analyzing short-term movements of the stock market, by looking at the possibility of excess returns, and by investigating how fast stock prices adjust to a new price level after relevant information has become available. With this, Fama focuses on those aspects of financial markets that are relevant for investors to overcome their problems. Concerning the form, the efficient markets hypothesis strives to deliver precise knowledge with clear implications. It advises investors to stop picking stocks and buy index funds instead. To deliver such precise knowledge that can guide everyday investment activities, mathematical deductivist models may well be indispensable (even though the degree of reliance on models has to be critically reevaluated after the financial crisis).

The efficient market hypothesis might indeed be a very useful linguistic device to overcome some of the problems that investors face. It helps investors understand important aspects of the market in which they are playing. In a lecture, Shiller (2008) tells his students: "The efficient markets hypothesis is a hypothesis that one should respect financial markets very much. . . . [I]t's tough to make money reliably and quickly in financial markets." The efficient market hypothesis points out that financial markets are often right. If an asset is sold relatively cheaply, the market might have a reason for this pricing. Investors should remember this well. Moreover, they should think twice before investing in actively managed mutual funds.

But neoclassical financial economists tend to misunderstand the efficient market hypothesis as an insight into the structure of financial markets. They assume that they have learned something about the essence of financial markets, about the way they really work. Many academics and regulators have therefore used the efficient market hypothesis as an argument for the deregulation of financial markets. Fama, for instance, seems to jump directly from his efficient market hypothesis (in which the problems at hand might allow us to ignore bubbles) to the denial that bubbles exist at all. "I don't . . . know what a bubble means," he says in an interview (quoted in Cassidy 2010, 30). As a consequence, he argues that financial markets cannot be the cause for the recent economic crisis (Cassidy 2010). He sees no need for increased regulation and claims that financial markets are best left to themselves. In this way, the efficient market hypothesis has (at least until the recent financial crisis) "informed a lot of regulation" (Shiller 2008).

Fama and others miss the point that different theories might be needed to overcome different problems.[8] When we move from optimization to regulation problems, the focus and form of our knowledge has to change. Theories that focus on bubbles and panics and are encompassing rather than precise (see, e.g., Shiller 2005; Minsky 1986) seem to be more promising candidates for addressing regulation problems. Again, one should not jump to the conclusion that these theories are better in grasping the essence of financial markets. This would be to relapse into the positivistic conception of theories. We can only argue that the theories of, say, behavioral finance are more helpful to overcome regulation problems. This does not necessarily mean that these theories will help us with our investment decisions. If Paul Samuelson argues that ultimately we have to judge behavioral finance on whether we can make money out of it (see Bernstein 2007, 39), he is simply wrong. The ultimate test for a theory is whether it helps overcome problems. And optimization problems are not the only problems. If behavioral theories help us overcome regulation problems, they are good theories.

Conclusion: Keeping Financial Theories Closely Tied to the Original Problems

Many financial economists strive for a unified description of all financial phenomena that could be used to solve all kinds of problems. According to Krugman (2009), the "clarity, completeness and sheer beauty that characterizes the full neoclassical approach" explains much of its theoretical appeal. We tried to show that such a unified description is not desirable. Theories are developed to solve specific problems in specific situations. They go astray if they become detached from the "original problem situations" (Kambartel 1989, 11). Financial economists, therefore, have the responsibility to keep their theories closely tied to these original problems.

As a consequence, a certain pluralism of approaches might be called for (see Lawson 2006, 2009). Breaking the dominance of mathematical deductivist models would allow financial economists to choose between different, well-developed theories, depending on the problems that need to be overcome. By critically reflecting the normative foundation of their discipline, financial economists could be confident that their theoretical endeavors contribute to the creation of justified financial markets.

Notes

1. Let us clarify how we use the words *theory, model,* and *hypothesis.* We use *theory* as a generic term that comprises different kinds of theories, such as models and hypotheses. While models (e.g., the Black-Scholes model) have a mathematical form, hypotheses (e.g., the efficient market hypothesis) can be explained without the use of mathematics. Positivistic finance limits its theoretical endeavors to these two kinds of theories. In section 2 we therefore speak interchangeably of either *models and hypotheses* or *theories.* In section 4 we show that complex, uncertain problems force us to develop other kinds of theories as well, such as frameworks.

2. The philosophical term *praxis* comprises all human activities (within a certain field). Here we are concerned with the praxis of financial markets, which refers to all human activities in financial markets. Obviously, every praxis is potentially confronted with problems that need to be overcome.

3. This has also eloquently been shown by the philosopher Richard Rorty (1989, 6): "The world does not speak. Only we do. The world can, once we have programmed ourselves with a language, cause us to hold beliefs. But it cannot propose a language for us to speak. Only other human beings can do that."

4. The sociologist Donald MacKenzie (2006, 15) makes a similar point by stressing "that economics itself is part of the infrastructure of modern markets." He talks of the performativity of theories. MacKenzie (2006) shows that the Black-Scholes model was increasingly used in the 1973 newly opened Chicago Board Options Exchange and that this led to prices aligning with the values calculated by the model.

5. The organizational theorists Paul Shrivastava and Ian Mitroff (1984, 22) see this similarly (we assume that what they write about the "organizational world" is also true for the financial world): "Metaphors permit the symbolical reconstruction of the organizational [for our context: financial] world in meaningful ways. They go beyond being mere embellishments of language by stimulating the understanding of assumptions through a creative process of comparison and crossing of images."

6. To address optimization problems, of course, presupposes that to help investors overcome their problems is to increase the overall productivity of financial markets and that this is beneficial for society as a whole (i.e., everybody, including the real economy). Without this assumption it would make no sense for academics (who are mostly paid with tax money) to help investors overcome optimization problems (it would be like offering classes on creative accounting or Ponzi-scheme construction). Since the financial crisis, the marginal utility of an ever-increasing financial system and the societal usefulness of more and more complex financial products have increasingly been called into question (Bhidé 2009; Chesney 2009). But this is not the place to critically discuss this assumption.

7. To illustrate this point, let us have a look at John Cochrane's reply to Krugman (2009). Cochrane (2009) writes: "Unless you [Krugman] are willing to elaborate your theory to the point that it can quantitatively describe how much and when risk premiums, or waves of 'optimism' and 'pessimism,' can vary, you know nothing. No theory is particularly good at that right now. Crying 'bubble' is empty unless you have an

operational procedure for identifying bubbles, distinguishing them from rationally low risk premiums, and not crying wolf too many years in a row." Cochrane's statement is certainly true for theories that should help investors to overcome optimization problems. They would need an "operational procedure for identifying bubbles." But this is not true for regulation problems. As mentioned, to impose a tax on all transactions, politicians and civil servants only need to know whether bubbles exist and why.

8. In an interview (Clement 2007) Fama says: "[T]he acid test [for theories] is, How good are the simplifications for your purposes? And for almost all purposes, market efficiency is a very good approximation. There is very little evidence that money managers can beat the market." We see that out of "all [possible] purposes" Fama focuses on those of the investors (money managers).

References

Akerlof, George A., and Robert J. Shiller. 2009. *Animal spirits: How human psychology drives the economy, and why it matters for global capitalism.* Princeton, NJ: Princeton University Press.

Bernstein, Peter L. 2007. *Capital ideas evolving.* Hoboken, NJ: John Wiley & Sons.

Bhidé, Amar. 2009. In praise of more primitive finance. *Economists' Voice* 6 (3): article 8.

British Academy. *Open letter to Her Majesty the Queen.* July 22, 2009. http://www .britac.ac.uk/events/archive/forum-economy.cfm.

Burrell, Gibson, and Gareth Morgan. 1979. *Sociological paradigms and organisational analysis: Elements of the sociology of corporate life.* London: Heinemann.

Cassidy, John. 2009. *How markets fail: The logic of economic calamities.* New York: Farrar, Straus and Giroux.

Cassidy, John. 2010. After the blowup. *New Yorker,* January 11, 28–33.

Chesney, Marc. 2009. Haben die Finanzmärkte den Kapitalismus verraten? *Der Schweizer Treuhänder* (8): 506–10.

Chesney, Marc. 2010. Enseignement de la finance: la crise a-t-elle eu lieu? *Le Temps,* October 18.

Clement, Douglas. 2007. Interview with Eugene Fama. *The Region: Banking and Policy Issues Magazine,* December, 15–23.

Cochrane, John H. *How did Paul Krugman get it so wrong?,* September 16, 2009. http:// faculty.chicagobooth.edu/john.cochrane/research/Papers/krugman_response .htm.

Colander, David, Hans Föllmer, Armin Haas, Michael Goldberg, Katarina Juselius, Alan Kirman, Thomas Lux, and Brigitte Sloth. 2009. The financial crisis and the systemic failure of academic economics. Working Paper 1489, Kiel Institute for the World Economy, Kiel, Germany.

Economist. 2009. Efficiency and beyond. *Economist,* July 18, 71–72.

Eichengreen, Barry. 2009. Origins and responses to the current crisis. *CESifo Forum* 9 (4): 6–11.

Fama, Eugene F. 1970. Efficient capital markets: A review of theory and empirical work. *Journal of Finance* 25 (2): 383–417.

Ferraro, Fabrizio, Jeffrey Pfeffer, and Robert I. Sutton. 2005. Economics language and assumptions: How theories can become self-fulfilling. *Academy of Management Review* 30 (1): 8–24.

Friedman, Milton. 1964. The methodology of positive economics. In *Essays in positive economics*, edited by M. Friedman, 3–43. Chicago: University of Chicago Press.

Habermas, Jürgen. 1966. Knowledge and Interest. *Inquiry: An Interdisciplinary Journal of Philosophy* 9 (1): 285–300.

Habermas, Jürgen. 1971. *Knowledge and human interests*. Boston: Beacon Press.

Habermas, Jürgen. 2003. *Truth and justification*. Cambridge: Massachusetts Institute of Technology Press.

Janich, Peter. 1989. Determination by reality of construction of reality? In *Constructivism and science: Essays in recent German philosophy*, edited by R. E. Butts and J. R. Brown, 257–269. Dordrecht: Kluwer Academic Publishers.

Kambartel, Friedrich. 1976. Bemerkungen zum normativen Fundament der Ökonomie. In *Theorie und Begründung : Studien zum Philosophie- und Wissenschaftsverständnis*, edited by F. Kambartel, 172–90. Frankfurt: Suhrkamp.

Kambartel, Friedrich. 1979. Ist rationale Ökonomie als empirisch-quantitative Wissenschaft möglich? In *Methodenprobleme der Wissenschaften vom gesellschaftlichen Handeln*, edited by J. Mittelstrass, 299–319. Frankfurt: Suhrkamp.

Kambartel, Friedrich. 1985. Where is more fog – In philosophy or in economics? In *Economics and Philosophy*, edited by P. Koslowski, 272–74. Tübingen: J. C. B. Mohr.

Kambartel, Friedrich. 1989. Statt eines Vorwortes. In *Philosophie der humanen Welt: Abhandlungen*, edited by F. Kambartel, 9–11. Frankfurt: Suhrkamp.

Kambartel, Friedrich. 1991. Versuch über das Verstehen. In *Der Löwe spricht und wir können ihn nicht verstehen*, edited by B. McGuiness, J. Habermas, K.-O. Apel, R. Rorty, C. Taylor, F. Kambartel, and A. Wellmer, 121–37. Frankfurt: Suhrkamp.

Kieser, Alfred, and Lars Leiner. 2009. Why the rigour-relevance gap in management research is unbridgeable. *Journal of Management Studies* 46: 516–33.

Krugman, Paul. 2009. How did economics get it so wrong? *New York Times Magazine*, September 6, MM36.

Lakoff, George, and Mark Johnson. 1980. *Metaphors we live by*. Chicago: University of Chicago Press.

Landry, Maurice. 1995. A note on the concept of 'problem'. *Organization Studies* 16 (2): 315–43.

Larsen, Peter. 2007. Goldman pays the price of being big. *Financial Times*, August 13, 25.

Lawson, Tony. 2006. The nature of heterodox economics. *Cambridge Journal of Economics* 30 (4): 483–505.

Lawson, Tony. 2009. The current economic crisis: Its nature and the course of academic economics. *Cambridge Journal of Economics* 33 (4): 759–77.

Lawson, Tony. 2009. Heterodox economics and pluralism. In *Ontology and Economics: Tony Lawson and His Critics*, edited by E. Fullbrook, 93–129. New York: Routledge.

Levine, David K. *An open letter to Paul Krugman*, September 18, 2009. http:www.huff
ingtonpost.com/david-k-levine/an-open-letter-to-paul-kr_b_289768.html.

Lorenzen, Paul. 1987. *Constructive philosophy.* Amherst: University of Massachusetts
Press.

MacKenzie, Donald A. 2006. *An engine, not a camera: How financial models shape markets.* Cambridge: Massachusetts Institute of Technology Press.

Marcuse, Herbert. 1964. *One-dimensional man: Studies in the ideology of advanced industrial society.* Boston: Beacon Press.

McGoun, Elton G. 1995. Machomatics in egonomics. *International Review of Financial
Analysis* 4 (2–3): 185–99.

McGoun, Elton G. 1997. Hyperreal finance. *Critical Perspectives on Accounting* 8 (1–2):
97–122.

McGoun, Elton G. 2003. Finance models as metaphors. *International Review of Financial Analysis* 12 (4): 421–33.

McGoun, Elton G., and Piotr Zielonka. 2006. The Platonic foundations of finance and
the interpretation of finance models. *Journal of Behavioral Finance* 7 (1): 43–57.

Miller, Merton H. 1986. Behavioral rationality in finance: The case of dividends. *Journal of Business* 59 (4): S451–S468.

Minsky, Hyman P. 1986. *Stabilizing an unstable economy.* New Haven, CT: Yale
University Press.

Mitroff, Ian I., and Richard O. Mason. 1980. Structuring III—Structured policy issues: Further explorations in a methodology for messy problems. *Strategic Management Journal* 1 (4): 331–42.

Nussbaum, Martha C. 1992. Human functioning and social justice: In defense of
Aristotelian essentialism. *Political Theory* 20 (2): 202–46.

Porter, Michael E. 1991. Towards a dynamic theory of strategy. *Strategic Management
Journal* 12 (S2): 95–117.

Rorty, Richard. 1989. *Contingency, irony, and solidarity.* Cambridge: Cambridge University Press.

Scherer, Andreas G. 1995. *Pluralismus im Strategischen Management. Der Beitrag der
Teilnehmerperspektive zur Lösung von Inkommensurabilitätsproblemen in Forsc-
hung und Praxis.* Wiesbaden: Gabler Verlag.

Scherer, Andreas G. 2003. Modes of Explanation in Organization Theory. In *The
Oxford handbook of organization theory,* edited by H. Tsoukas and C. Knudsen,
310–44. Oxford: Oxford University Press.

Scherer, Andreas G. 2009. Critical theory and its contribution to critical management studies. In *The Oxford handbook of critical management studies,* edited by
M. Alvesson, H. Willmott, and T. Bridgman. Oxford: Oxford University Press.

Scherer, Andreas G., and Michael J. Dowling. 1995. Towards a reconciliation of the
theory pluralism in strategic management: Incommensurability and the constructivist approach of the Erlangen School. *Advances in Strategic Management*
12A: 195–247.

Scherer, Andreas G., and Moritz Patzer. 2011. Beyond universalism and relativism:
Habermas's contribution to discourse ethics and its implications for intercultural

ethics and organizational theory. In *Philosophy and organization theory*, edited by H. Tsoukas and R. Chia, 155–80. New York: Elsevier.

Sharpe, William F. 1964. Capital asset prices: A theory of market equilibrium under conditions of risk. *Journal of Finance* 19 (3): 425–42.

Shiller, Robert J. 2005. *Irrational exuberance*. 2nd ed. Princeton, NJ: Princeton University Press.

Shiller, Robert J. 2008. *Financial markets: Lecture 6: Efficient markets vs. excess volatility*. http://www.academicearth.org/lectures/efficient-markets-excess-volatlity.

Shleifer, Andrei, and Robert W. Vishny. 1997. The limits of arbitrage. *Journal of Finance* 52 (1): 35–55.

Shrivastava, Paul, and Ian I. Mitroff. 1984. Enhancing organizational research utilization: The role of decision makers' assumptions. *Academy of Management Review* 9 (1): 18–26.

Skidelsky, Robert. 2009. How to rebuild a shamed subject. *Financial Times*, August 5, 11.

Sornette, Didier. 2009. Dragon-kings, black swans and the prediction of crises. *International Journal of Terraspace Science and Engineering* 1 (3): 1–17.

Spremann, Klaus. 2008. Alte und neue Paradigmen der Finance. In *Finanzstrategisch denken! Paradigmenwechsel zur Strategic Corporate Finance*, edited by G. Eilenberger, S. Haghani, A. Kötzle, K. Reding, and K. Spremann, 7–27. Berlin: Springer.

Steffy, Brian D., and Andrew J. Grimes. 1986. A critical theory of organization science. *Academy of Management Review* 11 (2): 322–36.

Willmott, Hugh. 2003. Organization theory as a critical science? Forms of analysis and "new organizational forms." In *The Oxford handbook of organization theory: Meta-theoretical perspectives*, edited by H. Tsoukas and C. Knudsen, 88–112. Oxford: Oxford University Press.

16 A Multilevel, Multisystems Strategic Approach to a Sustainable Economy

Mark Starik

The global financial crisis of 2008–2009 has been said to have had many causes that occurred at multiple levels of human society. Excessively risky real estate investments, overextended financial portfolios, disaggregated financial instruments, unregulated hedge funds, greedy bankers, and several other explanations for the worldwide financial meltdown illustrate the diversity of factors that may be associated with this complex, global economic situation (Shiller 2008). From a sustainability perspective, we might also consider that both the causes and the results of the financial crisis, as well as responses to it, can occur at multiple levels. These levels can include individuals, households, organizations, communities, networks, and societal institutions. Applying a model codeveloped by the author, this chapter analyzes the recent global financial crisis at these levels and accounts for natural environment-related inputs, processes, and outputs, as well as other systems-oriented phenomena at each level.

Such an approach is presented here because levels and systems analyses allow observers to adopt multifocal perspectives on societal phenomena. For example, to the extent that one of the many causes of the crisis was that risky home loans were made by financial institutions to homeowners who could not repay them, a sustainability perspective could include macro phenomena, such as continued human population growth and need for shelter, and micro phenomena, such as excessive heating and cooling bills exacerbating home-loan repayment. Similarly, regarding societal responses to these crises, in this case, recovery from economic crises, sustainability approaches might include reductions in overall human population growth, on the one hand, and installation of low-cost or no-cost residential energy conservation measures to reduce home energy consumption, on the other hand. Other examples of multilevel, multisystems perspectives on advancing sustainability in attempting to understand and address financial crises comprehensively could include residential, commercial, industrial, and institutional investment in improvements in air, water, and other resource quality, and a greater emphasis on eating lower on the food chain, for both human and natural environmental health benefits, both of which may have long-lasting financial aspects.

This chapter identifies the relevant multilevel and multisystems sustainability elements associated with the global financial crisis. It also suggests numerous strategies, policies, and practices that might help reduce the frequency or severity of such crises in the future. Though not a panacea, more sustainable approaches to a wide range of human behaviors may allow individuals, organizations, and societies to build economic and other systems that are more resilient than those that existed before these crises. In doing so, both human and natural environments might experience relief from unnecessary and unhealthy stress and coevolve in ways that enhance sustainability, here defined as long-term quality of life.

• • •

The recent worldwide economic downturn has prompted many observers to begin to question the sustainability of global economic systems. Such questions seem more numerous and serious than arose in past recessions, perhaps because the recent crisis has many potential high-profile causes, from the marketing of ill-advised investments in home loans to the disaggregation of financial instruments and overextended portfolios. Of course, a number of analysts, most notably and recently Thomas Friedman (2008) and Lester Brown (2009), have been pointing out for some time that our current economic systems, from the macro- to the microscale, have some glaring and potentially debilitating deficiencies. Numerous ecological systems on which all human economies are based are critically dependent on fossil-fuel, carbon-emitting resources, tragically exemplified by the Gulf of Mexico BP oil pollution catastrophe. A number of social systems, such as the ever-increasing human population (now more than 7 billion), are straining both ecological and human capacities to provide satisfactory levels of life's supporting services. This chapter identifies a strategic set of unsustainable ecological and socioeconomic policies and actions that may be contributing to this malaise and widespread dissatisfaction. The chapter also posits a number of current or proposed strategies that could move the world's economies in more sustainable directions. The framework that is used in this article is one that was developed in the mid-1990s (Starik and Rands 1995) and has been applied in a number of academic works. This framework accounts for multiple levels of human thinking and action, from individual (micro) through organizational, community, and network (meso) levels to societal or institutional (macro) levels. The framework also attempts to address each level of analysis from a systems perspective, including inputs, processes, and outputs. Where conceptually and practically appropriate, these levels and systems are integrated to provide a perspective on human economies that may be more comprehensive, consistent, and sustainable (in the sense of viable over the long term) than current approaches.

Individual Economic Level of Analysis

The first and most strategic aspect of this multilevel, multisystems analysis of the recent economic downturn is the widespread recognition that, especially at the individual level, humans generally, and children especially, have become disconnected conceptually from their natural environments (Louv 2005). That is, we as individual members of our species do not often consider ourselves to even be a species, that is, a subset, a building block, or an integral part of nature. At least in English, we refer to ourselves most often as the human race, rarely classifying ourselves as the animals that we are. Individuals in most modern human cultures and economies are often alienated from the natural environment, from other nonhuman living things, only occasionally recognizing that the rest of nature is not only centrally important for our own biophysical existence but also connected to us through all of our biophysical activities. It has been estimated that the average modern-day person spends as much as 90 percent of his or her time indoors (U.S. Environmental Protection Agency 2009), where the most salient forms of nonhuman nature are pets and houseplants. And to the extent that an ever-increasing amount of individual human time (at least in developed countries) is spent driving in a closed-in automobile means that even less human time is biophysically (as opposed to mechanically) connected to the rest of the natural environment. This alienation of the human individual is accompanied by a reciprocal nonrecognition that the natural environment makes up our component parts (inputs); maintains them to continue working together (processes); and produces solids, liquids, and gases (outputs) that will remain in the natural environment (until broken down) indefinitely. Perhaps more than ever in our human evolution, modern humans are often alienated even from their own biology, overconsuming food (and restricting physical movement) to the point of obesity, becoming addicted to harmful legal and illegal drugs, and ignoring health and safety warnings to put their physical health in jeopardy. This biophysical connection between humans and their natural environments, though generally unrecognized and nearly always underappreciated, exists whether humans are in their residences, workplaces, or social gatherings or are traveling between and among these sites.

The occasional exception to these alienating conditions often involve outdoor activities, from gardening and mowing the lawn to participating in an athletic event, or even just going for a walk in the park. The evolution of human societies in which human individuals are spending less of their time outdoors involved in primarily biophysical activities may have the tendency for these individual human economy producers and consumers to be less familiar with and have less of an affinity for ensuring that natural systems are respected and that their long-term viability is protected (Worthy 2008). Although the occasional environmental media program or speakers' event may moderately influence a fraction of human individuals that resource inputs (e.g., raw materials), processes (e.g., manufacturing), and outputs (e.g., air, water, land pollution) are consequential, few individuals may adjust their production and consumption behaviors only as a result of these well-intended efforts.

Clearly, at this individual human or micro-level of analysis, both current and possible efforts to move toward sustainability are plentiful. Environmental education appears to be on the increase in many cultures and economies, including the increased availability of quality environmental education materials (inputs); the offering of educational programs at multiple points of individual human development (processes); and the greater availability of employment positions that either focus on or include increased attention to environmental issues, concerns, and/or opportunities (outputs). Although such environmental educational approaches appear necessary to increase the amount of information human individuals possess to make better-informed decisions about the natural environment impacts of and influences on their production and consumption behaviors, these may be insufficient to actually change that behavior in sustainability directions (McKenzie-Mohr and Smith 1999).

Changes in individual sustainability-related behaviors may require involving individuals connecting with the natural environment more frequently and on a deeper beyond-rational basis. Some approaches that may help move individuals in this direction are to encourage the production, dissemination, and utilization of environmental information sources that help individual viewers or users deepen their connection to Earth's biophysical wonders. Such information-intensive strategies would likely be more effective if they included recommended actions or options for individuals to apply their more in-depth multisensory information in ways that can change their own behaviors, and perhaps those of other human individuals in their respective networks. For a popular, recent example, the movie *Avatar*, which many moviegoers watched in the graphically enhanced three-dimensional format, included a pro-environmental and pro-indigenous message, but it might have been more powerful in effecting human individual environmental change if it had included suggestions for individuals to join various efforts that promote indigenous environmental perspectives. The same could be said for much of the programming on the Disney, Discovery, and even the Green Channel on U.S. cable television. Even Al Gore's movie *An Inconvenient Truth* focused far more on rational analyses of global climate-change challenges than on either visceral reactions to the related damage or suggestions on how individual viewers should use that information. The systems perspective might have included using the input of the movie's message, going beyond the process of viewing the movie and moving in the direction of effective environmental decision and action outputs.

Another aspect of the recent global financial crisis is the obsession humans have with allocating far more cognitive attention and other resources to the immediate, short-term time frame than to medium- and long-term perspectives. Individuals who live for the moment often adopt a desperate, acquisitive worldview, and some observers have suggested that the modern era is one characterized by large number of people who want instant gratification. In the recent global financial crisis, for example, mortgages were made far too readily available to homeowners who were either not aware of or didn't care about their long-term ability to repay those loans, especially during down business cycles (Porter 2009). Because such cycles occur many times over the lifetimes of most adults, they are sometimes conveniently ignored in good times and a mentality of seizing on opportunities without considering their associated potential downsides can become frenetic. An extension of this short-term orientation is the difficulty most humans exhibit in making decisions that will have impacts well beyond their own lifetimes, such as the worst projected impacts of global climate change.

What can be done at the individual level to help reduce the frequency or intensity of financial crises? Increasing the breadth and depth of individual connections with the rest of nature could potentially encourage individuals to identify a more comprehensive set of human values. These could include in the long term highlighting the fact that more is not always better, either for humans or for their environments. Closer connections to nature could also allow humans to discover the value of reduce, reuse, and recycle, thus decreasing the need for humans to continuously overconsume. Finally, reestablishing effective, long-term relationships with human environments could enhance the value of living within limits, at least in the biophysical sense, again with advantages to both individual humans and their ecosystems.

Organizational Economic Level of Analysis

Although individuals can help advance global economies in more sustainable directions, when individuals collaborate, whether in households, organizations, communities, or networks, they likely have greater opportunities to influence the environmental behaviors of others. In addition, they also have opportunities to urge one another to broaden and deepen their own environmental commitments and behavioral changes, with potentially eco-positive economic effects. The field of social marketing has become important in this regard, and one prominent approach that includes significant attention to social norms, commitments, prompts, and pilot testing has developed several hundred case studies of pro-environmental projects (McKenzie-Mohr and Smith 1999).

At the organizational or meso level, apparently few finance-oriented firms exercised due care in counseling their clients and in training and motivating their employees to adopt prudent behaviors that were concerned with long-term stakeholder value. Such a perspective might have mitigated the rush-to-purchase frame of mind that pervaded the real estate market in the middle of the past decade. Rather, many financial advisers in that market encouraged their clients to become financially overextended, and news stories at the time of this writing are reporting that leading firms in the financial sector, like Goldman Sachs, routinely shorted their investments, often without informing the clients against whose interest they were betting. From a systems viewpoint, the problem was that one key set of inputs, the ability of borrowers to repay, was virtually ignored. And the information that many mortgages were unwise, which would be important decision inputs for purchasers of mortgage securities, was lost in the disaggregation of these securities and in the process of remixing them with other securities in different and often novel financial instruments (outputs). This narrowness of the decision inputs and remixing process resulted in critically information-deficient outputs (Munchau 2009).

A sustainability solution to this systemic problem at the organizational level is to expect and encourage that top management (including governing boards) in the financial and related sectors develop the values, plans, structures, and cultures within their respective organizations and value chains to ensure that as many stakeholder interests as possible, including long-term financial borrower and client interests, are treated as comprehensive inputs into the mortgage and investment purchase-decision process. One critical input, the borrower's ability to repay, needs to be factored into the front end of these transactions, and, to the extent feasible, continue to be associated with investment products related to those mortgages.

Of course, in addition to the mortgage being affordable and identified as such, a sustainability factor that is just as important is what products and services are being financed with those loans. Are the homes or other properties or assets that are being financed sustainable themselves? That is, do they support long-term quality of life? Are second and third homes, vehicles, and other household assets really necessary, and, if not, should organizations such as real estate brokers and car dealers market them as necessities? Manufacturing organizations might want to begin to question the size, operations, and type of their facilities and adopt more quality rather than quantity orientations. All organizations might examine their transportation profiles to identify opportunities for reducing energy consumption, such as through videoconferencing and hybrid fleets. Organizations overall could develop a systems view by studying how nature produces value and attempt to follow similar principles and processes (Hitchcock and Willard 2009).

In the past two decades, perhaps thousands of organizations in each of the three major societal sectors of business, government, and nonprofit organizations have developed a wide range of environmentally oriented policies, programs, and practices (Starik and Heuer 2002). These organizational-level sustainability approaches include now-familiar (but still not widely adopted) activities including pollution prevention, clean manufacturing, life-cycle analysis, design for environment, and sustainable supply-chain management (Starik and Marcus 2000). Although these green organizational approaches are certainly a welcome change from the norm of most of the past century, many of these efforts are still ad hoc, sporadic, and disconnected from the core missions of these organizations, some bordering on "green-washing" (MacDonald 2008). Similar to a deepening connection between human individuals and the natural environment, a greening economy would be composed of and encourage the development of households, organizations, communities, and networks that adopt and express more genuine integration with the rest of nature. One interesting and perhaps helpful approach would be organizational consideration of frameworks such as the business ecology model (Townsend 2008), in which businesses and other human organizations would adapt to and restore their biophysical environments rather than merely comply with environmental regulations, imperfect as they are.

Aggregations of human individuals at the community and/or network levels also have a role to play in advancing a more sustainable economy. When individuals collaborate, they can overcome some of their own limitations (Barnard 1938), especially information limitations, so encouraging community or network interest in sustainability at the local level and beyond may be prudent for those advocating ecological, social, and economic change. For example, numerous communities and stakeholder sets have engaged in community energy planning (processes), whether through past programs sometimes called integrated resource planning or more recently through the Transition Initiative movement. Where the former involved groups or organizations in the public and private sector developing long-term energy supply-and-demand plans, the latter are more likely groups of individual local residents who develop energy-descent plans and other projects to address climate change and peak oil concerns. Many other communities and stakeholder networks have emerged around the world to help advance sustainable economies, including those focusing on water, transportation, economic development, and other community needs (inputs). Communities and networks may be the meso-level entities from which customized sustainability approaches can be scaled up to make significant contributions to more sane economic systems. Co-housing, car sharing, community gardens, skill and tool libraries, childcare co-ops, and many other middle-range approaches can be effective, inspiring, and replicable.

One recent process phenomenon that has begun to play a role in advancing sustainable economies is the set of electronic social media Web sites, blogs, and wikis, including Facebook and MySpace, RSSs, Twitter, YouTube, Second Life, Planet Forward, BrightPlanet, and others. In addition to assisting individuals in communicating more frequently with others with whom they are familiar, social media also expands individual networks. Although many groups of individuals with special interests (inputs) have used these to advance group interests, those fostering more sustainable economies have done so to great advantage. Whether these are nongovernmental organizations (NGOs) raising money for Haitian earthquake relief, environmental lobbying, or environmental candidate election purposes (outputs), social media is becoming important to advocates of sustainable economies.

But the concept (and practice) of sustainability contains many paradoxes at each of the levels and within each of the systems components developed in this chapter, including the perspective that social media is a double-edged sword. For instance, at the network level, it has been suggested that the various so-called social media can play an important role in advancing personal and interpersonal sustainability. Each of these media allows users to exchange information, such as sustainability insights, practices, or issues, for benefits to both senders (enhancing message reinforcement and reputation) and receivers (enhancing peer motivation and idea generation). Besides informing one another about their sustainability ideas and activities, users of social media have also been involved in advancing political campaigns for political candidates perceived as sustainability oriented, as well as serving as an electronic avenue to building a sustainability archive as the first sustainability-oriented generation (i.e., baby boomers) begins to retire.

However, the social media are not always environmental media, as their excessive use can contribute to the alienation of humans from their natural environments because users can become enthralled with their electronic environments, spending excessive amounts of time with not only the social media but also with other computer technologies, including online games that simulate destruction of both other humans and various parts of the natural environment.

One approach to integrating the use of these media and a closer-to-nature approach can be considered high-tech and high-touch (Naisbitt, Naisbitt, and Phillips 1999). When applied to connections with nature, this development could include the use of geographic information systems, remote sensing, social media, and/or other technologically advanced techniques, in combination with field trips, collaborative experiments, and eco-sensitivity training. One well-known organization that has employed the high-tech and high-touch approach with significant long-term success is Earthwatch. This organization, started in the United States in 1982 and now operating in England, Australia, and Japan, regularly recruits citizen-researchers to both fund and assist in sustainability-oriented field research (Seitanidi and Crane 2009). In addition, Earthwatch uses advanced technology in conducting its research, most recently employing Earth imagery satellite technology to enable the organization to respond to sustainability crises (Perera 1999).

Similar to the individual human benefits of establishing more healthful connections with their ecosystems, households, organizations, communities, and networks could develop more comprehensive, long-term perspectives of their roles in society and in nature, thus developing alternatives to the overconsumption, frenetic free-for-all, hypercompetitive market behaviors that may have led in part to the recent financial crises. Conceiving, designing, and implementing programs that move toward a more holistic worldview that is consistent with long-term ecological survival might be more effective when collaborating at this level, both for the information and for the peer-support benefits. Pooling of financial resources to make energy conservation and renewable energy investments with reasonable paybacks is another reason collaboration at this meso level appears prudent.

Societal Economic Level of Analysis

Finally, at the societal or macro level, multiple causes of the global financial crisis can be identified. One major explanatory factor is the lack of an international financial system that can monitor the world economy for potential problems in key national economies that could trigger financial problems in other economies around the world. When problems such as the U.S. mortgage crisis was unfolding, such a worldwide monitoring system might have been able to warn financial decision makers throughout and beyond the United States to begin to make decisions and take actions to mitigate the infection in other economies. But such a system may not soon emerge in this era of continued dominance by sovereign, often-competitive, nation-states, so alternative approaches may need to be explored (Munchau 2009). These might include focusing more sustainability-oriented attention at the regional (subnational) and local (from metropolitan area to neighborhood) levels and, if successful, attempting to scale these solutions up to the national and international levels. Given that many environmental sustainability approaches focus on energy, water, waste, and human and ecosystem health, these may be the initial focal points of regional and local approaches. Distributed energy, which is typically generated via renewable energy resources, such as small-scale solar, wind, and biomass at the household and neighborhood levels, is a case in point. Numerous neighborhood solar cooperatives are emerging in many U.S. metropolitan areas, as are water and material recycling and community food-garden projects.

More generally, institution interactions with the natural environment are the most evident at the societal or macro level, both in nonsustainable and more sustainable economies. National governments and multinational businesses in particular have played major roles (inputs) in allowing, encouraging, and participating in natural environment deterioration, from involvement in armed conflicts to excessive, debilitating, and even toxic economic development. Numerous regional, national, and global environmental assessments over the past two decades confirm that the majority of the planet's ecological systems, whether air, water, land, or life phenomena, as inputs, are under severe stress (Brown 2009). Societal-level natural environment forestry, fishery, water-table, and marine-life depletion (processes) continue on a rampant pace, while waste (outputs) of all kinds mounts. Clearly, major international institutions in all three societal sectors need to address a wide range of macro-level sustainability inputs, processes, and outputs, which cross sectors, national boundaries, and socioeconomic stratas, including those related to sustainability issues that involve multiple ecological outputs. This macro-level sustainability need has been recognized by a number of multinational institutions, from inter- and intrabusiness, government, and civil society collaborations, such as the World Business Council for Sustainable Development, the United Nations, and the World Bank, to expansive religious or spiritual, educational, philanthropic, and even recreational societal collectivities. Other examples are the global public policy consortia, such as the World Dam Commission, that address sustainability issues; the effort to create more subnational, national, and transnational parks and other protected areas; and the attempts, especially by governments and NGOs to form peak associations and networks to address regional, and even global, sustainability challenges. Business has played some role in each of these partial solutions, but often the same businesses are engaged in working with the other sectors. Small and medium-sized enterprises (SMEs), which numerically dominate world economies and have often been said to drive societal innovation, have barely participated in these efforts, perhaps for the legitimate reason that they lack resources. So, if society wants to increase SME participation in societal sustainability challenges and solutions, more resources need to be allocated in this direction. However, given that most of Earth's ecological systems remain under increasing stress, far more is apparently necessary at this level, as well at each of the other levels.

Similar to the individual and household, organizational, community, and network levels, identifying and addressing sustainability issues at the societal level makes economic sense. Combining sustainability efforts at the international level especially pays off in the reduction of cross-border hostilities that are resource based, for example, and connecting major institutions to sustainability efforts helps set the norms for society, thus enhancing the prospects that individuals and others will voluntarily cooperate to reduce the need for unnecessary expenses, such as pollution control, and to increase wise investments in restoration to increase land or marine productivity, for another.

A To-Do List for a More Sustainable Economy

Sustainability prescriptions are nearly ubiquitous, but few identify the levels and systems aspects necessary for human actions in moving toward a greener economy. So, a number of suggestions are outlined in the rest of this chapter to highlight some of the more intriguing, and perhaps strategic, levels and systems possibilities.

At the individual level, numerous books, articles, and Web sites have identified some initial activities that might help move many of us toward creating and developing a greener economy. The most systems-oriented of these might be the development and use of a personal sustainability plan (PSP). Such a plan would use information, both quantitative and qualitative, about an individual's resource use (inputs), software, hardware, learning technology (processes), and carbon or other ecological resource use. A number of such personal sustainability plans have been suggested and put into effect by individuals in many countries. These have ranged in depth from the Walmart PSP (which usually addresses personal habit changing, such as dieting or smoking cessation) to some online, multiscreen programs that not only calculate ecological footprints but also help individuals customize programs to reduce their own impacts through behavioral changes. Of course, because most individuals on the planet share living, working, and other spaces and resources with other individuals, personal sustainability plans could be shared among households, worksites, and other small groups of individuals. Here, the obvious trade-off would be individual plan customization versus group plan standardization. One approach to be considered, if personal sustainability plans become popular, would be to encourage individuals to have more than one personal sustainability plan, including one that is customized and at least one more that is collaborative. This might follow the example of individuals who have both individual and household or worksite financial plans (Sarkissian et al. 2008; see also the Personal Sustainability Action Plan at http://kitch entablesustainability.com).

At the household, organizational, community, and network level, one of the more recent sustainability developments is the Transition Initiative (mentioned earlier), which is an effort that attempts to address local sustainability issues, often in conjunction with local government, NGO, and business organizations, and eventually to develop and implement energy-descent plans (Hopkins 2008). These groups, which number in the hundreds around the world, are concentrated in English-speaking countries and are primarily focused on climate change and peak oil. Their efforts have developed a wide range of projects to address these issues, with one of the most popular being local urban food production (Seyfang 2009). The program attempts to address the overall question, "For all aspects of life that this community needs in order to sustain itself and thrive, how do we significantly increase resilience (to mitigate the effects of "peak oil") and drastically reduce carbon emissions to mitigate the effects of climate change?" (http://www.transitiontowns.org, 2010).

Of course, many other organizational-, community-, and network-level sustainability efforts have preceded the Transition Initiative, including ISO 14001, Strategic Environmental Management, Natural Step, Local Agenda 21, and Integrated Resource Planning, among others. What appears necessary is that these efforts expand to include multiple aspects of sustainability (e.g., not only energy but also water, waste, and human and ecosystem health). One interesting and potentially replicable set of organizational-, community-, and network-level sustainability projects can be found in a recent edited volume by Stoner and Wankel (2008), and another that employs community-based social marketing is online (http://www.cbsm.com). Yet a third is contained in book cowritten by three chief executive officers called *Walking the Talk* (Holliday, Schmidheiny, and Watts 2001) and at the Web site of the World Business Council for Sustainable Development (http://www.wbcsd.org).

The challenge with all of these excellent sources and their organizations is to go beyond their initial awareness inventory effect to promote sustainability attention to the many other sustainability-related activities in which these and many other organizations and communities are engaged in on an ongoing basis. In addition, sustainability outlets need to identify and leverage opportunities for the replication of those that are successful and to encourage the development and application of methods to determine which of these are successful and why. One step in this direction has been taken by the

Canadian online organization etiquette.inc., which has developed the open-source sustainability case database "ethipedia." As of this writing, the site contained eighty-eight cases categorized in twenty industry sectors and highlighted fourteen different environmental and social benefit classifications, including energy conservation and renewables.

At the societal level, supraorganizations that might be described as global institutions have provided some overall leadership in helping move economies in more sustainable directions. These have included both individual institutions, such as the United Nations, which has fostered global climate-change and multiple other international sustainability negotiations, and combinations of global institutions and nonprofit organizations, such as the alliance between the World Business Council for Sustainable Development and the World Resources Institute to develop a global greenhouse-gas management protocol. What is difficult to assess, especially given the macro nature of these meganetworks, is the success of these institutions in advancing the world's economies toward sustainability. So, a major to-do activity, especially for sustainability advocates, is to research and assess these societal level entities and disseminate that information repeatedly and widely in multiple media for maximum impact.

Of all the suggestions for individuals, households, communities, networks, and society, in general, forwarded in this chapter, perhaps none is as important as the need for all of these entities to consider the values and prescriptions advanced in the International Living Building Institute's Living Building Challenge 2.0 (Zemtseff 2009). This set of ambitious, far-reaching sustainability prescriptions focuses on buildings, but its overall framework could be applied to multiple aspects of human life. In addition to 100 percent energy and water self-sufficiency, attention to both socioeconomic factors and aesthetics contributes to vaulting this emerging set of sustainability characteristics far beyond the U.S. Green Building Council Leadership in Energy and Environmental Design (LEED) Platinum standard, thus suggesting how all the levels identified in this chapter could take transformational steps toward sustainability. For instance, while individual building owners can practice total energy and water conservation, real estate developers at the organizational level and international development agencies at the societal level can advance these and other values in the challenge. Alternatively, sustainability advocates could advance other similar leading-edge approaches in economic sectors other than real estate to encourage other economic sectors to take transformational steps toward sustainability.

Conclusions, Implications, and Encouragement

This chapter has suggested that academics and practitioners who are interested in advancing greener economies might benefit from viewing our collective efforts on at least three levels and consider at least three systems elements. First, these perspectives offer a more comprehensive picture of both the challenges in moving the world's economies in more sustainable directions and the opportunities for doing so, hopefully without overcomplicating the analysis or overwhelming these potential agents. By viewing sustainability challenges and opportunities, individuals, organizations, and institutions are encouraged to connect the dots in identifying and leveraging the connections among these three levels of decisions and actions. For example, Chad Holliday, until recently a multidecade chair and chief executive officer of DuPont and, as of this writing, chair of Bank of America, has individually lobbied the U.S. Congress for a cap-and-trade carbon reduction policy, increased DuPont's orientation to sustainable product development while decreasing emissions, and developed institutions like the World Business Council for Sustainable Development (which includes more than two hundred corporate members) of businesses and nonprofit organizations that sponsor international conferences on sustainability and corporate performance.

In addition to a multilevel view of sustainable economies, a systems perspective can assist change agents in planning and implementing their sustainability decisions and actions. First, focusing on inputs encourages these individuals, organizations, and institutions to ensure they have the prerequisite initiative, ideas, personnel, infrastructure, and information resources before or as they begin their sustainability efforts, which would hopefully improve their prospects for success. Second, paying attention to processes, such as stakeholder collaboration, conflict resolution, or strategic information collection and analysis processes, can help sustainability decision makers (and action takers) add value to their inputs through organizing, focusing, transforming, or interpreting these resources in strategic sustainability directions. Finally, systematic attention to output (in which some writers may include outcomes and feedback) helps refine and communicate sustainability efforts to increase the likelihood that effects are realized. In addition, an output focus allows change agents to tailor their approaches to maintain or increase the likelihood of success into the future, in the event that adjustments to inputs or processes are necessary.

Overall, sustainability-oriented or green economy actors, from micro to macro levels, appear to need to redouble their efforts, and perhaps address their challenges and opportunities more systematically. Individuals may need to be more broadly and deeply involved both in practicing sustainability and in recruiting other individuals to do the same. The latter may require an evangelical, or at least a political, campaign sense of purpose of fervor and endurance of ridicule from potential skeptics or opponents. The time may be near for sustainability advocates to come out of the closet, be proud to be tree huggers, and stop acting as though the threshold-level change needed to significantly green human behavior can be done through sacrifice-free under-the-radar methods.

For organizations, extensions in breadth and depth of sustainability commitment and action may also be prescribed, but given the number of stakeholders and the multiplexity of their interactions, developing green economies through them is likely to be much more complex. Although a similar enrollment process to enlist colleagues or community members works to adopt sustainable behaviors, enrolling opinion leaders to do so may be a key sustainability strategy. For organizations, these are likely to be top managers, and for communities, the targets are likely to be political or social group leaders both in current and in upcoming generations. The need for and full range of net benefits of sustainability decisions and actions are apparently required to be emphasized and reemphasized again and again, often in different ways, by sustainability champions in both organizations and communities. Multimedia approaches may be effective among these potential green economic groups.

Finally, at the societal level, complexity of greening economics is likely at its greatest, as 7 billion potential decision makers and action takers constitute the human population. That number may provide a cue to institutions looking to advance green economies—develop goals, strategies, and programs that tend to reduce this complexity by reducing the growth of our human numbers. Given that the human species is still learning how to live sustainably both with nature and with ourselves, one prudent approach appears obvious: let's not make this huge educational feat any more difficult by continuously adding to our species! And because humans in the developed world often consume between twenty to forty times more resources than those in the developing world, it seems incumbent on those in developed counties to reduce their population many times faster than the rest of the world. Although a few nonprofit and government agencies have taken up this charge of reducing human overpopulation, these have often focused on developing countries; a refocusing on developed countries and an active involvement by the business sector in this campaign appears most prudent.

Of course, such an effort will need sophisticated approaches, as the subject of birth control is still a tricky one for all human societies. Such an effort can easily appear misanthropic, or quixotic, so although this recommendation may be one of the most strategic of any in this chapter, it is made with the utmost caution. Human reproduction touches on many sensitive issues, from those that are biological, sexual, and familial to those that involve religion and cultural values, such as freedom of choice.

One admittedly potentially controversial approach to resolve the population and consumption dilemma is to develop voluntary household, community, organizational, and societal resource budgets and provide both financial and nonfinancial incentives for these entities to attempt to stay within these budgets. Only minor adjustments would be made for additional household members, so that all households, regardless of size, used the targeted amount of, say, fossil fuels. As radical as this proposal may appear, if both human reproduction and consumption continue to increase unchecked in the coming several decades, societies will likely need to consider designing, implementing, and enforcing such resource rationing schemes just to prevent massive resource crises.

Implications for Academics

Research and teaching opportunities are numerous in the area of multilevel and multisystems approaches to green economies. Hopefully, the preceding pages have generated a number of research questions, including the following: What information inputs are necessary for individuals to reduce their consumption of limited resources such as energy and water? What communication processes work best in organizations and communities in inspiring their members to make better sustainability decisions? How can institutions increase their collaboration and reduce their complexities in moving their societies toward greener economies (the ultimate output)?

From a teaching standpoint, instructors need to identify and implement educational approaches that not only provide useful information for their students (at multiple levels of action) but also motivate students to take action on a broad and deep-enough basis to collectively and significantly have a positive effect. Primarily, instructors need to prepare future sustainability leaders for careers and lifestyles that incorporate sustainability responsibilities and actions throughout their careers as much as is appropriate. Transferring and leveraging instructor passion for sustainability would also likely be helpful.

Implications for Practitioners

As formulators and implementers of green economy policies, the bulk of responsibility for sustainability efforts rests with leaders and supporters in businesses, governments, and nonprofit organizations. Recognizing multiple levels and systems elements of their efforts may be a good first step in advancing the greener economies. Regarding levels, individual practitioners with similar green economy interests can be encouraged to join their efforts for greater effect. Those who lead business, government, and nonprofit organizations with similar or related green economy interests can also collaborate to advance their mutual sustainability goals.

At the practitioner institutional or societal level, multiorganizational and cross-sectoral collaborations, sometimes called peak organizations, can be advanced to move in greener economy directions. Examples of this phenomenon include community local currency programs; sustainability-related clearinghouses; and greener economy movements, such as the development of climate action and carbon-neutrality plans, and local organic food production and forest restoration plans, including within urban areas. Both formal and informal green economy associations could be encouraged at both individual and organizational levels. Affinity groups, clubs, task forces, and networks that advance greener economies need to be encouraged.

Final Thoughts

At all levels and in each system component, moving beyond initial emissions reductions, often referred to as low-hanging fruit, appears to be necessary in making significant strides toward greener economies. This more intensive effort appears necessary to make significant progress in reversing environmental damage that appears extant in most of the world's ecosystems. Meeting carbon reduction goals of 80 percent by 2050 appears to be very challenging, given that even some of the greener building practices, such as LEED Platinum, deliver only about half the emission reductions necessary for a healthful environment in that decade. Efforts to move toward greener economies will likely require crossing boundaries; scaling up; transforming cultures; and building coalitions and ongoing excitement, commitment, and strategic actions suggested in this chapter, including extending the values and practices of the Living Building Challenge 2.0 to other sectors of the human economy. Time is of the essence, and urgency in moving toward greener economies may need to be at the top of all of our personal and professional to-do lists.

References

Barnard, C. I. 1938. *The functions of the executive.* Cambridge, MA: Harvard University Press.

Brown, L. R. 2009. *Plan B 4.0: Mobilizing to save civilization.* New York: W. W. Norton.

Friedman, T. L. 2008. *Hot, flat, and crowded: Why we need a green revolution—and how it can renew America.* New York: Farrar, Straus, and Giroux.

Gore, A. 2006. *An inconvenient truth.* Emmaus, PA: Rodale.

Hitchcock, D., and M. Willard. 2009. *The business guide to sustainability: Practical tools and strategies for organizations.* London: Earthscan.

Holliday, C. O., S. Schmidheiny, and P. Watts. 2002. *Walking the talk: The business case for sustainable development.* San Francisco: Greenleaf Publishing.

Hopkins, R. 2008. *The transition handbook: From oil dependency to local resilience.* White River Junction, VT: Chelsea Green Publishing.

Louv, R. 2005. *Last child in the woods: Saving our children from nature-deficit disorder.* Chapel Hill, NC: Algonquin Books.

MacDonald, C. 2008. *Green, Inc.: An environmental insider reveals how a good cause has gone bad.* Guilford, CT: Lyons Press.

McKenzie-Mohr, D., and W. Smith. 1999. *Fostering sustainable behavior: An introduction to community-based social marketing.* Gabriola Island, B.C.: New Society Publishers.

Munchau, W. 2009. *The meltdown years: The unfolding of the global economic crisis.* New York: McGraw-Hill.

Naisbitt, J., N. Naisbitt, and D. Phillips. 1999. *High-tech, high-touch: Technology and our search for meaning.* London: Nicholas Brealey.

Perera, N. 1999. A view from above: Advanced satellites reduce risk. *Risk Management* 46 (7): 44–48.

Porter, M. 2009. *Financial crises.* Hamburg: MLP.

Sarkissian, W., N. Hofer, Y. Shore, and S. Vajda. 2008. *Kitchen table sustainability: Practical recipes for community engagement with sustainability.* London: Earthscan.

Seitanidi, M. M., and A. Crane. 2009. Implementing CSR through partnerships: Understanding the selection, design, and institutionalization of non-profit business partnerships. *Journal of Business Ethics* 85: 414–30.

Seyfang, Gill. 2009. *Green shoots of sustainability: The 2009 UK Transition movement survey.* Norwich, U.K.: University of East Anglia.

Shiller, R. J. 2008. *The subprime solution: How today's global financial crisis happened and what to do about it.* Princeton, NJ: Princeton University Press.

Starik, M., and M. Heuer. 2002. Strategic inter-organizational environmentalism in the U.S.: A multi-sectoral perspective of alternating eco-policy roles. *Business Strategy and the Environment* 11: 221–35.

Starik, M., and A. A. Marcus. 2000. Special research forum on the management of organizations in the natural environment: A field emerging from multiple paths, with many challenges ahead. *Academy of Management Journal* 43 (4): 539–47.

Starik, M., and G. P. Rands. 1995. Weaving an integrated web: Multilevel and multisystem perspectives of ecologically sustainable organizations. *Academy of Management Review* 20 (4): 908–35.

Townsend, A. K. 2009. *Business ecology: Why most green practices don't work and what to do about it.* Atglen, PA: Schiffer Publishing.

U.S. Environmental Protection Agency. 2009. *Buildings and their impact on the environment: A statistical summary.* Washington, D.C.: U.S. Environmental Protection Agency.

Wankel, C., and J. A. F. Stoner, eds. 2008. *Innovative approaches to global sustainability.* New York: Palgrave Macmillan.

Worthy, K. 2008. Modern institutions, phenomenal dissociations, and destructiveness toward humans and the environment. *Organization and Environment* 21 (2): 148–60.

Zemtseff, K. 2009. Living building challenge goes broader and deeper. *Daily Journal of Commerce* (Seattle), November 17. http://www.djc.com/news/en/12012170.html.

Comments

17 The Global Financial Crisis

A Perspective from India

Murali Murti and N. V. Krishna

The global financial crisis (GFC) is a term often used to describe the turbulence that shook major economies of the developed world during 2008 and early 2009. The GFC was characterized by economic recession, increased unemployment, the collapse of major banks, investment companies, and insurance companies, the collapse of the realty sector, and a sharp reduction in household and institutional credit. Further damage to the system was averted by huge bailout packages, with the Troubled Asset Relief Program (TARP) in the United States alone accounting for nearly $1 trillion.

The crisis also took a huge toll in human terms, with more than 100 million people slipping below the poverty line, workers in formal and informal sectors such as manufacturing, construction, and commerce being seriously affected, and more than 18 million people joining the pool of unemployed. It is also estimated that millions of children worldwide were affected by cognitive and physical disabilities resulting from malnutrition.

The United States and the developed economies of Western Europe were the worst hit by the crisis, whereas some other major economies, including China and India, escaped relatively unscathed. The focus of this chapter is on examining possible factors that led to a higher level of resilience of some economies, in particular, India. Resilience in this context denotes the ability to withstand the effects of an economic crisis with a relatively moderate impact, and the ability to recover rapidly from such crises. Given that such crises may recur in the future, it is critical that countries and economies move toward increasing the resilience of their systems.

In the present discussion, we examine resilience by considering a few key factors such as growth of gross domestic product (GDP); unemployment; financial asset values; and other asset classes, including realty and household and national debt. We also look at institutional failures as an indicator of resilience. In such a framework, it is observed that in the case of the United States, GDP growth fell sharply, realty values plummeted, values of financial assets were significantly destroyed, unemployment shot up, and housing finance companies, along with banking and insurance companies, either collapsed or had to be rescued. The impact of the crisis on India was less severe, with a slowdown in growth rather than a recession, moderate effects on property and other asset prices, little impact on unemployment, and not even a sign of failure in any bank or financial institution. It is on the basis of these differences that we state that India turned out to be more resilient than the United States.

We examine whether it is possible to identify specific factors related to the Indian economy, banking, and regulation that may have contributed to a higher level of resilience. We also look at cultural factors influencing behavior related to debt, savings, and credit, all of which played a key role in the crisis.

Another factor is the level of regulation and the role of the government in macroeconomic management. As we discuss later, India has evolved a strong regulatory framework and an effective central bank responsible for monetary policy, which has emphasized stability rather than growth. The United States, in contrast, has moved increasingly toward liberalization of markets, less or no regulation in many sectors, and an overarching view that less government is better. However, in responding to the crisis, many of these views had to be reversed in the United States, and the government ended up playing a dominant role in economic matters. Our view is that an explicit recognition of the need for a strong regulatory framework is essential and should not be considered a regressive measure in terms of free-market polemics. Similarly, it is necessary that the role of the government in macroeconomic management be clearly defined rather than focusing only on reducing its role and size. India's large domestic market, and relatively low dependence on exports, also insulated the economy from the effects of the crisis.

In the following sections, we examine the impact of the crisis and discuss a set of factors that may have led to certain economies like India being more resilient than others, like the United States. In terms of the impact, we examine data related to GDP, unemployment, and stock markets. This is followed by a discussion of social and cultural factors in which we discuss a key behavioral trait, the propensity to save, and how this differs significantly across countries, as well as the socioeconomic factors that impact the savings rate. We then discuss the role of the government, with a detailed discussion of the government's role in the banking sector. We also discuss financial regulation, followed by a section that examines the operational framework in the banking sector. This is followed by our conclusions, which attempt to bring together the various arguments in the chapter.

A Brief Analysis of the Crisis

The crisis in the U.S. economy started with the sudden collapse of the housing-asset bubble, followed rapidly by crises in the banking and financial sectors and thereafter in the real economy of manufacturing, retailing, and other sectors. U.S. house prices, which rose by 124 percent between 1997 and 2006, and contributed to more than half of U.S. GDP growth in 2005, declined by 26.6 percent between 2006 and 2008. Stock markets of many developed economies went into steep decline in 2008, affected by bank shares and commodity prices. London's FTSE index fell by 31 percent, Frankfurt's DAX by more than 40 percent, Paris's CAC by 42.7 percent, and the Japanese Nikkei by 42 percent, all within a one-year period. The banking sector went through an extraordinary crisis, with the U.S. government stepping in to save AIG, Citibank, Freddie Mac, and Fannie Mae (involving a guarantee of $12 trillion of debt)—and Merrill Lynch was sold to Bank of America. Table 17.1 presents certain key data related to the impact of the crisis on the U.S. economy.

It may be observed that the crisis affected the United States and Eurozone countries far more deeply than India. The GFC had a major impact on

TABLE 17.1 Economic indicators

Period	GDP Growth (%)			Unemployment (%)			Stock Indices	
	U.S.	Eurozone	India	U.S.	Eurozone	India	U.S. Dow	India BSE
Q3 2008	−2.7	−0.4	7.7	5.6	7.3	7.9	11,382	12,952
Q4 2008	−5.4	−1.8	5.8	6.6	7.5	7.9	10,831	13,056
Q1 2009	−6.4	−2.5	5.8	7.6	8.4	7.9	9,035	9,996
Q2 2009	−0.7	−0.1	6.1	8.9	9.0	7.9	7,762	9,901
Q3 2009	3.5	0.4	7.5	9.5	9.3	7.9	8,504	14,645

SOURCE: Constructed from data available from the Bureau of Economic Analysis, U.S. Department of Commerce (http://www.bea.gov), the Reserve Bank of India (http://www.rbi .org.in), and the Economist (http://www.economist.com).

the GDPs of both the United States and the Eurozone. Both regions showed negative GDP growth for twelve months and were therefore in recession for that period. In contrast, India's GDP dropped for three quarters but did not enter negative territory; in fact, it stayed above 5 percent for the entire period. Thus, it could be said that the Indian economy suffered a minor slump but was never in danger of a recession.

Unemployment rose steadily in both the United States and the Eurozone, and exceeded 9 percent in both areas by the beginning of the fourth quarter of 2009. In contrast, although reported figures are less exact, unemployment in India remained relatively constant throughout the period. Specific sectors, such as information technology services and textiles, are reported to have suffered a temporary drop but did not have a major impact on the employment picture in India as a whole.

The stock market, particularly in the United States, was adversely affected by the GFC. The Dow Jones Industrial Average suffered a net loss of 16 percent in the fifteen-month period from July 1, 2008, to October 1, 2009. The effect on shareholder wealth would have been correspondingly severe. In contrast, the Bombay Stock Exchange index, the BSE Sensex, gained 32 percent in the same period, although it also suffered losses from the end of 2008 to June 2009.

The Cultural Framework

In this section, we examine certain cultural and societal factors specific to India and whether they could have influenced the impact of the GFC in the country.

The first such cultural factor we consider is the propensity to save, as reflected by the gross national savings rate and its components. It may be observed in Table 17.2 that, historically, the Indian national savings rate has been relatively high in comparison to that of the United States, and it continues to be significantly higher.

The current savings rate of 29 percent in India may be compared to a rate of around 7 percent in the United States and 9 percent in Europe. It is also relevant to note that the component of private savings and household savings is much higher in India (well more than 20 percent), as compared to around 3 percent for the United States. Not only are the U.S. savings rates consistently and significantly lower than in India; they also indicate a declining trend over the past twenty years. For example, the U.S. household savings rate declined from around 7.5 percent in 1991 to −0.5 percent in 2005. During the same

TABLE 17.2 Comparison of savings rates, India and United States

	Indian Gross Domestic Saving				U.S. Gross Domestic Saving		
Year	House-hold Sector	Private Corporate Sector	Public Sector	Total	Household Savings Rate	Net Private Savings Rate	Net National Savings Rate
1985	—	—	—	—	—	11.1	7.0
1986	—	—	—	—	—	9.5	5.2
1987	—	—	—	—	—	8.8	5.6
1988	—	—	—	—	—	9.5	7.0
1989	17.9	2.4	1.7	22.0	—	8.5	6.2
1990	19.3	2.7	1.1	23.1	—	8.3	5.1
1991	17.0	3.1	2.0	22.1	—	8.7	4.6
1992	17.5	2.7	1.6	21.8	7.5	8.9	3.6
1993	18.4	3.5	0.6	22.5	5.6	7.9	3.2
1994	19.7	3.5	1.7	24.9	4.7	7.2	3.9
1995	18.2	4.9	2.0	25.1	4.4	7.6	4.7
1996	17.0	4.5	1.7	23.2	3.7	7.1	5.5
1997	17.6	4.2	1.3	23.1	3.0	6.9	6.7
1998	18.8	3.7	−1.0	21.5	3.8	6.2	7.3
1999	21.3	4.5	−0.9	24.9	1.7	5.1	7.0
2000	21.2	4.1	−1.8	23.5	1.6	3.9	6.0
2001	22.0	3.6	−2.0	23.6	1.4	3.6	4.2
2002	23.1	4.1	−0.7	26.5	2.2	5.2	2.1
2003	23.5	4.4	1.0	28.9	2.0	5.3	1.3
2004	22.0	4.8	2.2	29.0	1.9	4.9	1.0
2005	—	—	—	—	−0.5	3.0	0.1

SOURCE: Constructed from data available from the Bureau of Economic Analysis, U.S. Department of Commerce (http://www.bea.gov) and the Reserve Bank of India (http://www .rbi.org.in).

period, the corresponding rate for India increased from around 17.9 percent to 22 percent. It is to be noted that the high savings rate also coincided with a gross national product growth rate of around 7 percent, thereby reducing the need to borrow.

It is significant, in the context of the GFC, that the propensity to save appears to have declined across the board in the United States over the 1990–2005 time frame, whether measured by personal or corporate or governmental data. In sharp contrast, during the same period, the savings rate actually increased across the board in India. Our argument is that a higher savings rate indicates a conservative attitude to personal finances, and the same conservatism inhibits taking on debt and repayment obligations.

In the following discussion, we examine various factors affecting the propensity to save, how India is positioned with respect to these factors, and some additional factors rooted in cultural practices.

In a cross-country study of national savings rates, Kirsanova and Sefton (1996) identify a set of factors that influence the savings behavior of countries. These factors include demographics, welfare programs from the state, retirement behavior, constraints on borrowing, income distribution over one's lifetime, income uncertainty, and capital gains accounting. Uncertainty about one's future income expectations, for the cited reasons, is a driving factor for increased savings. It is relevant, in this context, that 92 percent of the Indian workforce is employed in the informal sector, which is characterized by a high degree of income uncertainty, no retirement benefits, constraints on institutional credit, and limited benefits from the state in terms of welfare measures. For example, household expenditure on health in India is estimated to be more than 80 percent of the total health expenditure, a very poor level of provisioning by the state. The basic thrust of the study is that the national savings rate is inversely proportional (though not directly so) to the citizen's expectation of retirement benefits, benefits delivered by the state, certainty of income over one's lifetime, ease of access to institutional credit, and the average retirement age. All these factors tend to increase the savings rate in the Indian context, and the outcome is reflected in the relatively high and stable savings rate exhibited by the Indian economy. In contrast, the United States provides its citizens with far higher levels of support, including social security, education, civic amenities, and health insurance. The proportion of the labor force employed by the organized sector is much higher, and the incidents of unemployment and poverty are far lower. All these positive factors result in reduced risk perceptions, and hence lower propensities to save.

Another key factor leading to the GFC was the behavior of individuals with respect to credit, savings, and debt, all of which are closely interrelated. Housing loans in the United States, widely considered a major causal factor of the crisis, were aggressively sold to clients who could not realistically meet their repayment obligations. Indians, by and large, are far more conservative in terms of taking on debt-based obligations, and Indian banks and financial institutions are rigorous in their due-diligence requirements for extending such loans. Indeed, as we discuss in more detail later, Indian bankers are driven by nonperforming assets (e.g., bad loans) and their control rather than by growing the size of their loan portfolios. This is one cultural factor that surely mitigated the risk of bubble formation, specifically in the housing sector. An important aspect of housing finance in India is that the typical Indian buyer has far more equity in a house that is partly financed by a loan than does his or her U.S. counterpart. Among other factors, this is because of the widespread prevalence of black money (a term commonly used in India to describe unaccounted, unrecorded, and untaxed cash flows that constitute a parallel economy) in the realty sector, which is neither reported nor accounted for but leads to a situation in which the homeowner actually has much more equity in a house than what is recorded. This skewed ratio leads to a much better rate of repayment for housing loans and much lower rates of delinquency.

Another important aspect specific to India is the low proportion of the population that has access to institutional credit of any type. Credit card penetration is less than 1 percent of the population, whereas credit facilities from institutional sources are used by less than 14 percent of the poor (annual income of $1,000 or less). Microfinance clients as a group probably constitute the largest group with access to institutional credit, currently estimated at 50 million people, or approximately 4.3 percent of the population. Thus, the low proportion of the population with access to institutional credit also lowers the vulnerability of the system to misuse and abuse of credit.

The Indian economy was characterized by shortages of all kinds of goods and services for many decades following independence in 1947, with extensive controls in terms of regulatory and licensing regimes exercised by the government. It was a common experience for citizens to wait for many years for a telephone connection, a cooking-gas cylinder, a car, or a motorcycle. Thus, entire generations grew up with a mind-set that was quite used to postponing expenditure and focused on savings, commonly the only source for funding the purchase of assets. Even though the Indian economy has changed significantly since the 1990s and has been liberalized and globalized to a great extent, the same approach to debt and savings continues among a large proportion of the population.

Despite the significant heterogeneity in terms of religion, language, culture, and ethnicity, social structures in India show evidence of stratification and continuity across generations and centuries, as seen by the caste system, prevalent across the country, particularly in the "traditional" sector of the economy, which accounts for around 80 percent of the population. Decision

making by individuals is strongly influenced by family and caste considerations, including decisions regarding credit and debt, as well as occupation
and marriage (Munshi and Rosenzweig 2009). Such societal factors tend to
encourage conservative behavior in terms of savings and debt. In comparison, we see that the U.S. and Eurozone economies are far more individual
oriented, with higher levels of social mobility and much better entitlements
and provisioning in terms of social support systems, such as health, unemployment insurance, social security, and access to credit. Thus, there are some
major societal differences between India and the Western economies that affect credit-related behavior and mitigated the effects of the crisis in India.

The foregoing discussion identifies certain cultural and societal factors in
India that influenced credit- and debt-related behavior and possibly helped
the country avoid the worst effects of the GFC. However, it is worth considering whether these factors are in fact desirable, whether one may expect the
same state to continue, and whether there are lessons appropriate for other
countries.

The Role of Government

One of the more unexpected fallouts of the GFC was the reemergence of the
government as a key factor in economic management. Starting with the aggressive interventions by the U.S. Federal Reserve in September 2008, followed
by the swift takeover of many banks and financial institutions, and culminating in the $800 billion TARP at the end of 2008, the role of the U.S. gov-
ernment strengthened immeasurably in the formulation of economic policy.
With the takeover of General Motors, the term *state capitalism*, previously applied only to a few countries, notably China, could well refer to at least a part
of the U.S. economy, and the Eurozone as well. This represents a dramatic
reversal of the doctrine of deregulating the economy and financial markets, a
trend that had gained ground since the 1980s.

It is sometimes overlooked that state capitalism is the major mode of
economic organization in many sectors and regions of the world (Brammer
2009). The key role of the state in the management of the economy, including financial systems, was well accepted by the Western economies for about
thirty years following the end of World War II, a period when a new global
economic order emerged, although this role of the state was then reduced
steadily in the United States in particular over the following thirty years.

The energy market provides a good example of the dominant role of the state. The world's thirteen largest oil companies, measured by reserves (e.g., Saudi Armco, Gasport, China National Petroleum Company), are controlled by governments. Exxon Mobil, the largest private sector oil company, is fourteenth on the list. State-controlled companies now control more than 75 percent of global crude-oil reserves. Investors and corporate leaders have to recognize that free-market globalization is no longer the unchallenged economic paradigm, particularly in view of the performance of the Chinese economy.

Is state capitalism as efficient as the free market? Is there any consideration other than efficiency that requires a place for state capitalism? Many of the stimulus packages and other forms of active intervention have been accepted as a necessary part of the government's role. Indeed, it has been argued that excessive deregulation of the financial markets, including the repeal in 1999 of the Glass-Steagall Act, was a significant factor leading to the GFC (Skidelsky 2009). It is clear that the role of the state and state capitalism are important aspects that are in a state of flux and need to evolve to effectively address the challenges of managing economies and nations in the future.

In this section, the discussion focuses on the history and the present status of the Indian banking industry as an example of state capitalism, as data in this regard may provide some pointers to the performance of the Indian economy during the GFC. It is a remarkable fact that there has not been a single bank failure in India during the GFC.

After independence, successive Indian governments promoted what was referred to as a mixed economy, meaning that the private sector would co-exist with the government-owned or public sector. The banking sector was no exception, and starting in 1969, the Indian government nationalized the twenty largest banks. Unlike in the United States, the Reserve Bank of India, the central bank, had been a state-owned entity since independence. Thus, virtually the entire banking sector came under state control. Following the 1991 reforms, however, the banking sector came to include many private and international players.

Currently, there are more than 290 scheduled banks (a term used in India to describe banks registered with the Reserve Bank of India, the central bank) in the country, with sixty-six thousand branches. The total asset base of Indian banks is approximately US$335 billion, with total deposits of more than $279 billion. Public-sector banks account for 72.5 percent of the asset base.

In a study comparing the performance of Indian public-sector and private-sector banks, Mittal and Dhade (2007) created two indices: a profitability index based on a combination of financial ratios and a productivity index based on a combination of relevant indicators. Tables 17.3 and 17.4 summarize their findings.

On the basis of Tables 17.3 and 17.4, we can infer that the Indian banking sector continues to be dominated by the public sector—in terms of geographic spread, asset base, and customer base, the public sector is far larger than the private sector. Second, the profitability of the Indian public sector is lower than that of foreign banks operating in India but compares approximately to that of the Indian private-sector banks. Third, the cost structure of the public-sector banks is lower as a result of lower salaries and lower infrastructure costs.

Therefore, on the basis of profitability analysis, it can be concluded that public-sector banks are less efficient financially than their private-sector counterparts. This finding in turn is supported by the figures for productivity. The productivity of Indian public-sector banks is less than 50 percent of their private-sector counterparts and less than 30 percent of their foreign banking counterparts. Some of these discrepancies can be attributed to the charter under which public-sector banks operate, that is, the requirement to

TABLE 17.3 Profitability indexes of Indian banks

	1999–2000	2000–2001	2001–2002	2002–2003	2003–2004
Public sector	0.47	0.34	0.57	0.76	0.89
Private sector	1.59	0.61	0.64	0.85	0.79
Foreign banks	−1.72	−0.70	0.12	1.50	1.60
Total	**0.65**	**0.31**	**0.56**	**0.82**	**0.91**

SOURCE: Mittal and Dadhe 2007.

TABLE 17.4 Productivity indexes of Indian banks

	1999–2000	2000–2001	2001–2002	2002–2003	2003–2004
Public sector	1.25	1.6	1.91	2.15	2.47
Private sector	2.64	3.06	4.01	4.44	5.27
Foreign banks	6.99	9.03	10.07	10.31	9.57
Total	0.65	0.31	0.56	0.82	0.91

SOURCE: Mittal and Dadhe 2007.

offer services to as wide a cross section of the Indian business and consumer markets as possible, including the socially needy sectors.

However, this inefficiency has also acted as a brake on the growth of the financial services sector in India. In fact, the Indian financial services sector has been demonstrably less aggressive in offering new and financially innovative products to the consuming public. This may also have inhibited, to some extent, the growth of the Indian economy itself. Had the profitability and productivity of the Indian public-sector banks matched those of their private and foreign counterparts, there may have been a significant impact in terms of GDP growth. Such growth, however, may well have fueled asset bubbles along the lines of the GFC in the West.

Thus, a startling conclusion might be that it is state capitalism that, despite its observed inefficiency as compared to market-driven capitalism, has shielded the Indian economy from the worst negative side effects of financial efficiencies in the United States and the Eurozone.

The Role of the Central Bank

The financial sector in India is regulated by the Reserve Bank of India (RBI), India's central bank. It is fully owned by the Indian government. The main functions of the RBI are common to those of most central banks, such as creating monetary policy, regulating and supervising the financial system, managing and regulating foreign exchange reserves and markets, issuing and exchanging currency notes and coins, performing the role of banker to the banks, and so on. Where the RBI differs is in its mandate to facilitate development through a wide range of promotional functions in support of national economic objectives.

In the context of the GFC, it is useful to compare the policy-making approach of the RBI with that of other central banks, notably the U.S. Federal Reserve. For example, a major objective of monetary policy in India has always been price stability. Containing inflation has been a priority for the RBI over the years. In contrast, a historical point of worry for the Fed has been deflation.

During the first half of 2008, as a result of the high growth rates of the Indian economy, the inflation rate had reached high levels. Therefore, the RBI consciously instituted a policy of tightening liquidity by raising interest rates. A side effect of this tight money supply was to discourage excessive speculation in the financial derivatives markets. Thus, to some extent, the effects of the GFC were mitigated even before they had struck.

Most important, the RBI's policies are consciously countercyclical, unlike the approach in many other countries, especially the United States (Reddy 2002). This approach is based on the principle of ensuring stability of the economy rather than growth. Therefore, the buildup of risks in the global financial system had been articulated by the RBI as early as 2005. The RBI also instituted some proactive preventive measures, including addressing liquidity issues specifically through tight regulation of interest rates; providing self-insurance through the buildup of foreign exchange reserves; and moderating capital inflows while simultaneously liberalizing outflows, especially from households and corporations. Banks were encouraged to concentrate on traditional retail banking rather than wholesale or capital market operations. Training programs were undertaken to enhance skills in the financial workforce capable of dealing with the new financial instruments. The regulatory framework was extended to systemically important financial institutions.

Despite these measures, there was a perceptible impact of the GFC on India: slower growth. One important reason for this was the greater integration of the Indian economy with the global economy. Therefore, any global downturn was bound to cause a ripple in India. The withdrawal of foreign institutional investment from the equity markets, the reluctance of banks to lend, and the reluctance of borrowers to borrow, in view of uncertain economic conditions, and possibly a simultaneous but autonomous downturn in the domestic economic cycle, were other contributing factors.

The relative rapidity with which India has come out of the GFC can be attributed to proactive and conservative policy measures. These included monetary measures, such as reduced interest rates, reduced bank reserve requirements, and liberalized refinance facilities. Governmental measures also helped, especially the stimulus packages launched in December 2008.

Governance and Operational Processes in the Banking Sector

Good regulation in itself is of no benefit unless it is supported by good corporate governance and operational processes that ensure long-term stability. This section focuses on some of the key aspects of governance and operational processes in Indian banks and discusses how these may have mitigated, to some extent, the effects of the GFC.

As already noted, the Indian banking sector is dominated by public-sector banks (PSBs). Governance of PSBs is well structured, as the banks are state owned. Structurally, the governance of a PSB rests with the board of directors. The composition of the board generally follows a standard pattern that has been legislated over the years. The chair, managing director, and executive directors of all PSBs are appointed by the government. This ensures that all PSBs function in accordance with policies directed by the government and the RBI, with much less independence of action than most banks in a fully free-market economy.

The boards are required to set up a number of committees to manage the affairs of the PSB, such as management, risk management, asset liability management, audit, and several other committees. As a significant measure of oversight, the audit committee of a bank must necessarily include the chartered accountant directors on the board, but the chair is not a member.

Appointment of auditors is done through a very detailed procedure based on a panel of approved auditors circulated by the RBI. Appointment and removal of auditors requires prior RBI approval. Through legislation, the RBI is empowered to appoint a director on the board of a bank if it believes that the situation at the bank calls for such a measure.

Another distinctive feature of the Indian banking sector is the existence of self-regulatory organizations (SROs) since before independence. At present, there are four SROs in the financial system: the Indian Banks Association (IBA), the Foreign Exchange Dealers Association of India (FEDAI), the Primary Dealers of India (PDAI), and the Fixed Income Money Market Dealers of India (FIMMDAI)

The IBA, established in 1946 as a voluntary association of banks, strives to strengthen the banking industry through consensus and coordination. It also acts as a forum for conducting negotiations between bank managements and employee unions.

In the area of foreign exchange, FEDAI has refocused its role by giving up rate fixing, but it plays a multifarious role in training bank personnel, accounting standards, the creation of risk measurement models, and accreditation of foreign exchange brokers.

In the financial markets, the PDAI and FIMMDAI are of recent origin, established in 1996 and 1997, respectively. Both have been proactive and are closely involved in contemporary issues relating to development of money and government securities markets. The representatives of PDAI and

TABLE 17.5 Ratio of net NPAs to net advances (%)

	2003	2004	2005	2006	2007
PSBs	4.5	2.9	2.0	1.2	1.0
Private	4.4	2.0	1.6	0.8	0.9
Foreign	1.3	1.0	0.8	0.9	0.8

SOURCE: Constructed from data available from the Reserve Bank of India (http://www.rbi
.org.in) and the Ministry of Finance, Government of India (http://www.finmin.nic.in).

FIMMDAI are members of important committees of the RBI, both on policy
and operational issues.

Although corporate governance standards and SROs are indeed essential
for the routine functioning of the banking sector, the experience in the developed world during the GFC has illustrated the importance of operational
process control to prevent extreme swings in the dynamics of the financial
system. In this regard, the PSBs have developed a culture over the years in
which abundant caution accurately reflects the RBIs own self-prescribed
guideline of stability over all else. The most important feature of this culture
is a clear focus on nonperforming assets (NPAs) as a measure of performance
rather than only profitability. This is a policy that has been driven by the Indian government and the RBI. Table 17.5 illustrates this focus well.

Table 17.5 offers some explanation of why toxic debt accumulation as evidenced in the West before the GFC has not taken place in India.

Executive compensation is another area that is tightly controlled. Salaries
at PSBs are fixed and based on government pay scales for equivalent levels
of responsibility, qualifications, and skills. Salaries are worked out through
a collaborative negotiating process in which the RBI and the IBA are actively
involved.

There are no incentives or bonuses linked to performance. Promotions
and important assignments are the only form of reward. Although this system
undoubtedly stifles managerial initiative, it has the positive effect of discour-
aging excessive risk taking at operational levels and huge bonuses—a major
cause of the GFC.

Conclusions

Resilience is the characteristic of being able to manage the impact of large-
scale shocks to the macroeconomic and financial sectors of a nation-state, so

that the impact is minimized and recovery is rapid. It may be that the long-term sustainability of socioeconomic systems, including nation-states, will require the ability to survive shocks from time to time, given the complex nature of interdependencies in the world economic order. In an increasingly globalized world, the butterfly effect is clearly of great relevance. India was able to fall back on the domestic market to a large extent, as its overall dependence on overseas markets was limited and the size of its internal market is so significant. The regulatory framework inhibited exposure to banking and financial market risks. The government played an active and interventionist role in terms of monetary and fiscal policies, focusing on stability rather than growth.

The role of the government is an important aspect that emerges from our discussion of the Indian experience. As mentioned in earlier sections, the government's role, in terms of many dimensions, went through a dramatic reduction in the 1990s in the United States and other Western economies, and the same economies had to resort to massive intervention by the government to mitigate the effects of the crisis. This experience should be a key input in determining the magnitude and scope of the government's role in the evolution of the global economic order.

High propensity to save, less focus on current consumption, and conservative attitudes toward debt are all factors that contributed to India's ability to cope with the crisis. These factors are real challenges for the United States, as its economic doctrine requires ever-growing consumption and an underlying philosophy that more is better. Indeed, the imperatives of profit and top-line growth, which drive the U.S. corporate sector, face the most significant challenges in terms of aligning with the needs of sustainability. As M. K. Gandhi (1958) said, the world has enough to meet people's needs but not their greed. The pursuit of happiness needs to be delinked from the acquisition of material assets and the consumption of resources.

References

Brammer, Ian. 2009. State capitalism and the crisis. *McKinsey Quarterly*, July 2009.

Gandhi, M. K. 1958. *Towards new horizons, part 2: Mahatma Gandhi the last phase.* Ahmedabad: Navajivan Publishing House.

Kirsanova, T., and J. Sefton. 2006. A comparison of national savings rates in UK, USA and Italy. Discussion Paper No. 192, July, National Institute of Economic and Social Research, London.

Mittal, M., and A. Dhade. 2007. Profitability and performance in Indian banks: A comparative study. Paper presented at the annual conference of the Association of Indian Management Scholars, Hyderabad.

Munshi, K., and M. Rosenzweig. 2009. Why is mobility in India so low? Social insurance, inequality and growth. Working Paper No. 14850, April, National Bureau of Economic Research, Cambridge, MA. http://www.nber.org/papers/w14850.

Reddy, Y. V. 2002. Public sector banks and the governance challenge. Paper presented at Brookings Institution Conference on Financial Governance, New York.

Reddy, Y. V. 2009. *India and the global financial crisis.* New Delhi: Orient Blackswan.

Skidelsky, Robert. 2009. *Keynes: The return of the master.* New York: Penguin Books.

In Lieu of a Conclusion

Paul Shrivastava and Matt Statler

When we began this project, we fully intended to arrive at a series of firm conclusions about how to resolve the financial crisis by building sustainable, creative, and reliable organizations and economies. We have been humbled by a journey that has opened up more questions than it has answered. Many of the chapters have laid bare the false assumptions of traditional finance and management theories and practices, and some have offered pathways for creating alternatives. Collectively, the chapters open up alternative visions of how the postcrisis recovery might unfold—and yet many questions remain unanswered.

At least this much seems clear: the global financial system cannot sustain unfettered growth due to constraints that ultimately are ecological. For some people, this conclusion may recommend slow growth or low growth; for others, it calls for no growth or contraction. In any case, economies will need to be managed within the constraints of changing climate, declining biodiversity, and eroding ecological conditions. Under such circumstances, a successful recovery cannot occur without human creativity—including aesthetic perceptions and judgments of fit, appropriateness, and beauty—and a focus on reliability and resilience that can sustain organization forms and economic relations even in the face of extreme uncertainty.

Despite the hopeful message of the chapters in this book, our own observations about the reality that we are living with are rather sobering. First, all the major economies of the world are scrambling to stem the damages of the financial crisis. Yet nearly three years on, the largest economy (United

States) is looking at a double-dip recession and possibly a decade before it recovers. Whatever that word means to policy makers, we do not discern in mainstream political discourse any coherent direction or consensus on sustainability. Instead, we sense a kind of unmanaged general drift, the kind of inertial momentum that Jared Diamond (2005) has identified in association with societies on the brink of ecological collapse. For example, even when there is a clear scientific consensus about the urgent need for action, as in the instance of the 2009 Copenhagen climate treaty, existing vested interests and ingrained habits of thought and action thwarted the articulation and implementation of meaningful change.

Second, we are witnessing the continued failure of national and global leadership to seize the opportunity for radical transformation of economies and organizations toward sustainable, creative, and reliable development. When we started this project two years ago, Barack Obama's election as president of the United States symbolized a hope for change for the whole world. Since then, his own leadership potential has appeared to diminish, in part because his administration has become tangled up in the myriad tentacles of government bureaucracies, national politics, and geopolitical calculations, and in part because of unprincipled and relentless assaults on his legitimacy to serve in the office from unlikely coalitions of racists and industrial polluters (Mayer 2010). In light of Obama's current predicament, we wonder whether perhaps it is time to give up on conventional ideas of leadership and look for some form of antileadership in which the public takes responsibility for its own domains of influence instead of waiting for leaders to show the way. And yet, inasmuch as the Tea Party itself purports to be precisely such a movement, we remain skeptical about the extent to which any such political activism could gain significant influence without succumbing to the redemptive and ultimately narcissistic hero worship that appears endemic to contemporary media culture.

Third, we observe that some economies, such as India and Canada, have been more resilient than others in dealing with the financial crisis. India's resilience may be tied to the fact that before the crisis, it had limited and deliberately government-managed coupling to the global economy. Canada was shielded partly by its own conservative and regulated banking practices. One reaction to the financial crisis is a reassessment by many countries about how tightly they wish to be connected to global markets, the importance of economic self-sufficiency, and the search for ways to control their own destinies. Over the long term, this may put some brakes on the process of economic globalization that seemed unstoppable a few years ago. Prioritizing national interests over global ones was one of the reasons for failure of the Copenhagen Accord, and it raises sharp challenges for governance of global commons.

Finally, we notice a striking lack of focus and use of human creativity and human potential in the past economic regimes. The design of economies and organizations in the past treated humans as a source of labor—a hangover from the industrial era. In the context of the agricultural and industrial societies, this meant physical labor. In the emerging knowledge economies of the future, it is not physical labor but creative intellectual ideas, binding social relationships, and emotional work that contribute to success. Making human creativity central to processes of production and consumption will be a key to sustainable organizations and economies of the future. Despite the centrality of creativity (and a lot of lip service paid to it), mainstream management education remains steadily straitjacketed within narrow and limited technocratic ways of thinking within functional areas. Only recently have educators and managers attempted to break out of traditional, siloed thinking into more holistic and systemic ways of addressing human problems.

Moving forward, if we wish to take up the challenges posed by the contributors to this volume, who collectively lay the groundwork for responses to the contemporary crisis that are creative, reliable, and sustainable, the possibilities for action are many. To put it crudely, this whole mess could unfold in many directions. And granting the critique of metaphysical assumptions that perpetuate the attempt to predict future events using statistical methods, history may or may not be a guide to the future.

Thus, in lieu of firm conclusions, we close with an account of how each of us, the editors, is personally navigating the post–financial crisis situation in our own work and networks. We are currently engaging as scholars, teachers, and organizers in a humble but nevertheless dedicated manner to create a more reliable and sustainable future global economy. The following account of our current activities is driven not by hubris but by a pragmatic desire to invite collaboration and even critique, in hopes that readers of this volume will be able to address the challenges that the contributors have raised.

· · ·

Matt Statler currently serves as the Richman Family Director of Business Ethics and Social Impact Programming at New York University's Stern School of Business. This position allows him to frame the global financial crisis in terms of business education, as a problem pertaining both to overall curriculum design and to classroom pedagogy.

In this respect, it seems clear that business education has in recent generations sought to provide students with tools and techniques that can be used to generate consistent results even if they are applied in different contexts. Broadly speaking, the paradigm of scientific management has held sway, leading researchers to seek to identify universal laws and immutable principles of organizational practice and leading instructors to present economic and management theories as if they held the same predictive validity as the laws of physics. The adage "if you can't measure it, you can't manage it" has led scholars and strategists to focus on variables that lend themselves to measurement with relative ease and has shifted focus away from the ambiguous and often irreducibly qualitative feelings, perceptions, and expressions that make up everyday life.

And yet the complexity and uncertainty that characterize today's global economy have frustrated attempts to manage exclusively by the numbers. Business educators are increasingly realizing that the concepts and methods associated with empirical science cannot suffice to prepare future leaders for the challenges they will face on the job. For this reason—not to mention the wake-up call provided by the global financial crisis—the pendulum in business schools is swinging away from objectivity and toward subjectivity, away from the sciences and toward the humanities, away from facts and toward values. This is not to say that the scientific analysis of objective facts has no role in the economy of the future but simply that business educators are increasingly recognizing that its role, whatever it may be, cannot totally exclude the subjective interpretation of human values.

The Carnegie Foundation for Excellence in Teaching recently conducted a three-year study of the integration of what it calls liberal learning in the undergraduate business school curriculum, and its findings suggest that the future of business education will look more like a philosophy seminar and less like a physics lab.

The undergraduate college at the Stern School of Business has over the past decade developed a series of course offerings that exemplify this trend. The Social Impact Core Curriculum is required of all undergraduate business students, and it includes one course for each year of study: Business and Its Publics, a freshman course that is focused on the interface between the institution of business and other institutions, including government and nonprofits; Organizational Communication and Its Social Context, a sophomore course that takes a rhetorical perspective on the relationships between and among various stakeholders; Law, Business, and Society, a junior course that inquires into the relationships among laws, social norms, and ethical principles; and Professional Responsibility and Leadership, a senior course that addresses individual-level decision making in reference to ethical principles and institutionalized sources of value.

Over the past year, many of the more than seventy faculty members teaching these four courses gathered on a regular basis for the Social Impact Pedagogy Seminar. The primary purpose of this seminar was to promote coherence across the four courses while developing a more robust culture of sharing ideas and teaching practices. Through this process, the following principles were articulated to describe what Stern undergraduate students do in the Social Impact Core Curriculum:

- Become more aware of multiple stakeholder perspectives on important business issues
- Develop a more nuanced understanding of the many relationships among corporations, governments, nongovernmental organizations, market economies, and civil society
- Begin the process of developing professional ethics in harmony with their own personal values
- Learn to articulate, defend, and reflect critically on a point of view

Students seek to achieve these learning objectives in the context of twenty-person discussion groups that resemble humanities seminars more than unidirectional lectures or case analysis sessions that typify traditional business education. They write critical essays about real-world business problems that enable them to integrate analysis, dialectic, and reflective judgment into a process of practical reasoning about what should be done and why.

Again, Stern is in this regard merely representative of a broader trend sweeping across the field of business education that includes the MBA Oath, the Principles for Responsible Management Education, and many other coordinated initiatives. Cynics may view such phenomena as mere window dressing or, worse, as an ultimately insincere and ineffectual apologia designed to deflect lawsuits and divert attention away from the real business at hand, namely producing another generation of ruthless oligarchs. In our view, although such cynicism is not entirely unfounded, the students themselves provide the clearest indication that the future need not simply resemble the past.

Incoming students are painfully aware that public trust in business leaders is at an all-time low. Moreover, as representatives of the millennial generation, they seek meaning as well as money. Indeed, the most popular MBA student club at Stern is currently the Social Enterprise Association, which provides an umbrella point of focus for a range of activities that would have seemed impossibly idealist even five years ago at such an elite American business school: socially responsible investing, social entrepreneurship, microfinance, and environmental sustainability.

In this light, the ongoing attempts to develop and integrate curricular and cocurricular programming that focuses critical reflection on the relationship between business and society at the Stern School of Business (as well as other universities) provide one set of examples of how to create more reliable and sustainable future economies.

· · ·

Paul Shrivastava's work at the David O'Brien Centre for Sustainable Enterprise (DOCSE) explores pragmatic solutions to challenge global sustainability. Several themes exemplify this work.

First is the Breaking the Silos project. Business school research on sustainable enterprise and the green economy is highly fragmented and lacks cross- and interdisciplinary integration. It has evolved in functional silos of management, accounting, finance, information systems, operations, and marketing. Just within the management silo, as represented by the Academy of Management, there are more than twenty smaller divisional silos. Beyond business research, there are many areas of the social sciences, engineering, biological science, arts, and the humanities that are very pertinent to understanding the required transition of the global economy toward sustainability.

Sustainability of enterprises requires holistic integrated thinking to find complete, systemic, and practical answers. We must break out of the silos, bridge between them, and develop a more integrated field that draws on the strengths of separate disciplines but is more holistic in character. The Breaking the Silos project is a series of meetings, conferences, research collaborations, and cultivation of cross-disciplinary communications. It seeks cross-functional theorizing and collaboration needed to fully understand what will constitute the sustainable enterprise of the future.

Second is the Learning by Doing Urban Resilience project, which seeks to first build creative and sustainable solutions and learn from them in the process of doing. It is focused on the perennial and global problem of homelessness. Every major city has a homeless population. The financial crisis is increasing the number of homeless and cutting resources of the philanthropic charities that deal with it. L'Itinéraire is a street news magazine produced and sold by the homeless. It has a simple business model in which homeless people sell the magazine on the street for Can\$2 and keep \$1 for themselves. They buy twenty magazines at the beginning of the day and replenish their stock every few hours on the basis of demand. The project also provides social and psychological services to its clients. There are more than one hundred street newspapers around the world that work on this basic model, employing thousands of homeless people in major cities around the world. Our project is developing a social business franchise to multiply street newspapers. It is packaging the technologies, news services, financial model, training, and advertising in a simple, convenient format that allows any charitable organization or social entrepreneur to create a street newspaper in his or her own city.

Third is researching in the discomfort zone. For far too long, management researchers have been researching safe topics in the comfortable environment of management suites, research labs, and academic classrooms. Sustainability in the meantime is happening (or not happening) in the streets, in homes, and in third-world slums, and in lands, seas, and the forests around the world—places in which we academics are not very comfortable operating. One example of an ongoing research project in the discomfort zone is our Off the Grid Solar Communities project. It is an attempt to bring (sustainable) development to the disenfranchised. It seeks to create business models that will let poor, rural, nonelectrified communities to have on-site economic development and avoid having to migrate to city slums. It is being implemented in Jharkand, the poorest state of India, where 80 percent of the population is tribal and lives below the poverty line. A cluster of villages is being electrified off the main grid using solar power. This power is used to light homes, as well as a community center, a power rice mill, a mobile irrigation pump, and other facilities for producing economic value. We are developing business models that will create a local economy, local markets, and local education and healthcare facilities.

In the area of arts and sustainable enterprise, in collaboration with ICN Business School's Art Technology and Management Program, DOCSE researchers are exploring the use of the arts and arts-based methods for understanding sustainability issues. The project examines the dynamic relations among art, aesthetics, and sustainable development of organizations. Art influences the sustainability of companies through architecture, aesthetics of workspaces, design of products and services, graphic art in advertising, and arts-based training methods. Arts also allow us to study those aspects of organizational sustainability that are a strength of aesthetics inquiry, such as sensory and emotional experiences often ignored in traditional management studies. The project also develops instrumental ways to use the arts techniques (e.g., music, dance, painting, photography) for teaching and training on sustainability issues.

• • •

The various projects and activities currently being undertaken by the editors of this volume provide illustrations of what can be done in the hopes of creating more reliable and sustainable economies. If we had a similar account of the projects being undertaken by the contributors to this volume, it would doubtless illustrate a greater range of possibilities. Building alternative visions of how the postcrisis recovery might unfold is a task we invite readers to engage in their own professional work, their institutions, and their personal lives. We hope this volume will serve as impetus for such engaged scholarship and action.

Contributor Biographies

Can M. Alpaslan is associate professor in the Department of Management, College of Business Administration and Economics, at California State University–Northridge. He received his Ph.D. from the University of Southern California. His latest book (with Ian Mitroff), *Swans, Swine, and Swindlers: Coping with the Growing Threat of Mega-Crises and Mega-Messes*, is published by Stanford University Press.

. . .

Ralph Bathurst is a practicing musician turned organizational theorist. His Ph.D. is in management from Victoria University of Wellington, and his primary research interests focus on how artistic engagement assists leadership practice.

. . .

Michael Berkowitz is the chief operating officer for Deutsche Bank's Corporate Security, Business Continuity, and Operational Risk Management group. He has been with the firm since 2005 and has held several positions, most recently as the CSBC head in Asia Pacific, based in Singapore. Before that he was deputy commissioner of the New York City Office of Emergency Management. At the office from 1998 to 2005, he led the city's planning efforts in response to coastal storms, biological terrorism, and the creation of its Citywide Incident Management System. Additionally, he responded to various incidents, including the 9/11 terrorist attacks, the 2003 Northeast blackout, the crash of

American Airlines Flight 587, and the anthrax letters of 2001. From 1995 to 1998, he was the editor of *Emergency Preparedness News*, a Washington, D.C.–based newsletter for emergency management professionals.

• • •

Nathaniel I. Bush is a Ph.D. student at the Goldman School of Public Policy, and a predoctoral research fellow at the Center for Catastrophic Risk Management, at the University of California, Berkeley. His research interests include sustainability, systems' resilience, technological innovation, and resource management and conservation. Before attending Berkeley, he studied at Pomona College and University of California, Los Angeles, and he worked as an analyst and project manager for several boutique consulting firms.

• • •

Margot Edwards earned her Ph.D. from Massey University in management, and her research integrates sports and arts-based leadership processes into the organizational arena. Her recent work extends these elements into how the arts provoke sustainability awareness and the development of community-based arts programs.

• • •

William R. Gruver joined Bucknell University in January 1993, when he retired as a general partner after a twenty-year career at Goldman Sachs, the international investment-banking firm. As the Howard I. Scott Clinical Professor of Global Commerce, Strategy, and Leadership, he is teaching courses in investments, investment banking, strategy, international relations, and leadership. His work has been published by (among others) *Directorship, Financial Times, Los Angeles Times, New York Times, New Republic,* and Public Radio International. He remains active in finance and business as a board member of Diversified Information Technologies (an international document-processing firm); Hirtle, Callaghan (a $20 billion investment adviser); TheStreet.com (also chair of the compensation committee for a publicly traded publisher of financial and investment advice); and TBIC Asset Management (a Zurich-based investment adviser).

• • •

Pierre Guillet de Monthoux is professor of Management Philosophy at Copenhagen Business School, Denmark, and guest professor to University of

St. Gallen; Switzerland. His research connects aesthetics, art, humanities, and management. He has published *The Art Firm: Aesthetic Management and Metaphysical Marketing* (Stanford University Press, 2004) and coedited *Aesthetic Leadership* (Palgrave-Macmillan, 2007). As head of the CBS Department for Management, Politics, and Philosophy, Guillet de Monthoux is currently engaged in research and educational programs bridging humanities and liberal arts to management.

· · ·

Pat Kane is a writer, musician, consultant, and activist based in Glasgow and London. He is the author of *The Play Ethic: A Manifesto for a Different Way of Living* (Macmillan, 2004). The Play Ethic (http://www.theplayethic.com) is also an innovation consultancy that has worked with organizations like Lego, BT, Bartle Bogle Hegarty, Nokia, the U.K. Cabinet Office, and the Scottish government, among many others. Kane speaks regularly on the power of play throughout the world, in the last year speaking in New York; Washington, D.C.; London; and Istanbul. He has spoken to many educators in both Scotland and Australia about the role of play in educational reform. He is still one-half of the pop duo Hue and Cry (http://www.hueandcry.co.uk), which is currently making its fourteenth album. The group has recorded with jazz titans like the Brecker Brothers, Ron Carter, Mike Stern, Tito Puente, Jon Faddis, and Tommy Smith, and has opened for U2, Madonna, James Brown, Van Morrison, Al Green, and Ray Charles.

· · ·

N. V. Krishna is adviser, Centre for Budget and Policy Studies, and director, Microsense, in Bangalore, India. He holds a degree in engineering from the Indian Institute of Technology, Madras, and a graduate degree in management from the Indian Institute of Management, Calcutta. He has more than thirty-four years of professional experience in industry, during which time he has also pursued academic interests.

· · ·

Peter F. Martelli is a Ph.D. candidate and a predoctoral research fellow at the Center for Catastrophic Risk Management at the University of California, Berkeley. His research interests are in evidence-based management, knowledge translation, expertise, social networks, and risk. He has participated in the Center's work on patient safety, wild-land fire, and civil and industrial infrastructure, and he currently cochairs RhoNet, the Center's initiative to promote reliable health care. Before attending Berkeley, he studied at the University of Pennsylvania and Thomas Jefferson University, and he was a research coordinator at the American College of Physicians, where he helped establish and manage the ACPNet national practice-based research network.

• • •

Emilio Marti is a Ph.D. candidate at the Department of Business Administration of the University of Zurich and affiliated with University Priority Research Program Ethics of the University of Zurich. He holds a master's degree in philosophy and is about to finish a second master's degree in financial economics. His research interests are in philosophy of science, theories of justice, and business ethics.

• • •

Skip McGoun is professor of finance at Bucknell University. He is the creator and organizer of nine conferences on alternative perspectives on finance, which aim to broaden the dialogue in finance and encourage research that is interdisciplinary or that challenges prevailing beliefs. McGoun's own research investigates finance as a pop-culture phenomenon. He has explored such topics as the parallels between motoring and personal investing, as well as the likeness of Wall Street's structures and institutions to theme parks or theater, with the employees and customers playing their fantasy roles as popularized by Madison Avenue and Hollywood.

• • •

Brett S. Messing is the chief operating officer of the C40 Cities Climate Leadership Group and a senior adviser to the Bloomberg Foundation. He is also the Terence M. Considine Visiting Research Fellow in Law, Economics, and Business at Harvard Law School. He previously worked for Los Angeles Mayor Antonio R. Villaraigosa as a senior adviser and chief operating officer of the Office of Business and Economic Policy. Messing began his career at Goldman Sachs, where he was a vice president; he also worked at Lehman Brothers as a managing director. Thereafter, he was the managing partner and founder of GPS Partners, a $2 billion hedge fund focused in the energy sector. Messing is a graduate of Brown University and Harvard Law School.

• • •

Ian I. Mitroff is university professor at Alliant International University, adjunct professor at the College of Environmental Design, and senior research associate at the Center for Catastrophic Risk Management at the University of California, Berkeley. He is also professor emeritus at the Marshall School of Business and the Annenberg School of Communication, University of Southern California, and adjunct professor of health policy in the School of Public Health at St. Louis University. His formal degrees are from the University of California, Berkeley. His latest books, *Dirty Rotten Strategies: How We Trick Ourselves and Others into Solving the Wrong Problems Precisely* and *Swans, Swine, and Swindlers: Coping with the Growing Threat of Mega-Crises and Mega-Messes*, are published by Stanford University Press.

• • •

Murali Murti is professor of management at PES Institute of Technology, Bangalore, India. His work experience spans more than three decades in industry and academics. He holds a degree in electrical engineering from the Indian Institute of Technology, Bombay, and a graduate degree in management from the Indian Institute of Management, Calcutta.

• • •

Robert Richardson is the director of correspondence for the Office of the Mayor in New York City. In this role, his portfolio has included a number of projects that combine elements of public affairs, communications, social media, content management, and operations. Most recently, he and his team helped design and launch pilot programs for NYC's internal and external crowdsourcing platforms. Upcoming projects include establishing the information architecture for the new digital archive and managing the implementation of a citywide enterprise content management solution. He holds a B.A. in philosophy and history from Wheaton College and an M.A. in philosophy from Pennsylvania State University.

• • •

Karlene H. Roberts is a professor at the Walter A. Haas School of Business, at the University of California, Berkeley. She is also chair of the Center for Catastrophic Risk Management at Berkeley. Roberts earned her bachelor's degree in psychology from Stanford University and her Ph.D. in industrial psychology from the University of California, Berkeley. She also received the docteur honoris causa from the Universite Paul Cezanne (Aix Marseilles III). Since

1984 Roberts has investigated the design and management of organizations and systems of organizations in which error can result in catastrophic consequences. She has studied both organizations that failed and those that succeed in this category. Roberts has worked in such industries as the military, commercial marine transportation, health care, railroads, petroleum production, commercial aviation, banking, and community emergency services.

. . .

Perry Sadorsky is an associate professor of economics in the Schulich School of Business at York University in Toronto, where he teaches business students at both the undergraduate and graduate (MBA) level. He researches business interests related to energy, the natural environment, and financial markets. He has published extensively in these areas. He has been involved in several international organizations and international working groups.

. . .

Andreas Georg Scherer holds the Chair of Business Administration and Theories of the Firm at the Department of Business Administration of the University of Zurich. His research interests are in business ethics, corporate social responsibility, international management, international relations, and organization theory. He has published nine books and most recently coedited *Handbook of Research on Global Corporate Citizenship* (with G. Palazzo). His work has appeared in *Academy of Management Review, Advances in Strategic Management, Business Ethics Quarterly, Journal of Business Ethics, Journal of Management Studies, Management International Review, Organization,* and *Organization Studies.*

. . .

Henrik Schrat has studied painting and stage design in Dresden, Germany, and completed a master's in fine art media at the Slade School at UCL in London in 2002. He has shown his work internationally in group and solo shows, among others Global Players (Tokyo, 2005) and Eat the Food (MOCCA, Toronto, 2007), he painted the mural in the casino of the Deutsche Bundestag (*Milk & Honey,* 2002), and he has realized numerous site-specific works. His doctoral thesis "Meanwhile . . . Wham! Comic and Its Communication Value in Organizational Context," was recently submitted at the Essex Business School, University of Essex (supervisor: Heather Höpfl). He lives and works in Berlin.

. . .

Paul Shrivastava is currently the David O'Brien Distinguished Professor and director of the David O'Brien Centre for Sustainable Enterprise at the John Molson School of Business, Concordia University, Montreal. He also serves as senior adviser at Bucknell University and the Indian Institute of Management, Shillong, and leads the International Chair for Arts and Sustainable Enterprise at ICN Business School, Nancy, France. Shrivastava was part of the team of professionals who helped found Hindustan Computer, one of India's largest computer companies. He founded the nonprofit Industrial Crisis Institute in New York, and he has published in *Industrial Crisis Quarterly*. He founded *Organization and Environment* (published by Sage Publications). He was founding president and chief executive officer of eSocrates, a knowledge management software company, and the founding chair of the Organizations and the Natural Environment Division of the Academy of Management.

· · ·

Mark Starik is professor in the Department of Strategic Management and Public Policy at the George Washington University School of Business. In the department and throughout the university, he develops programs, researches, teaches, and advises organizations and individuals in the areas of strategic environmental management, environmental and energy policy, environmental entrepreneurship, and climate action policies and practices. His teaching has included executive management, doctoral, graduate, and undergraduate student programs and courses. In addition to numerous academic articles and edited volumes, he has written several business sustainability cases, made numerous presentations to both academic and practitioner audiences, and organized many sustainability events that integrate those audiences. He is a cofounder of several sustainability-oriented organizations, including the Academy of Management Organizations and the Natural Environment (ONE) Division, and he is a board member of several nonprofit organizations. He has published widely in a variety of sustainability and management academic and practitioner outlets and has provided sustainability consulting services to numerous business, government, and nonprofit organizations. Starik's additional practitioner experience includes working with several organizations as an environmental and energy analyst and managing a residential energy conservation organization. He is an avid conserver of resources and user of renewable energy products and services.

· · ·

Matt Statler is the Richman Family Director of Business Ethics and Social Impact Programming and clinical assistant professor of management and organizations at the New York University Stern School of Business. Before joining Stern, Statler served as the director of research for the university's Center for Catastrophe Preparedness and Response, where he focused on how businesses can become more strategically prepared for crises. Statler initially developed this research focus while serving as the director of research at the Imagination Lab Foundation in Lausanne, Switzerland. He has published dozens of journal articles and book chapters, and he has written or edited several books, including the recent *Encyclopedia of Disaster Relief* (Sage, 2011). Statler earned his B.A. in philosophy and Spanish literature from the University of Missouri at Columbia and his Ph.D. in philosophy from Vanderbilt University. He spent one year at the University of Heidelberg as a Fulbright scholar.

· · ·

Aida Sy holds a doctorate from the Sorbonne with first-class honors. She is currently assistant professor of accountancy and taxation at Marist College in New York, coeditor of *IJCA* and *IJEA*, visiting researcher at the University of Paris–9 Dauphine and University of Bordeaux–4 Montesquieu, and editorial board member of several journals. She participates in several international conferences as presenter, discussant, and chair and is the coorganizer of the International Conference of Critical Accounting. She was the plenary speaker at the University of St. Andrews, the International Congress of Accounting Historians, and the first WAFS. She is a member of the Ph.D. Project (KPMG), the American Accounting Association, the European Accounting Association, and the Critical Accounting Society. She has published several chapters in books on accounting, editorials, and more than twenty refereed articles.

· · ·

Steven S. Taylor is an associate professor in the Department of Management at the Worcester Polytechnic Institute in Massachusetts. His research focuses on the aesthetics of organizational action and reflective practice. Recently, his academic work has focused on theorizing the use of arts-based process within organizations and exploring beautiful action within organizations. Taylor is also a playwright whose work has been performed in England, France, Poland, Canada, New Zealand, and the United States.

· · ·

Tony Tinker is professor of accountancy at Baruch College, City University of New York (CUNY), and he is or has been visiting professor at St. Andrews, Scotland, and UNISA, Australia. He is founder member of the AIA, and CUNY On-Line Programs. He is a fellow of the ACCA and twice past council member of the American Accounting Association (AAA) and past chair of the AAA Public Interest Section. He has authored or coauthored *Social Accounting for Corporations, Paper Prophets,* and *Policing Accounting Knowledge,* and he has published numerous articles. He is coeditor of *IJCA* and holds numerous editorial board memberships. He has appeared on CNN, BBC, CBC, Pacifica Public Radio, and New York Public Radio, and has had articles published in *Newsweek* and the *Wall Street Journal.*

Index

Italic page numbers indicate material in tables or figures.